Old Chillicothe

Old Chillicothe

Shawnee & Pioneer History

TECUMSEH

William Albert Galloway

COMMONWEALTH BOOK COMPANY
St. Martin, Ohio

© 1934 by William Albert Galloway
© 2022 by Commonwealth Book Company
All rights reserved. Printed in the United States of America.

ISBN: 978-1-948986-40-3

Commonwealth Book Company, Inc.
St. Martin, Ohio

COVER ILLUSTRATION: Battle of Tippecanoe (1811). Chromolithograph by Kurz and Allison, circa 1889. Pictured is an American force commanded by William Henry Harrison, and the Native American party led by Tecumseh's brother, Tenskwatawa, also known as The Prophet.

DEDICATION

In living memory of an ancient "Pact of Peace"—1797—and its reenactment—1926—this book is dedicated by its author

*To his friend
Thomas Wildcat Alford
(Gan-waw-pea-se-ka)
great-grandson of Tecumseh, Shawnee patriot, orator, statesman and general.*

Our history records that your people were a nation of warriors who battled with unfaltering courage to preserve your home and heritage in the Northwest Territory.

You lost!

Our victory was won by reason of superior equipment and resources; its motive was a persistent determination to possess your fair and fertile land.

We won!

In this same land, where you once raised your tepees and wigewas, kindled your camp-fires and chanted your war-songs, the boy, the youth and the man who followed, call aloud to hear the stories of your day.

You yet remain!

WILLIAM ALBERT GALLOWAY

WILLIAM ALBERT GALLOWAY

FOREWORD

By C. B. GALBREATH[1]
*Secretary and Librarian of
Ohio Archaeological and Historical Society*

OLD CHILLICOTHE, a Story of Conflicts and Romances, by William Albert Galloway, A.M., M.D., LL.D., is a book of rare interest to every citizen of Ohio and to many readers and students beyond the limits of that State.

The author, the late William Albert Galloway, was well qualified in many ways to write such a volume.

He was a lineal descendant of James Galloway, Sr., who was a member of General George Rogers Clark's expedition against the Indian Town, Old Chillicothe, in 1782. After the treaty of Greenville in 1795, this pioneer ancestor moved in 1797 with his wife and five children from Lexington, Kentucky, to a new home location in the neighborhood of Old Chillicothe. Here members of the Galloway family have made their home up to the present time.

Dr. William Albert Galloway was born in Xenia, April 8, 1860. He was the great-grandson of James Galloway, Sr., at whose home the Indian chieftain Tecumtha had at many times been a visitor. Dr. Galloway had grown up in contact with the interesting history of the region in which he was born. From early life that history had a special appeal to him.

He was President of the Greene County Historical Society, and a life member of the Ohio State Archaeological

---

[1]The death of Dr. Galbreath occurred February 3, 1934

FOREWORD

and Historical Society, to whose Museum he made valuable contributions, including the famous tomahawk which had been presented to his great-grandfather by Tecumtha.

For years he had been industriously engaged in the preparation of this work for the publication of which provision was made at the time of his death.

In later years he was in frequent and intimate correspondence with Thomas Wildcat Alford, the great-grandson of Tecumtha. Alford had translated the Four Gospels into the Shawnee language, in order, as he declared, to preserve that language in its purity before the last of the Shawnee tribe, qualified to make such a translation, had passed away. Dr. Galloway, a short time before his death, to the gratification of Mr. Alford, published, in the Shawnee tongue, the Four Gospels. Alford made personal visits to the home of Dr. Galloway and furnished the information in regard to his Shawnee Indian ancestors.

Old Chillicothe, in the formative period of Ohio and the Nation, was a point of unusual interest, and the historical collections by Dr. Galloway deserve a permanent place in the record of the region and the period to which they are devoted.

C. B. GALBREATH

INTRODUCTION

By THOMAS WILDCAT ALFORD

Head Committeeman and Custodian of the Tribal Records of the Absentee Shawnees

IN THIS story of *Old Chillicothe, Kahtv Cvlvhgrfagi,* many of my nation's traditions have been given a first opportunity to become written history. It is a matter of great satisfaction that its author came to us to obtain our traditions of the place, and our part in the stirring events of this story, and that at a time when the old traditions of our people are fast disappearing, owing to influences of civilization; and that he has faithfully interpreted them as though the spirit of our dear Uncle Joe had entered into his spirit.

The historic connection of his family with my people extended from 1782 to 1813, and a part of it became an important historic influence in our destiny, and also in the subsequent events which helped to determine that of Canada. Traditions of 1797 which have descended with us through our great-grandfather, Gikuskawlowa, who signed several treaties with the United States in its earliest days, also entitled the author of this to the Shawnee Indian histories he has used and which are embodied in correct relation in *Old Chillicothe,* as to our names, narratives and historic events.

It is proper for me again to say that tradition is the only way my people have had or could have to transmit our histories of the past, and whenever they could be checked by your written records, they have been found to be reliable in substance, and often more explanatory in detail. I,

INTRODUCTION

therefore, feel certain that the stories herein related are reliable Shawnee history.

The visit of the author produced in us a profound spiritual impression. Here was a perfect stranger whom we never saw before, but who was armed with the Tomahawk-pipe of friendship which we knew as though the spirits of our two departed ancestors came with it. *Pvyaqw biaci uqrkvni nili Wihgrnewi Daghrkvni-uqrkvnvli brsi galv nihki niahkvki neswi ni-gahgirmaurki ucvjrlvhku mwvhi u biaci medfamr-wrli nili.* This ancient Pipe introduced our guest, and the natural result followed—the Renewal of the Pact of Friendship, which was rarely celebrated in ancient times, and never with an alien, except under our certain conviction of the worthiness of the recipient *nvhekv ya-iqslafici inv wa-tfakutv.* This Renewal of 1926 is a solitary incident of this kind in our history, and is notable for this reason, and also from the fact that the principals in the Renewal were blood descendants of like relationship (great-grandsons), to the two men who first enacted it in 1797. The Renewal, 129 years later, again establishes this ancient relation and its obligations. Its historic significance is rendered more sacred by the ceremonial use again, and for a like purpose, of the Tomahawk-pipe of our great chief Tecumseh, which he presented to his friend, James Galloway, Sr., to keep, *ne tabawa tfwi gikvtu gita neswrpitvgi gita jrkvtfwi,* a material gift, binding the compact. It was used in confirming the ceremonial of 1797 and that of 1926; but, unfortunately, in the latter ceremonial we lacked the kinnikinick (*gilaginikv*) and other unessential things, owing, as our forefathers would say, *bofi takuhsiyawi-lanvwawewa,* to too much civilization.

I feel certain that the reading of this story will renew interest in my people and in *Old Chillicothe, Kahtv*

INTRODUCTION

Cvlvhgrfagi iahgi yadryrga macimi n'uhfanrki, our old home and the home of our fathers. I deem it a privilege to have lent however little of my aid to its author in his efforts to give only authentic Shawnee Indian details wherever their interesting history enters into his story. The reader may feel assured that these details are held by us to be dependable and **authentic**.

Thos. W. Alford

CONTENTS

	PAGE
FOREWORD by C. B. Galbreath	v
INTRODUCTION by Thomas Wildcat Alford	vii
INTER UMBRAS	1
General George Rogers Clark	1
General Simon Kenton	4
Colonel Daniel Boone	7
OLD CHILLICOTHE	10
The Numerous Ohio Chillicothes	15
THE SHAWNEE INDIANS	18
The Five Clans or Septs	21
Clan Names in Many Forms	22
The War of the Iroquois	24
Once More the Young Red Man Goes West	29
Pucksinwa, the Father of Tecumtha	37
Migrations to and from "Old Chillicothe"	40
HISTORIC BACKGROUNDS	43
Old Cha-lah-gaw-tha Town	43
The Indian Village	43
The Kentucky Forters' Period	45
The Miami Valley Campaigns of 1779-1790	49
The Battle of Oldtown and the Shawnee Historical Background	54
The Battle of Oldtown	55
Plan of March, 1780	66
Catahecassa or Black Hoof	71
Plan of March, 1782	79
Celebration of 1832	86
Logan—1786	90
General Josiah Harmar's Expedition—1790	94
General Harmar's Defeat	96
Traces of Expeditions Against Shawnees	99
"Shawnee Highways" in Greene County, Ohio	101
TECUMTHA	106
A Notable Family	106
The Birthplaces of Tecumtha	107
The Galloway Family	121
Ruddell's Account of Tecumtha	128
A Pioneer Romance	135
Brothers by Blood	139

CONTENTS

The Sacred Slab 151
The Death of Tecumtha 152
"If A Man Die, Shall He Live Again?" 162
Dedication of Tecumtha's Birthplace 163
The Pact of Peace and Friendship, 1797 . . . 166
The Renewal of the Pact of Peace, 1926 . . . 167

SHAWNEE DOMESTIC AND TRIBAL LIFE 170
Boys' and Girls' Names and Games 171
Homes and Family Life 173
Religion and Morals 177
Education 179
Tribal Government 180
Food and Its Preparation 183
Ceremonials and Records of Time 189
Social Life of the Shawnees 194
The Passing of A Loved Mother 198
Mourning Song of the Shawnees 200
Shawnee Sunrise Love Song 201
Pioneer Records of Shawnee Customs 201
The Indian Burial of Black Hoof 204

PIONEER STORIES WHICH MUST NOT BE FORGOTTEN . . 207
General Thomas Worthington 209
The Historic Banquet at Adena, 1807 213
The Story of Josiah Hunt 217
The Centinel and *The Maxwell Code* 219
William Smalley 232
The Camp at Waynesville (Waynesburg) . . . 238
The Scott Encampment 239
Rev. Robert Armstrong 245
Kenton, the Patriot 254
 Kenton's Run of the Gantlet 256
 The Kenton Elm 257
The Captivity and Escape of Daniel Boone . . . 258
 Boone's Own Story 260
Concerning Stephen Ruddell 263
Captain Thomas Bullitt 266
A Pioneer Funeral 268

INDIAN STORIES 270
Indian Joe 270
The Second Bend in the River 276
Non-hel-e-ma, Shawnee Princess 283
The Two Wyandotte Camps in Greene County, Ohio . 295
Weh-yah-pih-ehr-sehn-wah (Blue Jacket) . . . 298
Legend of the First Meeting of the Cha-la-kaw-tha and
 Tha-weg-ila Clans of the Shawnees . . . 303

xii

ILLUSTRATIONS

APPENDIX	313
Shawnee Vocabularies of 1818, 1854 and 1926	313
The Translation of the Four Gospels	323
Descendants of Tecumtha	324
AUTHORITIES QUOTED	329
INDEX	331

ILLUSTRATIONS

William Albert Galloway	*Frontispiece*
	FACING PAGE
Thomas W. Alford	vi
Site of Shawnee Indian Town of Old Chillicothe	10
Hills Adjoining the Site of Old Chillicothe	22
Marker at the Site of Old Chillicothe	40
Simon Kenton's Station in 1794	52
Monuments Erected at Old Chillicothe	70
James Galloway, Sr., and Treasurer's Receipt	88
Drake's Map of the Miami Country	102
Tecumtha	108
Absentee Shawnee Governing Committee of 1901	116
Memorial to Tecumtha	120
Rebecca Galloway	134
The Sacred Slab	150
Ceremonial Tomahawk-pipe of Tecumtha	160
Thomas Wildcat Alford and Family, and the Author	168
Guest Chair of the Pioneer Galloway Home	182
General and Mrs. Thomas Worthington and Gift of Indian Commission	210
The Maxwell Code and *The Centinel*	222
Home of Oren and Martha North, Old Chillicothe	254
Memorial to Daniel Boone and 27 Salt Makers	262
The Second Galloway Pioneer Home	280
Woodland in Which Wyandotte Indians Camped	296

INTER UMBRAS

GENERAL GEORGE ROGERS CLARK

GENERAL George Rogers Clark, General Simon Kenton and Colonel Daniel Boone were intimately connected with the militant life of Old Chillicothe from 1779 to 1794. Events of their declining years, which are of significant and lasting interest, are noted in Judge Burnet's "Letters to J. Delafield, Jr.;"[1] in Colonel Boone's Diary;[2] and Timothy Flint's pen picture of Boone.[3]

Melancholy interest not infrequently attaches to events which attend the later years of men who were yesterday's leaders of conquest.

The letters of Jacob Burnet, one of Ohio's pioneer United States senators and a distinguished jurist, to J. Delafield, Esq., give intimate accounts of the sombre events that gathered about General George Rogers Clark and General Simon Kenton, both of whom he knew personally and visited in their declining years.

Mindful how great is the unpaid debt we owe to these leaders for their service in the conquest of the Northwestern Territory, the notations, now rarely read, are here appended.

On one of Judge Burnet's trips from Cincinnati to Vincennes, he was accompanied by Governor Arthur St. Clair's son. After a night at Louisville, they decided to go out in the country seven or eight miles and pay their respects to General George Rogers Clark, who then lived with his brother. Judge Burnet's indictment of his

---

[1] *Hist. and Phil. Soc. of Ohio, Transactions*, Pt. 2, V. 1.
[2] *Ohio Arch. and Hist. Quarterly*. 13:265-277.
[3] Flint, Timothy. *Life and Adventures of Daniel Boone.*

country's neglect of General Clark and its obligations to him for the conquest of our richest and most important economic area, the Northwestern Territory, is here given:

We were received with kindness and pressed to spend the day. At that time, the exploits of General Clark were fresh in the recollection of the country. He was admitted to be one of the greatest military geniuses of any age or country. It was known that in 1778, with no other means furnished by the State of Virginia than his commission and a warrant to raise men, and make contracts on the credit of the commonwealth, he collected a small band of heroes in the wilds of Kentucky, and having inspired them with his own spirit, and attached them most ardently to his person, he proceeded to Kaskaskia and took the posts on the Mississippi. This expedition was scarcely exceeded in difficulties and hardships by the memorable march of Arnold to Quebec, in the winter of 1775. At that time, Governor Hamilton was at Fort Vincennes with a superior force, meditating the capture of Clark and his band of heroes, which he considered inevitable. The American general, however, aware of his purpose and of his own danger, determined to anticipate his enemy by a forced march through swamps and quagmires to the Wabash. This plan succeeded, Hamilton was surprised, and his fort carried by storm. With his little corps, General Clark suceeded in retaining military possession in that extensive country till the close of the war, and by that means, saved it to the United States; the fact being well understood that in arranging the articles of the treaty of peace with Great Britain, our claim to the Northwestern Territory rested principally on his conquest and occupancy.

The cruel ingratitude with which this great man had been treated by his country, and the consequent poverty which had made him a pensioner on the bounty of his relatives, by whose charity he then subsisted, was more than he could bear. It drove him to intoxication. He sought the inebriating bowl as though it contained the water of Lethe and would cause him to forget what he had been and what he was. When I was induced to visit him, by the veneration I felt for his talents and services, his health was much impaired by intemperance, but his majestic person, his dignified deportment and strong features bore the impress of an intelligent, resolute mind; and immediately brought to my recollection the personal appearance of Washington, to which it seemed to approximate. The first impression made on my mind was that he was born to command, and that nature had fitted him for his destiny. I saw him with deep regret, and left him under a conviction that he was, or had been, richly endowed with the personal and mental qualities of a consummate general; and that he was then falling a victim to his own strong sensibility and to the ingratitude of his native State, under whose banner he had fought and conquered.[4]

Very respectfully,
J. BURNET

J. Delafield, Jr.

The value of Judge Burnet's public services during the development period of the Northwestern Territory and in the early period of newborn Ohio is evidenced in the character of his public addresses and letters which may be found in the histories of that period. After more than one hundred years, even a casual reading of these documents reveals the perfect definitive selection of terms used to express his views on the important issues of his day. His choice language may be likened to the tones of Felix Salmond's 'cello. Nothing can be added to complete its expression.

The only duty performed at the first assembly on February 4th, 1799, of the Representatives chosen under the Ordinance of 1787 by the electors of the Territory, was the nomination of ten freeholders, from whom President Adams appointed five, to constitute "The Legislative Council of the Territory of the United States, Northwest of the River Ohio." These were David Vance, of Vanceville; Jacob Burnet and James Findley, of Cincinnati; Robert Oliver, of Marietta, and Henry Vanderburgh of Vincennes.[5] Of Judge Burnet's work in this conspicuous and influential body, it is recorded by Mr. A. A. Graham that—

---

[4] Burnet, Jacob. "Letters relating to the Early Settlement of the Northwest Territory, in a Series addressed to J. Delafield. Jr., Esq." In *Hist. and Phil. Society of Ohio Transactions*, Pt. 2, V. 1:61-63.

[5] *Ohio Arch. and Hist. Quarterly*, 1:309-310.

Not only did he draft a majority of all laws passed, but he also compiled a code of rules for both houses, prepared an address to Governor St. Clair, also one to President Adams, and acted in many other useful places. When the troubles concerning the jurisdiction of Kentucky over the Ohio River arose, his careful investigation induced a settlement between the two commonwealths satisfactory to all.[6]

GENERAL SIMON KENTON

The events of General Simon Kenton's declining years show in him the qualities of true greatness that could rise above "the slings and arrows of outrageous fortune." From a man in most affluent circumstances, his descent to poverty and dependency was rapid and seemingly unbroken till he, like General Clark, was given home and food by a son-in-law. For the one, is recorded declining years of broken spirit and bitter memories; for the other, declining years enriched by contentment. General Kenton's financial misfortunes must have become acute as early as 1823—13 years before his death. At that period, the Ohio Creditors' Law permitted seizure and imprisonment of the person of a debtor unable to meet his obligations.

A valuable historical record from "Some Documentary History of Ohio" by George Davenport Kratz is here quoted:

The following document is a receipt for special bail of Simon Kenton, bail being furnished by John Daugherty and Robert Renick. The incident involved in this transaction is not known to history:

"Received of John Daugherty and Robert Renick special bail for Simon Kenton in a case where Samuel Need and Abraham Need and plaintiffs and said Simon Kenton is defendant in court of common pleas for Champaign County, the body of said defendant who has this day been surrendered by said special bail before Samuel Hill, Esquire, one of the associate judges of our said court of common

---

[6]*Ohio Arch. and Hist. Quarterly*, 1:312.

pleas in persuance of the statute in such case made and proceeded.

    5th Sept. 1823   F. Ambrose, Shff.
                                  of Champaign County

Receipt for the body of
    Simon Kenton
from Shff. Champaign."

No record, however, has been found of Kenton's actual imprisonment in this case.[7]

But for Kenton's unconquered, unquenchable spirit of optimism, one might write at its conclusion, "Sic transit gloria mundi."

When I first became acquainted with Kenton, (writes Judge Burnet) his house was always open to strangers as well as friends. Every traveler who called was received with kindness, treated with hospitality, and pressed to stay, till himself and his horse should be recruited. His residence was then in the vicinity of Washington, Kentucky, where he cultivated a farm of a thousand acres of the finest land in the country. In 1797, on my way from Limestone to Lexington, I stopped and spent a day at his house and partook of his hospitality with great satisfaction. He pressed me to stay with him longer, but my business would not permit me to do so.

Unfortunately, he was illiterate and altogether too confiding. Judging others by himself, he was not conscious of the danger to which his unsuspecting mind exposed him—he believed men were generally honest, nor did he awake from that delusion till he was cheated out of his whole estate. This was done principally by one of his own relatives to whom he had confided the management of his affairs. At an advanced age he was reduced from affluence to abject poverty, and left dependent on the charity of a humane son-in-law, who was himself poor and depended on his daily labor for his daily bread. Yet he was cheerful and happy and, although he saw the children of his treacherous friend living in affluence at his expense, he told me that he would not exchange situations with them for twice the amount of their ill-gotten wealth. "I can," said he, "sleep

---

[7] *Ohio Arch. and Hist. Quarterly*, 21:402.

quietly, while they are suffering the pangs inflicted by a guilty conscience."

Before I became a member of the Senate, General Vance, who was in the House of Representatives, had made several efforts to obtain a pension for this unfortunate, but meritorious pioneer. When we met in Washington City in 1828 we determined to make another effort in his behalf. A bill was introduced in the House of Representatives granting him a pension, and, by the persevering energy and personal influence of General Vance, was carried through. It came to the Senate, late in the session, and was referred to the appropriate committee. I advocated it in the committee-room and found no difficulty in convincing them of the justice and equity of the claim. They reported it back to the Senate with an opinion that it ought to pass. The case did not come within the provisions of any of the pension laws on the statute book. It was opposed on that ground and resisted by the strict constructionists as a dangerous precedent. But the effect of their opposition was finally defeated by a full and faithful exhibition of the services and sufferings of the applicant. It was shown that his life had been one succession of exposure and suffering in defense of his country, from the Battle of the Kanawha, before the Declaration of Independence, to the last victory of Harrison on the Thames. The friends of the bill, contended that the case could not become a dangerous precedent because there was no parallel to it; that the claim was one, *sui generis*, and could never be referred to, for the purpose of sustaining other claims; but that if it could, if there were many cases presenting the same evidence of exposure and suffering in the defense of the country, they would form a new class as meritorious as any which had yet been provided for, not excepting those of the army of the revolution. During the discussion, the feelings of General Smith of Baltimore were very much enlisted. He made a brief appeal to the humanity and justice of the Senate in favor of the claim; in which he declared that if there was no law for the relief of such heroes as Kenton there ought to be; but whether or not, he would give him a pension. The bill passed by a large majority and, as it referred back to the date of the first application, it gave him an ample support for the remnant of his life.[8]

Very respectfully,

J. Delafield, Jr.

J. BURNET.

---

[8]*Hist. and Phil. Soc. of Ohio, Transactions*, 178-180.

INTER UMBRAS

General Kenton's final years—1825-1836—were lived in a single room log cabin apparently twelve feet square. Three of the four original corner-stones on which the little structure stood are in place. On one of them the following legend is chiseled:

> The corner-stone of the house in which
> Gen. Simon Kenton died, April 29, 1836
> Do not move it.

The cabin was close to a good spring which yet flows out of a hollow log placed on end for a container. There is a nearby excavation in the hillside, probably a cave for storage of fruits and vegetables. The single room log cabin with a "lean-to" at the rear to increase its living capacity rarely had a cellar under it, in pioneer days. The "cave" was constructed near the cabin, if a hillside was available. These "caves" served a double purpose, they were excellent as vegetable cellars and were safe retreats in times of heavy wind-storms of that period. The cabin site is in the hill country of Logan County, Ohio, near the settlement formerly known as New Jerusalem. General Kenton died at the age of eighty-one. He was buried on a spot selected by himself, on the crest of a hill adjoining his cabin. His remains were removed in 1852 to Oak Dale Cemetery, Urbana, Ohio. A fitting monument, designed by the noted American sculptor, J. Q. A. Ward, and erected by the State of Ohio, marks this noted pioneer's final resting-place.

COLONEL DANIEL BOONE

Daniel Boone's final years were spent with his sons, Daniel, Morgan and Nathan, and his daughter, Jemima, who was then Mrs. Flanders Calloway, at Charette Village, Missouri, on the north side of the Missouri River. He was surrounded by every pioneer comfort that these devoted children could provide. His last years were marked by contentment of spirit and the philosophy which blesses the thoughts of men who have traveled life's journey always close to nature and nature's God. The voices of the forest had called to him and he understood them. He was not a warrior or statesman. He developed few indeed of the ideals or attributes of Clark or Kenton. He was essentially a pathfinder, scouting for an ever-advancing wave of civilization, and as it followed and crowded onto him, he moved on. Even in his final days this instinct to push farther west from Missouri was a ruling passion. Timothy Flint, one of Boone's biographers, describes him as "sociable and kind in his feelings, very fond of quiet retirement, of cool self-possession and indomitable perseverance. . . . Never was old age more green or gray hairs more graceful."[9] But let Boone speak for himself:

> Two darling sons and a brother, I have lost by savage hands, which have also taken forty valuable horses and an abundance of cattle. Many dark and sleepless nights have I spent, separated from the cheerful society of man, scorched by the summer's sun and pinched by winter's cold, an instrument ordained to settle the wilderness. But now, the scene is changed: peace crowns the sylvan shade.[10]

Probably every sort of adventure in the experience of a pioneer scout and Indian fighter occurred to Boone at some time during his eventful historic career. His last years were spent largely in his favorite environment, the forest. There, he occupied himself with hunting, his lifelong vocation. Often he was out for days at a time; sometimes alone with his faithful, well-loved dogs, and at other times, members of his devoted family accompanied him. One of the outstanding experiences of his life was his capture, in 1778, and his adoption by the Shawnee Indians from whom he received the Indian name of "Big Turtle." The more intimate details of this eventful four months of his life, narrated in one of the stories which follow,[11] will be of increased interest in connection with the Shawnee tradition of Boone's escape given to history for the first time in this story.

Like his friend, Simon Kenton, he, at one time, pos-

---
[9]Flint, Timothy. *Life and Adventures of Daniel Boone*, 249.
[10]*Ohio Arch. and Hist. Quarterly*, 13:277.
[11]See "Captivity and Escape of Daniel Boone," on a later page.

sessed large tracts of fertile Kentucky land, but lost them through defective titles to tracts which he sold with warranty deeds.[12] Following losses which totaled more than his entire estate, he removed to Boonslick, Missouri, in 1797. It was a quiet departure. The lure of Kentucky had gripped him. He joined her fortunes, and lived the life of her pioneer day, her greatest son, her "instrument ordained to settle the wilderness." Beloved then, as now, by every Kentuckian worthy of the name, Boone is the hero of her history. All that is mortal of him rests in her own warm blue-grass soil at Frankfort.

"HOME IS THE HUNTER FROM THE HILLS"

---

[12]Defective land records impoverished many of the earliest Kentucky pioneers. Overlapping boundary lines in the Virginia military lands, between the Scioto and Little Miami Rivers, north of the Ohio, were sources of extended litigations and attendant losses. Tomahawk rights, corn-growers' deeds and squatters' claims were familiar designations in the court records following the first waves of immigration into these territories. An outstanding effort to extend illegally the boundary lines, for personal gain, may be found in the court records reported in the issues of the *Ohio Federalist*, April 6, April 10 and June 6, 1815, and the *People's Press*, No. 101, March 1, 1827. The prominence of the promoter lends regretful interest to these records.

View taken from Bryson's Hill, 3½ miles north of Xenia, Ohio, on the Springfield-Xenia Pike, the Bullskin Trace of pioneer days. Simon Kenton's Run of the Gauntlet, 1778, in a lane of rows of 600 Indians, and probably with 800 looking on, extended from the buildings at the extreme left of the picture, across the valley in the foreground, to a point near the barn shown in the extreme right.

The distance across the valley is one half-mile. The village extended for a half-mile along the ridge shown at the extreme right in a S. E.-N. W. direction. This is now Oldtown, Ohio. To the far right, the dim tree line of the Little Miami River is seen. Between it and the village ridge was the drill-ground of the Greene County Militia, under the Ordinance of 1784. This ordinance was repealed in 1844.

OLD CHILLICOTHE

THE DESIRE to preserve the story of the notable historic events from 1778 to 1813, closely connected with Old Chillicothe, will recall authentic records and also traditions from our own and from Shawnee sources heretofore unpublished. The history of Old Chillicothe, the principal village and home of the Cha-lah-kaw-tha clan of the Shawnee Indians, is of deep interest. Previous to 1770, it was known as Peckuwe or Piqua, then the home of the Peckuwethage. The bounds of the pickets which surrounded the Msi-kah-mi-qui (Council-house) of the Shawnee Indians at Old Chillicothe — now Oldtown, Greene County, Ohio,—are known; the location and designation being both legally and historically accurate. This was the place of Colonel Boone's captivity; of General Simon Kenton's Run of the Gantlet, in 1778, following his capture for the theft of seven Shawnee horses; and of Jennie Cowan's captivity. Nearby was the birthplace of Tecumseh, and the scene of Rebecca Galloway's romantic courtship. In the Msi-kah-mi-qui, or temple, usually referred to as Council-house, many solemn councils were held during the period when the Shawnee clans were unable to decide whether they would join their paleface enemy in peace, or fight until every Shawnee warrior fell in the struggle.

The following data are definite as to the village and its location: Colonel Boone's personal narrative of his captivity locates "Old Chillicothe" as the "principal Indian town on the Little Miami." An accurate copy of this valuable narrative, contributed by the writer, may be found in the *Ohio Archaeological and Historical Society's Publications*.[1] The writer's great-grandfather, James Galloway, Sr., was a member of General George Rogers Clark's second punitive expedition against the Shawnee Indians at Old Chillicothe

---

[1] *Ohio Arch. and Hist. Quarterly*, 13:263-277.

in 1782. The court-house records of Greene County, Ohio, verify the exact location of this village by his testimony in the case of John Stevenson vs. Peter Vandolah, in the Greene County Superior Court in Chancery, before Josiah Glover, Master Commissioner, at the house of Abner Reed, June 15, 1818. On the foundations of this pioneer brick house of Abner Reed, a frame dwelling-house has been erected, west 160 yards from the marker placed on the Springfield-Xenia highway by Catherine Greene Chapter, Daughters of the American Revolution, which locates both the village site and Simon Kenton's historic gantlet run in 1778.

After testifying that he first saw "Old Chillicothe" and the Little Miami prairie bottoms in 1782, to the question, "Are you now sitting in the place called 'Old Chillicothe'?" James Galloway answered: "I am sitting within the bounds where the pickets were."

The writer possesses a certified copy of General Simon Kenton's deposition in the Seventh Circuit Court for Ohio District, wherein James McDonald is plaintiff, and Richard Cost, James Galloway, Jr., and others are defendants, date of April 13, 1826, from which the following is taken:

Q.: Were you acquainted with the country northwest of the Ohio River between the Little Miami and Scioto Rivers in the year 1787 and before and after that time?

Ans.: I was through that country twice in the year 1778. The first time I was on Paint Creek; and on my second trip in that year, I took horses from the Indians near the Chillicothe town on the Little Miami River, and have frequently been through that country since, until the present time. From the year 1778 to 1794, I was often on the Scioto with parties of men under my command, and traversed the country between the Little Miami and Scioto Rivers in various directions, as high up the Little Miami as Old Chillicothe, and as high up the Scioto as to the mouth of Paint Creek, and above where the town of Chillicothe now stands. I was pilot to General Clark's army on his campaign in 1780. I was pilot and commander of a company with General Clark in his campaign in 1782. In 1786, I was pilot, and commanded a company with Colonel Logan in his campaign in that year, and was often afterwards through that country with scouting parties under my command until the year 1794.

Nothing is needed to strengthen these two court records, although the testimony of other soldiers of Clark's 1780 expedition is available. Both deponents were notable pioneer citizens acquainted with the facts narrated; both were reliable. This, therefore, was one of the principal locations of the Shawnee Indians who were described in history as "the Spartans of their race; the first to enter battles, and the last to sign treaties." We may expect, therefore, to meet unusual situations in this historical study. Over this ground, the footsteps of notable Indian chiefs have trod, and their voices have echoed; the Logans; Cornstalk (Hokolesqua); Black Hoof; the talented Little Turtle, the enemy of General St. Clair; Silver Heels; Blue Jacket —who was Marmaduke Van Sweringen, a captured white boy who had been adopted. Blue Jacket was first in command of the Indian forces that defeated General St. Clair; and second in command of the allied Indian army defeated by General Wayne at the Battle of Fallen Timbers. Here also was the home of the Kispokotha chief Pucksinwah, and his sons, Chiksika, Tecumseh (Tecumtha) and Tenskwatawa, "The Prophet," and their sister, Tecumapese. Likewise, notable white prisoners have sojourned here, some quite willingly, others very naturally under protest: Daniel Boone, greatly loved and adopted into the tribe; Simon Kenton, soundly feared and genuinely hated. There were many men, women and children who were captive here, some of them from the best Kentucky and Virginia pioneer families. Jennie Cowan, grand-aunt of the late Rev. Dr. James Gillespie Carson, was captured in Tennessee. The Virginia captives included members of the Cunningham, Hamilton and McKee families and Mrs. Jennie Gilmore, with her son, John, and two daughters, Betsy and Margaret, who remained captives for seven years. Israel Donalson and Mrs. Dennis were among the well-known captives of this settlement. The 27 salt-makers taken captive with Daniel Boone at Salt Licks in Kentucky in 1778 were captives here.

ON THE LITTLE MIAMI

A few years ago, Dr. Charles Eastman, an influential Sioux Indian, graduate of Dartmouth College, was the writer's guest and visited this village site. He quickly noted the extended hard soil ridge for residence; its excellent water-shed; a fine spring near by; rich prairie lands on both sides of the ridge; the Little Miami River affording good fishing and canoeing to the Ohio River;[2] and all surrounded by hills which, in Indian days, were heavily wooded, making an ideal covering for game. Fortunately a good description is found in the *Draper Manuscripts* of Old Chillicothe and its inhabitants of date, June 1779:

In the spring of 1779, the village was inhabited by 100 warriors and 200 squaws and children—*Tabawa nanvudoki chena nesana tabawa iqaki macimi vpalufvki*. Four hundred warriors and their families, estimated at 1000 to 1200 Shawnees, had migrated, settling near the present site of Cape Girardeau, Missouri. Restlessness and mass movement were Shawnee characteristics. So the village, by June 1779,—the date of the first punitive expedition against it—was three-fourths under-populated (a fortunate condition, indeed, for the invading expedition). In the center of the village stood the large Council-house (*Msi-kah-mi-qui*)—about sixty feet square, built of strong notched hickory logs, with open gables at each end, and upright posts in the center supporting the roof. There were a dozen board huts on the southern slope of the ridge, besides many log ones scattered along the ridge quite far out to the southwest. North of the ridge were many ordinary huts, some well built.

The Indians had long since learned from white prisoners the use of the ax, saw, auger and wooden pin, their purchase having been available to Indians at the French and English trading-posts for half a century or more. Huts located on the bottom lands were pretty well scattered, and occupied much of the land north of the ridge to Massies Creek and the Little Miami River. There were likewise a number of tepees among the huts.

The village had been built to accommodate, also, the

---

[2] The Ohio River was called Spay-lay-wi-theepi by the Shawnees, and Ouabachi by Father Jacques Gravier in 1700.

1000 or 1200 Shawnees who emigrated to Spanish Territory in March, 1779, and later became known as "The Absentee Shawnees." These were the advocates of peace measures with the whites. Those who remained were war advocates. The migration was the first outcome of years of solemn deliberation by the Shawnees, in representative meetings at Old Chillicothe, to determine the future policies of their nation with the whites—whether peace and amalgamation, or war and annihilation. The historic fact of these deliberations was noted by Alford on the occasions of his designation to the officers of the Greene County (Ohio) Chapters, Daughters of the American Revolution, of the birthplace of Tecumseh "in the neighborhood of Old Chillicothe."

Black Fish was the tribe's principal civil chief when it was attacked before daylight by Colonel James Bowman and 264 Kentucky volunteers. Black Hoof, according to Shawnee tradition, was then residing at the village, and was the battle chief. This, the first organized punitive expedition against the village, occurred in June, 1779. Its organization was reported in detail to General George Rogers Clark by Colonel Bowman on June 13, 1779. The "open season for Indians" of the Miami Valley began in 1778, at Boonsborough, Kentucky, where a number of Shawnees had taken an active part in its attack. The Bowman expedition was a punitive adventure. The underlying contention between the Indians and the pioneer whites of that period was the determination of the Shawnees to maintain the Ohio River as their south boundary line as designated in the first Fort Stanwix Treaty in 1768.

This was the only boundary treaty acknowledged by all of the tribes as binding. The various representative Indians participating in the Treaty (1768) had been designated by their tribal conferences, and authority to attach their signatures was given to those delegates who participated in this treaty conference. The second Fort Stanwix Treaty was not thus authorized, so far as the Indian interests were concerned and, consequently, was repudiated by them. The determination of the *whites* was to disregard the first Fort Stanwix Treaty, in which the Ohio River was made the southern limit of the territory belonging to the Indians. In the darkest hours of the Revolution, when defeat seemed inevitable to the colonial military forces, General Washington and other leading Revolutionary officers associated with him, looked to the Northwest Territory, which included the Indian lands, as the place of retreat and re-establishment in the event of defeat of the colonial arms.

After the Treaty of Paris, General Washington in 1787 bought four surveys in Clermont County, Ohio. They totaled 3051 acres. Three surveys were choice bottom lands. The fourth was heavy oak-timbered upland. They were located: one on the Xenia State Road, then known as the Bullskin Trace, a notable north and south Indian trail which became Ohio's first highway by Legislative Act on February 4, 1807; the others were in Pierce, Miami and Union Townships. Nine hundred and seventy-five acres were located near Camp Dennison, Ohio. The President was a good judge of land. His choice was decided by the heavy oak-timber growth. Among the Virginia Revolutionary soldiers who located surveys near the President's, was General Richard Clough Anderson, aide on the staff of General LaFayette. He was the grandfather of Major Robert Anderson who defended Fort Sumter, and of Governor Charles Anderson, of Ohio. General Washington's estate lost all of these lands through defective records.[3] Detailed history of "Washington's Ohio Lands" is found in an accurately prepared paper by the late E. O. Randall.[4]

THE NUMEROUS OHIO "CHILLICOTHES"

The spelling and pronunciation of Cha-lah-kaw-tha[5] by pioneer writers as *Che-le-coth-e*, and anglicized to *Chilli-*

---
[3] See footnote 12, page 9.
[4] *Ohio Arch. and Hist. Quarterly*, 19:303-318.
[5] The Shawnee spelling of this word is *Cha-lah-kau-tha*, pronounced *Chaw-lah-koh-tha*, *ch* as in *church* and the final *a* as in *father*. The first three syllables are guttural, the major inflection being upward on the third (Alford).

cothe, arose from phonetic interpretation of an alien tongue. The Shawnees had no written language by which they could preserve their own pronunciation, and few of the white pioneers had either the time or the inclination to enter into the difficulties of Indian vocal inflection and phonation. Such details were of little consequence to the pioneers whose efforts were largely to destroy, and not preserve, living characteristics of a race which courageously opposed their acquisitions. In Shawnee pronunciation, all the laryngeal muscles are used in giving a low guttural sound difficult to acquire except in part and after practice. This is especially notable in words of several syllables where there is a tonal difference to each succeeding syllable. James Galloway, Sr., pronounced "Chillicothe" as though spelled "Chelicothe" and pronounced Chee-le-kauth-e. John Williams, in *The American Pioneer* writes:

Those valleys—the Scioto and Paint Creek valleys—were favorites of the Aborigines also, in each of which they built their Che-le-co-the which is understood to be an Indian name signifying town or city.[6]

In the September number of the same publication, in an article on Logan, Felix Renick, Esq., writes:

Captain Parsons informed me that he was in the town where Logan then resided and where he delivered his speech. He called it Chi-le-coth-e, sounding each syllable as it would be, detached from the rest.[7]

The philology of the word as given by Alford is interesting and authentic. He explains its several and significant uses as applied to clan and residence conditions. Chillicothe, he says, does not mean town or dwelling-place in the Shawnee language, but is the Anglicized name of one of the five original Shawnee clans which composed this nation. Each clan's dwelling-site took the name of the particular clan dwelling there. In the Shawnee nation, there were originally five clans:

---
[6]*Amer. Pioneer*, 1:205 (June, 1842).
[7]*Amer. Pioneer*, 1:332 (September, 1842).

(1) Thawegila
(2) Chalahkawtha (Chillicothe)
(3) Peckuwetha (Piqua)
(4) Maykujay
(5) Kispokotha

The "Chillicothe" clan built or occupied, for a greater or less time, all the five Ohio Chillicothes. The Peckuwetha clan built and occupied the Piqua towns. To illustrate: If the "Chillicothe" clan built and occupied a town, it would be called "Chillicothe." If later they moved away to another location, and the Kispokotha Clan (Tecumtha's clan) moved into and occupied it, the name of the town would be changed to Kispokothage. Shawnee tradition relates that the Peckuwetha clan first located and built Old Chillicothe on the Little Miami, and resided there for a time. The town's name then was Peckuwe or Pique. Later the Chalahkawtha clan predominated in numbers and the town automatically changed names becoming "Chillicothe." As the Chalahkawtha clan's residence there became longest in moons and seasons, the name became "Old Chillicothe." In the event that the village was occupied by several clans, the town would take the name of the clan to which the head chief belonged.

The late Professor R. W. McFarland's article on "The Chillicothes" gives the same meaning to the Shawnee designations as Williams's. He locates the five Ohio villages known as "Chillicothe": (1) on the site of the present city of Piqua; (2) Chillicothe, often called Old Chillicothe, now Oldtown, three miles north of Xenia; (3) Chillicothe, also often called Old Chillicothe, at or near the village of Westfall, four miles down the Scioto River from Circleville, on the west bank; (4) Chillicothe, now Hopetown, three miles north of Chillicothe, Ross County, also called Old Town in early Ohio history; (5) Chillicothe, now Frankfort, also called Old Town. Indian names, he states, were usually significant, as were Old Jewish names.[8]

---

[8]*Ohio Arch. and Hist. Quarterly*, 11:230-231.

THE SHAWNEE INDIANS[1]
By Thomas Wildcat Alford

FROM THE early days, even after the settlement of North America by the white race to the present time, the history of the Shawnee Indians is wrapped in obscurity. They moved about so incessantly, and were so often divided in their migrations, that we are unable to track the various clans or natural divisions. I think the historians all agree that they were the most restless, energetic, warlike, and adventurous of all the Indian tribes.

Their original home from time immemorial was in what is now the State of Kentucky and northern part of Tennessee, from which they went forth in their war or hunting expeditions in all directions, and back again; sometimes they were driven out by their enemies, but they soon returned. Here they had a common home and a common town, which they called "Skipakithiki" or "Place of Blue," which appears in history as, "Eskipakithiki," said to have been located on a branch of the Red River of the Kentucky which we call "Cantucky," or "Long Flowing." They had prehistoric villages scattered over this territory from which their wanderings extended east to the shores of the Atlantic Ocean; south to Georgia, to the Carolinas, and even to Florida; west to the Mississippi River, beyond the Cumber-

---

[1] My Dear Friend, Dr. Galloway:
　　I am sending you this history in order that it may be of service to you in the article you are preparing about the Shawnees from their viewpoint of their history.
　　Necessarily, I have to send you a sketch based upon notes I have collected to use in writing a history of my people which, if God spares my life long enough, I hope to finish; these notes are based upon Shawnee tradition in so far as it is corroborated by records of your people. I have had great difficulty in getting at the truth; so many statements of your people are at variance with our tradition and vice versa, that at times I get almost discouraged. Following is the outline, so far gathered, of the history of the Shawnee Indians.
　　　　　　　　　　　　　　　　　　　　Thos. W. Alford.

land River which they call "Skipaki Theepi," or "Blue River"; and north to the Great Lakes. At any time in the early days they could be found here, in greater or smaller numbers, and sometimes they rudely fortified themselves therein and defended their country against their numerous enemies. Their Town, "Skipakithiki," was undoubtedly rebuilt, time and time again, as often as their enemies destroyed it, and in the same vicinity. The surrounding country was then known to the sons of the forest as the "Middle Ground," or the "Dark and Bloody Ground."

In describing the locality of the town rebuilt during historic times, one pioneer said, "The locality of 'Eskipakithiki' was extremely beautiful, on a small prairie with a more level region adjacent, and a better quality of land than was generally found in the country." Another said, "I know but one other place to please the eye as well"; and still another, "O bears and buffaloes, elk and deer, the number was legion; and at many of the large salt-licks of the country they congregated in such prodigious herds that the sight was truly grand and amazing." Its site is said to be about eleven miles east of Winchester, in Clark County, Kentucky, and the present hamlet of Indian Fields marks the site. It was subsequently know to the early traders as "Pick Town," or "Pickque," or "Blue Lick Town," or "Pickawilany," from "Peckuwe," name of one of their clans, and "ilani," man; therefore "Peckuwe-lani," "man of Peckuwe," who perhaps occupied the town at that time.

Here, it is said, the French first met the Shawnees. "M. Charleville, a French trader from Crozat's colony at New Orleans, came in 1714, and traded with them." It is said his store was built on a mound near the present site of Nashville, where the Shawnees "had fortified themselves and maintained a protracted war for the possession of their home country." When the English traders first came here is not known, but it is a matter of history that one, Robert Smith, while trading here with the Shawnees, picked up two teeth of a mastodon in 1744, and gave the same to Christopher Gist in 1751.

Perhaps I should not go into detail too much, for lack

of time, to show where they were found by your people in the early settlement of North America. However, they were perhaps first referred to, as subsequently known, in 1586, by Ralph Dane, commander-in-chief of Sir Walter Raleigh's colony on the Roanoke Island. Dane states, "To the northwest the farthest place to our discovery was to 'Chawannocks,' from 'Sawanwaki'; a Shawnee name for Shawnees, plural; Distance from Roanoke about 130 miles." He also states that "they are about 700 fighting men." The Town of Chawanocks is shown on John White's map of 1586. Captain John Smith, who arrived in America in 1607, speaks of them as living in Virginia. They were also located to the west of the Susquehanna on its banks. On the maps of the earliest Dutch and Swedish navigators in 1614 is depicted a nation called "Sawwanew" (Shawnee) living on the east bank of the Delaware near its mouth.

In 1632, Captain Henry Fleet found "Shaunetowa," or "Sawanwiutawa" in the Shawnee language, which means Shawnee town, at the head of navigation of the Potomac, which was under an "emporor," Powhatan perhaps, the father of Pocahontas, or Matoawka. Here I may be excused for saying that I am convinced that both Powhatan and his daughter were Shawnees, at least they bear Shawnee names. Powhatana was his full name from which your people left the last *a* out, and it means "Shake it up."

In 1640, "Sawanoos" (Shawnees) were enumerated as one of the tribes of the Delaware River; and in 1656, "Sauwanoos" are located as between the Upper Schuylkill (and westward therefrom) and the Delaware.

The map of New Netherland of 1676 also places them between these two rivers, but much lower down, and to the mouth of the Schuylkill, under the name of "Sauno."

In Robert Morden's 1687 map of Carolina and Virginia, the "Sauna" are located in Upper South Carolina beyond the headwaters of the Broad and Wateree Rivers.

Other facts may be cited showing their presence east and west, and north and south of their original home at the beginning of white settlements on the Atlantic coast. How they came to be there, or what brought them there, is, of course, beyond conjecture. Perhaps they were driven there by the Iroquois and Catawbas, their hereditary enemies, or by their natural inclination to wander.

THE FIVE CLANS, OR SEPTS

The Shawnees were originally or naturally divided into five clans, or septs, of the nation; and had a way of naming each town or village after the name of the clan that built or occupied it; and following are the names of these clans:

1. Thawegila, (has no particular meaning).
2. Chalahgawtha, (has no particular meaning).
3. Peckuwe, or Peckuwetha, (one of ashes or dust).
4. Kispugo, or Kispokotha, (has no particular meaning).
5. Maykujay, (big-bodied, fat).

Out of either of the first two comes the principal, or national chief, because the *Meesawmi*,[2] or token of life of a clan, is equal in power in each of these two. The rest are subordinate, having each its own Meesawmi and its own chief, who is independent of the principal chief in matters pertaining to his own clan, but not those affecting the nation as a whole. Under its own *Meesawmi*, each clan has a certain duty or peculiar office to perform for the nation, for instance, the Peckuwe has charge of maintenance of duty and celebration of things pertaining to God, or Maneto; the Kispugo, of things pertaining to war; the Maykujay, of health and medicine, that is, he is the doctor; and the two chief clans, Thawegila and Chalahgawtha, of things political, or things affecting the nation as a whole.

Thawegila, Peckuwe and Kispoko are and have been from time immemorial, more or less, closely related, politically and morally; and Chalahgawtha and Maykujay also. These two general divisions of the clans were less marked in the early days, but gradually grew more promi-

---

[2]For explanation of *Meesawmi*, see chapter, "Indian Stories."

nent as the settlements by the Americans advanced westward, owing, it is presumed, to natural rivalry of the two chief clans, and to the sides taken by each faction in the wars and contentions of all races in America. The locations of these two general divisions seem to be well-defined and apparent in the colonial records by a line drawn from their "home land" east to the Atlantic, and west to the Mississippi. South of this line was the hunting or "wandering" ground of the Thawegila faction, whose settlements scattered over the south, even to Florida, and, therefore, they were the Southern Shawnees; and the Chalahgawtha faction were the Northern Shawnees whose hunting-ground was north of this line, or, generally speaking, north of the Ohio River. Their settlements also scattered over this territory to near the Great Lakes. It is a fact that none of the latter faction ever settled south of what are now the states of Kentucky and Tennessee, and never east of the Alleghany Mountains. These seemed to be their locations when the English came to America.

CLAN NAMES IN MANY FORMS

The names of all these clans have been preserved in colonial history to this day, in many forms which perhaps confuse persons not acquainted with these natural divisions of the Shawnees. If you ask a Creek Indian the name of a Thawegila town, he is likely to say "Sawakola," or "Sawokla," or "Sawokli," as preserved in the south where the Creeks lived; if a Delaware Indian, he is likely to say, "Assiwikala" or "Sewickley," in which form are preserved the names of two streams known as Big Sewickley Creek, one entering the Youghiogheny from the east, two or three miles below the village of West Newton, in Westmoreland County, and the other entering the Ohio from the north, about two miles above Logstown Bar, and forming a part of the boundary line between the counties of Allegheny and Beaver in Pennsylvania, near the neighborhood of which was the residence of the Delawares and the Thawegila clan of Shawnees about 1730. Other forms may be cited.

HILLS ADJOINING THE SITE OF OLD CHILLICOTHE

Here Simon Kenton secured and drove off seven horses. The Shawnees captured him with the horses at the Ohio River. See Kenton's affidavit on page 11

What is said about Thawegila is also true as to the rest of them. Peckuwe, or Peckuwetha, is written "Pequea," "Pequa," "Pekwes," "Picque," "Pickaway," and "Pick;" and "Pechoquealin," "Pecquealin," "Pickawillany," the latter three forms meaning "Man of Peckuwe," as explained before. The form "Pickaway" is preserved in the name of a county in the State of Ohio, and "Piqua" in the name of a town in the same State.

The name of Chalahgawtha clan is changed in form less than all the rest. It is almost uniformly written as "Chillicothe." It is said that in Daniel Boone's day, several Chillicothe towns were destroyed by the Kentuckians, and rebuilt again and again by the Shawnees in different localities. One Chillicothe town was located at the mouth of the Scioto, which the traders called "Lower Shawnee Town." Another was at or near the village of Oldtown, on the Little Miami, three miles north of Xenia, Greene County, Ohio; and others in the same and other states.

Maykujay is written as "Maquck," "Mequck," "Muquck," "Macqeechaick," "Mecquachake," "Machachac," "Macqueechaick," and all are supposed to be plural, especially the last four forms, "Maykujayki." It is said a town of "Moquck," or "Macqueechaick," stood in 1751 on the east side of the Scioto, above, on what are known as Pickaway Plains, which were formerly called by the Indians and traders as the Great Plains or "Maquck," or "Maykujay," in Pickaway County, Ohio.[3]

The name of the clan Kispugo is written, "Kispoko," "Kispicotha," "Kiskapooke," "Kiskapoke," etc. The latter two forms are plural, "Kispugoki." This clan of the Shawnees was more or less affiliated with the Creek, or Muskogee Indians in the south in the early days, and it is said by historians that the town of "Tukabatchi" of the Upper Creeks on the Tallapoosa River, one and a half miles below its falls, was anciently settled by the "Ispokogi," a Creek name for the members of this clan.[4]

---
[3] Modern spelling, Macacheek.
[4] Modern spelling, Kispoko, or Kispokotha.

THE WAR OF THE IROQUOIS

About the year 1670, the Iroquois again turned their arms and waged an unrelenting war against the Shawnees, and drove them from their towns in the Ohio Valley, some into the country of the Creeks in the south, and others among the Pgewilaneki, or the Miamis, in the northwest. But they would not submit, although all that was required of them was to acknowledge the Iroquois as better warriors than themselves. However, the Iroquois claimed to have conquered them, and claimed their land. But it is doubtful. Sometimes a faction of the Shawnees was compelled to submit to their dictations, and was driven time and time again from their home in the Ohio Valley, but they soon returned. So in this, their last effort to conquer them, most of the Shawnees returned to their home land on the Blue River, afterwards the Cumberland, and on the Kentucky before the expiration of ten years. From there, in the spring of 1681, one of their chiefs who commanded 150 warriors, appealed to the French for protection against their enemies the Iroquois who were allies of the English, and in the summer of 1682, LaSalle brought about an alliance with the Miamis, Illinois, Shawnees and others for common defence against the Iroquois. A little later, some of them joined the French and were with LaSalle at his Fort of St. Louis in 1683 on the Illinois River. Their village of 200 warriors, perhaps 600 or 800 souls, was located a year later on the south side of the river, behind the fort.

In the struggle which began in 1689 between England and France to determine which people should be masters of North America, the Shawnees hesitated to join the English in the beginning of the war because the Iroquois were allied on that side, although most of the Shawnees preferred the English friendship, especially those who had previously been in the east where they had better acquaintance with them and their goods, and had traded with them. Those who remained in the south and west, and who had more acquaintance with the French, were inclined to side with them. But all were against the Iroquois, who proved rather a hindrance to the English on account of this enmity.

THE SHAWNEE INDIANS

About 1690 or later, about half of the Shawnees began an eastward movement for the last time to seek peace and protection in eastern Pennsylvania, where some of them arrived from the south and joined their brothers, a portion of the Peckuwe clan. The latter came there in 1692 with their chief, Miawawluway, or "Meaurroway," and all settled near the mouth of the Susquehanna on the Peckuwe, or "Pequea," Creek in what is now Lancaster County, and later at Paxtan on or near the site of Harrisburg. Another party of the same clan who left LaSalle's Fort at St. Louis, with their chief Kawkawatchikay, or "Kakowatgheky," came in the same year and settled among the Delawares on the Delaware River in what is now Monroe County. The town on that river was known later as Peckuwelani, or "Pechoquealin," man of Peckuwe. The rest, headed by Wawpaythi (Swan), or "Opessa," proceeded down to the head of the Chesapeake Bay and settled in what is now Cecil County, Maryland, and later in 1697, by permission of Pennsylvania and the Conestoga Indians, they joined their brothers at the Pequea Creek. There was another band conducted by Arnold Viele from the Ohio Valley who joined those on the Delaware in the summer of 1694. Two other settlements of Shawnees from the south were made later on the Upper Potomac, one on what is now the site of Oldtown in Allegany County, Maryland, which was known later as Opessa Town, and the other, of those of Thawegila, a little farther west on the same river.

Governor Fletcher of New York admitted the Shawnees to the covenant chain of friendship in 1694.

On May 26, 1698, the old chief, Miawawluway, for the last time, attended a conference held at Steelman's trading-house. He was brought there on horseback on account of his great age. His death undoubtedly occurred soon after, but the exact date is unknown. After his death, Wawpaythi, or "Opessa," became chief of the Peckuwe clan, of those of "Pequea" on the Susquehanna, and on April 23, 1701, he represented his clan, with other Indians, in the treaty of alliance with William Penn at Philadelphia. This was perhaps the first treaty ever made by these Indians, because the Shawnee chief, Kawkawatchikay, was informed on May 21, 1728, by Governor Gordon that, at the time of William Penn's first treaty with the Indians in 1682 or 1683, the Shawnees were not in this country. They came long afterwards and desired leave of the Conestoga Indians and of William Penn to settle in this country. Opessa was undoubtedly very happy with his people at this time, for he told Governor John Evans, who visited him in 1707, that his people were happy to live in a country at peace, and not as in those parts where they formerly lived; for then, upon their return from hunting, they found the town surprised, and their women and children taken prisoners by their enemies. He continued as chief of his clan at Peckuwe on the lower Susquehanna until 1711, when his people disagreed with him, and he voluntarily abandoned both his chieftainship and his clan, and sought a home among the Delawares. On June 14, 1715, in the Court-house at Philadelphia, with a companion, he took part in the Great Ceremony of the Pipe of Peace, with rattles and songs. The pipe was offered first to the king, to the governor, council, and all other English present, and afterwards to all their Indians, and then, with the same ceremony, it was put away again. Later Opessa left the Delawares and removed to one of the Shawnee towns on the Upper Potomac, which, since 1722, was known to the traders as "Opessa Town," now Oldtown, Maryland. He refused to return to his people, although he was repeatedly urged to do so. Therefore, Quakuntawayna was chosen as their chief, but he had the name only, without authority. There was no real chief among them until Lawpkaway, the son of Wawpaythi, or Opessa, attained his manhood. Opessa died about 1729.

 The Iroquois were not at peace with the Shawnees in 1704, notwithstanding the admittance of Shawnees into the covenant of friendship by Governor Fletcher in 1694 and the treaty of alliance of William Penn in 1701. Their secret enmity against them continued, together with the intrigue of the French in the north and west, and the Catawbas, their hereditary enemies in the south, which caused the Shawnees, including others, to remain comparatively quiet.

 This resulted in the decrease of the fur trade among

the English. As early as 1691, the English took notice of this and urged the General Assembly of New York "that communication be opened and peace be made with the far nations of Indians, with a view to increasing the fur and peltry business." When a report reached the Provincial Council on May 18, 1704, that the Iroquois Indians intended shortly to come down and carry off the Shawnees, both those settled at Pequea and elsewhere, "they being their enemies," the Council sent messages accompanied by belts of wampum to the Five Nations in behalf of the Shawnees, "our friends and allies." During the following August, eight or nine chiefs of the Iroquois visited Philadelphia in response to these messages, and a new treaty, favorable to the Shawnees, was made between them and the Provincial Government.

The main body of the Shawnees which did not move to Illinois, and from thence to Pennsylvania, consisted of those who remained on the Cumberland and the Kentucky after those that Arnold Viele conducted to the Delaware left the Ohio Valley, and those who remained in the south after those who migrated into Pennsylvania, left there. They maintained communications with all settlements by visits to each other during all of the time of their separation. These settlements, villages, or towns, their names and approximate dates of their locations, are given in the colonial records. But names are different in form because derived from different nations of Indians. For instance, the Shawnees on the Savannah River were known to the English in the south as "Savannahs," and were mentioned in Archdale's *Description of Carolina*. Those who remained in what is now the State of Kentucky are located by Father Jacques Gravier on the Cumberland River, although he calls the Ohio "the Ouabachi" in his narrative descriptive of his journey down to the mouth of the Mississippi in 1700 (printed from manuscript, by Shea).

The Shawnees who came east to seek peace and who had signed treaties for peace expected adequate protection from the English, who seem to have failed to give it, and the excuses given by the Iroquois of whom they had natural suspicion, seemed to them too readily accepted. This caused them growing unhappiness, and they naturally looked for protection elsewhere. Of this the French were not too slow to take advantage. When later the French secretly approached them through a Frenchman named Cavillier, some readily listened and even visited Canada for this purpose about 1722. Ahkuwila, or "Ocowellos," chief of the Upper Shawnees on the Susquehanna, informed the Council at Philadelphia on May 28, 1723, of his past visits, and that "they intended shortly to make another to the Governor of Canada." In response, the Governor and Council wrote him, discouraging the proposed trip to Canada, and sent them five gallons of rum "to cheer their hearts at the hearing of his words." Marquis de Vaudreuil had adopted measures in 1724 to bring nearer to his colony the nation of the Chaouanons (Shawnees), who he says consisted of over 700 Indians who were unhappy near the English.

In 1724, the Delawares moved west to the Allegheny country from their homes, chiefly in the vicinity of Shamokin, now Sunbury, in Northumberland County, Pennsylvania. They settled and built their first town on the Allegheny "some ten miles below the mouth of the Mahonoy, which they called 'Kithenning,' or 'Kittanning'." The reasons for their removal were the same which caused the Shawnees to remove westward to the Allegheny. The Peckuwes at Paxtan preceded the Delawares in 1724 as the advance guard. They were told by the Iroquois at Jaylasquahgi, or "Chillisquaque" in 1726, that "our land is going to be taken from us. Come, brothers, assist us. Let us fall upon and fight with the English." But they answered. "*No*, we came here for peace, and have leave to settle here. We are in league with them, and cannot break it." About a year later, after denouncing them and the Delawares, looking upon them for the future "as women and not as men," since they would not hearken to them nor regard what they had said to them, they ordered the Shawnees to "look back toward Ohio, the place from whence you came, and return thitherward, for now we shall take pity on the English, and let them have all this land." They further said, "Now, since you are become women, I'll take

'Peckoquealin' (Peckuwe-lini) and put it on 'Meheahoming' (Wawwiyawmi, or Wyoming), and I'll take 'Meheahoming' and put it on 'Ohioh,' and 'Ohioh,' I'll put on 'Woabach,' and that shall be the warrior's road for the future." This was related by the Shawnee chiefs to Governor Gordon in a letter, June 7, 1732.

ONCE MORE THE YOUNG RED MAN GOES WEST

Here they lived comparatively in peace for about thirty-two years, except for causes cited and the continual decreasing of the game, driven away by the English, whose contentions with the French through their allies, the Iroquois, whom most of the Shawnees preferred to be on the opposite side, led them to begin once more, and for the last time, a westward movement toward the land of their ancestors in the Ohio Valley. This they completed during the years 1728 to 1730. The immediate cause of their removal was that, in the early part of this year, disorders were committed by some of their young men "through the connivance of Peter Chartier, a half-blood Shawnee and a trader among them on the opposite side of the Susquehanna from 'Peixtan' near what is now Harrisburg." The victims were men and women of the Conestoga Indians, who resented it so highly they threatened to cut off the whole nation of Shawnees. On May 20, 1728, Kawkawatchikay, or "Kakowtcheky," chief of the Peckuwe clan at Peckuwe-lani, or "Pechoquelin," sent a verbal message through the traders of that place to Governor Gordon to the effect that he, having heard that Conestogas were come with a design to make war upon our Indians, had sent eleven of his men, armed, to inquire into the truth of this report, with orders to assist our brothers in case the same should be true; that their provisions failed them and they were obliged to get from the inhabitants wherewithal to subsist; but that they offered no rudeness until the white people treated them ill and fired upon them; that he was very sorry for what has happened; but that one of them was wounded and lost his gun, which he desired might be sent. On September 1, they sent for John Schonhoven, one of the traders of Durham in Bucks County to bear a message for them to the governor, desiring to make a treaty with him, having collected furs for that purpose. While he was among them in Peckuwe-lani, a message came by an Indian from the Susquehanna, upon receiving which, the Shawnees, with their wives and children, went off from Peckuwe-lani, leaving their corn standing; that the hurry they seemed to be in, gave cause for apprehension of some mischief that was on foot. This was reported to the governor. Outbreaks occurred simultaneously among the Shawnees of Peckuwe, Paxtan, in Lancaster County, and "Jaylasquahgi," or "Chillisquaque," and those of the two Peckuwe-lani towns in the present counties of Warren in New Jersey and Monroe in Pennsylvania. This occurred after the advance guard of the Shawnee Emigration westward had reached the Allegheny country. The fact was that Manawkyhickon, a noted Delaware chief, and a near relative of Wequela, who was hanged in New Jersey the year before, much resented his death, and had sent a black belt of wampum to the Iroquois who "sent the same to the Miamis, with a message desiring to know if they would lift up their tomahawks and join with them against the Christians, to which they agreed." The governor was not much surprised to hear this report, as the message from Susquehanna might be supposed to come from the chiefs of the Iroquois then said to be about Conestoga; but he stated that he was surprised to receive a report of the removal of the Delawares and Shawnees from their towns, and of their war spirit.

Chief Kawkawatchikay and his clan of Peckuwe Shawnees had really made their first move in the direction of the Ohio, and many of them went there directly from "Peckuwe-lani," or "Pechoquealin," above Delaware Water Gap. The majority, however, had gone only as far as the "Wawwiyawmi," or Wyoming Valley, where they settled on the west bank of the Susquehanna of the North Branch, at a place subsequently known as the Shawnee Flats, immediately below the site of the present town of Plymouth in Luzerne County. This continued to be an important town of the Shawnees until 1743. In the summer or fall of that year the chief and his people removed to the Ohio River and settled at Logstown, about 18 miles below Pittsburgh, and just below the site of the present village of Economy, Beaver County, Pennsylvania.

The lower Susquehanna, the upper Potomac Shawnees, and those at Jaylasquahgi, or "Chillisquaque," on the west branch of the Susquehanna, likewise took up their belongings and followed their brothers over the mountains, establishing themselves on the Allegheny and along its tributary, the Conemaugh, or "Kiskiminetas," and on what was known after its abandonment by them as Chartier's Old Town. This was probably at the mouth of Bull Creek, near the present borough of Tarentum, Allegheny County. This was one of the principal villages of the Shawnees until 1745, and this and the Delaware town of Kittanning, with two or three smaller villages between, and three or more along the banks of the Kiskiminetas, constituted a centre of Indian population and influence known for many years in Pennsylvania colonial history as "the Allegheny."

After the death of their chief, the Potomac Shawnees, having been attacked by their southern enemies in 1729 at Wawpaythewi Odayway, or "Opessa Town" on or near the site of the city of Cumberland on that river, took their wives and children over the mountains to the Conemaugh and the Allegheny. If their chief here referred to as having died was Wawpaythi, or "Opessa," for whom this town was named, then the date of his death is approximately given as that of 1729 or before. After the treaty at Conestoga in 1728, several Shawnees settled at Allegheny, and went to the governor of Montreal to seek protection from the French against the Iroquois, whom they suspected would hinder their settling at Allegheny.

By 1730, most of them, excepting Kawkawatchikay and his clan still at Wyoming, were on their several settlements on the Allegheny and numbered about 115 families, 360 fighting men, as reported by traders to Governor Gordon on October 29, 1731, including names of their chiefs. On the Conemaugh, or Kiskiminetas, there were three towns,

95 families. 300 men. Fifty families of these and 100 men were of Thawegila, or "Asswikalas," or "Sewickley" clan settled on the Youghiogheny River at the mouth of Big Sewickley Creek, in what is now Westmoreland County, "lately from South Carolina to Potomac," whose chief was Ahquiloma, or "Aqueloma," true to the English; of the others, Ahkuwila, or "Okowela," or "Ocowela," or "Ocowellos," was the chief who was "suspected to be a favorer of the French." He was the chief of the Upper Shawnees on the Susquehanna, who had settled at the mouth of the Jaylasquahgi, or "Chillisquaque" Creek and who had mentioned his past visits to the governor of Canada in 1723.

In "Ohesson" on the Juniata at the mouth of Kiskahkuwila, or "Kishacoquillas" Creek, on or near the site of the present Lewiston in Mifflin County, were 20 families, 60 men, under chief Kiskahkuwila or "Kissikkahquelas."

Although Ahkuwila was represented as chief in this report of the Upper Shawnees on the Susquehanna, now settled on the Conemaugh with 200 men and 45 families, Nawchikana, or "Neuchconeh," was the real acting chief at Allegheny during the minority of Lawpkaway or "Loyparcowah," Wawpaythi's, or "Opessa's" son.

The French began building trading-posts about this time near the Ohio River, and the English traders there seemed to be under great apprehension on this account. A Seneca chief reported to Thomas Penn that the French came to Ohio in the fall of 1731 "to build houses there to supply the Indians with goods." On May 14, 1732, Edmund Cartlidge, a trader, likewise reported to the governor that the French had come again and were going to settle there. He also reported that a trader John Kelly told the Shawnees at Allegheny that the Iroquois were "ready to eat them up and drive away the French if the English governor should say the word." This information put the Shawnees in such a state of alarm and anger that they were about to begin war on the English traders at once, and were restrained only by the efforts of Peter Chartier and the French, who persuaded them that the news was false.

In a meeting at Philadelphia on August 23, 1732, the

proprietor suggested to the chiefs of the Iroquois that they compel the Shawnees to return eastward from the Allegheny country, and locate themselves on a reservation which had been surveyed for them in their former place of residence, the Cumberland Valley. This the Iroquois agreed to do, and to this end they labored over them for two years. In their final effort, in October, 1734, when their messengers asked them to return towards Susquehanna, the Shawnees answered that they would remove farther north, towards the French country, and at the same time, sent a belt of wampum to the Delawares, intimating that as they were to seek out a new country for themselves, they would be glad to have them go along. Whereupon some chiefs of the Iroquois set out to speak with them and they met at Allegheny, but without success. The Shawnees refused to leave Allegheny which, they said, was more commodious for them. The speaker for the Iroquois on this occasion was a Seneca chief who lived in the neighborhood. He "pressed them so closely" that they took a great dislike to him, and some eleven months after the chiefs returned, some young Shawnee warriors seized this speaker and murdered him, and then fled down the Ohio, fearing vengeance of the Iroquois. "It was supposed they returned to the place from whence they came, which was below Carolina." One of the chiefs of the Iroquois, after informing the Governor and Council of his failure, added that "one clan of these Shawnees had never behaved themselves as they should, and the Six Nations were not satisfied with them, as they seemed to harbor evil designs. This clan was called the Shaweygira (Thawegila), and consisted of about 30 young men, ten old men, and several women and children." The Seneca chiefs informed the government of New York, July 29, 1735, that they "heard there is a number of them departed down the River" (Ohio), and "we desire to know so soon as possible where those people are travelled to." John and Thomas Penn answered their request and said that they "understood those who murdered the Mingo Chief at Allegheny came there about four years since from the westward or southward to Ohio, but we do not know from whence they came nor to what parts they have gone."

It is not to be wondered at that the members of the Thawegila clan should be accused by the Iroquois of this murder. In any case, they were sure they would be because of the hatred these enemies had against them above all others, and knowing this and fearing the consequences "a number of them departed down the River" Ohio. They might have committed the murder, or it might have been done by others, but in either case they knew they would be blamed because "they had never behaved themselves as they should" and would not submit to their enemies, who "seemed to harbor evil designs" against them, and, therefore, "the Six Nations were not satisfied with them." Chief Ahquiloma, who brought some of this clan from South Carolina to Potomac, and from thence to Allegheny with 50 families and 100 men, was reported as "true to the English." Therefore if this act was really committed by his men, it was an act against the Iroquois and not the English. Thawegila always stood the foremost against all claims made by those, who naturally wished the members of this clan to return "to the place from whence they came, which was below Carolina." If this phrase was originated by them, it seems like a blind thrown in for others, including the English, who persisted in using them as a tool. However, it was apparent that the Shawnees grew more and more distant, notwithstanding the presents showered upon them by the English. Governor Thomas observed, in a message to the Pennsylvania Assembly, July 31, 1744, that there was but one of the Shawnees from Ohio present at the treaty with the Iroquois held at Lancaster during the month of June, and that he had since been informed that they and the Iroquois were far from being on good terms. The former had been endeavoring to draw the Delawares from Shamokin to Ohio, and the Iroquois feared that, in case they themselves were involved in the war which actually began between the English and the French, they would be obliged to fight the Shawnees and, perhaps, the Delawares also. The Governor adds, "Indeed, it is observable that the closer our union has been with the Six Nations, the greater distance the Shawnees have kept from us. I wish any method could be fallen upon to secure them effectually to the British interests, as they lie upon one part of our frontier, and our most valuable trade for skins is with them; but considering their frequent intercourse with the French, and their inconsistence, I almost despair of it." This was proven in the following year in the battle of Laurel Hills where General Braddock was defeated on July 8, 1775, by the French and Canadian Indians, with whom many Shawnees fought against the English and their allies. Among these was the celebrated chief Catahecassa, or Black Hoof, and perhaps his brother also, Chief Kikuskawlowa, or Notched Tail.

It seems that the Shawnees were the first to advocate prohibition of strong drink. On April 24, 1733, the chiefs at Allegheny wrote Governor Gordon, acknowledging presents received from him, and complaining of the number of new traders coming among them "bringing nothing but rum, and requested that orders be sent them to break in pieces all kegs so brought; and by that means the old traders will have their debts (paid), which otherwise never will be paid." Again on May 1, 1734, they dictated a letter to the Governor and Council of Pennsylvania, repeating what they said before regarding debts and unlicensed traders coming among them, and begged the Council "that no trader be allowed to bring more than thirty gallons of rum into the cabin where he lives directly, and not to hide any in the woods; and that every trader bring his license with him. For our part, if we shall see any other traders than those we desire among us, we will stave their kegs and seize their goods." In one of their towns on the Allegheny, they were attacked by Catawbas in 1736, and later informed the Proprietor that they were strongly solicited by the French to return to them; that every year they send them powder, lead and tobacco to enable them to withstand their enemies by whom they have often suffered; that they have gone so far back that they could not go further without falling into their enemies' hands, or going over to the French, which they would willingly avoid; that if they should return to Susquehanna, as the Pennsylvania government has often pressed them to do, they would starve, there being little or no game; and they, therefore, requested that they be furnished with arms and ammunition for their defense against their enemies, and to secure their continuance at Allegheny. The Council in return sent them a small present and invited the chief to visit Philadelphia with a view to renewing their treaties. On March 20, 1738, they acknowledged the receipt of this present "of a horseload of powder, lead and tobacco," and repeated that "they have a good understanding with the French, the Iroquois, the Ottawas and all the French Indians;" that the land reserved for them on the Susquehanna did not suit them; that they desired to remain where they were all together and make a strong town, "and keep our young men from going to war against other nations at a distance." The chiefs added, "after we heard your letter read, we held a council together to leave off drinking for the space of four years. The proposal of stopping the rum and all strong liquors was made to the rest in the winter, and they were all willing. As soon as it was concluded, all the rum that was in the towns, belonging to both the Indians and the white people, was staved and spilled. The quantity consisted of 40 gallons, which was thrown in the streets. We have appointed four men to stave all the rum and strong liquors that are brought to the town hereafter, either by the Indians or white men, during the four years." This "was accompanied by a pledge, signed by 98 Shawnees and two traders, agreeing that all rum should be spilled, and four men should be appointed for every town, to see that no rum or strong liquor should be brought into their towns for the term of four years."

In compliance with the invitation, the chiefs of the Shawnees from Wyoming and Allegheny came to Philadelphia, July 27, 1739, and held a council with Governor Thomas Penn. A new treaty of alliance and friendship was concluded, in which it was set forth that the Shawnees had removed westward to the Allegheny for the benefit of the hunting. This was signed, on behalf of the Shawnees at Ohesson on the Juniata and Susquehanna, by Kiskahkuwila, Palakikawcowthawta and Maiatahkula; those of Wyoming on the Susquehanna by Kawkawatchikay; and those at Allegheny by Nawchikana and Tomminipaquah, or "Tomenebuck."

Four years later, in the summer or fall of 1743, Chief Kawkawatchikay, with his clan, removed from Wyoming Valley in compliance with the invitation by his brothers, and settled at Logstown, on the right bank of the "Spaylaywi Theepi," or Ohio River, about eighteen miles below the Forks, now Pittsburgh, where he died about the year 1756. A few years after his departure from Wyoming, he was succeeded there as chief by Pucksinwa, or "Packsinosa." The latter had removed from Paxtan to the settlements of the Delawares, where he learned to speak their language, and from thence to Wyoming, as his contemporary, Chief Wawpaythi, did in 1711, after he had voluntarily abandoned his chieftainship and moved among the Delawares.

We shall now give our attention, in closing, to

PUCKSINWA, THE FATHER OF TECUMTHA

His name appears in the historical records in many forms, such as "Pucksinotha" or "Paxinosa," or "Puckshenose." These three names are affectionate names, as your people say "Willie" for "William." The same may be said of "Puckshinwau," or "Puckshenoath,' or "Puckeeshano," or "Packisheno." The son of Tecumtha also has names that appear as "Pugeshashenwa" and "Puchethei" which were probably given him by the Pottawatomie and Kickapoo Indians who have such names, and to whom he was well known. But these are positively not Shawnee names.

As to when Pucksinwa, the father of Tecumtha, came into eastern Pennsylvania from the south and whether Tecumtha's parents came with the Peckuwe Shawnees, who settled in 1692 at the "Pequea" Creek in Lancaster County, or if they came later and settled at "Paxtan," on or near the site of Harrisburg, is an open question. Some historians have the opinion that this Shawnee town "Paxtan" or "Paxton" or "Paxtang," derives its name from Peckuwe, or "Peckquea," the name of the clan of Shawnees that settled just below there in 1692. I have a suspicion that it might have been originally a "Paxinosa's" town from the name of this chief; later shortened into "Paxtown" or "Paxton," or "Paxtan," and other forms. However, that may be, "Paxinosa" certainly came from "Paxtan" when he removed north to the settlements of the Delawares, and from thence to the east or north branch of the Susquehanna, and settled at the Shawnee Town, Wyoming, now Plymouth, Luzerne County, where Chief Kawkawatchikay, with part of the Peckuwe Shawnees, had removed in 1728 from Peckuwe-lani, or "Pechoquea-lin," on the Delaware River in Monroe County. A few years after 1743, the date when Kawkawatchikay removed from Wyoming to Logstown on the Ohio River, about eighteen miles below Pittsburgh, Pucksinwa succeeded him as chief at Wyoming.

On August 22, 1749, Pucksinwa joined, with a number of others, in executing a deed to the Penns, conveying the land between the Delaware and Susquehanna, north of the Blue Mountains, and south of Wyoming. In 1756, he and his people followed the Delawares to Tioga, and in May of that year he acted as interpreter for them in a council "because he talk good Delaware." In 1757, he lived at Otseningo, now Binghamton, Broome County, New York. "He remained true to the English during the trying years from 1755 to 1758." In 1758, he with his entire family was met by Benjamin, a Delaware Mohegan, near Tioga. He told Benjamin that, as he had heard that the English had very bad designs against the Indians, he was going to his land at the Ohio where he was born. He undoubtedly joined Chief Kawkawatchikay's clan of Peckuwe Shawnees at Logstown, where they had removed fifteen years before from Wyoming. This clan is closely related with his.

The Chalahgawtha, or "Chillicothe" clan had a settlement lower down the Ohio, at the mouth of the Scioto, which they called "Chalahgawtha," and the traders, the "Lower Shawnee Town." This town was destroyed by an unusual flood some time between 1752 and 1753, and they partly rebuilt it on the Ohio, opposite the mouth of the Scioto, with few log cabins. They invited their Peckuwe brothers living at Logstown to come and live with them, and quit the French. After the destruction of their town, some moved up the Scioto and were joined by those who left Logstown in 1758, and settled at the Great Plains of Maykujay, or "Moquck," now known as "Pickaway Plains," where part of the Chalahgawtha clan and the Kispoko, with its chief Pucksinwa, established themselves on the Scioto opposite their brothers, the Maykujay. The rest of the Chalahgawtha, with the Peckuwe and Thawegila clans, moved northwest towards the Little Miami where they settled. The town of the former was known as Kispoko, or "Pucksinotha's Town" and as "Chalahgawtha Town," while the town of the latter was known as Peckuwe or "Chalahgawtha" on the Little Miami. This removal of the Shawnees from Logstown took place during the same year that Pucksinwa told Benjamin that he was on his way to his land at the Ohio "where he was born"—about 1758. George Croghan, a trader and Indian agent, said in his *Journal*, that he arrived at Logstown in the night of November 28, 1758, and found the town deserted by the late inhabitants, the Shawnees. Upon inquiring the reason of their speedy flight, the Delawares who were with him informed him that the Shawnees of Lower Shawnee Town had removed off the Ohio River and up the Scioto to a great plain called Maykujay, or "Moquck."

On November 25, 1758, General Forbes occupied Fort Duquesne, and two years later, on August 12, 1760, Pucksinwa, or "Pucksinosa," attended a conference held at Fort Pitt by General Monckton with the chiefs of the Iroquois, Miamis, Delawares, Ottawas, Wyandots and Shawnees.

The defeat of the French, and consequently the surrender of all their lands by the King of France to the King of England in 1763 awakened their minds to the power of the English, and aroused important discussions among them as to what should be done for the future welfare of the Shawnee nation in order that it might survive. Secret councils were held among the several clans of the nation, regarding the meaning of their tradition, pertaining to their several *Meesawmis*, which grew out of the sides taken by the clans in the war for and against the English. Many warriors were for continuance of opposition and war against them and their allies, while other chiefs were for living in peace with them. Evidently a disagreement finally took place, which caused their final division into two factions. Each was headed by one of the two chief clans— Thawegila and Chalahgawtha—as it is today. This division may almost be likened to the denominations among your people who, however, barely mentioned this, and only in common parlance, as "medicine," whatever that means. In these secret councils, which lasted for several years, no outsider was permitted, and only the chiefs of the *Meesawmis* and those specially instructed and deputized for that purpose took part. The Peckuwe clan had a Council-house, or Msi-kah-mi-qui, at the Peckuwe Town on the Little Miami, (afterwards Chalahgawtha Town), where at times these councils were held. To be with these Peckuwes, with whom his clan was closely related, Pucksinwa, with his clan, moved thither in 1768, *and on the journey he camped just outside of the town to await his son Tecumtha's birth.* Pucksinwa was killed at the battle of Point Pleasant in 1774.

MIGRATIONS TO AND FROM "OLD CHILLICOTHE"

After this battle, the final division began to be carried out, first, the members of one of the two chief clans— Thawegila—led by Kikusgawlowa, went south, and united with the rest of the clan among the Creeks (see *History of American Indians*). Later, these returned to the shores of the Ohio to their "home land" for the last time, and left the United States, and then went into "New Spain" the year 1785. As their own statement attests, in a treaty council held at St. Louis in 1815 by William Clark and others, they said, "Brothers, it is thirty years since we came to this country. When we arrived among the Spaniards to look

MARKER AT THE SITE OF OLD CHILLICOTHE

Erected at Oldtown by Catharine Greene Chapter, Daughters of the American Revolution, Greene County, Ohio

for a suitable piece of land to settle ourselves on, and after we found a place we liked, we informed the Spanish officer of it, and that we intended to settle ourselves there." How long it took them to find it is not stated, but in 1793, the Spanish government through Baron de Carondelet, a Spanish nobleman, granted them land 25 miles square, near Cape Girardeau, Missouri, "the records of which are in St. Louis." A second party, the Peckuwe and Kispoko clans, migrated in 1779 with about 1200 warriors, women and children from Old Chillicothe, and joined their brothers at Cape Girardeau. A third and last party joined later, those spoken of in the Congressional records as "a hostile party who had gone to New Orleans; from thence to Pensacola, where Governor O'Neal received them and gave them presents; from thence to the Creek Nation, where they were in 1792; and from thence to Cape Girardeau." This completed the division, as it has remained ever since.

The Chalahgawtha and Maykujay only remained north of the "Spaylaywi Theepi," or Ohio River, on their original territory. They later removed northwest and settled near Hog Creek and Great Auglaize River, as their treaty of September 29, 1817, stipulates, at a place they called "Wapaghkonetta." Tradition says the Maykujay clan has lost its *Meesawmi*, and hence it ceased to exist as such. Its members became scattered among other clans, specially the Chalahgawtha, and also intermarried with their former enemies, the Senecas and Wyandots, and others. A few still remain with them, known as the Eastern Shawnees, living in the northeastern part of Oklahoma today. In 1833, about 300, whom we know today as the Ohio Shawnees, moved from Wapaghkonetta, Ohio, to the land assigned them west of the Mississippi by treaty of July 20, 1831, "to contain sixty thousand acres within the tract of land equal to fifty miles square." This land was granted to the Missouri Shawnees, not the Absentee Shawnees, in lieu of their land at Cape Girardeau which they ceded to the United States, November 7, 1825. It was located west of Missouri and south of the Kansas River in what is now the State of Kansas. Thus the Ohio Shawnees became the Kansas Shawnees to us, who sold out all this land in 1854 without the knowledge or consent of the Absentee Shawnees. After the Civil War, they removed into the Cherokee Nation of Oklahoma, into which they were incorporated in 1867. They are there now, a part of the Cherokee nation.

The Missouri Shawnees of Cape Girardeau are now known as the Absentee Shawnees of Oklahoma. They are so called because they were absent when their lands, which they received in lieu of those at Cape Girardeau, were sold out by those in Kansas, and their money disposed of without their knowledge or consent.[5]

---

[5] The final disposition of the claims of the Absentee Shawnees for their lost lands is shown in Mr. Alford's letter to the author, dated August 3rd, 1928: "The government has engaged me to help find out the heirs of the old claimants of our war lost-property claims, which have been pending before Congress for over a half-century, and for which appropriation has been finally made by the last Congress for their settlement. I am working in the Indian office at the Shawnee Indian Agency, here (Shawnee, Oklahoma), under Judge Tutwiler, Examiner of Inheritance, assigned for this work. This final settlement was advanced by the information given to us by you in 1926, of Colonel Bowman's Report to General George Rogers Clark, of the attack under his command on Old Chillicothe in 1779, in which he states that three months previous to his attack, 1000 or 1200 of the Shawnee Indians had emigrated from Old Chillicothe to Cape Girardeau, Spanish territory west of the Mississippi, and settled there. From this point on, the history of the Absentee Shawnees was readily traced to the satisfaction of the large claim for lost property."

HISTORIC BACKGROUNDS

OLD CHA-LAH-GAW-THA TOWN
(Old Chillicothe)

* * *

From 1779 to 1790, five organized military invasions were directed against this village, either as a primary or a strategic point of attack on the Shawnee Indians of the two Miamis and the Mad River Valleys.

* * *

They were commanded by:

Colonel John Bowman	1779
General George Rogers Clark	1780
General George Rogers Clark	1782
Colonel Benjamin Logan	1786
General Josiah Harmar	1790

* * *

THE INDIAN VILLAGE

DURING THE five invasions of the Miami country from 1779 to 1790, Old Chillicothe was destroyed four times—1780-'82-'86-'90, and four times rebuilt by the Shawnees on the same site.

In General Harmar's daily log of his invasion in 1790, he adds two more Chillicothes and gives their locations: a Chillicothe on the St. Mary's River, two miles from the Miami (Maumee) village at which he camped on October 17th, 1790—and destroyed upon leaving—and a Chillicothe —possibly Girty's Town—on or near the present site of St.

Marys. He does not mention destroying this village. The Miami village, Harmar says, consisted of eighty tepees and huts.[1]

Each of the invasions destroyed the Indian villages in the territories they covered, which included Old Chillicothe on the Little Miami; Old Piqua and the Mackachek villages —including Wappatomica and Pidgeon Town on Mad River; upper and lower Piqua on the Great Miami; and the Miami villages and Chillicothe in the St. Marys and St. Joseph River territory. The extensive orchards, cornfields and gardens in the Auglaize country (about Fort Defiance) which were a base of food supplies, were not reached until General Wayne's campaign, ending in the Battle of Fallen Timbers, 1794. There was real hunger among the Indians the winter following this battle when England withdrew her support. This "base of supplies" explained the lack of serious damage done in the destruction from 1779 to 1790, of sectional villages and supplies, for as long as any food lasted it was Indian common property.

General Harmar wrote in the daily log of his march, on Saturday, October 30th, 1790: "All these Chillicothys are elegant situations—fine water near them and beautiful prairies. The savages knew how to take a handsome position, as well as any people on earth. When they leave a Chillicothe, they retire to another place and call it after the same name."[2] Old Chillicothe was located in a choice position and was quickly rebuilt on that account; also—an important Indian consideration—the waters of the Little Miami River, one-half mile distant, had not been polluted during battles by the blood of their own people. An Indian village of the Shawnee type was easily rebuilt. It consisted of tepees, requiring poles, bark and skins. Huts were built of round logs, a single room roofed with bark. There were no chimneys or windows. If fire was used inside, the bark roof pieces were shifted so a draft could be obtained and the smoke escape. A single entrance was closed when desired, or in bad weather, by buffalo or other pelts. The

---

[1] *Ohio Arch. and Hist. Quarterly*, 20:92.
[2] *Ohio Arch. and Hist. Quarterly*, 20:94.

white pioneers used the same "door" as noted in the Maxwell story. Cooking was usually done out of doors. The few tools necessary for hut construction were well known to the Indian at that time. They had been sold to him for a number of years by English and French trading-posts. Some skill in their use had also been acquired from white prisoners who were recipients of favors during captivity if skilled in axcraft. As the materials for huts and tepees were easily available near by, the rebuilding of the villages which the invaders burned from 1779 to 1790, was not a difficult task.

The expeditions against Old Chillicothe remained only a few days before returning to Kentucky. The location was desirable—rich prairie, building ridge, clear spring water, river and forested hills—so rebuilding was soon begun; in fact, began with the invaders' return march to the Kentucky settlements.

Returning to the old village site was characteristic of this nation, and is noted elsewhere by Alford.

The narrow line of the invader's march from Fort Washington to Old Chillicothe, did not disturb the game in the forest. The Little Miami River continued to teem with fish. Sugar trees, indigenous to this section, still furnished sugar, and the forests surrounding the village site remained ideal hunting-grounds. His own method of fighting and his knowledge of the country enabled the Indian to meet the invaders with small loss of life and quickly replaceable loss of property.

The Shawnee came back each time. Sixteen years of warfare and the Treaty of Greenville were required to dislodge him from the Miami Valleys.

THE KENTUCKY FORTERS' PERIOD

Many pioneer families from the colonies braved the dangers and hardships of Boone's wilderness trail, and hastened overland to Kentucky on the news of the riches of this trans-Appalachian Eldorado. Others, including many adventurers of the period, chose the easier but more perilous Ohio River way into the uncharted western and northwestern territories of Virginia. Many families, who had become impoverished from sacrifices and service in the American Revolution, found themselves compelled to migrate west in search of new homes and a new chance at life's fortunes. After they had located in Kentucky, the dangers that thickened about them and the disasters that came with unexpected frequency were met with superlative courage and endurance considering the small resources of defense at their command.

A study of the military and other limitations at the time of the five pioneer invasions against Old Chillicothe and the Indians of the Miami valleys, gives a more adequate appreciation of the difficulties of pioneer isolation, and helps us to visualize the adverse conditions under which the Kentucky forters wrote their strenuous history into the records of the closing decades of the eighteenth century.

A present-day motor trip from Old Chillicothe and other Indian village centers in the Miami valleys, to Harrodsburg, Fort Asaph's (Stanford, Kentucky) and the site of Boone's Fort, gives personal contact with the marching distances from points of initial assembly of the Kentucky pioneer invasions to their objective—the hostile Indian settlements north of the Ohio River. The burdens and sacrifices entailed in any one of these invasions, on the men who went and the women who were left to keep open their isolated cabin homes in Kentucky's forests, can never be truly described. Only the highest type of physical stamina and moral courage could have endured and survived.

The long marches, after the assembling of the militia at its Kentucky rendezvous, the mouth of the Licking River, now Covington, Kentucky, were made by foot or horseback overland. There were no roads or bridges across streams; no camps with supplies nor organized medical care for the ill or footsore. An axe, a mess kettle and other necessary supplies were transported by packhorses, one to each six soldiers. There were no tents or other shelters for the rank and file. Lucky indeed was the soldier who could forage enough branches or leaves, at the end of the day's march, to keep his bed above the damp ground. A few small prairies relieved the monotony of march through otherwise unbroken forests. The trail avoided swamps and fallen trees and crossed rivers where fords could be found. Where none existed, as at the Ohio, the horses and cattle were made to swim the river, and crude boats or rafts transferred the men and camp impedimenta. The same surface conditions were met north of the Ohio for 60 miles, to the first Indian village, Old Chillicothe, on the Little Miami River.

The militia-men were clothed in tow or linsey-woolsey homespun garments. There was no warm underclothing. The moccasions were homemade and often required repair at the end of a day's march. The men were armed with their own flint-lock rifles, many of which had forty-two or forty-four inch barrels. The gun measured about four feet, nine inches, over-all. Its average weight was ten pounds. It was bored either 54 or 40 caliber (32 or 40 bullets to the pound of lead). Powder was carried in homemade "steer's horn" receptacles hung independently by a leather strap slung across the shoulders. In a homemade deerskin bag, three extra flint chips and lead for one hundred or more bullets and bullet-molds were carried; likewise the precious "one gill of salt" ration. A small buffalo-horn containing emergency powder was carried in a pocket, as were some extra bullets, so that the loss of the pouch and large powder-horn in a hand-to-hand conflict, would not render the rifle useless. An additional tanned deer's hide pouch containing parched corn was usually tied on the body belt, while pieces of jerked buffalo meat were carried in the large pouch.

These three articles of food, with some flour from the commissary, when such could be obtained, constituted the rations of the invaders.

The serious problems which confronted the settlements following the Indian attack on Boonsborough in 1778, may be studied with clearer historic retrospect from first papers and manuscripts of the period available.

After 1777 Indian raids into Kentucky, with increasing loss of life and property among the forters, so discouraged settlers that many returned to their former homes east of the Alleghanies. At one period those left in Kentucky settlements numbered less than 150 men—about 40 families—and the protective centers were reduced to three forts: Boonsborough. Harrodsburg and St. Asaph's (Logan's Fort). It was about this time, and probably as a result of the reports borne back to Virginia, that Colonel John Bowman and two companies of Virginia militia hastened to Fort Logan as a protective measure. His presence restored confidence and the tide of emigration began its return flow. Colonel Bowman, who settled south of the Kentucky River, quickly determined that the center of Indian activity should be attacked by a punitive expedition. He did not know the location of Old Chillicothe in the Little Miami country. Neither, it seems, was its exact location known by the Kentuckians themselves. He therefore directed Simon Kenton to select two other scouts and, with them, to locate the Shawnee settlement and determine a suitable line of march against it. Kenton selected George Clark and Richard Montgomery as associates. Disguised as Indians they had no difficulty in locating the village without being discovered. Had they followed orders and returned with this information, no misfortune would have befallen them. Unhappily, they found a drove of horses pasturing in a prairie meadow northeast of the village. Many of these horses had been taken from Virginia and Kentucky in the numerous Shawnee raids of the period. The temptation was too great, and the seven fine horses they took back with them proved to be their undoing. They were overtaken at the Ohio River while trying in vain to get the horses across stormy waters to the Kentucky shore. Kenton was captured; Montgomery was killed; George Clark escaped and bore back the information desired.

Colonel Bowman gathered his force of attack in May, 1779, at the mouth of the Licking River. After crossing the Ohio, his line of march followed the Little Miami River to

Old Chillicothe, the present site of the village of Oldtown. Clark, who had escaped capture by the Indians the year before, and William Whitley were the two guides of Bowman's forces. On leaving the Ohio River 32 of Bowman's force of 296 men, remained to guard the boats till the expedition returned. Bowman's Invasion with its historic background is given under the title "1779"—*Draper MSS.*,[3] quotations from which are kindly granted to the writer.

THE MIAMI VALLEY CAMPAIGNS OF 1779-1790

After the Treaty of Wautega was signed, Chief Dragging Canoe took the hand of Boone and said: "We have given you a fine land, Brother, but you will find it under a cloud and a dark and bloody ground."

The misfortunes that befell the Kentucky settlers who located in the Licking River country within protective distances of Hinkson's (later Ruddell's) and Martin's Forts, culminated on June 22, 1780, in a disaster unequaled in the history of the Kentucky pioneer period. The narrative of Mrs. W. T. Lafferty, historian and descendant of Charles Lair, on whose land Hinkson's Fort was located, causes us to pause in these times of assured security and endeavor to realize something, at least, of the dangers that beset the earliest settlers in the Licking River valley.

Mrs. Lafferty writes:[4]

The main facts concerning Byrd's invasion and the attack on Ruddell's and Martin's Forts are as follows: Captain John Hinkson and his companions came down the Ohio and up the Licking in the spring of 1775. At "The Cedars," which is the old Charles Lair home, they built a fort, with a cabin for each of the 15 men. It was completed about the midle of March, 1775, before "Boonesborough" was started, on April first of that year. A few of the men brought their wives to the fort, but the Indian depredations were such that it became unsafe; some "went

---
[3]Draper MSS., 5 D 1-20.
[4]Lafferty, Mrs. W. T.—Letter to W. A. Galloway, December 1, 1928.

back to the settlements," some took their wives to McClelland's Fort at Floyd's Big Spring, where Georgetown is now, and some to Harrod's Fort at Harrodsburg. Hinkson's Fort was deserted.

In the meantime, Captain Isaac Ruddell and his companions were on their land at Ruddell's Mills on Hinkson's Creek some miles away.

When the Indian invasion of 1780 was planned to avenge the conquest of Clark in 1778-'79, the news of it reached the Kentucky settlements and caused general consternation. Isaac Ruddell, at Ruddell's Mills, found his people too exposed to remain there. He took them to Hinkson's old deserted fort (at "The Cedars") which he enlarged and fortified.

On the twenty-second of June, 1780, Captain Henry Byrd of the 8th Regiment of His Majesty's forces, aided by Simon Girty, McKee and the Indian chief, Logan,[5] came leading British Regulars, Indians, Tories and Canadian officers from Detroit, the western post. This invasion was organized, not only to exterminate the Kentucky forts, but also to force the Virginia frontier back east of the Alleghanies; to regain Kentucky as the Happy Hunting Ground of the Indians, and true to the policy of Great Britain in the Revolutionary War, to prevent the western growth of the American colonies.

In executing their plan, they waged the War of the American Revolution on Kentucky soil, demanding surrender in the name of King George III and making official report to Sir Frederick Haldemand, the British lieutenant-general who, at the time, was governor of Canada. His papers, which have been bequeathed to the British Museum, cover 232 volumes of manuscript and record the atrocities committed against the Kentucky pioneers.

Coming by boat down the Great Miami, and up the Ohio and Licking Rivers, the invaders disembarked at Falmouth where North and South Licking join. Beside the small arms with which England had provided them, there

---

[5]Of St. Asaph's, located at the present town of Stanford, Kentucky, Dr. Louise Phelps Kellogg writes: "From this fort, Colonel Benjamin Logan made his long lopes to the settlements, for militia to come to the aid of hard-pressed settlers. And over this path they did come to Kentucky's preserving—Bowman, Todd, Dillard, Harlan, Smith, and many others who formed the elite of Kentucky's fighters during the American Revolution."

were six pieces of artillery, French swivels mounted on horseback and a cannon on wheels. Putting up huts to shelter stores and baggage from the weather, they cut the first road through the North Kentucky forests over which wheels could travel in order to transport the cannon to Central Kentucky. See Byrd's War Road on Filson's Map of 1784.[6]

The invaders crept along the south fork of Licking, down the dry creek bed of Snake Lick, where they effected a crossing at a sweeping curve of the river near Boyd Station, by building a temporary ford of logs laid crosswise, then lengthwise across the river. Over this they hauled their cannon and, fording Raven Creek, Mill Creek, and Gray's Run, where the latter empties into the Licking at Cynthiana, they again crossed South Licking at the Buffalo Ford near Lair, and creeping cautiously up the steep embankment just at dawn, they attacked Ruddell's Fort. They demanded surrender in the name of King George III, firing the cannon, which struck terror to the hearts of the forters, as they beheld the logs of the blockhouse give way.

Realizing that defense was impossible, Captain Ruddell agreed to surrender and set to work on the articles of capitulation. After the white flag had passed back and forth several times, the invaders agreed that each man should keep his small arms, and the women and children be left in safety at the nearest fort. But alas! The moment the gates were opened, there followed a scene of frightful carnage. Byrd's Indian contingent, giving the war-whoop, rushed into the stockade and, choosing their victims, began a bloody massacre. Wives were snatched from their husbands, children from their parents; about twenty were tomahawked and scalped. The baby of Mrs. Ruddell was torn from her arms and thrown into the fire before her eyes. Captain Ruddell pleaded in vain for mercy, for Captain Byrd was unable to control the Indian warriors he had loosed upon the forters.

Drunk with blood and success, they demanded to be led four miles farther on to take Martin's Fort. It was located on Stoner Creek where the Buffalo Trace crossed it, just back of Runnymeade, the historic home of Colonel Zeke Clay of Bourbon County.

Captain Byrd agreed to go, after the chiefs had given solemn promise that the women and children should become

---

[6]In Filson's *Kentucke*, ed. by W. R. Jillsin. Frontispiece.

prisoners of the British and the Indians have the booty. Their promise was kept and Martin's Fort was taken without bloodshed.

Then the Indians, mounting the horses of the forters, in order to ride in comfort, loaded their prisoners down with plunder from their own cabin homes and drove them along with their cattle and hogs on the journey northward. Can you visualize that tragic scene and with your mind's eye see 470 men, women and children bowed down under the weight of their household goods and their sorrows, driven like dumb animals over the narrow trail by a thousand British Regulars, wearing the uniform of the mother country; by Green Coat Rangers from Canada, Mingos, Delawares, Shawnees, Hurons, Ottawas, Tawas, and Chippewas in war paint and feathers; driven into a captivity which lasted 14 years (until the Treaty of Greenville, Ohio, was effected by General Anthony Wayne), a captivity in which families were separated and, in some instances, were never gathered together again?

The story of their wanderings far up into Canada—some even reaching the Atlantic Coast—and of the hardships they endured were recited by these forters, for at least 30 families of them finally reached their Kentucky homes. One told how the men were made to haul stone to build a mill, as though they were horses; another of kindlier treatment of women who demanded a home to live in and got it, earning their living by making the ruffled shirts of the British officers. There is an old adage that "it takes three generations of needlewomen to make a lady" and these Virginia women were ladies and expert needlewomen, and had all the work they could do, rolling and whipping the fine linen ruffles and making a dainty edge which pleased their captors. One woman had been forced by the Indians who captured her, to carry a copper kettle on her head on her long journey, and the hair never grew again, so she was compelled to wear a cap the rest of her days.

The abandoned fort was later used by Charles Lair as a stockade for his mules. My father, who was born in 1815, told me it stood next to the cemetery which was just back of the Lair home called "The Cedars." I have many interesting stories of the Buffalo Trace near which the fort stood, and other material which may prove interesting to you.

Ruddell's Fort was about four miles from Cynthiana, the county seat of Harrison County. Though built by

SIMON KENTON'S STATION IN 1794

Located on the Maysville and Lexington Pike, near Washington, Ky. Note the port-holes used in defense. The rock is part of the old fort near Maysville, Ky.

HISTORIC BACKGROUNDS

Hinkson, Ruddell's and Hinkson's were one and the same.

You are quite right, Clark's attack on the Piqua towns was the retaliatory measure following Byrd's invasion.

Stephen Ruddell, according to our records, was adopted by the Indians and after the Treaty of Greenville, he brought his Indian wife and children to Kentucky to visit his parents. He became a Christian and a Baptist missionary among the Indians, and records of the Cooper's Run Meeting-house describe his visits in most interesting fashion, telling of Indian gifts and wampum which they sent in grateful appreciation of the gospel and interest in their spiritual welfare.

Martin's Fort is in Bourbon County, about six miles from the county-seat, which is Paris. Bryant's Station is about the same distance from Lexington, the county-seat of Fayette. Logan's Fort was just outside of Stanford, the county-seat of Lincoln County.

Logan built his fort, frequently called St. Asaph's,[7] in April, 1775, at the Buffalo Wallow. It withstood many Indian attacks and its history is one of thrilling episodes. In an old cemetery nearby are the bones of those first forters. Such cemeteries were built just outside the walls of those early forts and sometimes help us to locate the fort sites. All of these forts are close to Lexington and are most interesting.

There were three outstanding forts in Kentucky in 1777—Logan's, Boone's and Harrod's. At the close of the Revolution, there were sixty, stretched like cities of refuge along the Wilderness Road and the Buffalo Trace so that settlers coming into the country could travel by day from one to the other and sleep in safety within the stockaded walls of a friendly fort at night.

Yours very truly,

(Signed) MRS. W. T. LAFFERTY, Secretary,
Woman's Club Service,
University of Kentucky,
Lexington, Kentucky.

* * *

---

[7]See p. 50, footnote No. 5.

OLD CHILLICOTHE

THE BATTLE OF OLDTOWN, MAY-JUNE, 1779, AND THE SHAWNEE HISTORICAL BACKGROUND

By THOMAS W. ALFORD

It was about the year 1763 when the Shawnee Indians began to be agitated as to whether they should continue their fight for their country, or make a lasting peace with the white man. Many warriors were for continuance of the fight until the whites were exterminated; but many chiefs said, "Let us seek peace and make a permanent friendship with the English."

The serious discussion of this matter began after the defeat of the French, and consequently the surrender of all their lands by the King of France to the King of England in 1763, which awakened their minds to the power of the English. This led to secret councils among the chiefs of the several clans, or septs, composing the tribe or nation, and to consulting the meaning of the *Meesawmi* which each clan possessed. This *Meesawmi*, it is claimed in their tradition, was handed to each clan by the Great Spirit away back in the beginning. It is known today as medicine, whatever that means to us; but it means more than that to them. These secret councils lasted several years, and finally grew into general councils of the tribes in which discussions were made as to what should be done for their future welfare, in order to survive. Evidently they could not agree; therefore the two factions gradually resulted in the final split of the Shawnee Nation which still exists.

It was during the times of these councils, in the spring of 1768, that Pucksinwa stopped to await his son, Tecumtha's birth at the spring a few flights of arrows distant to the southeast of Old Chillicothe, now Oldtown, Ohio, before attending the council which was being held in the Msi-kah-mi-qui (Temple) or Council-house situated in this town. This was then an important town and a great meeting-ground of the Shawnees up to the time of its evacuation by them, just a few months before its first invasion and its defeat under Colonel Bowman, "Otahemine-

gesfoki," or, in Strawberry month. He found only a few Indians here to oppose him.

THE BATTLE OF OLDTOWN

In the month of May, 1779, Colonel John Bowman, with 264 men in line, marched against the Shawnee town Chalahgawtha (Old Chillicothe) on the Little Miami River. The party rendezvoused at the mouth of the Licking River, or "*Skopabewe Fheepi,*" and on the second night came in sight of the town undiscovered. It was determined to wait until daylight before making the attack; but by the imprudence of some of the men whose curiosity exceeded their judgment, the party were discovered by the Indians before the officers and men had arrived at the several positions assigned them. As soon as the alarm was given, a fire commenced on both sides and was kept up, while the women and children were seen running from cabin to cabin in the greatest confusion and gathering in the most central and strongest places for defense. At daylight, it was found that Bowman's men were about 100 yards from the cabins in which the Indians had gathered. Bowman having no other arms than rifles and tomahawks, it was thought imprudent to attempt to storm strong cabins as well defended as these were. In consequence of the warriors' gathering in a few cabins contiguous to each other, the remainder of the town was left unprotected; therefore, while a fire was kept up at the portholes, which engaged the attention of those within, fire was set to 30 or 40 cabins, which were consumed, and a considerable quantity of property consisting principally of kettles, blankets, fur robes and silver ornaments were taken from those cabins. In searching the woods near the town, a drove of horses was rounded up and a large number were captured. One hundred and sixty-eight were gotten across the Ohio River to their camp on the Licking.

About ten o'clock Bowman and his party commenced their march homeward, after having nine men killed. What loss we Indians sustained is not known, except our principal chief, Mkahday-wah-may-quah, or Black Fish, was wounded in the knee, and one warrior was killed in the pursuit. After receiving the wound, Black Fish proposed to surrender, being confident that his wound was dangerous, and believing that there were among the white people surgeons who could cure him; none among his own people could do it. The party had not marched more than eight or ten miles on their return before the Indians appeared in considerable force in their rear and began to press hard on that quarter. Bowman selected his ground and formed his men in a square; but the Indians declined a close engagement, and kept up only a scattering fire. It was believed by the whites that their object was only to retard their march until they could procure reinforcement from the neighboring village.

This statement was undoubtedly based on the fear and imagination of Bowman's invaders during their precipitous retreat, and also upon the statement that 75 warriors escaped through a "gap" between Logan's and Bowman's command before daylight on the morning of the attack. There is no record in American history that 75 Shawnee warriors ever ran away from any enemy without putting up a stiff fight, especially when their women and children and a part of the warriors—about 35 men and boys included—were trapped, but were standing off the attacking force, with great bravery and without any loss of life. And as subsequently learned, at that date, May 31-June 1, 1799, the Shawnee population in the Miami and Mad River villages was at its ebb, owing to the emigration.

Three months before Bowman's attack, 1000 to 1200 Shawnees, who were peace advocates, had emigrated to Cape Girardeau, Spanish Territory, west of the Mississippi River, there to reestablish their homes and lives free from war with the white man.[8] This depletion in numbers of nearby and available fighting reinforcements is borne out by the facts developed during Bowman's retreat; the number of pursuit Indians is not mentioned as larger than that

---

[8]See Bowman's *Reports to the Governor of Virginia*.

engaged in the Council-house defense of Old Chillicothe by Logan, Bedinger and other white men who were Bowman's leaders. The pursuit attack began between ten and twenty miles south of Old Chillicothe. The Bowman retreat was greatly handicapped by an attempt to save all the plunder taken at the village. As soon as a strong position was taken by Colonel Bowman, the Indians retired, and he resumed the line of march, when his rear was again attacked. Colonel Bowman again formed for battle, again the Indians retired, and this was repeated several times; at length, John Bulger, James Harrod and George Michael Bedinger—with 100 others on horseback, according to the Draper MSS.— rushed on the Indian ranks and dispersed them in every direction; after which the Indians abandoned the pursuit. Bowman crossed the Ohio at the mouth of the Little Miami and, after crossing, the men dispersed to their several homes. (It will be noted with satisfaction that our history of this battle coincides so closely with yours as to this and other major periods.)

Early writers estimate that as many as 300 horses were captured at the Battle of Oldtown. It was the break-away of men from the ranks to secure them, after they had been located, that disorganized Colonel Bowman's command and destroyed the discipline of his troops during and following the battle. Whatever the original number of horses found in Shawnee pastures, the invasion succeeded in reaching camp, at the mouth of the Licking River, with 165, in addition to other articles of value taken in the cabins and wigwams, such as fur robes, silver ornaments, kettles, and loot easily transported. After a short rest in camp, this booty was disposed of by an auction, the total of which amounted to 32,000 English pounds, or about $500.00 continental currency for each man. Following the sale, those whose accounts amounted to more than their proportion, gave notes for the difference to those whose purchases were less. They then disbanded and each man sought his own home in his own way. There is no record that these notes were ever paid, for reasons that are apparent to the reader, and that were unavoidable at that period in pioneer Kentucky, where the movements of its population were uncertain and its banking facilities were nil. Colonel Bowman was severely criticized at the time for failure of leadership at this battle-front, and Colonel Logan was openly praised as a leader.

From that date till his death Logan continued to increase in public estimation, both as a military and civil leader. His influence, always for public welfare, became as widespread as the boundaries of his adopted State. He comes down through history as one of the two greatest of the patriots and leaders in the pioneer period of Kentucky.

Following the unfortunate events at Gnadenhutten,[9] and in eastern Ohio early in 1777, and the murder of the great Shawnee chief, Cornstalk and his son, Elinipsico, the Indians commenced their invasions of the settlements south of the Ohio. The Shawnees became infuriated, and started upon the war-path from their towns upon the Scioto and Miami Rivers. Before the end of the year, a large portion of that nation had taken up the hatchet. In the spring, as there were but very few men interested in retaining possession of the posts on the north side of the Kentucky River, they broke up—their occupants removing, on the thirtieth of January, either to Boonsborough or Harrodsburgh. The whole population was then in these two forts. . . . As the months wore away, both posts were attacked but neither was taken. In the meantime, Logan's fort near the site of the present town of Stanford, Lincoln county, was occupied; it too, was assailed by the Indians, but their attack proved unsuccessful. So troublesome had they been throughout the year—so discouraging had their hostilities proved to immigration—that, at its close, the settlements were restricted to the three forts just mentioned.

The siege of Boonsborough was the great event of the year 1778, in Kentucky. Preparations for this, at the principal town of the Shawnee Indians north of the Ohio, tended for a length of time to restrain small parties of savages from their incursions into the settlements. Still, there were Indian depredations before and after that event. . . .

The time had arrived with the opening of the spring of

---

[9] See page 79.

1779, when it was very evident to the settlers of Kentucky that, of all the Indians at that time invading the country, the Shawnees were the most active and bloodthirsty. It seemed exceedingly plain to them that from Chillicothe, on the Little Miami, came most of the war-parties marauding in the now increasing settlements. "Why should not that prolific hive of mischief be destroyed?" was a question then frequently asked. And it was finally determined by the settlers to free themselves from danger and their settlements from savage inroads, by carrying an expedition against it. John Bowman, residing at Harrodsburgh, as colonel of militia and lieutenant of Kentucky, called for volunteers and resolved to take the command of them in person—the first regular enterprise to attack, in force, the Indians beyond the Ohio, ever planned in Kentucky. Bowman, the year previous, had contemplated an expedition to the same town, and sent Simon Kenton with two others to Chillicothe to make discoveries. The settlers were to plant their corn and be in readiness to rendezvous in May, at the mouth of Licking. The Shawnees seem not to have had any apprehensions of such a retaliation for their frequent invasions of the Dark and Bloody Land. The place of meeting for the volunteers of the interior was fixed at Harrodsburgh; whence, under Benjamin Logan and Silas Harlan as captains, they marched to Lexington, meeting at that point a company from Boonsborough commanded by Captain John Holder. These two companies were there reinforced by another headed by Captain Levi Todd. They marched from Lexington by way of the Little North Fork of Elkhorn, encamping the first night near its mouth. Their second encampment was on a small branch of Mill Creek, about two miles north of Lee's Lick. Thence, they went down the Licking, until they finally reached its mouth—opposite what is now the city of Cincinnati, then a wilderness—the place appointed for the general meeting of the army, on the site of the present city of Covington, Kentucky. . . .

Early in the morning of the 28th of May, 1779, and immediately below the mouth of Licking River, Colonel John Bowman and his army crossed the Ohio. Thirty-two men remained to take care of the boats. Two hundred and sixty-five, including officers, formed into marching order with George M. Bedinger as adjutant and quarter-master and commenced their march along an Indian trace for the objective point of the expedition—the Shawnee town, on the east side of the Little Miami, distant about 65 miles in a northeast direction, piloted by George Clark and William Whitley. The men were mostly on foot, not very heavily encumbered with provisions—a peck of parched corn and some "jerked" meat to each man was all. Firing was interdicted after crossing the river and the whole force marched rapidly on their way, making directly for the Little Miami, which stream they were to follow to the Indian town. The volunteers were armed with rifles and tomahawks. They arrived within ten miles of Chillicothe at dusk on the 29th, when a halt was ordered. During the whole journey not an Indian had been seen, and the commander was sanguine enough of being able to surprise the savages.

A council was now called to determine upon the time of attacking the town. It was resolved to march that night and invest the place and commence the attack at daybreak the next morning. A point a few hundred yards southwest of the village, in a prairie, was reached a little after midnight. Bowman and his captains went forward to reconnoitre. They were gone about an hour. Upon their return, a disposition of the force was made preparatory to the attack. The men were separated into three divisions: one under Captain Logan was to march to the left of the town; another under Captain Harrod to the right until they met on the north side; the other division under Captain Holder was to march directly in front of the village, but to stop some distance away. By this arrangement there would be an opening south of the two first-mentioned companies through which, when the alarm was given, the Indians might escape;—they would be allowed to go some distance from their cabins before encountering, immediately before them, the company of Holder. This was a very ingeniously contrived plan; for, if all the men were to rush up at once, the enemy would be forced to remain in their wigwams where they could fight their assailants at a great advantage on their side. Silently and undiscovered, the three divisions took the positions assigned them and impatiently awaited the appearance of day, so as to begin the battle. The men under Harrod and Logan, at a given signal, were to commence the attack; while Holder's were to lie in ambush, to await the out-rushing of the frightened savages and pour in upon them, as they appeared, a deadly fire. It was understood if the men should be discovered before daylight, Holder's division was to endeavor immediately to fire the cabins. It was not long before the Indian dogs set up a loud and persistent barking. Their owners came out, in some instances, and encouraged them as if they were apprehensive of danger. . . .

The center of Old Chillicothe was about 170 rods east of the Little Miami. Skirting along on the east side of the town was a small stream, afterward called Oldtown Run, which, with a course nearly north empties into Massie's Creek at no great distance away. On the west side of the village was a fine spring, the waters from which run in a southwesterly direction, soon to mingle with those of the Little Miami. A prairie lay adjoining the town, on the south, and cabins were built some distance upon one, on the north. A ridge south of the spring extended from the skirts of the village in a southwest course to the river; another, just across the run to the east, has a northeast trend to Massie's Creek. The site of the village is about three miles north of the present town of Xenia, county-seat of Greene County, Ohio.[10]

At the time of this expedition against the Shawnees, their whole number of warriors at Wapatomica, Mackacreek and Piqua on Mad River and at Chillicothe on the Little Miami was about 500, of whom 100 were in the latter village with about 100 squaws and children. About a month previous, true to the wandering instincts of that nation, 400 of their warriors with their families, under their chiefs Black Stump and Yellow Hawk, accompanied by the French trader, Loramie, migrated west of the Mississippi, settling

---

[10]Note reference to "Old Chilicothe (Chillicothe), the principal Indian town, on Little Miami," Filson's *Kentucke* (1784), 63.

upon Sugar Creek, a little distance above Cape Girardeau, in what is now the State of Missouri, then under Spanish rule. The principal chief of the Shawnees at Chillicothe when the town was invested by Bowman, was Black Fish. His subordinates were Black Hoof and Black Beard. Northeast of the center of the town stood the Council-house, a large building, one story high; said to have been 60 feet square; built of round hickory logs, with gable ends open and upright posts supporting the roof. Black Fish's cabin was some 30 yards west of this structure. There were several board houses or huts in the south part of the village —some ten or twelve. . . .

While the army of Bowman lay quietly around Chillicothe, a Shawnee hunter was returning to the threatened village. As he neared Holder's division, he suddenly stopped, fearful of falling into a trap, and made a kind of interrogative ejaculation, as much as to say, "Who's there?" when one of the men very near him shot, and the savage fell, at the same time giving a weak, confused yell. Immediately another soldier ran up, tomahawked and scalped him. The firing of that gun set at naught many of the wise plans and well-laid schemes depending upon daylight for their execution. A few Indians came out in the direction of the report, to ascertain the cause. As they approached Holder's line, the men lay close and still, with cocked guns. But this was enough to alarm the vigilant savages who hastily retreated, receiving a volley as they fell back. Black Fish was severely wounded, the ball ranging from his knee along up his thigh and out at the joint, shattering the bone; showing that he received the wound in a squatting position. He was taken to his cabin by three warriors. He called upon them not to leave him but to stand their ground and all die together.

The return of the party of observation and the volley fired by Holder's men, fully aroused the slumbering occupants of Old Chillicothe. There was immediately a great outcry and confusion. The squaws and children and a few men made a rush for the Council-house. According to previous orders Holder's division now advanced and set fire

HISTORIC BACKGROUNDS

to the town. The men reached the board shanties on the south, and at once began the work of plundering, giving the savages ample time to fortify themselves by fastening securely the door of the huge building they had congregated in. The houses were set on fire as fast as they were plundered in the darkness. This attracted the attention of the other divisions, portions of which, without orders left their positions and joined in the work of securing valuables.

No sooner were the cabins all ablaze than an attempt was made to capture the Council-house; but the assailants were so warmly received that they were glad to fall back. It now began to grow light in the east and Bowman, satisfied that it would be impossible to capture the stronghold of the enemy, sent word to Logan's and Harrod's divisions to fall back to the south of the town. Meanwhile, in front, a desultory fire was kept up between some of Holder's men and those within the Council-house; the stragglers from the other divisions also took part. When it became broad daylight, a few men, in their endeavor to get as near the building as possible in hope of killing some of the inmates, found themselves so much exposed that to attempt to retreat would be certain to draw upon them a volley from the Council-house. They had taken a position behind a large white oak log not over 30 yards from the enemy. Some of the party in moving to get a good position for delivering their fire, were killed. The survivors finally heard a voice calling to them to retreat; but how this was to be done was the question. Adjutant Bedinger concluded to make the attempt. The spot where the men lay was southeast of the Council-house about 300 feet. Bedinger sprang, ran a zigzag race across the stream east, and escaped unhurt, although a volley was fired at him. The rest of the party immediately ran to an empty cabin near by, reaching it before the enemy had time to reload their rifles.

The men remained in the hut some time, trying to devise means to escape. Finally a novel plan was hit upon. Each one provided himself with a plank and holding it upon his back slantingly so as to protect his body from the bullets of the savages, started upon the run. This movable backwork—rather than breastwork—proved amply sufficient to save the lives of all; for they all escaped over the fork of Massie's Creek near by; dropping, each one, his plank as he entered in safety the cornfield at that point.[11]

During all this time the scenes being enacted within the Council-house were of a strange character. Assatakoma, a conjurer nearly one hundred years old, kept constantly calling out, encouraging the warriors congregated there—not over 25 in number, with about 15 boys who could shoot; but quite a number had no guns to use. The squaws and children kept up a great noise, screaming and whooping. The Indians managed to make what answered for portholes, between the logs and in the roof of the building, through which they fired. Joseph Jackson, who had been a prisoner of the Shawnees since February of the preceding year, calmly surveyed the scene, tied as he was to a post in the midst of the shrieking crowd. At the first alarm, he had seized a rifle and started for the woods, but was overtaken by a warrior, brought back, and secured.

As soon as Bowman determined not to attempt the capture of the Council-house, deeming it too strong to be assailed with rifles only, and had called back the divisions to the southwest of the town, the principal effort was to secure horses—a large number being found near by in a kind of common—evidently driven in from the woods by the flies. One hundred and eighty were captured. The army was thus engaged when the surviving stragglers who had been in such close quarters behind the oak log, arrived. The sun was then about two hours high. The amount of plunder taken from the cabins that had been burned and from others in the west side of the town not fired was considerable, consisting of silver ornaments (of which a large number was found) and clothing. By nine o'clock, everything being arranged, marching orders were given and the army started upon its return having lost nine men killed in exposing themselves to the fire of the savages within the Council-house and one wounded. The trail out was the route taken; the men, as is usual with volunteers and militia

---

[11] Verified by statement to James Galloway, of a reliable Indian, who took part in this battle. See *Draper MSS.*

upon such occasion, being at first in considerable confusion. The principal cause, however, was this: soon after daylight a Negro woman came out of the Council-house as if having escaped the savages, and reached the army without harm. She declared that Simon Girty with 100 Shawnees from Piqua—12 miles distant—was hourly expected. The commander gave little credence to this tale; but the story getting among the men and the number of Girty's savages increasing to 500 by the time of starting, caused some consternation—resulting in a disposition of many to be off, regardless of the manner of their going; but order was soon restored and the march continued.

After making 14 miles, Indians were discovered in pursuit, who soon commenced an attack. Bowman with great courage and steadiness called a halt, formed his men in a hollow square, ready to meet the savages should they appear in force. It was soon discovered that there were but few of them; but as they continued their annoyance, wounding some of the men, a small detachment charged out and routed them. One of their number was killed and scalped. Bowman had three of his men wounded during the afternoon; none killed. After this, they were not again molested by the Indians. Early on the first day of June, the army reached the Ohio just above the mouth of the Little Miami, where they found the boats in waiting. The men were soon conveyed across the stream, the captured horses swimming. The number of the latter that reached the Kentucky shore, was 163. The boatmen, while the army was absent, had remained in their bateaux and canoes, moving up and down the river, for greater safety.

The army now feeling greatly at ease, moved leisurely some three or four miles to the rear of the elevated hills which skirted the Ohio until a fine spring was reached, when it halted. Hunting and fishing soon supplied the camp, and the rest and sleep enjoyed, soon gave new life and vigor to all. They were again in Kentucky where peavines, wild clover and wild rye furnished an abundance of food for the half-famished horses. It was agreed to have a sale of the horses and other booty; and an equal division was made of the amount realized. The captains were to keep an account of the amount purchased by their respective companies and if it were found that any one had bid in property exceeding the amount of his dividend he was to pay the surplus—having a credit of one year—to his commanding officer. The several sums thus collected were to be divided among such as did not purchase to the full amount of their dividend. The vendue realized a little over £32000, giving to each one of the 296 about £110 Continental currency. Many purchased more than that amount; but, as these debtors were scattered afterward from Red Stone Old Fort on the Monongehela to the Falls of the Ohio and Boonsborough, no collections were ever made, or if made were never paid over to those who were justly entitled thereto; so, it resulted in each one securing in most cases, just what was struck off to him at the vendue.

The party of Monongaheleans who had joined the invading army now took to their canoes and made their way up the Ohio to their homes; while the residue scattered to their various places of abode—the general impression being that the expedition was a failure. The amount of booty obtained was large; the march had been conducted outward with great secrecy; and it was evident to all, but for the accident of the return just at that inauspicious moment of the Shawnee hunter, the whole village would have been captured. As it was, not only many of their cabins were burned, but much corn destroyed. It is very evident from the journals of that day that the enterprise was looked upon as a success.[12]

* * *

PLAN OF MARCH, 1780

General Clark's campaign against Old Chillicothe in 1780 was quickly organized to invade the Miami country

---

[12] *Ohio Arch. and Hist. Quarterly,* 19:448-459. From Draper MSS. An interesting side-light is thrown upon Bowman's successfully reaching Old Chillicothe, by the fact that he chose a night on which the moon was totally eclipsed. See *Virginia Gazette,* July 10, 1779, quoted in *Ohio Arch. and Hist. Quarterly,* loc. cit., 459, note.

and avenge the disaster at Ruddell's and Martin's Forts. Captain Byrd and his captives had scarcely reached Detroit before Clark's forces had invaded the Miami Valley, destroyed Old Chillicothe, and fought the battle of Old Piqua. Although both villages were destroyed, the invasion resulted in little change in the Shawnee status, as no occupancy of the invaded territory was attempted, or indeed was possible. The population in Kentucky in 1780 was heavily drawn on for the limited service time given by the militia and volunteers in both of General Clark's Miami country invasions. There were neither men to be spared nor means to maintain them, nor were there orders from Virginia authorizing occupation of the successfully invaded territory. On the other hand, disapproval and regret because of Clark's second invasion and its probable effect on peace negotiations then in progress, was sharply expressed in a communication from Governor Harrison of Virginia to General Clark, after his invasion of 1782. Destruction of the Indian maize fields and villages was believed by the Kentuckians to be a severe and weakening blow to the Indians—a delusion which should have been obvious with succeeding invasions, and was so in 1791, when there was no battle at Old Chillicothe. The Indians abandoned the village on Clark's approach, and fled to Old Piqua on Mad River fourteen miles north, where the battle-field topography was more to their liking. General Clark halted for a day to give his men time to burn what remained of the town and to destroy the gardens and all of the cornfields south of the village in the prairie land, except about five acres left for the army's use on its return march. On the morning of the sixth of August, 1780, the army marched by sunrise and, having a level open way, arrived in sight of Piqua, crossed the ford of the Mad River and engaged the Indians in battle about two o'clock p. m.[13]

---

[13] After General St. Clair's defeat, it became apparent that none of the preceding invasions of the Indian country had seriously depleted their civil resources or their military spirit. Relatively few of them had been killed during these invasions. They had quickly rebuilt their "villages," and food was available as needed from the Auglaize country, an unknown source until Wayne's campaign in 1794. A new generation of youths likewise, had

OLD CHILLICOTHE

Since there is some confusion concerning the three Piquas and their historical events, similar to that noted in the various accounts of the seven Chillicothes, the description of Piqua on the Mad River, as given by Major James Galloway, follows:

The principal part of Old Piqua on Mad River stood upon a plain, rising fifteen or twenty feet above the river. On the south, between the village and river, there was an extensive prairie; on the northeast, some bold cliffs, terminating near the river; on the west and northwest, level timbered land; while on the opposite side of the stream, another prairie of varying width stretched back to the high grounds. The river sweeping by in a graceful bend; the precipitous, rocky cliffs; the undulating hills with their towering trees; the prairies, garnished with tall grass and brilliant flowers combined to render the situation of Piqua both beautiful and picturesque. At the period of its destruction, Piqua was quite populous. There was a rude log hut within its limits, surrounded by pickets. It was, however, sacked and burnt on the 8th of August, by an army of 1,000 men from Kentucky, after a severe and well-conducted battle with the Indians who inhabited it. All the improvements of the Indians, including more than 200 acres of corn and other vegetables then growing in their fields, were destroyed. The town was never after rebuilt by the Shawnees. Its inhabitants removed to the Great Miami River, and erected another town which they called Piqua, after the one that had just been destroyed and in defense of which they had fought with the skill and valor characteristic of their nation.

In *The Life of General George Rogers Clark*, Doctor James notes that Fort Jefferson was Colonel Byrd's point of attack but the arrival of Colonel George Slaughter with reenforcements for Fort Jefferson, at the Falls of Ohio, probably influenced Colonel Byrd to direct his invasion to Ruddell's and Martin's Forts. This expedition came by boat down the Great Miami River to the Ohio. The turn of their prows up, instead of down the Ohio, added new and melancholy chapters to both Kentucky and Miami Valley history.

---

grown to warrior age, thoroughly imbued with war spirit. They distrusted and hated the white man as deeply as he did them.

When word of Colonel Byrd's intended attack on Fort Jefferson reached General Clark at Kaskaskia, June 5, 1780, he started at once for Harrod's Fort to organize *defense forces*.[14]

This journey by rowboat up the Ohio and afoot across an uncharted wilderness to Harrod's Fort was both difficult and dangerous. All rivers and streams in western Kentucky were swollen and dangerous to cross at this time, due to unusually heavy and prolonged rainfalls. The Tennessee and Kentucky Rivers required log grape-vine rafts for crossing. The difficulties and dangers that squarely confronted General Clark would now be deemed insurmountable. A short time after his arrival at Harrodsburg, word reached the Fort of Byrd's change of plan and his destruction of Ruddell's and Martin's stations. Clark's purpose changed at once. In place of an *army of defense* for the protection of Fort Jefferson, he threw all the forces of his personality into the organization of an *army of reprisal* against the Shawnees and their allies. All Kentucky was calling for revenge. Clark "took the law into his own hands." He blocked all exits from Harrodsburg; stopped land speculation, then at its height; drafted available men, whether native or transients; likewise all available resources "without compunction of conscience." He sent runners with orders for mounted militia to rendezvous at the mouth of the Licking River, by August 1, 1780, ready to cross the Ohio and march on Old Chillicothe. There is record of material objection to General Clark's method at this time of getting "what he wanted when he wanted it," but all Kentucky was fighting mad and calling for a retaliatory invasion with General Clark as its leader. On August 1, 1780, the forces he had demanded had reached the rendezvous at the mouth of the Licking River, and an army of one thousand men was ready to cross the Ohio River and go forward on its avowed mission of retaliation.

On August 2, 1780, General Clark and his forces crossed the Ohio opposite the mouth of the Licking River. He left 40 men to guard the boats and a small reserve store-

---

[14]James, James A. *Life of George Rogers Clark*, 209-210.

house, and started to Old Chillicothe, the Indian capital. Dr. James, who refers to Clark's account of the expedition, August 22, 1780, makes no mention that a small blockhouse was erected on the north bank of the Ohio by this expedition.[15]

Interesting personal incidents center in Old Chillicothe history and are recalled as Clark's first invasion approached close to "the capital of the Shawnees on the Little Miami River." Simon Kenton, who was pilot of Clark's 1780 invasion and was with General Clark in his Vincennes campaign, had reason to know Old Chillicothe and its location all too well. In 1778 he had been taken prisoner by the Shawnees while scouting with Montgomery and Clark for its location and the best trail to it from the mouth of Licking River. He was finally saved from death at the stake, by the extraordinary efforts of Simon Girty, a friend of other days, but now an Indian ally, and by the diplomacy of Logan, the great Mingo chief.

Early Greene County traditions relate that Simon Girty and his brother, with four Indians, were camped a few miles down from the village on the west bank of the Little Miami River. Kenton, who had been sent out by General Clark with a party to scout the line of march along the east bank, chanced near this camp. Girty and his party discovered their presence, and with the advantage of location, were able to escape quickly. After scouting the invading army, they hastened to Old Chillicothe with the word of the approaching invasion and ordered the Indians to "set fire to the town and retreat to Piqua." This was the warning the Indians had of General Clark's impending attack. Tradition relates that the Indians fired the town as they were leaving it. General Clark states the town was burned by his orders.[16] Both statements can be true. General Clark's men had both time and inclination to finish what the Indians may have undertaken, but failed to complete on account of their hurried departure.

---

[15]"George Rogers Clark Papers, 1771-1781," in *Ill. Hist. Society Colls.*, 8:451-453.
[16]"George Rogers Clark Papers. 1771-1781," in *Ill. Hist. Society Colls.*, 8:451-453.

MONUMENTS ERECTED AT OLD CHILLICOTHE, NOW OLDTOWN, GREENE COUNTY, OHIO

HISTORIC BACKGROUNDS

CATAHECASSA, OR BLACK HOOF

The celebrated chief of the Shawnees was born in Florida, and had bathed and fished in the salt water before he settled on Mad River. He was present at the defeat of Braddock, near Pittsburgh, in 1755, and was engaged in all the wars in Ohio from that time until the Treaty of Greenville in 1795. He was a man of sagacity and experience; of fierce, desperate bravery, and well informed in the traditions of his people. He occupied the last position in his nation and was opposed to polygamy and the practice of burning prisoners. He was a man of good health; was five feet, eight inches in height. He died in Wapakoneta at the age of one hundred and ten years, A. D. 1831. Mr. Thomas F. McGrew in his address on the occasion of the Shawnee Centennial in Springfield, Ohio, August 9, 1880,[17] says:

I believe that this Indian was a chief leader in the defense of Piqua when the place was invested by General Clark.

On the second of August, 1780, General George Rogers Clark moved from the point named (a blockhouse that he built on the site where Cincinnati now stands) to the Indian towns on Mad River located in and near the territory which is now included in Clark County, Ohio. The distance to be marched was about 80 miles through an untracked forest over which with great labor the soldiers cut and bridged, when necessary, a road for the passage of horses and pack mules and one six-pounder cannon.

The old Indian town of Piqua was situated about five miles west of the present site of Springfield, on the north bank of Mad River. In going there from Springfield, you pass down Mad River where the stream runs in a westerly direction out into a large basin or prairie which gives some evidence of having been at one time the bottom of a small lake. At the time the Indians occupied the place the prairie was about three miles long and about one mile wide. At the time referred to, there was on the south side of the river another prairie bordered by low hills in the distance. Over this prairie ran the road from the old Indian town of Chillicothe about 12 miles south of Piqua, which road reached

---

[17]See Springfield *Gazette* for this date.

the river on the south bank nearly opposite the latter town. About two-thirds of the distance down the prairie on the north side of the river, any further progress was obstructed by what might be called the Willow Swamp, stretching across the prairie from the southwest to northeast, stopping about 100 or 200 yards short of a limestone cliff, rising out of the border of the basin of the prairie. Behind the Willow Swamp was located the town of Piqua. . . .

The soldiers marched without tents, beds or personal baggage; their rations for 30 days' campaign were six quarts of corn, one gill of salt, with what green corn and wild game they might pick up on the march, sometimes green plums were cooked and eaten by the men. The impression obtained not only in settlements but with the soldiers, was that if the army were defeated none of the men would escape, and that in such event the Indians would fall on the defenceless women and children of Kentucky and massacre them. It seemed that either the white settlers or the Indians must be destroyed and both parties regarded it in the same light and acted with the calmness and bravery usual to forlorn hope.

On the sixth day of August, 1780, the army arrived at the Indian town Old Chillicothe, only to find it burned and the inhabitants gone. On the seventh, some days sooner than the Indians had expected, it drew up in front of Old Piqua. A soldier had deserted to the Indians before the army had arrived at the mouth of the Licking and gave notice of the approaching expedition.

The plan of the siege as presented here, is slightly changed from the published accounts, but at the same time agrees in the main with all I have met here and conforms in all particulars with the nature of the locality. I have obtained the following details:

The attack commenced about two p. m. on the eighth of August, and lasted until five in the evening. The assaulting forces were divided into three separate commands. One under Colonel Lynn was ordered to cross the river and encompass the town on the west side. To prevent this move from being successful the Indians made a powerful effort to turn the left wing of the assaulting party, which Colonel Lynn successfully defeated by extending his force a mile to the west of the town.

Colonel Logan, with 400 men under his command, was ordered to march up the south side of the river (concealing, if possible, the move from the observation of the Indians), and cross over the stream at the upper end of the prairie, and prevent their escape in that direction. General Clark remained in command of the center, including one six-pounder cannon. He was to assault the town in front. This disposition of the forces, with a simultaneous assault made by the separate commands, promised, if well executed, the capture of the town, and a complete rout of the Indians, with the death of a great number. According to the custom of the times, no prisoners were made. All that were captured were put to death.

The Indians, according to their plan of defense, could not safely retreat, if defeated, over the round-topped hill, for the elevation would bring them within sight and range of the American rifles, and the cannon, with the command of General Clark, which, in appearance and sound, created more fear than it did harm.

Neither could they escape out of the upper end of the prairie for Colonel Logan and his 400 men had been sent to intercept them there;[18] nor to the north for this route was too much obstructed by the rocks; nor to the west or lower part of the town, the location of the stockade fort, for at this point the battle raged with the greatest fierceness, under the command of Colonel Lynn. The constant crack of the rifle in its deadly work, the shouts of the white soldiers, the yells of the Indians ... the distant roar of the cannon, disclosed this to be the point where defeat was to be accepted or victory won.

Simon Girty, who was never a constant friend to any party, gnashing his teeth in impotent rage, ordered his 300 Mingo Indians to withdraw from what may have appeared to him an unequal contest.

The Shawnees, disheartened by the withdrawal of their allies, and pressed by the fierce, rather desperate fighting of the whites, which they denominated "madness" or fate, so reckless were the soldiers in exposing their lives, lost heart. Against "madness" the Indians never contend. They gave up the fight, and slowly fell back up the prairie, partly concealed by the tall grass, the wigwams and the trees in the willow swamp. They fought, as they retreated, not for victory, but for their lives, until they reached the rocks,

---

[18]The entire background of the village was an unguarded forest, open to their unpursued retreat. The round topped hills were then in native forest, and offered in case of retreat, the ideal Indian cover.

beneath which they had concealed their women and children.

Their situation was now worse than it had been at the commencement of the conflict, for they had passed all the low ground, making a retreat to the north practical, with the exception of the opening cut-down from the cliffs already described, and up through this, tradition claims, they marched out into the hills. . . .

Some persons assert that Colonel Logan marched to a point where Mad River meets with the waters of Buck Creek before he crossed the river, and then marched down the east side thereof to execute his part of the general plan. He made about three miles, according to all authorities, and that is the distance from the site of Old Piqua to the mouth of Buck Creek. It follows that if he did go so high up the river as the point named that he would have traveled six miles before he could bring his men into action.

This view of the maneuvering after looking over the location of the battle-field seems so unmilitary that I cannot accept it. I presume that he made a detour from the river, that his force might not be observed, as secrecy was one of the conditions of success. To accomplish his part of the general plan, he may have marched three miles, but certainly not six. Let this point be settled as it may, there is no dispute about the fact that when he got his men into position the battle had been fought and won, and the Indians were gone. The loss was about equal—20 men on each side.[19]

The Piqua town is described as built after the manner of the French settlements. It extended along the northwest foothills of Mad River for a distance of three miles east of the ford. The cabins, in many places, were more than 20 poles—302 feet—apart. Colonel Logan, therefore, in order to flank the town on the east according to orders, marched his divisions three miles up the east bank of Mad River where he expected to find a ford. In this he was disappointed. By this maneuver two divisions of General Clark's forces became unavailable for the fight, and are said not even to have seen an Indian during the action of the afternoon.

---

[19]Rockel, W. M. *Hist. of Springfield and Clark County, Ohio*, 51-54.

HISTORIC BACKGROUNDS

It seems probable, from histories of this battle, that the women and children, with the household goods of the settlement, had been removed to a safe point in the heavy woodlands north, or west in the direction of the present city of Piqua in Miami County where their new village home was located after the battle. Likewise that most, if not all, of the available warriors were engaged against Floyd, Lynn and Harrod's forces beyond the lower end of the village where access for retreat into the forest was open and unguarded, in case they were not able to maintain themselves in the fight.

General Clark, himself, with Colonel Slaughter's U. S. troops and the mounted field-piece—which he captured at Vincennes—followed the first division across the ford and took the middle position facing the village in preparation for a front attack. This did not materialize, as the Indians seem to have centered practically all their force of 300 against the western division of Clark's army under Floyd, Lynn and Harrod.

The Indians evinced great military skill and judgment in their attack on the western division and their strong effort to turn its left wing. Floyd, Lynn and Harrod, to prevent being outflanked, were compelled to extend their lines a mile below the ford where the first Indian forces engaged them. The battle continued warmly contested on both sides, with the Indians slowly retreating until they reached the timbered foothills. From this point, they were driven eastward toward the location of the blockhouse at a point now marked by an imposing monument erected in memory of George Rogers Clark and his soldiers who won the Battle of Old Piqua.

At about five o'clock in the afternoon, "the Indians disappeared everywhere unperceived except for a few in the village." The field-piece which had not been in use before, after a half-hour's delay, was trained upon the blockhouse and nearby cabins. A few shots served to dislodge some of the Indians who had taken cover in them. This remnant formed a short battle-line facing General Clark's division; but they, however, quickly gave way to a charge attack after a few maneuvers which led General Clark to believe they intended to surrender. This short contest over, they retreated as the others had done, into the forest beyond the settlement. The battle ended with the withdrawal of all the Indians' forces, except a few prisoners. Bradford notes:[20]

The action was so severe a short time before the close that Simon Girty, a white man who had joined the Indians and who was made a chief among the Mingos, drew off 300 of his men, declaring to them it was folly in the extreme to continue the action against men who acted so much like madmen as General Clark's men, for they rushed into the most extreme danger with a seeming disregard of the consequences. This opinion of Girty, and the withdrawal of the Mingos, so disconcerted the rest, that the whole body soon after dispersed. It is a maxim among the Indians, never to encounter a fool or a madman (in which terms they include a desperate man), for they say, with a man who has not sense enough to take a prudent care of his own life, the life of his antagonist is in much greater danger than with a prudent man.

The death of Joseph Rogers, Clark's nephew, while trying to escape from Indian captivity to his uncle's command, was the melancholy incident of this battle. He was shot by a Kentuckian while trying to make himself known as he approached Clark's command, and died a few hours afterward amid such attentions as his uncle was able there to provide.[21]

The official information of the destruction of Old Chillicothe and the battle of Old Piqua is found in General

---

[20]Bradford, John. *Historical Notes on Kentucky*, from the *Western Miscellany*. . . . New ed. by J. W. Townsend, San Francisco, Grabhorn, 1932, pp. 97-98.

[21]Rogers was taken prisoner by the Shawnees in 1777 at McClelland's Fort, Georgetown, Kentucky. Rogers' fate was not known after the Georgetown fight until his death at Old Piqua. In this fight, John Gabriel Jones was killed. Jones was a distinguished pioneer and co-delegate from Fincastle County, Virginia, (later Kentucky) with George Rogers Clark to the Virginia Assembly at Williamstown, Virginia, in 1776. Jones was one of Kentucky's ablest men. His death, like that of Captain Estill, was an irreparable loss to the Kentucky of that day.

Clark's short report to Governor Jefferson. The report was dated at Louisville, August 22, 1780, thirteen days after the battle, and contains the essential history of the invasion from the dates of rendezvous at the mouth of the Licking River to the disbandment of the army at the same place. The facts, as therein narrated by General Clark may be accepted as the correct history of the adventure, however much other and later narratives may vary in their "historical records."

By every possible exertion, and the aid of Colonel Slaughter's corps, we completed the number of 1000, with which we crossed the river at the mouth of Licking on the first day of August and began our march on the 2nd. Having a road to cut for the artillery to pass, for 70 miles, it was the 6th before we reached the first town, which we found vacated, and the greatest part of their effects carried off. The general conduct of the Indians on our march, and many other corroborating circumstances, proved their design of leading us on to their own ground and time of action. After destroying the crops and buildings of Chillecauthy, we began our march for the Picaway settlements, on the waters of the Big Miami,[22] the Indians keeping runners continually before our advanced guards. At half-past two in the evening of the 8th, we arrived in sight of the town and forts, a plain of half a mile in width lying between us. I had an opportunity of viewing the situation and motion of the enemy near their works.

I had scarcely time to make those dispositions necessary, before the action commenced on our left wing, and in a few minutes became almost general, with a savage fierceness on both sides. The confidence the enemy had of their own strength and certain victory, or the want of generalship, occasioned several neglects, by which those advantages were taken that proved the ruin of their army, being flanked two or three different times, drove from hill to hill in a circuitous direction, for upwards of a mile and a half; at last took shelter in their strongholds and woods adjacent when the firing ceased for about half an hour, until necessary preparations were made for dislodging them. A heavy firing again commenced, and continued severe until dark, by which time the enemy were totally routed. The cannon

---

[22]Mad River is a tributary of the Big Miami River.

playing too briskly on their works they could afford them no shelter. Our loss was about 14 killed and 13 wounded; theirs at least triple that number. They carried off their dead during the night, except 12 or 14 that lay too near our lines for them to venture. This would have been a decisive stroke to the Indians, if unfortunately the right wing of our army had not been rendered useless for some time by an uncommon chain of rocks that they could not pass, by which means part of the enemy escaped through the ground they were ordered to occupy.

By a French prisoner we got the next morning, we learn that the Indians had been preparing for our reception ten days, moving their families and effects: that the morning before our arrival, they were 300 warriors, Shawanese, Mingos, Wyandotts and Delawares. Several reinforcements coming that day, he did not know their numbers; that they were sure of destroying the whole of us; that the greatest part of the prisoners taken by Byrd, were carried to Detroit, where there were only 200 regulars, having no provisions except green corn and vegetables. Our whole store at first setting out being only 300 bushels of corn and 1500 of flour; having done the Shawanese all the mischief in our power, and after destroying the Picaway settlements, I returned to this post, having marched in the whole 480 miles in 31 days. We destroyed upwards of 800 acres of corn, besides great quantities of vegetables, a considerable portion of which appear to have been cultivated by white men, I suppose for the purpose of supporting war parties from Detroit. I could wish to have had a small store of provisions to enable us to lay waste part of the Delaware settlements, and falling in at Pittsburg, but the excessive heat, and weak diet, shew the impropriety of such a step. Nothing could excel the few regulars and Kentuckyans, that compose this little army, in bravery and implicit obedience to orders; each company vying with the other who should be the most subordinate.[23]

---

[23]"George Rogers Clark Papers," in *Illinois Hist. Soc. Collections*, 8:451-453; Draper MSS., 8 J 136. This document was published under the title. "Gen. Clark's Campaign, 1780.—Official Letter. Richmond, (Virginia), October 4. Extract of a letter from Colonel George Rogers Clark to his Excellency the Governor, dated Louisville, August 22, 1780." The present copy is from the transcription by Dr. Draper.

After the battle and the Indian retreat at Old Piqua came the mayhem of the gardens and cornfields and the destruction of the wigewas and other types of dwelling at Old Piqua along the

HISTORIC BACKGROUNDS

PLAN OF MARCH, 1782

Early in 1782 forays and battles broke forth with fresh fury in the Ohio Valley between the Red Men and their enemies, the pioneer settlers. Calamity seemed to beset the posts and settlements north and south of the Ohio River. Events that form the historic background of General Clark's 1782 expedition against the Shawnees in the Little and Great Miami Valleys began March eighth, 1782, north of the Ohio. On this date at the Indian Mission village of Gnadenhutten, 90 non-resisting Moravian Christian Indians were massacred by militia under command of Colonel Williamson. The massacre was unprovoked. Three days were taken by the captors for deliberation before the final verdict of death was determined. Two boys only escaped.

The Indians north of the Ohio River were infuriated, especially the Delawares, who were relatives of the martyred Moravians. On May 25, 1782, Colonel William Crawford led a command organized near Pittsburgh, at Mingo Bottoms, against the Upper Sandusky Indian settlements. Information of this invasion and its purpose to destroy the Wyandotte and Shawnee settlements "with fire and sword," was obtained from various sources by these Indians. Captain Caldwell with a mixed force of several hundred rangers and Indians was sent from Detroit to reinforce the settlements about Sandusky. They were joined by bands of Wyandotte and Delaware Indians and on June fourth the

---

foothills and cliffs for a distance, said by some writers, to have been three miles. No effort was, or could be made at pursuit. Night in the shadows of the forest, and the serious food shortage facing General Clark, provided safe conduct for retreat of the Indians to the Great Miami River. There they re-located in two villages, Upper and Lower Piqua, and were established in their usual village life, two years later, when General Clark's second invasion reached them.

On the tenth of August, two days after the battle of Piqua, the army began its march homeward over the trail it had cut through the forest from the Ohio River to Old Piqua. Its first encampment was made at Old Chillicothe where, on the 11th of August, it cut down the small field of corn that had been left for the men and horses on their return. There is no historical reference to other camp points between the Little Miami River and the mouth of the Licking where the army dispersed and each individual made his way home.

battle began which resulted in the defeat and tragic death of Colonel Crawford and a number of his soldiers. An attack on Hannastown followed Crawford's defeat. It was destroyed with the loss of a number of forters, and outside settlers killed or made prisoners. Captain Estill's death and the attack on Holden's post by Wyandottes, were followed by the turning back toward Kentucky of an invasion against Wheeling commanded by Captains Caldwell, McKee and Joseph Brandt. Wheeling as an objective was abandoned, and Bryant's Station, Kentucky, became this invasion's point of attack.[24]

During the short and unsuccessful investment of Bryant's Fort, the growing corn, gardens, and stock of the forters were killed and their horses driven away with the retreating forces toward the Licking River. A two days' march was required to reach it and dispose of the invading forces in ambush, where they awaited the pursuing Kentuckians, with every advantage in numbers and position favorable to the invaders. The pursuers, gathered from various nearby posts at Bryant's Fort, refused to wait for Colonel Logan and a strong force known to be hurrying to their aid from St. Asaph's Fort at Stanford, Kentucky. Rash councils prevailed, followed by an attack on the invaders which met with the quick defeat of the forters and the loss of 70 men, including a number of the ablest pioneer leaders then living in Kentucky.

History can find no justification for the rash and overconfident advice on which this most unfortunate attack was made. Especially was this true with Colonel Logan known to be hastening forward with 470 mounted men. On September 2nd, 1782, 37 settlers were captured at Kincheloes Station. These were some of the major incidents that formed the historic background of General George Rogers Clark's second invasion of the Shawnee country on the two Miami Rivers occurring in quick succession; each attack causing large loss to the Kentucky forters, consternation seized these pioneer settlements.

---

[24]James, James A. *Op. Cit.*, 265-271.

HISTORIC BACKGROUNDS

The unanimous call that went out to General Clark from the Kentucky Forters to head an invasion of reprisal into the Shawnee country north of the Ohio was answered by his organization in October of an invading force of 1050 Kentucky militia-men at the mouth of the Licking River opposite the present city of Cincinnati, Ohio. Edna Kenton in her recent interesting volume, *Simon Kenton*, writes of the assembling of Colonel Logan's forces for Clark's 1782 invasion:

Logan, with whom Kenton served, commanded the troops of the interior, and when they left Lexington, the men scattered through the country, to hunt by the way and so provision themselves, and to meet by a certain day at Byrd's old encampment in the forks of Licking. They killed a good supply of buffalo and deer, and jerked the meat at night—each mess with its packhorse kept together. There was one packhorse to each mess of six. The men took from home enough parched corn to last them to the Indians' towns—a handful a day being a ration.[25]

All the county lieutenants provisioned their men likewise, and the united forces finally met across the Ohio, opposite the mouth of Licking where Cincinnati now is. Logan and his men arrived on the morning of the designated day and Clark came up in the evening. On the fourth of November, at the head of more than a thousand men, Clark set out for the Shawnee towns, Kenton, Boone, and Waters piloting.[26] Logan went on with one hundred and fifty horsemen to Loramie's trading-store at the head of the Miami and burned the large supplies there.

The two principal towns destroyed on the Great Miami were Lower Piqua, situated on the site of the present city

---

[25]Kenton, Edna. *Simon Kenton*, 159-160.
[26]Simon Kenton states in his deposition of April 13, 1826, before Levi Barwood, Zane Township, Logan County, Ohio, Associate Judge of the Court of Common Pleas, that he was scout and captain of a company in General Clark's invasion of 1782.
Kenton states in this deposition that he was pilot of George Rogers Clark's 1780 expedition, which came north through Lebanon, crossed the Little Miami River and camped two miles from the Little Miami on Caesar's Creek, thence to Glady's Creek and Old Chillicothe three and one half miles north of Xenia, Ohio.

of Piqua, Miami County, Ohio, and Upper Piqua, three miles above. Loramie's store was 14 miles north of Upper Piqua at the mouth of Loramie creek. (See Colonel John Johnson's map, 1845). Dr. James A. James states in his admirable Life of Clark:

Parched corn, buffalo meat and venison were quickly collected, but other supplies were gotten together with great difficulty. The credit of the State was worthless and Clark's own available resources were exhausted. *He finally exchanged 3,500 acres of his own land for the flour necessary for the expedition.* On the fourth of November 1050 mounted men, with Clark in command, set out for Chillicothe, the main Shawnee stronghold. Rigid discipline was maintained during the march of six days.[27]

Colonel R. C. Ballard Thurston, President of the Filson Club, Louisville, Kentucky, has generously permitted the writer to quote, from the unpublished manuscripts of Colonel Cave Johnson, an important record bearing on General Clark's invasion of 1782:

In the year, 1782, General Clark headed an expedition against the Indians in the Miami country. My brother Robert commanded a company from Bryant's Station. Jeremiah Craig and myself were his subalterns. Every man fit for the campaign, except a sufficiency to take care of the fort and the families in it, was called out. Colonel Benjamin Logan was second in command.

One wing of the army marched up the river from the falls, the other from Lexington and Bryant's Station. They met in general rendezvous on the ground now occupied by Cincinnati when General Clark took immediate command. We then marched through Old Chillicothe, on the Little Miami, to the Indian town of Pickway, on the Big Miami. We had one piece of cannon, I think, a six-pounder. The Indians fled and gave us no general battle. They did come one dark night and fired on us, which caused us to extinguish our fires, but kept at such a distance that they hurt none of us. Some scouting parties killed a few of them and took some prisoners, I don't remember how many, and

---

[27]James, James A. *Op. Cit.*, 277.

HISTORIC BACKGROUNDS

destroyed their corn and all the villages we could find. We then marched home. This was in November.[28]

Harmar's invasion of 1790 followed this trail, as noted in Harmar's *Journal*, entries of Oct. 2nd, to 6th inclusive.[29]

The route of Clark's 1782 invasion is established by these references. Old Chillicothe was the only Indian village situated on the Little Miami River. In further verification of Clark's disputed 1782 route, are Clark's own order and a letter here added; and references from a sketch of Colonel Robert Patterson, by John W. Vancleaf from data furnished him by his son Jefferson Patterson:

In the latter part of September, Clark assembled an army at the mouth of the Licking to avenge the defeat of the Blue Licks by an invasion of the Indian country. Colonel Patterson served as colonel in the expedition. The towns on the Little Miami and Mad River and the Pickaway town on the Great Miami were destroyed, but the Indians retired before the army without giving them a battle.[30]

The only Indian village in the Little Miami Valley was

---

[28] In a trial before Josiah Glover, Master Commissioner of Chancery of the Superior Court of Greene County in the case of John Stephenson vs. Peter and J. Vandolah in the matter of a bill in equity filed July 4th, 1815, with a final entry on July 21. 1818, pp. 322-349 inclusive found in the Greene County records of the Superior Court, James Galloway deposed:

Q. "How long have you known Old Chillicothe on the Little Miami River, where you now are?"

Ans. "I have known it since the month of October or November, 1782. It was at that time and has continued to be a place of notoriety in the Miami country."

Q. "Are you now sitting in the place called Old Chillicothe?"

Ans. "I am now sitting in the bounds where the pickets were."

James Galloway took part in the Battle of Blue Licks and was a member of General Clark's invasion of 1782. Otherwise, he could not have been there on that date. He was treasurer of Greene County from its organization in 1803 till June, 1819, and was a pioneer of outstanding influence in his community from the date of his settlement with his family near Old Chillicothe in 1797 until his death in 1836.

[29] *Ohio Arch. and Hist. Quarterly*, 20:90.

[30] *Amer. Pioneer*, 2:346-347.

OLD CHILLICOTHE

Old Chillicothe, the principal town of the Shawnee Indians three and one-half miles north of Xenia. The other villages mentioned in Boone's narrative were located, one on Wills Creek (Willstown) five and one-half miles from Old Chillicothe, and the others on the Great Miami River, at and not far distant from the present city of Piqua, Miami County, Ohio. This place and Loramie's store, 14 miles north of Upper Piqua on the Great Miami, were the "high water" marks of Clark's 1782 invasion. These villages were destroyed a few days later before Clark began his return march to Kentucky.

For the reader who may be interested in Kenton's difficulties and responsibilities as pilot in a hostile Indian country, a trip on foot from the mouth of Caesar's Creek to Clark's 1782 camp two miles east, will help visualize 1782 conditions of unbroken terrain. The same conditions are found along Massie's Creek east from Wilberforce University, from the former site of King's mill, and in isolated pieces of woodland, still standing on the Polecat Road, Clark's line of march from Old Chillicothe to the 1780 battlefield of Old Piqua, on Mad River.

Further evidence of Clark's invasion at Old Chillicothe, "the principal Shawnee town Chillecauthy," is found in Clark's general orders—Nov. 9th, 1782—and in his letter to General Irvine, Nov. 13, 1782:

Clark's Order to His Army Before the Battle of Old Town (Old Chillicothe), 1782

Chelecothe, November 9, 1782.
Gen'l orders as an action with the Enemy may be hourly Expected the Officers are Requested to pay the Strictest attention To their duty as Suffering no man to Quit his Rank Without leave as Nothing is more dangerous than Disorder. If fortunately any prisoner Should fall in to our hands they are by no means to be put to Death without leave as it will be attended with the Immediate Masseerce of all our Citizens that are in the hands of the Enimy and Also deprive us of the advantage of Exchanging for our own people, no person to attempt to take any Plunder untill Orders Should Issue for that purpose under penalty of Being punished for Disobedience of orders and to have no Share of Such plunder himself. The Officers in

perticular are requested to Observe that the Strictest Notice be paid to this Order, as much Depends on it all plunder taken to be Delivered to the Quarter Master, to be Devided among the Different Batallions in proportion to their Numbers any person Concealing Plunder of any kind Shall be Considered as Subject to the penalty of the Above Order.[31]

Signed G R CLARK

—*Excerpt from George Rogers Clark's Papers.*

Clark to William Irvine, November 13, 1782
(Draper MSS., 11J24,—Transcript)

Miami, 13th Nov., 1782

Sir: I fell in with your late Expresses on the 2nd Inst at the mouth of Licking Creek—Was happy to find that our designs was likely to be well timed—We march'd on the third, the 10th surprised the principal Shawnee Town Chillecauthy, but not so compleatly as wished for, as most of the Inhabitants had time to make their escape.—We got a few Scalps and Prisoners—I immediately detached strong parties to the neighbouring Towns and in a short time laid five of them in ashes, with all their Riches—The British trad'g post as the carrying place shared the same fate—I can't learn by the Prisoners that they had any Idea of your second design & hope that you will compleatly surprise the Sanduskians—I beg leave to Refer you to Mr. Tate & his companion for particulars for reason well known to you.[32]

I am Sir with respect
Your Obdt Servt
G. R. CLARK.

As soon as General Clark heard of the disaster at Blue Licks, he determined to chastise the Indians and, if possible, destroy them. To this end, he called for one thousand men, to be raised from Kentucky, making their headquarters at Cincinnati, where he was to meet them, at the head of a part of an Illinois regiment, of which he then had command, bringing with him one brass field piece.

The exultant savages had returned to Old Chillicothe, and had divided their spoil and their captives. Colonel Boone was immediately sent for to take part in this expedition. Clark's army crossed the Ohio, and marching very rapidly up the banks of the Little Miami, arrived within two miles of Chillicothe before they were observed. Here

---

[31]*Ill. Hist. Soc. Coll.*, 19:151.
[32]*Ill. Hist. Coll.*, 19:152-153.

they discovered a solitary straggler, who instantly fled to the village, yelling like a demon at every jump. The troops pressed on with all possible speed, but upon entering the town found it deserted. So precipitate had been their retreat, however, that the enemy left the fires burning, pots boiling, and meat roasting on sticks. This was a treat to the almost famished Kentuckians, who, after full indulgence, proceeded to destroy the town, corn and everything tending to support the savage foe. It is said that on the approach of the army, men, women and children fled to the forest, leaving everything behind them. Five towns, during this expedition, were left in ashes, and the work of destruction was complete. This campaign so thoroughly crushed the Indians, that no more organized raids were made against the surrounding settlements, and the termination of the Revolutionary War left them to their own resources.[33]

CELEBRATION OF 1832

The band of intrepid pioneers under the command of General George Rogers Clark, stationed at the mouth of the Licking, on the fourth day of November, 1782, resolved that all the survivors should on that day 50 years afterward, meet on the same ground in a semi-centennial celebration on the fourth of November, 1832. The call for this meeting was extensively published in the newspapers in the west.[34]

---

[33] Dills, R. S. *Hist. of Greene County, Ohio*, 252-253.
The three Greene County Histories, Dills's 1881, Broadstone's 1898, and Robinson's 1909, contain positive statements of General George Rogers Clark's 1782 invasion, attacking Old Chillicothe, on the Little Miami River, on its incoming line of march against the Indians of the Miami Valleys. All local history of Dills's edition, 1881, was written by the late Prof. George S. Ormsby, Supt. of the Xenia City Schools for many years. Prof. Ormsby's Greene County historical work was known to be carefully and critically compiled, and may be depended upon to be historically reliable.

[34] The call was addressed to the veterans who had fought with General George Rogers Clark, at Kaskaskia, Cahokia and Vincennes and those who remained of the men Clark led in his second punitive expedition against Old Chillicothe and the Upper and Lower Piquas in Miami County. The appeals for this meeting signed by General Simon Kenton and by Kenton and James Galloway addressed to "The Citizens of the Western Country" have been preserved in the *American Pioneer*. They were prepared for these two aged veterans by Major James Galloway, Jr., a fre-

HISTORIC BACKGROUNDS

General Kenton's Address to the Citizens of the Western Country:

The old pioneers, citizen-soldiers, and those who were engaged with us in the regular service in the conquest of the western country from the British and savages, fifty years ago, have all been invited to attend, with the survivors of General George Rogers Clark's army of 1782, who purpose the celebration of a western anniversary according to their promise made on the ground, the 4th day of November, in that year. Those, also, who were engaged in like service subsequently, and in the late war, have been invited to attend, and join with us in the celebration on the said 4th of November, at Old Fort Washington, now Cincinnati. I propose that we meet at Covington, Kentucky, on the 3rd; the 4th being the Sabbath, to attend divine service; on Monday meet our friends on the ground where the old Fort stood; and then take a final adieu, to meet no more, until we shall all meet in a world of spirits!

Fellow-citizens of the West! this is a meeting well worthy your very serious consideration. The few survivors of that race, who are now standing on the verge of the grave, view with anxious concern the welfare of their common country; for which they fought against British oppression and savage cruelty, to secure to you our posterity, the blessings of liberty, religion and law. We will meet and we will tell you what we have suffered to secure to you these inestimable privileges; we will meet, and if you will listen, we will admonish you face to face, to be as faithful as we have been, to transmit those blessings unimpaired to your posterity; that America may long, and we trust forever, remain a free, sovereign, independent, and happy country. We look to our fellow-citizens in Kentucky and Ohio, near the place of meeting, to make provision for their old fathers of the West. We look to our patriot captains of our steamboats, and patriotic stage contractors and companies, and our generous inn-keepers, to make provision for the going and returning to Cincinnati, from all parts of the West. We know they will deem it an honor, to accommodate the gray-headed veterans of the West, who go to meet their companions for the last time; for this may be the only opportunity they will ever have to serve their old fathers, the pioneers and veterans of the West.

---

quent contributor to the press of that period under the pseudonym of "Pioneer Junior." They were written at the old Galloway home during a visit of General Kenton to his old comrade, James Galloway.

Fellow-citizens! being one of the first after Colonel Daniel Boone, who aided in the conquest of Kentucky and the West, I am called upon to address you. My heart melts on such an occasion; I look forward to the contemplated meeting with melancholy pleasure; it has caused tears to flow in copious showers. I wish to see once more, before I die, my few surviving friends. My *solemn promise,* made fifty years ago, binds me to meet them. I ask not for myself; but you may find in our assembly some who have never received any pay or pension, who have sustained the cause of their country, equal to any other service; who in the decline of life are poor. Then, you prosperous sons of the West, forget not these old and gray-haired veterans on this occasion; let them return to their families with some little manifestation of your kindness to cheer their hearts. I add my prayer; may kind heaven grant us a clear sky, fair and pleasant weather—a safe journey and a happy meeting, and smile upon us and our families, and bless us and our nation on the approaching occasion.[35]

Urbana, Ohio, 1832. (Signed) SIMON KENTON.

An address signed by Simon Kenton and James Galloway, dated June 22, 1832, and the one a short time before this date, signed by Simon Kenton, were printed in many newspapers of the period, and in that way probably reached all of the survivors of General George Rogers Clark's army of 1782. The meeting—November fifth, 1832,—was well attended as the following note from the *American Pioneer* indicates: "From some sickness, General Kenton did not attend the 50th year celebration, but although the cholera prevailed in Cincinnati at the time, many attended, and the corporation generously voted the old veterans a dinner."[36]

The address of these two pioneer veterans, on June 22, 1832, shows the deep interest they both had in the approaching memorial meeting, and their great desire to meet with those veterans of 1782, who yet survived the intervening 50 years, since they last clasped hands and bid each other good-bye at their final camp on the Licking River. It was addressed:

---

[35] *American Pioneer*, 2:156-157.
[36] *American Pioneer*, 2:153-154.

JAMES GALLOWAY, SR.

TREASURER'S RECEIPT

In the handwriting of James Galloway, Sr., who was treasurer of Greene County, Ohio, 1803-1819

HISTORIC BACKGROUNDS

To the surviving Officers and Soldiers who served under General George Rogers Clark, on a campaign against the Indians in the year 1782.

Fellow Soldiers—In the year 1827, General Green Clay and Captain John Kenton made some exertions to ascertain the names and the residence of such of us, as were then living, who served on the above campaign, and to call our attention to a promise which, at the instance of Captain M'Cracken was made to him, and to each other, on the 4th November, 1782, when encamped opposite the mouth of Licking, where Cincinnati now is, that as many of us as should be living, would meet on that ground on that day fifty years, which will be on the 4th day of November next. You will no doubt all recollect Captain M'Cracken. He commanded the company of light-horse, and Green Clay was his lieutenant. The Captain was slightly wounded in the arm at the Piqua town, when within a few feet of one of the subscribers; from which place he was carried on a horse-litter for several days; his wound produced mortification, and he died in going down the hill where the city of Cincinnati now stands. He was buried near the blockhouse we had erected opposite the mouth of Licking, and the breastworks were thrown over his grave to prevent the savages from scalping him.

Since 1827, Green Clay and John Kenton have both died. It is not known what number of us they ascertained to be then living, nor where they reside. John Kenton, in a letter to one of us in that year, states that he only knew of about twenty who were then living, but was informed that there were many more living in the State of Kentucky. We have resided for upwards of thirty years in the State of Ohio; all our comrades of 1782, with whom we were acquainted in this State, and many who lived elsewhere, are dead. We know of not one survivor but ourselves, but hope there may yet be many others. We are both old men, and have survived the ordinary term of human life; but still our hearts are warmed with a portion of youthful feeling when we look back to the times of the first settlement of the West —times which tried men's souls; and also when we look forward to the near approach of that time, when we promised to meet on a spot which was then a forest, but is now a city, rivalling in numbers, wealth and enterprize, many cities whose history goes back for centuries; a time when we hope to take by the hand, and to exchange congratulations with those whom we once knew in the prime of life, in youthful manhood, full of patriotism and love of country;

but whom we now can only expect to see, bowed down with age, with hoary locks and tottering limbs, with every feeling blunted, but that of love of country, and attachment to our free republican institutions.

We would earnestly invite and entreat all our companions who can, by any means, attend, to meet us in Cincinnati on the 3d (the 4th being Sunday) day of November next. We also respectfully request that editors of newspapers would give circulation to this notice, particularly in Kentucky.[37]

June 22nd, 1832   (Signed) SIMON KENTON
             JAMES GALLOWAY

LOGAN—1786

From March 18, 1776, the date of General Benjamin Logan's permanent establishment of his family home at St. Asaph's, now Stanford, Kentucky, he became an outstanding leader in the pioneer military activities of the territory now known as Kentucky. He has been properly described as "a leader whom no danger ever appalled or confused, and whose best faculties were called into action in the midst of conflict." The authorities of Virginia, in recognition of his signal ability to command, conferred on him the rank of Brigadier General, and in this capacity he joined General George Rogers Clark's expedition against the Wabash Indians in 1786, bringing with him about four hundred men from the Lincoln County district.

Following these orders, on September 14, 1786, General Logan left camp at once for St. Asaph's and assembled from Lincoln and Fayette Counties, 790 Kentucky mounted men for this expedition, 500 of whom furnished their own mounts and equipment, including rations. By October sixth, this invading force reached the Mack-a-chack villages, about 300 miles north of Stanford, and destroyed this scattered cluster of small Shawnee settlements.[38]

---

[37]*American Pioneer*, 2:166-167.

[38]General Richard Butler, who conducted a large trading post at Old Chillicothe previous to the American Revolution, gives the list of Indian towns, in "Letters of an American Planter" and a map of

HISTORIC BACKGROUNDS

General Logan's invasion of the Mackachack settlement was characterized by a series of running skirmishes. There was no defined battle-front; a number of isolated parties of Indians were pursued at several points and a dozen killed. The most important event connected with the invasion was the surrender of the Old Chief Moluntha with his three wives, of whom Grenadier Squaw is mentioned as one, and a party of women and children, among whom seem to have been two white women prisoners with their two young daughters. Solomon Clark's deposition[39] gives a clear descriptive detail of the event and is probably as reliable as any data now available. He mentions "Grenadier" as one of Moluntha's wives. He does not identify her, however, as the famous sister of Cornstalk, though she was mentioned in General Butler's journal as being present with her daughter at the Treaty of Fort Finney. She is there called Catherine, or Katy for short. She was the most remarkable of all western aboriginal women. Moluntha was well known to many of the Kentucky invaders, and also well thought of and quite naturally was the center of attraction after his surrender. Captain Hugh McGary, whose rash leadership has been held responsible for the disaster at Blue Licks, hearing the King of the Shawnees had been taken prisoner, came to see him and found it was Moluntha, one of the Blue Lick Shawnee leader chiefs. Moluntha, who was smoking a pipe and passing it to others of the crowd about him, held out his hand to McGary, who took it and asked him if he was at the Blue Lick defeat. Moluntha answered that he commanded the warriors of his town there. Then McGary, in a rage exclaimed "G— d— you, I'll give you Blue Lick play." He seized a tomahawk and

---

the Upper Scioto Country. The towns were: Mamacomink, Puckshauoses, Maquechaick, Blue Jacket's Town, Pecowick, Kispoco, Waccachalla, Chillacote. These were all situated on Alluman Creek and Deer Creek. Cornstalk's town was situated on the north side of Scippo Creek, along the Scioto Trail—State Route No. 4—four miles south of Circleville, Pickaway County, Ohio. Across the creek, south within a quarter of a mile, was his sister's town. She is known as the Grenadier Squaw. Her Indian name was Non-helema and her English name Catherine. For short many pioneers called her Katy.

[39] *Draper MSS.*, ICC 3-4.

sunk it in the old chief's head, causing immediate death.[40] The commotion among the Kentuckians and their disapproval of this inexcusable act after the surrender of this distinguished prisoner was positive, and though McGary escaped personal violence there, he was later brought to court martial for this act. There were four counts in the indictment:

1. The killing of Moluntha who had surrendered and was a prisoner of war (consequently entitled to protection).
2. Disobedience of orders.
3. Disorderly conduct as an officer and threats to kill Colonel James Trotter who was his superior in rank and did not approve McGary's act.
4. Abusing other field officers (for the same reason).

The court records the following findings:
1. Guilty.
2. Not guilty.
3. Guilty.
4. Part guilty.

The sentence was suspension from command for one year. At the end of this time history finds McGary again active in Kentucky affairs. He subsequently attained the rank of major.

Interesting details of Logan's invasion on which history is entirely silent, may be found in the Draper files. Mackachack, McKeestown, Moluntha's town and Wapotomica were destroyed by parties of invading forces on the following day, October 11, at their leisure, the Indians having deserted them. The area of corn-fields destroyed is not given, but manifestly was large. Considerable booty and a number of horses were taken. This loot, with all prisoners, was removed to Moluntha town and guarded there till the return march began. The loot was comparatively small, amounting to only $2.50 per man for the 885 men

---

[40]Green, Thomas M. *Historic Families of Kentucky*, 137.

entitled to participate. The prisoners accompanied the invaders to Kentucky and were kept at Danville until exchanged. It has been difficult to select the most reliable basis for this history. Green's *Historic Families of Kentucky* so far as it treats of Logan, is recommended. Howe's *History of Ohio*,[41] which gives the battle story of a boy of 16, is like most historical narratives given from memory 50 years after, distorted by the increasing egotism that mirages passing years. This is so evident that Howe himself adds corrective comment at the close of the chapter. The following notes are taken from the ably written history of General George Rogers Clark by Judge Temple Bodley of Louisville, Kentucky. They, with the reference above, give a wide field for the study of the first source information on this subject.

"The facts about Logan's expedition have been grossly distorted in history." Thus Wither's *Chronicles of Border Warfare*,[42] says that in carrying out his expedition he practically revolted from Clark, and Logan destroyed eight large towns, killed about 20 warriors, and captured 70 or 80 prisoners.[43]

Contemporary reports show that the Shawnee warriors had gone against Clark and that almost none but old men, women and children were left in the towns. (*Michigan Pioneer Collections*,[44] Denny's Journal,[45] Harmar's Report, Library of Congress, Continental Congress, Letter to Sec'y of War,[46] *St. Clair Papers*,[47] *Draper MSS*.[48])

"This expedition gave Logan his first and only inde-

---

[41] Howe, Henry. *Historical Collections of Ohio*, 2:98-99.
[42] Withers, A. S. *Chronicles of Border Warfare*, 386. Note.
[43] Withers, A. S. *Chronicles of Border Warfare*, 386.
[44] *Mich. Pioneer and Hist. Collections*, 24:34-39.
[45] Denny, Major Ebenezer. *Military Journal*, 93-94.
[46] Library of Congress. Continental Cong. Letter to Sec. of War No. 150. v. 11:163-164.
[47] *St. Clair Papers*, 2:18-19.
[48] Draper MSS., 11 F 61. (Rept. of Indian Councils. Mohawk Chief's Speech).

pendent command, and he did not depreciate his performance when reporting it to the Governor."

The following relates to General Clark's 1786 Wabash invasion and Logan's authority to conduct the Mackachack campaign:

> General Clark, after reaching Clarksville with his forces, organized for the campaign against the Indians of the Wabash Valley, learned from his spies that the Shawnees, despite their treaty promises, had joined the hostile confederacy; and, to compel them to desert and discourage their allies, he ordered Logan to return to Kentucky, gather troops there and lead them against the Shawnee towns. As the Lincoln and Fayette people regarded the Shawnees as their special enemies, Logan readily gathered 790 men, all but 85 of them mounted volunteers, and fell upon the Shawnee towns. The attack was wholly unexpected and there was little or no resistance; for 400 warriors had gone against Clark and few, save old men, women and children, and a few warriors as guards, were left in the towns. Even the leading sachems who remained had gone some distance to attend an Indian Council. General Logan destroyed their houses and crops, killed ten Indians and took thirty-three prisoners. Amongst the killed was the old chief, Moluntha, who had long been friendly to the Americans. He had surrendered, but, while shielding himself with the American flag and holding up the recent treaty, was cut down. This killing of the old chief led to acrimonious disputes between some of the officers and later to court martial and lasting enmities.[49]

GENERAL JOSIAH HARMAR'S EXPEDITION—1790

In the four years which elapsed after General Benjamin Logan invaded Old Chillicothe and the Miami and Mad River Valleys, the federal government made numerous efforts to arrive at peace terms with the Shawnees and their allies. The ease with which these tribes had met the Bowman, Clark and Logan invasions, the small loss of life and property attending them, strengthened their belief that they would be able to mainain a successful defense, and

---

[49]Green's *Historic Families of Kentucky*.

continue to retain possession of the territory promised them by the first Fort Stanwix Treaty. To all advances of the government, therefore, the response of the Indian was: "Withdraw your settlement west of Pennsylvania and north of the Ohio River if you desire peace." In the interests of peace they even suggested a plan of equitable settlement with the squatters and their removal from the disputed territory.

Futile treaties with the Shawnees were entered into at Fort Finney, January third, 1786, and at Fort Harmar, January ninth, 1789. During the interval between these two dates, commissioners of high standing appointed by the government, made various attempts to extend the boundary lines for emigrant settlement of the eastern part of the Northwest Territory, but all to no avail.

By 1790, renewal of hostilities in Kentucky and along the Ohio and Wabash Rivers became acute, largely due to continued territorial aggressions. A communication on the Indian menace to General Knox, aroused military officers at Washington to the belief that organized hostilities should no longer be delayed.

On July ninth, 1790, General Knox directed General Harmar to confer with Governor St. Clair and organize a punitive expedition against the Indian "Maumee towns located above the Wabash River." The authority had already been vested in General Harmar by General Washington, to issue a call for 1000 Virginia militia (this included Fincastle County, later Kentucky) and 500 militia from Pennsylvania. Four hundred United States troops were made available for this call. These troops were subsequently used as a training nucleus for the less experienced militia. The 1453 men finally enlisted under General Harmar for this invasion were classified as follows in Lieutenant Denny's report to Major General Butler, President of the Court of Inquiry, following General Harmar's defeat:—

    3 Battalions of Kentucky Militia,
      1 Battalion of Pennsylvania Militia and
      1 Battalion of Mounted Militia   1133
    2 Battalions of Federal Troops   320

                              Total 1453

GENERAL HARMAR'S DEFEAT

As all overtures of peace failed and the depredations continued, an attempt at coercion became inevitable. The President, by and with the consent and advice of Congress, dispatched General Harmar on the 30th of September, 1790, with 320 federal troops and 1133 militia to attack and destroy the principal villages and supplies of the Indians in the Miami country.

The troops after seventeen days' march from Fort Washington reached the Great Miami village, without any other molestation than that of having a number of their packhorses stolen. On their arrival they found the village deserted and all the buildings set on fire by the Indians. After a short delay, the troops proceeded to the neighboring villages without molestation, and destroyed five of them. A quantity of corn, computed at fifteen thousand bushels, which they found buried in different places, and very large quantities of vegetables of every kind were found and destroyed.

The first opposition was met when a party of about 150 Kentucky militia and 30 regular troops, all under the command of Colonel Hardin, of Kentucky, were detached from the main body lying in the Great Miami village, to pursue the trail of a party of Indians, which had been discovered the day before. After pursuit of about six miles, they came up with, and were attacked by a body of Indians who were concealed in the thickets on every side of a large plain. On the first onset the militia without exchanging a single shot, made a most precipitate retreat and left the regular troops to stand the whole charge of the Indians; the conflict was short and bloody, the troops were soon overpowered by numbers, and all fell except two officers, and two or three privates, who used their bayonets with the greatest possible obstinacy. Ensign Hartshorn was one of the officers who providentially escaped by a very lucky circumstance. He fell over a log in retreating and by that means screened himself from the eye of his pursuers. Under any other circumstance he would have been lost. Captain Armstrong, who commanded the party, likewise made his escape, by plunging himself into a pond or swamp within two hundred yards of the field of action, where he remained the whole night a spectator to the horrid scene of the war dance performed over the dead and wounded bodies of the soldiers that had fallen the preceding day. The Indians were under the command of Little Turtle, ablest of all Miami war chiefs.

After this, a few skirmishes followed, until the second capital action, two days after the army left the Miami village. At ten miles distance from the town, the general ordered a halt, and detached from 400 to 500 militia, and about 60 regular soldiers, under the command of Major Wyllys and Colonel Hardin, who were ordered to march back to the town. On their first entrance a small body of Indians appeared and immediately fled, decoying the whole body of the militia, by making their flight in different directions, and encouraging the militia in divided parties to pursue. By this stratagem the few regular troops were detached from the main body of the militia. The Indians commenced the attack with their whole force, excepting the flying parties that had divided the militia. Although they soon found some part of the militia returning at their backs, they pursued their object of routing and destroying the troops, as the only sure plan of success; which after a most bloody conflict on each side, they effected, Little Turtle again being in command.

Nothing could exceed the intrepidity of the savages on this occasion. They appeared to despise the militia, and with all the courage conceivable, threw down their guns, and rushed upon the bayonets of the regular soldiers. A number of them fell, but being so far superior in numbers, they soon overpowered the regulars. While the soldier had his bayonet in one Indian, two more would sink their tomahawks in his head. The defeat of the troops was complete; the dead and wounded were left on the field of action, in possession of the savages. The number of Indians in the attack has been estimated at one hundred. One hundred and fifty is the largest estimate given by Harmar's officers.

The following is a copy of the official return of the killed and wounded in the expedition:

Killed of the Federal troops: one Major, two Lieutenants, 73 rank and file—total 76. Wounded—three rank and file.

Killed of the Militia: one Major, three Captains, three Lieutenants, one Ensign, 25 rank and file—total 33.

All but nine of the regular troops, including two commissioned officers, were killed. Among the slain was Major Wyllys, and a number of brave and valuable soldiers. The Indians, it appeared, did not think it prudent to pursue their successes from the field of action, so most of the troops that were not killed or badly wounded, made their escape.[50]

General Harmar's orders for mobilization at Fort Washington and Fort Steuben were issued about July 15, 1790. Many of the militia who answered this call were unfit for Indian or any other service. They came to Fort Washington poorly equipped, their arms generally bad and unfit for service; destitute of such simple camp equipment as axes and kettles, and many of them being either old and infirm, or boy substitutes. This was the material out of which General Harmar had to make his "army" ready in two months to go against Indians, whom General Harrison later described as "a body of the finest light troops in the world."[51] With this impossible material and two months' training, he set out to invade a country, every foot of which was familiar to the enemy and unknown to the invader.

They were whipped before they left Fort Washington on September 26th, 1790. Colonel John Hardin, an unfortunate commander of the invasion, was the ranking colonel by seniority and entitled to command. From some

---

[50] *The People's Press*, Xenia, Ohio, Wednesday, June 28, 1826. In view of the disastrous results of the engagement on this occasion, it is amusing to read the report made by General Arthur St. Clair to the Secretary of War, *Ohio Arch. and Hist. Quarterly*, 20:87-88.

[51] Harrison, General W. H. "Discourse on the Aborigines of the Valley of the Ohio," in *Hist. and Phil. Soc. of Ohio*, 2:255.

cause not evident, he was so unpopular with the Kentucky militia that they refused to go forward under his command. Both officers and men openly declared that unless Colonel Trotter commanded them they would return to their homes in Kentucky. This was the first of several disagreements of men and plans that contributed to General Harmar's defeat. Later Colonel Hardin took the place of Colonel Trotter and was badly defeated.

The Harmar line of march north followed the east bank of the Little Miami River to Old Chillicothe,[52] thence northwest to the Maumee settlements. This line of march is still traceable for a short distance on the Isaac Evans farm south of Spring Valley, Greene County, Ohio. Interesting events occurred in this invasion at Old Chillicothe, General Harmar's first point of Indian contact, 65 miles from Fort Washington on Sunday, October 17th, 1790.

TRACES OF THE EXPEDITIONS AGAINST THE SHAWNEES

General Harmar's line of march from Cincinnati to Old Chillicothe may be followed by reference to McBride's *Pioneer Biography,* synopsis of which march is here quoted.[53] The added distance of each day's march equals the present distance by railroad between these two points—

Sept. 30, 1790: The army moved from Fort Washington at 10:30 A. M., northeast 7 miles, to a branch of Mill Creek. Oct. 1st: The advance was 8 miles west of north to a small branch of Mill Creek. Oct. 2: 10 miles, a N. W. course, then 5 miles N. E., then E., then S. E. to Muddy Creek, a branch of the Little Miami River, in all 15 miles. Oct. 3: two miles, where the forces under Col. Hardin were joined. Oct. 4: N. E., crossing the Little Miami River to its east side, then Sugar Creek (Sugar Creek, as known today, would not be crossed on the line of march. Caesar's Creek,

---

[52]McBride, James. *Pioneer Biography,* 1:122 *passim.* See Harmar's Journal, in *Ohio Arch. and Hist. Quarterly,* 20:89-96.

[53]McBride, James. *Op. Cit.,* 1:118-119.

a few miles below Spring Valley in Greene County, Ohio, is probably meant. It would be necessary for Gen'l Harmar to cross this creek which is yet quite large where the crossing is noted), in all 9 miles. Oct. 5; From Sugar Creek, N. E. up the Little Miami River to Glade Creek (now Glade Run), in all 10 miles. From this point, the distance to Old Chillicothee is less than 5 miles. Gen. Harmar crossed the Little Miami River at Old Chillicothe, and proceeded N. W. to the Little Miami villages in the Auglaize River country.

At Roxanna, his trace seems to pass through the woodland of the farm of Isaac Evans.

The line of this march is here given in full detail, since it followed the trace taken by General George Rogers Clark in his expedition against Old Chillicothe and Pickaway in 1780. The line of General Harmar's march after leaving Old Chillicothe and until he reached Pickaway, or Old Piqua, where Clark's battle of 1790 took place, is as follows:—After crossing the Little Miami River at Old Chillicothe, he took a N. E. course to this day's camp, October 6, 1790, nine miles distant. On October 7, his course was N. and N. W. across the Pickaway Fork, or Mad River, to a camp one mile beyond the ford, in all nine miles.

The Army, says McBride, "followed the trace made by General George Rogers Clark in his expedition against the Indian towns, October, 1780, as far as the Piqua town." This trace, given above as Harmar's line of march, presented no difficulties of ford or terrain. The same line of march from the mouth of the Licking to Old Chillicothe was followed by Clark in 1782, but he did not go farther north on it than Old Chillicothe in 1782.

From that point his march is a northwest course, crossing Mad River (some distance above Dayton, Ohio). His objective was Upper and Lower Piqua.

As the line of General Logan's expedition is of record, coming by way of Kenton's trail to Old Chillicothe, we may now reasonably be sure of the traces taken from the Ohio River to Old Chillicothe by four of the five military expeditions against the Shawnees of the Little Miami River settlement. Logan's route from Maysville, north, was via the

Winchester Trace to the point where it intersected the Kenton Trail. This is known today as "The Old Urbana Road." It passes through the present towns of Bloomington, Bowersville and Jamestown, Ohio. The Kenton Trail leaves this trail at a point about two miles north of Jamestown and goes in a directly west course about ten miles, ending at Old Chillicothe.

Colonel Bowman's expedition in 1779 has left the story of his line of retreat. This was south, past the present site of Xenia to Caesar's Creek, and along its course to the Little Miami River, which he followed till he reached his camp at the mouth of the Licking River. In his rapid retreat which, at first, was nearly a rout, it is very probable that he followed the same trace as he had used in his advance. Scant written history of these pioneer expeditions left many events of the period that can now be covered only by traditions. However, these, where they can be harmonized, are as valuable and reliable as much of that period's history of record, especially that part of which was compiled from the recollections of those who were participants of the events of that stirring time, but who had grown old before their recollections were made a matter of record. Abner Thompson notes the inaccuracies attending such records in his own narrative of the Battle of Piqua. This historical account is found in Howe's *History of Ohio*.[54]

"SHAWNEE HIGHWAYS" IN GREENE COUNTY, OHIO

The Scioto Trail   The Bullskin Trace
The Winchester Trace   The Kenton Trail
     The Old Xenia Road

Indian traces through Greene County, Ohio, centered at Old Chillicothe on the Little Miami River. The locations of three primary Indian traces are historically well known. A fourth short trail was located and used by General Simon Kenton. In General Logan's campaign against the Shawnees in 1786, Kenton, who was Logan's pilot and also

---

[54] Howe, Henry. *Op. cit.*, 1847:192.

captain of a company, led this invading force of 790 men the final fifteen miles of their march to Old Chillicothe along the trail he had blazed, and which is yet known by his name.

The Winchester Trace was a north continuation of the *Buffalo Trace* from Limestone—now Maysville—to the Kentucky salt-licks, and on to Lexington, Kentucky. Beginning at Aberdeen, on the north bank of the Ohio River, opposite Limestone, its course across Ohio lay in a north-northwestern direction. Entering Greene County in its southeast section, it followed a general northwest direction to Old Chillicothe where it ended. At the point where the trace crossed Todd's Fork of Caesar's Creek in Greene County, there was a small Indian settlement without name, so far as now known. The village site on the hills of the north bank of the creek, was near "warm springs," the waters of which were relished by many birds, observed to tarry there over season during their migrations.

A branch from the Winchester Trace connected Old Chillicothe with Peckuwe, which the Peckuwe clan occupied on their removal from Old Chillicothe, a few miles southwest of Springfield, Ohio. This village was built on Mad River and is best known by its pioneer name of Old Piqua, and was probably this tribe's most eastern village location. General George Rogers Clark's forces destroyed it on their final invasion of the Shawnee country in 1780.

From Peckaway, or Piqua, this trace went on to the Miami villages on the Auglaize River, which were destroyed by General Anthony Wayne on his march to the Battle of Fallen Timbers, August 20, 1794. In a letter written from Grand Glaize, August 14, Wayne gave this description of the valley then under cultivation by the Indians: "The margins of these beautiful rivers, the Miamis and the lake and the Auglaize, appear like one continued village for a number of miles, both above and below this place, nor have I ever before beheld such immense fields of corn in any part of America from Canada to Florida."

The Scioto Trace began at Old Chillicothe, and was used by the Shawnees there to reach their settlements on

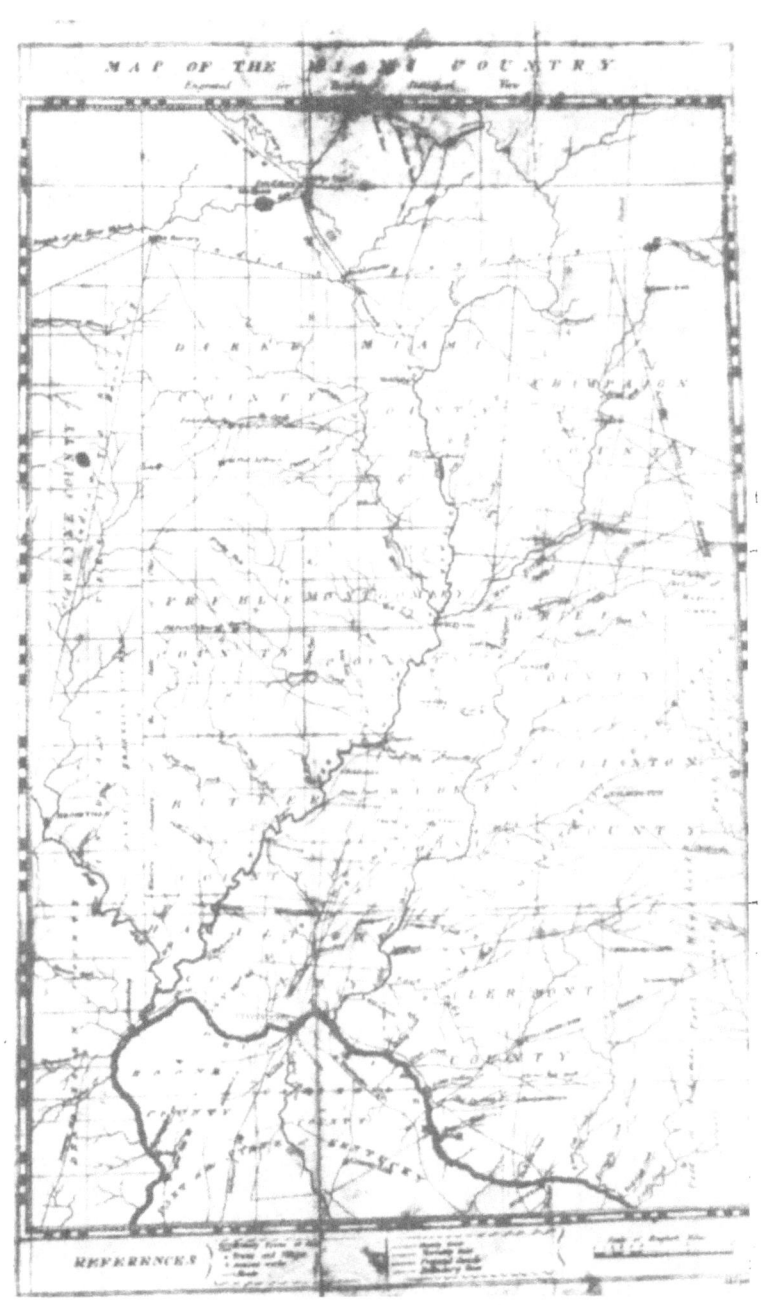

Drake's Map of the Miami Country

the Scioto and Muskingum Rivers. Its direction was eastward on the highlands, paralleling Massie's Creek to the mound-builders' fortifications at Cedarville, Ohio; thence in an east by south-east direction over the extended upland plateau of Greene and Fayette counties to the Shawnee settlements on the Pickaway Plains. Here, it intersected various other traces which led north, east and south to the numerous Indian settlements in the eastern half of Ohio, and beyond. This *Scioto Trace,* most often used by the Shawnees of Old Chillicothe and their trusted white captives, led to the salt springs of southeastern Ohio by intersecting traces centered at the Scioto settlements. In point of use, this was their principal and only east and west trail. It was without terrain or ford difficulties. This "Shawnee highway" was established in 1756 between the Scioto villages and the newly located village of Peckuwe, later Old Chillicothe, on Massie's Creek and the Little Miami River.

Another trace, running directly north through Old Chillicothe and on to Detroit, began at the mouth of Bullskin Creek where it empties into the Ohio River. This was known to the earliest pioneers as *The Bullskin Trace.* This trace, by legislative enactment on February 4, 1807, became "The Xenia State Road." The enactment provided for a road right-of-way sixty-six feet wide throughout its course. Appropriations were carried by the enactment to be used in its initial improvement. Some parts of this road between Williamsburg and Harveysburg are now closed to traffic, but the state's title is clear. Its course, beginning at the mouth of Bullskin Creek, where it empties into the Ohio River at Chilo, is through Felicity and Bethel to Williamsburg; thence to Dickey's Tavern, and on to Van Camp's corner (Slab's Camp) and Edenton. It crosses Route 28 near Edward's Schoolhouse, and goes on to a point about one mile west of Clarksville, and one-half mile east of Harveysburg. From its intersection with the Waynesville and Wilmington Pike, it is an improved highway to New Burlington, Xenia, Oldtown (Old Chillicothe), Springfield, Urbana, and on to Detroit. A map, marking the entire course of this road, and shown in this narrative, is taken from Drake's *Beauties of Cincinnati and the Miami*

Country, published in 1815. By reason of its early official establishment "The Old Xenia Road" may be considered the mother of Ohio's present system of state-maintained highways.

The Kenton Trail. The fourth Greene County trace, which was located late enough in northwestern territorial history to be called "a trail," was located by General Simon Kenton. A part of this trail lies along the north borderline of the Virginia Military District lands given by that state to General Horatio Gates as a recompense for his distinguished services during the American Revolution. It was less than fifteen miles in length, but in connection with the Winchester Trace, to which it was tangent, it became the pioneer route of choice from Kentucky to the Miami country.

A branch of the Winchester Trail, the Aberdeen-Limestone, location of which is noted above, passed through Bloomington and Jamestown, Ohio, directly north to Urbana. It was known in early Ohio history as the Urbana Road, but it is now State Route No. 72. Kenton's Trail, which had Old Chillicothe as its objective, left the Urbana Road north of Jamestown, Ohio, and crossed Caesar's Creek near the present residence of O. T. Wolford, at a point known in pioneer days as Jacob Brown's saw mill; thence west to Old Chillicothe. The terrain was upland, permitting easy and rapid marching.

The story of "the trace," which preceded and followed the location of the American Indian in the Miami country, is of much interest. Its origin and development were described by Senator Thomas H. Benton in a speech delivered in the United States Senate. General John C. Fremont, "the pathfinder" who was Senator Benton's son-in-law, had located a wagon-route, beginning at the Mississippi River, and ending at the Pacific Ocean, with mountain passes of gradient suitable for a transcontinental road. To the objections voiced in the Senate, that "only scientific men could determine the best and easiest passes for such a road," Senator Benton replied: "There is a class of scientific engineers older than the schools. . . . They are

HISTORIC BACKGROUNDS

the wild animals which traverse the forests, not by compass, but by instinct which leads them always the right way to the lowest mountain passes . . . and the shortest route between two distant points. The Indian first, then the hunter follows this same trail. After that, it becomes the wagon-road of the immigrant, and lastly, the railroad of the scientific man." In these few words, Senator Benton described the genesis and evolution of our roads. From the upland paths of the migratory fauna of the prehistoric period, we derive the name "highway" by which we designate the principal roads of the present period.

The tracks of the pioneer and his family, in quest of a new home in the Northwest Territory, first followed the trace. The hardships of such journeys cannot now be visualized, for the luxury and travel speed of our day dim the atmosphere of historic vision. As population increased, the trace grew into the trail, the road, the stage road, then the post road when mail was coming over it. The toll-pike and the free turnpike followed, and finally the admirable system of state and national hard surfaced highways of today. One hundred and thirty-three years ago, the Treaty of Greenville was consummated. In two decades of that time, the trace has lifted its path above the clouds to causeways over which we may be transported with unbelievable speed to distances heretofore impossible. The conquest now turns to the paths of the sky, where the limits of distance and time are conquered; but the trace of the pioneer—the beginning of it all—remains a record of antiquity near enough our time to be honored as the "Old Xenia Road" has been, with a monument that marks its place in the history and growth of *The Northwest Territory.*

TECUMTHA

A NOTABLE FAMILY

MY FAMILY tradition, verified by Shawnee tradition, is of a residential period, at Old Chillicothe, of the Shawnee Chief Pucksinwa, from March, 1768, till he lost his life at the Battle of Point Pleasant, 1774. He was the father of America's most distinguished Indian family. Chiksika, the oldest son, was with his father at this battle, and into his care, the passing chief gave the rearing of the six other children. Of the seven children, Chiksika and his sister, Tecumapese, have places in pioneer contemporary history; Tenskwatawa, "The Prophet," in Northwestern Territory and international history.

Tecumseh (Tecumtha) (Tikomfa), the fourth child, who was born in 1768 "in the neighborhood of Old Chillicothe on the Little Miami," and killed at the Battle of Thames, October 5, 1813, became the most notable Indian in American history. His character and home life, when a boy, were under the direction and care of his sister, Tecumapese, whom Rebecca Galloway declared to be "attractive in face and form, and in character far more so." Tradition and history speak only admiring and respectful words of this woman. It was the eldest brother, Chiksika, who took his father's place in the rearing of this notable family, and the sister, Tecumapese, who early instilled into Tecumtha the humanity for which he became noted *in* history.

After the loss of their father, family ties marked by devotion and self-sacrifice—traditional details of which still remain—give glimpses of conditions in the household, which must have become formative influences in the remarkable careers of its members. Indians like Massasoit, Pontiac and King Philip have left impressive individual records in American history, but this is the only instance where several members of the same Indian family became historically notable. Tecumtha attained international recognition. His remarkable military ability is credited by Young, an English historian, as being responsible for the preservation of Canada for the British empire. "No one," he writes, "can fully calculate the inestimable value of those devoted red men, led on by brave Tecumseh during the struggle of 1812; but for them, it is probable we should not now have a Canada."

Tecumtha was notable as a hunter, warrior, orator and Indian statesman. A true son of his Spartan race, he was undismayed, unfaltering and uncompromising in the final years of the struggle of his people to retain the heritage of their fathers, even when it became apparent that their manifest destiny was to be racial defeat and subordination. In the closing months of his notable career he attained the rank of brigadier-general in the British army, in command of the Indian forces at the Battle of the Thames, where he lost his life, October 5, 1813.

THE BIRTHPLACES OF TECUMTHA

The extensive collection of Tecumtha history assembled in the Congressional Library at Washington, D. C., and there available for students who may be interested in the study of this great American Indian's career, consists largely of the books and manuscripts of American writers. The few volumes and monographs of English and Canadian authors very naturally have followed the extended associations and services of this noted Indian leader after he became an ally of Great Britain.

Some are more artful in descriptions; others in portraitures of events and associations, and others have been admirably facile in deductions and individual elaborations. Having read one, however, the student may feel fairly acquainted with the limited facts available to most white writers of these essays on Tecumtha's life. He likewise recognizes the same halos and illuminations which with one or two exceptions, are made to surround the final years of this distinguished American by the annotators of his career.

Articles in the Bulletins issued by the United States Bureau of Ethnology have been contributed by Indian writers associated in the Indian work of this Department. *Tecumtha* is here given as the great leader's name, by Dr. James Mooney, his biographical contributor,[1] as given by the Shawnee historians of this date, and by Dr. Moorehead and Mr. McWhorter.

So far as now known, no Tecumtha history has been contributed by Shawnee writers familiar with the history and traditions of the Kispokotha sept of this nation, the sept of the noted chief, Pucksinwa, the father of Tecumtha. Methotase, his mother, was of the Peckue sept. The approximate date of the birth of this, their fourth child, destined to attain a distinguished place in American history, is now recorded officially by the memorial of the Absentee Shawnee Business Committee[2] as March, 1768, and the place of his birth located by it, as the Great Springs, a short distance southeast of Old Chillicothe, then their principal town—now Oldtown, three and a half miles north of Xenia, Ohio.

There is no confusion among Tecumtha authors as to the place of his burial. *There was but one place.* Concerning its exact location, the warriors who retrieved his body after the Battle of the Thames, and bore it to its resting-place still maintain their vigil with racial fidelity in Indian sorrow and silence. No white man has been entrusted with this secret, although its general location is indicated by Drake.[3]

Since it has fallen to the lot of Tecumtha to be classed with the bard Homer, and such distinguished men as Columbus, Kingsley and Gladstone, whose birthplaces have been claimed at numerous points and in widely separated locations, extracts from the texts of noted authors who have written Tecumtha's several birthplaces into history,

---

[1] U. S. Bureau of Ethnology, Bulletin No. 30.

[2] Appointed originally by the U. S. Government. They take the place of the chiefs of old times.

[3] Drake, Benjamin. *Life of Tecumseh and His Brother the Prophet,* 202 *passim.*

TECUMTHA

are here given. The texts vary, from statements that designate these birthplaces without reference to a source of information, to those which give sources and references for student research.

Since two of these locations are at widely separated points—Old Piqua on Mad River, Ohio, and Hacker's Creek, Virginia,—and both are given as birthplaces of Tecumtha, the Shawnee's viewpoint of all of these various locations becomes interesting and is significant of the estimate the Indian puts on many of *our* recitations of *his part* in *our history*. He says—"The controversy about the birthplace of Tecumtha is a white man's quarrel, in which we have no interest. The Shawnee knows where his great chief, Tecumtha, was born and where he was buried. The white man has not heretofore sought us for our side of the story. He glorifies only his own imagery of history."

The Alleged Birthplaces of Tecumtha
References From American Writers

BENJAMIN DRAKE

Drake writes:

Some diversity of opinion has prevailed as to the birthplace of Tecumtha. It is generally supposed and indeed is stated by several historians to have been in the Scioto Valley near the place where Chillicothe now stands. Such, however, is not the fact. He was born in the valley of the Miamis, on the bank of Mad River, a few miles below Springfield, and within the limits of Clark County. Of this, there is the most satisfactory evidence. In the year 1805 when the Indians were assembling at Greenville, as it was feared with some hostile intention against the frontiers, the Governor of Ohio sent Duncan McArthur and Thomas Worthington to that place, to ascertain the object and disposition of these Indians. Tecumtha and three other chiefs agreed to return with these messengers to Chillicothe, then the Ohio seat of government, for the purpose of holding a "talk" with the Governor. General McArthur, in a letter to Drake, under date of 19th of November, 1821, says, "When on the way from Greenville to Chillicothe, Tecumtha pointed out to us the place where he was born. It was in an old Shawnee town, on the northwest side of Mad River, about six miles below Springfield."[4]

Drake then follows with a quotation from a letter dated January 17, 1822, written by Stephen Ruddell, who became Tecumtha's adopted brother after 1780, and most intimate associate during his lifetime. This letter was obtained while Ruddell was living in Missouri, by Major William Graham. Ruddell, Drake calls "a man of veracity." He continues the narrative following General McArthur's version of Tecumtha's birthplace, as follows:

This fact is corroborated by Stephen Ruddell, the early and intimate associate of Tecumtha, who states that he was "born in the neighborhood of 'Old Chillicothe' in the year 1768.[5] (The Old Chillicothe here spoken of was the Shawnee village situated on Massie's Creek, three miles north of where Xenia now stands and about ten or twelve miles south of the village pointed out by Tecumtha to General McArthur as the spot of his nativity.)

The statements of the two letters are wholly contradictory. Ruddell does not even inferentially mention Old Piqua as the place, or that it was located in "the neighborhood" of the birthplace of his adopted brother, Tecumtha.

General McArthur does not mention Old Chillicothe as near the location designated by Tecumtha. Neither place needed the other to identify its location. Each place was well known to every Indian and white man of that period in Ohio. Many had fought at both places and some thousands of each had marched through or near to both village sites in the various earlier invasion of the Miami Valleys by organized Kentucky forces.

The Ruddell letter and other Draper manuscripts of the Wisconsin Historical Society state that this great chief of the Shawnees was born, as the Keepers of the Shawnee nation's records have affirmed, at Old Chillicothe, but the

---

[4] Drake, Benjamin. *Op. Cit.*, 66.
[5] Drake, Benj. *Op. Cit.*, 66.

exact location given is beyond this village at springs "several arrow flights," southeast; not between it and Old Piqua. The only Indian village known at one time to have been located between the two was Willstown, five or six miles west of north of Old Chillicothe, and it was a small settlement at best.

If Stephen Ruddell had meant to designate Old Piqua as Tecumtha's birthplace, he would have done so. The place was Tecumtha's and his own Indian village home in 1780. He knew this place, its location on Mad River as well as, or better than he did Old Chillicothe and its location on the Little Miami River and Massie's Creek. John M. Ruddell's letter of May 12 and 13, 1868, states "Stephen and Abram were adopted by the Indians by different families in the same village, and Stephen knew Tecumtha in his youth; they played and slept together at Piqua." This was after Byrd's attack on Ruddell's Fort in 1780, when these two Ruddell brothers were taken captive. It was six years after the death of Pucksinwa, Tecumtha's father, whose residence was located at Sexton Point, Old Chillicothe, after his migration to that place in 1768; and twelve years after Tecumtha's birth on the Sexton lot, in the neighborhood of Old Chillicothe.[6]

Another Tecumtha birthplace alleged to have been so designated by himself personally to a Miss Mitchel was located on Hacker's Creek, Virginia. An interesting narrative of this place and event is found in chapter six of *Border Settlers of Northwestern Virginia*, by L. V. McWhorter, author, noted student of Indian affairs and of Virginia history during the Northwest Territory period. In this chapter he sums up the claims of several American locations that are claimants for the honor of being the birthplace of this great American Indian, and completes his argument with the artistry of a true historian dealing with a question in which there is an historical doubt at his time of writing, though admitting none in his own mind or conclusions. He concludes:

---

[6]*Draper MSS.* 21 S 252-254.
The McKay Land Plat, from Greene County, Ohio, Records.

Without entering into a discussion as to the probability of which of these tribes was the last to abandon a continuous occupancy of the valley, or whether they were contemporaneous; summing up the facts, I regard this claim of Hacker's Creek to the honor of being the birthplace of Tecumseh, supported as it is by his own statement, as worthy of consideration and probably correct. Let Virginia then add to the long list of her warriors, patriots and statesmen, the name of Tecumseh; really Tikamthi, or *Tecumtha*, the "meteor" or "shooting star"; the "crouching panther," "I cross the path, or way." Even if born at Old Chillicothe or on Mad River, Tecumseh was still a Virginian; for all that part of the territory northwest of the Ohio River belonged to Virginia until after the Revolution.[7]

SAMUEL G. DRAKE

Drake in his *Biography and History of the Indian of North America* asserts:

The place of this renowned warrior's birth was upon the banks of the Scioto River, at what is now Chillicothe. His father's name was Puckeesheno, which means, "I light from flying." He was killed in the Battle of Kanawha in 1774. His mother's name was Meetheetashe, which signifies "a turtle laying her eggs in the sand."[8] She died among the Cherokees. She had at one birth, three sons,[9] Elkskwatawa, which signifies "a door opened"—was called the "Prophet," Tecumseh, which is, "a tiger crouching for his prey," and Kumskaka, "a tiger that flies in the air."

DR. WARREN K. MOOREHEAD

Dr. Moorehead, in one of the ablest of research articles on "The Indian Tribes of Ohio,"[10] quotes the Bureau of Ethnology as authority for the spelling of Tecumtha, and

---

[7] McWhorter, L. V. *Border Settlers of Northwestern Virginia*, 77.

[8] Drake, Samuel G. *Biography and History of the Indians of North America.* Ed. 1, 339.

[9] There is no mention or intimation, in Shawnee history, of Tecumtha being one of triplets. Tenskwatawa, The Prophet, was four years younger than Tecumtha. Twin or triplet brothers, were born to his parents about 1772, two years before the Battle of Point Pleasant.

[10] *Ohio Arch. and Hist. Quarterly*, 7:80-81.

notes that Hatch's History gives 1775 as his birth-year.[11] He is inclined to accept Dr. Mooney's statement of 1770 as the correct date. The article quotes extensively from Professor Gatschet of the Bureau, on the origin of the name Tecumtha.[12]

Moorehead credits the statements of General Simon Kenton, that Tecumtha was born at the family cabin on the bank of Stillwater and the Great Miami River.[13]

H. C. SHETRONE

Mr. Shetrone, author, director and archaeologist, in an extended and valuable monograph on "The Indian in Ohio" designates "Piqua, a few miles south of the present city of Springfield, in Clark County, as the birthplace of Tecumtha in 1768," but does not quote references. This monograph and that of Dr. Moorehead, cover an extensive research field. They both give invaluable source references of Indian history in the Northwestern Territory and the Ohio Valley.[14]

HON. E. O. RANDALL

For the student of Ohio Indian life, the references cited by the Hon. E. O. Randall more closely concern his story of "Tecumseh, the Shawnee Chief."

A painstaking investigation as to the place and date of Tecumtha's birth leads to the clear conviction that he was born at (Old) Piqua, in the spring of 1768. Confirmatory of this, we have the written testimony of the Ruddells and John Johnston. . . . John Johnston was United States Government Indian Agent for all the Indians of Ohio for some 30 years. He knew Tecumtha, and often conversed with him. He states Tecumtha was born at Piqua. . . .[15]

---

[11]Hatch, Col. W. S. *A Chapter of the History of the War of 1812 in the Northwest*, 96.

[12]U. S. Bureau of Ethnology, *Annual Report*, No. 14.

[13]*Ohio Arch. and Hist. Quarterly*, 7:79-80.

[14]*Ohio Arch. and Hist. Quarterly*, 27:430.

[15]*Ohio Arch. and Hist. Quarterly*, 15:494-495.

The statement of Benjamin Kelly, who gives Old Chillicothe as Tecumtha's birthplace[16] is found in several places; and in an article by Rev. Th. S. Hinde to John S. Williams, Editor of the *American Pioneer*,[17] also Draper MSS.[18] Benjamin Kelly, then a lad of twelve, was with the salt-makers who were captured by the Shawnees, February 8, 1778, while making salt at the Kentucky Salt Licks for the Kentucky settlements, and lived with the Shawnees until the Treaty of Greenville, 1795.[19] These prisoners were either adopted into the tribe at Old Chillicothe or taken on to Detroit for ransom (the ransom price paid by the British for a living prisoner was then $100.00; that for a scalp was $50.00). The ransomed prisoners were usually paroled home by the British commandant. Kelly[20] was retained, as was Stephen Ruddell, a lad of his own age, who was taken prisoner at the attack on Ruddell's Fort in 1780. These two boys were adopted by the Shawnees, some writers record by Tecumtha's own family. They grew up playmates and, with him, adventurous soldiers. They openly shared his views and fortunes. Neither one mentions Old Piqua as Tecumtha's birthplace; both designate Old Chillicothe. Both men subsequently became Baptist ministers of recognized standing. Chillicothe, as designated in this article, was located three and a half miles north of Xenia, Ohio, on U. S. Highway No. 68. It is now the village of Oldtown.

The adoption, mentioned in the Draper MSS. of Kelly, Tecumtha and the Prophet by Black Fish (marked "error" by Draper), presents no difficulties to the reader who understands the relations the leading civil chief of the Shawnees bore to the social and economic order of tribal life.

Pucksinwa, Tecumtha's father, was a war chief. He

---

[16] Draper *MSS.* 21 S 252-254; *Ohio Arch. and Hist. Quarterly*, 15:496.
[17] *Amer. Pioneer.* 1:328.
[18] Draper *MSS.*, 4 G 84.
[19] *Ohio Arch. and Hist. Quarterly*, 13:271.
[20] Kelly's statement was given after both of the Sexton land transfers. See McKay plat drawings.

led his Kispokotha sept forces in the Battle of Kanawha—Point Pleasant—and there lost his life. He was then the most prominent Shawnee war chief, next to Cornstalk and Black Hoof. The oversight and care of a battle chief's family, because of rank and services, became the peace chief's duty until time and circumstances eased their necessities. Even then such relationship, usual to Indian custom, would remain unbroken.

Methotasa, the mother of Tecumtha, was a member of the Peckue tribe—not a Cherokee as frequently noted by early writers. The J. M. Ruddell letter, May 12-13, 1868, shows her to have returned to her sept at Old Piqua at the time of General Clark's Battle of 1780. This was the same year Stephen Ruddell was captured, and two years after Benjamin Kelly was captured with Boone's salt-makers.

The chronology and migrations of the Tecumtha family may be followed by dates now available; the migration of the Kispugotha sept, led by its war chief, Pucksinwa, in the spring of 1768 from the Pickaway Plains to "join their brothers at Old Chillicothe"; the place of his residence at Old Chillicothe, "on the point recently occupied by Mr. Sexton"; and the subsequent date of his death at Point Pleasant in 1774, followed by the Ruddell date of Tecumtha's and Stephen Ruddell's residence in Old Piqua, 1780.

A critical reading of Stephen Ruddell's statement that Tecumtha was "born in the neighborhood of 'Old Chillicothe'" and the accurate location by Drake, of "The Old Chillicothe" here spoken of on Massie's Creek, three miles north of where Xenia now stands, places a different interpretation on the Drake birthplace narratives and Mr. Randall's conclusions.

Colonel John Johnson, in his sketch of Tecumtha says, "He was born on the Scioto, near Chillicothe, was a Shawnese by father and mother."[21] Stephen Johnston states, "His birthplace was near Springfield, Ohio."[22] Another

---

[21] *Draper MSS.* 11 YY 17.
[22] *Ibid.*, 11 YY 4.

writer, name not known, says, "he was born at Upper Piqua,"[23] and Draper marks "error" after this statement. No Ruddell correspondence even remotely mentions Old Piqua as Tecumtha's birthplace.

Stephen Ruddell's narrative stating that Tecumtha was "born in the neighborhood of Old Chillicothe in 1768,"[24] was the narrative secured for Drake by Wm. R. Graham. As far as yet found, Draper never obtained any other statement from the Ruddells—father or sons—about Tecumtha's birthplace. Other valuable Tecumtha history is found in later letters of the sons: Jett Ruddell, Marcelline, Ill., Oct. 19, 1883; J. W. Ruddell, Marcelline, Ill., May 15, 1863, and Nov. 15, 1884, and John M. Ruddell, May 12, 13, 1868.[25]

Randall's paper on "Tecumseh, The Shawnee Chief," says:

> A grandson of Tecumseh, son of Pugeshashenwa, was known as Big Jim. He was Chief of the Absentee Shawnees, located in Oklahoma. He died in Mexico, August, 1901. A great-grandson of Tecumseh, grandson of Pugeshashenwa, (by a sister of Big Jim), was Thomas Washington, who was also an Absentee Shawnee chief. He visited the President at Washington in 1901. This the writer, E. O. Randall, learned through correspondence with Mr. M. J. Bentley, ex-Special United States Indian Agent, at Shawnee, Oklahoma.[26]

Thomas Washington, great-grandson of Tecumtha, whose Shawnee name was Wayl-way-way-se-ka, was, as his photograph shows, a man of distinguished appearance, tall, erect and strong. In 1901, he, with Thomas Rock and Gan-waw-pea-se-ka, (Thomas W. Alford)—all then members of the Absentee Shawnee Business Committee—visited Washington, D. C., on the important mission of securing long-delayed settlements for Civil War losses. They were accompanied east by a beloved Quaker missionary—Auntie

---

[23]*Ibid.*, 11 YY 8.
[24]*Draper MSS.* 2 YY 120.
[25]*Ibid.* 2 YY 12.
[26]*Ohio Arch. and Hist. Quarterly*, 15:496.

ABSENTEE SHAWNEE GOVERNING COMMITTEE OF 1901

1. *Se-ku-nah* or *Thomas Rock*.   2. *Gan-waw-pea-se-ka* or *Thomas W. Alford*.   3. *Wayl-way-way-se-ka*, or *Thomas Washington*.

This committee was appointed by the United States Government in 1885 to assume and exercise all governing authority over the absentee section of the Shawnee nation.

The committee functions in place of the chiefs of old times. In 1901 it visited Old Chillicothe, now Oldtown, Greene County, Ohio, and located the birthplace of Tecumtha at the Great Springs, now the Ohio State Fish Hatchery, two miles northeast of Xenia, Ohio.

TECUMTHA

Kirke—who visited with her people in Ohio till the delegation returned from Washington. On the delegation's return, Gan-waw-pea-se-ka stopped for Mrs. Kirke, while Washington and Thomas Rock came to Old Chillicothe to visit the birthplace of Tecumtha, the great-grandfather of two of the delegation, and the home of other ancestors, who had passed away at Old Chillicothe and were buried nearby. Mr. Henry Slagle, a well-known and reliable Xenian, gives the following story of their 1901 visit:

In January, 1931, Dr. W. A. Galloway asked me in to see a large photograph he had received of some prominent Shawnee Indians. I recognized, at once, the tall Indian in this picture as one with whom I had tramped about Oldtown (Old Chillicothe) thirty years ago. Dr. Galloway informed me that the name of the tall Indian was Thomas Washington.

In 1901, while fishing near Oldtown, in the Little Miami River, I came upon two Indians, one very tall and one of medium build, but strong and sturdy. As we three went on together, the tall Indian, in broken tongue, recounted the times of his Shawnee ancestors, formerly of this place. At various points, he told something about his experience here once before, and described the difference in appearance over that time. This tall Indian had to talk slowly in his broken English as he recounted the scenes of his ancestors' life here, and reconstructed the last days of the Shawnee Indians on this, their stamping-ground; thereby verifying and dovetailing several interesting historical incidents in my boyhood life.

He pointed, with his long arm and hand, to "Injuns' buryin'" in the direction where Henry Crowl, a half-breed, and another Indian, called Comanche Jim, had located it about the year 1876. I was then a boy of fifteen and went with these two Indians to the place they believed to be their ancient graveyard. This was between Shawnee Creek and Towler Road, a short distance west of Xenia, Ohio. The Pennsylvania and Baltimore and Ohio Railways make a sharp curve out through the gravel-bank at this point. These two Indians, like many other pairs of their race, stayed only a day or two and were not again seen here.

After meeting up with Thomas Washington and Thomas Rock at Oldtown in 1901, I came to believe that the frequent visits of Indian men to their old stamping-ground

OLD CHILLICOTHE

here, during the generation before my own, was due to love for their old home and devotion to memory of their dead. When we three reached the narrows at the south entrance to the prairie village site, I did not meet the head Indian who, I understood, was with the Commission. Washington stopped and closely scanned the beautiful landscape seen on all sides from the railway, and pointed to the creek that threads the valley, coming from the southeast into Old Chillicothe and its prairie site. He gazed long and in silence at every landmark about him; then, with a sweep of his long arm, he marked a course from the Old Chillicothe village site, *southeast,* along the curving course of Stoner Creek—now Oldtown Run—and said: "Old Injun Trail, big springs, Tecumtha star shoot, he born by 'em." At this point, they left me and took their way southeast along the creek that leads past the great fisheries' springs.

Colonel William Stanley Hatch

Hatch's *Chapter of the History of the War of 1812 in the Northwest* records:

Tecumtha was the youngest of three brothers at the same birth. This event, so extraordinary among Indian tribes, with whom even a double birth is quite uncommon, struck the mind of his people as supernatural, and marked him and his brothers with the prestige of future greatness —that the Great Spirit would direct them to the achievement of something great.

They were born in a cabin or hut, constructed of round saplings chinked with sticks and clay, near the mouth of Stillwater, on the upper point of its junction with the Great Miami, then a pleasant plateau of land, with a field of corn not subject to overflow.

These facts were communicated to me a short time after the council at Springfield in 1806 (in the presence of Colonel Robert Patterson, one of the original proprietors of Cincinnati), by General Simon Kenton, who was more familiar with the Indian chiefs and Indian tribes of the Northwest at the period of their greatest power, both in war and in peace, than any other man. He stated that he well knew all the brothers; had been in the cabin where they and the family lived, and that other Indians whom he knew to be perfectly reliable, and who were intimately acquainted with the family of Tecumseh, had fully confirmed the above statement as to the triple birth and the location of their parents' residence at the time of their birth.[27]

Judge William Mills, founder of Yellow Springs and of Antioch College, gives public reference to Greene County as the birthplace of Tecumtha, in his formal centennial historical address at Greene County's greatest mass meeting celebration, July 4th, 1876. Quoting from this oration, we find:

For many years prior to its first settlement, in 1780-1790 and 1791, both soldiers and officers of General Clark's, Harmar's and St. Clair's campaigns, as well as scouts and prisoners of war, from Kentucky, had passed through this section of Ohio, always a favorite resort and cherished home of the aborigines, the birthplace of the renowned warrior, Tecumseh. With the keen insight of pioneer adventurers, they beheld its beauties, richness and great agricultural resources . . . It only remained for their bold and daring spirits, thus schooled in the midst of dangers and surrounded by a relentless foe, when seeking new homes, to find their way, one by one or in groups, to this fair and beautiful land.

The large number of officers and men of standing and character who permanently settled in Greene County after 1796—many of whose families still remain here—have given narratives heretofore known only as traditions which have been verified into written history from collections of Northwest Territory documents now available, and from carefully written histories long out of print, such as Green's *Historic Families of Kentucky*, or reprints like Filson's *History of Daniel Boone*. These give unusual authority and unanimity to the county's early history.

Traditions that center about the various birthplaces of Tecumtha that have passed through intermediary pioneer narrators, are naturally omitted. They are too varied in statements to use in an argument to establish historical facts.

---

[27] Hatch, W. S. *Op. Cit.*, 88-90.

OLD CHILLICOTHE

The designation by the Absentee Shawnee Business Committee of Old Chillicothe as Tecumtha's birthplace is conclusive so far as this nation's history is concerned. The members of the Committee have subscribed to the following memorial, which appears on a tablet erected by the author at the site of the Shawnee village:

U MKVWALAMAKUFEWA

TIKVMFA

INV MSI SRWVNOWI NRGRNI-ILAFITV, UGIMV, MACIMI PLIGITIYAWI CINVLI INI INGLASI-MRN-EWI SVMRKV-NAGI, U MVMAGOLI CINVLELI SIR ISAAC BROCK SIFOLI INA 1812 LVGITVHFOWA-NAGI.

USGI-LANVWAWI INA MARCH, 1768 LVGITVHFO-WA-NAGI. INI TVHDAGI MSI TIGIKVMI LRKUFWA-LANV WV IKUSGRGI ILANVLU YALRWVHQAGI TAKV-WIHI WATVH-KUFVGI INI PVSIDOWI CVLVHGRFAGI UCI.

NFAQI INA OCTOBER 5, 1813 LVGITVHFOWA-NAGI, IAH BAMI NEGRNIWI WECI-NVHGAMRCI NI NANVUDOMANVHI INI TVH NOCHADEMRWRCI NIHI TAKUHSI-YAWI NOCHADE-WANHI THAMAS SIDOTA, CHETHAM, BECI-DRMQA ONTAR-IO, KANADEGI.

YOMV MKVWALAMAKUFEWA LRCIMOWA SRWVNWV U GAHDRCIMOWA PVYACI SI LANVWAWICI UCI. UD RYECI GICITVWA-LADRNRWV NIHKI WVYRKUTV-GIKI PVYACI IGI SRWVNWV UTWALOWA.

Translation:

MEMORIAL TO TECUMTHA

THE GREAT SHAWNEE LEADER, CHIEF, AND BRIGADIER GENERAL IN THE BRITISH ARMY, BY APPOINTMENT OF GENERAL SIR ISAAC BROCK IN 1812.

BORN MARCH, 1768, AT THE GREAT SPRINGS, A FEW ARROW FLIGHTS SOUTH-EAST OF OLD CHILLICOTHE.

KILLED, OCTOBER 5, 1813, WHILE LEADING OUR WARRIORS AGAINST THE AMERICAN FORCES AT THE BATTLE OF THE THAMES, CHETHAM, PROVINCE OF ONTARIO, CANADA.

THIS MEMORIAL RECORD IS FROM SHAWNEE HISTORY, FAITHFULLY PRESERVED BY THE HISTORIANS OF THE SHAWNEE NATION.

MEMORIAL TO TECUMTHA

Erected in 1931 by Dr. William A. Galloway at Oldtown, Greene County, Ohio. Thomas Wildcat Alford, great-grandson of Tecumtha, is standing beside the monument

TECUMTHA

Authorized by the Absentee
Shawnee Business Committee

GAN-WAW-PEA-SE-KA   THOMAS W. ALFORD
QUA-LAY-PATH-KA-KA   JOHN E. SNAKE
NANA-QUAW-COMS-KA-KA   THOS. B. HOOD
NAH-KE-PEAS-KA-KA   JACOB BUCKHEART

Erected by
William A. Galloway, M. D.

THE GALLOWAY FAMILY

James Galloway, Sr., was a member of General George Rogers Clark's second expedition against Old Chillicothe in 1782. After the Treaty of Greenville, in 1795, had opened the Miami Valley land to white settlers, he moved in 1797 with his wife and five children from Lexington, Kentucky, to a new location in the neighborhood of Old Chillicothe. He and other Kentuckians who settled this Miami Valley were Scotch Associates of means and character who were opposed to the attitude of Kentucky on the slavery question. His gravestone in Stevenson cemetery relates he was "a soldier of the Revolution in 1776, an honest man and a pious Christian." He was treasurer of Greene County, Ohio, from its organization in 1803 until 1819. His daughter, Rebecca, was born October 7, 1791, and lived within five miles of her girlhood home near Old Chillicothe until her death, February 25, 1876. Her grandchildren—including the writer—were old enough in 1876 to recollect her description of her pioneer home; the story of Tecumtha's suit for her hand; and interesting details of Indian and pioneer life of her girlhood.

Old Chillicothe was the largest village inhabited by Shawnees when her father settled there in 1797, although 1000 to 1200 Shawnees had emigrated to Fort Girardeau in 1779. James Galloway mingled with them—a generous and well-wishing neighbor—and was so received by them. Hospitality in those days was never curtailed in the homes of leading and influential settlers of comfortable means. James Galloway's home was central and the frequent meeting-place of first settlers of his type—Rev. Robert Armstrong, Joseph Kyle, Sr., Lieutenant John Gregg, David

Laughead, Sr., Stephen Winter, William Bull, Sr., and Lieutenant Colonel Alexander McHatton. Revolutionary soldiers and able men—as they would be now if living—were the household's neighbors and guests; likewise many others, for James Galloway's pioneer home was on the Winchester Trace from Maysville, Kentucky. This migration "trace" passed through Old Chillicothe to Old Piqua, and thence to the Northwest. The Bullskin Trail running north from Bullskin Creek crossed the Winchester Trace at Old Chillicothe.[28] Its continuation to Detroit, through Yellow Springs, Springfield, and Urbana is shown in Drake's 1815 map of the Little Miami country. Of equal character and standing were their neighbors, thirteen miles away at Sugarcreek—the McKnights, Lammes, the father of Governor Vance, and others. These men and their families were Scotch Associates (Seceders) and Presbyterians.

    Tecumtha was a frequent visitor in the Galloway home, where he found books and household comforts that were a part of the home life of the first pioneers who settled at Old Chillicothe and Bellbrook on the Little Miami River. He also found there new experiences, in religious and domestic ethics that held his attention and exerted a marked influence on his subsequent career. The blessing of God (his Great Spirit) was asked before each meal, and thanks returned to Him after it was finished. The household usually gathered about the family altar for prayer before each day's work, and always before each night's retiring. Psalms were sung by all, and the simpler messages of the Bible were read aloud by the host—a member of Rev. Armstrong's Massie's Creek congregation. What was done here was understood by this distinguished Shawnee, for he then understood English and could also speak it with some fluency. It is probable that Tecumtha's knowledge of English began with a white prisoner boy, Benjamin Kelly, who was his adopted brother and remained with his family seven years, and Stephen Ruddell, a prisoner fifteen years, who was also Tecumtha's playmate and adopted brother, and who was his own age. They grew up together and, naturally, these

---

[28]See page 103.

three boys attained considerable use of both languages. Ruddell was long and intimately associated with Tecumtha; and later became a Baptist missionary in the Shawnee nation. For many years following 1797, Tecumtha maintained unbroken friendly relations with his host and family and continued to be a welcome guest at the Galloway home. He was an astute man with human experience and a clear knowledge of all contemporary events that affected the interests of his nation.

He knew Indian treaties in detail, and the sinister significance to his race of those which followed the first Fort Stanwix Treaty of 1768. The books of the household held his continued interest. The story of the Exodus of the children of Israel, and the miracle of the parting waters interested him. An exodus tradition, he informed his host, was a part of his nation's history. He was respectful at all times to the religious customs and beliefs of his host, but remained unshaken in the belief that the Great Spirit in his ministrations to his Indian children, had given them spiritual truths they could better understand and interpret for guidance in their daily duties and obligations.

The white man's development of printing and writing impressed him deeply with its advantages over any scheme the Indians had, or might have, for record and communication. He could listen to the reading of other men's thoughts, thus permanently preserved. Rebecca Galloway was a good reader and free commentator, and Tecumtha was a good listener with a remarkably retentive memory. As time passed, a good part of his visits were taken up with her reading to him and their discussions. She naturally became interested in his use of English, and as she was the daughter of a family accustomed to correct expression, she instructed him in a better use of her native tongue. It became a pleasure to her, and his aptitude was such as would be expected in one who, a few years later, was recognized by many as the most remarkable man of his race. The Associated Press[29] gives an interesting reference to this story

---

[29]In a story released for publication January 26, 1927.

which is here quoted as a succinct statement of a part of this notable courtship:

Tecumtha fell deeply in love with the girl. Their contact was frequent, for the chief was often an invited guest at the Galloway home. From her, Tecumtha learned the almost perfect command of English that marked his speech. She read to him from her father's books. She told him the story of the Bible, and explained to him the white man's religion.

The books available included her pastor's library, as well as her father's—a list of about 300 volumes—embracing the best publications of the period. These books had been carried by wagon or horseback across the Alleghany Mountains; thence by boat down the Ohio River to Stoner Creek and Lexington, Kentucky; thence by wagon or pack to Old Chillicothe. Hamlet was a character admired by Tecumtha. His reaction to the white man's Scotch Associate religious fundamentalism is given above; likewise his views that his own people would not understand or benefit by it beyond the revelations of the Great Spirit already given to his red children. The fact, as history relates, that he was one of the finest looking men of his time, certainly did not make his entertainment, with its element of instruction, much of a task for this daughter of the household, who then was about sixteen—the beginning of a girl's most romantic period. When he brought a birch-bark canoe for her use on the river near-by, taught her how to use it; and came with a present of a large silver comb, it became apparent to the family that this great chief's aptitude in studying English, and his frequent visits to the household, had a motive other than that of friendly interest.

True to his racial instincts, however, no expression escaped his lips, and no unusual action betrayed itself to her. He went first to her father, James Galloway, Sr., and with great dignity requested the hand of his daughter, Rebecca, in marriage. Here, indeed, arose a delicate situation. Rebecca had not thought of him except as the most interesting and brilliant man she had ever known. He was a man of another race. He was forty and she sixteen. He had enacted the Indian pact of peace and friendship between the Galloway family and the Shawnee Indians, and confirmed it by the gift to the father of his ceremonial tomahawk-pipe. He had "broken bread" many times in this home and sat in his host's guestchair. The daughter, who had never been in love and was yet fancy free, awoke to find herself confronting not a theory, but an acute situation. If it could not be met favorably, it must be handled delicately. Indeed, so great was the respect of the entire family for Tecumtha that any course which would wound his feelings was unthinkable. After a serious family conference, it was decided to let Rebecca, herself, determine and announce her own decision in her own way, and in her own time. The situation in the Galloway home changed in a day. Tecumtha the guest, had become Tecumtha the suitor. Since this romance has long been noted as Ohio's early historic pioneer romance,[30] it is only fair to each to give some description of the man and the girl as they were known to the family about 1806-1808.

Tecumtha was then in the prime of physical development. He had been married to an Indian girl, Manete, who had passed away. She is described by one historian as a beautiful girl, and by another as a woman older than he, and of different type. One son, May-thah-way-nah, who was born to this union, was destined to survive his father and perpetuate the family. "Little Jim," or Toh-tah-mo, a chief of the Peckuwe clan of Shawnee Indians now on the Shawnee Reservation in Pottawatomie County, Oklahoma, is a lineal descendant of Tecumtha and Manete, as is also Thomas W. Alford, Chairman of the Business Committee of the Absentee Shawnees, which occupies the place of chiefs and councilors of old. This Committee was appointed by the U. S. Indian Bureau, and is the recognized head of this sept.

Tecumtha's appearance has been described by prominent men and officers of his day. A pen-picture of his physical appearance, which compares closely with Shawnee

---

[30]See page 135.

OLD CHILLICOTHE

tradition, is here quoted from Hatch's *History of the War of 1812*. This description is of date August 17, 1813, seven weeks before his death at the Battle of the Thames:

The personal appearance of this remarkable man was uncommonly fine. His height was about five feet nine inches; his face oval, rather than angular; his nose handsome and straight; his mouth beautifully formed like that of Napoleon I, as represented in his portraits; his eyes clear, transparent, hazel, with a mild, pleasant expression when in repose or conversation, but when excited in his orations, or by the enthusiasm of conflict, they appeared like balls of fire; his complexion more a light brown or tan than red. His whole tribe, as well as their kindred, the Ottawas, had light complexions. His hands and arms were finely formed; his limbs straight; he always stood erect, and walked with a brisk, elastic and vigorous step. He was invariably dressed in tanned buckskins; a perfectly fitting hunting-frock descending to the knee was over his under clothes of the same material, the usual cape and finish of leather fringe about the neck, cape edges of the front opening, and bottom of the frock; a belt of the same material in which were his side-arms (an elegant silver-mounted tomahawk and a knife in a strong leather case), short pantaloons, connected with neatly fitting leggins; a mantle of the same material, used as a blanket in camp, and as a protection in storms.[31]

His face expressed power, with a fine chin, eyes dark hazel, an aquiline type of nose, an expressive mouth and fine teeth. From these descriptions of his personal appearance; the excerpts of his Osage speech; references from Drake and from Young's *English History* and the evidences of intellectual range manifest during frequent visits with James Galloway, and his associate pioneer neighbors, a fine estimate can be made of the personality and personal appearance of this remarkable Indian. No painting or reliable sketch of him was made during his lifetime. The one usually printed is little more than a caricature, and for this reason, the writer has gathered for preservation such physical details of his appearance as are available from

---

[31] Hatch, W. S. *Op. Cit.*, 113-114.

Shawnee and other sources believed to be historically reliable.[32]

He seemed to have been as impressive to white men as he was to men of his own race. In the Galloway home, he was dignified and well-mannered, and fell easily into the amenities of his host's abode. Rebecca stated that his appearance was notably attractive, that always he was well and neatly dressed in the typical Indian garb of his rank, and that he possessed a remarkable mind, with never a descent into the realms of commonplace except once, and for that error—intoxication—his repentance was complete. Later, he and his brother, the Prophet, became America's earliest active apostles of prohibition. The Prophet openly proclaimed prohibition to be a fundamental tenet of his new and inspired religion. The historic stand of the Shawnees against intoxicants shows them to have been America's earliest protagonists of prohibition.

Many Indian leaders of that period were outspoken enemies of the liquor traffic as then forced upon them by white traders. The restraint of this traffic by officials of that period was feeble and ineffective to a marked degree. The result on Indian life and happiness was deplorable.

Letter from Stephen Ruddell

Clarksville, Mo.
Jan. 17th, 1822

Dear Sir,

I received yours a few days ago and with pleasure have endeavoured to comply with your request. I have stated as many facts concerning my old friend and brother as I can recollect at this distant period of time. I presume you can collect from authentic sources all that passed in which Tecumthe was an actor after the peace of Greenville. If you cannot I will at any time communicate to you what I know of him. I will refer you to Gov. Worthington, Gov.

---

[32]From description given by Rebecca Galloway to members of her family yet living, a resemblance in face lines and complexion may be observed in the picture of his great-grandson, Thomas W. Alford, taken when he was forty and one of the illustrations used in this narrative.

Cass and Gen'l McArthur for the particulars of a meeting that took place at Greenville old fort, and also at Chillicothe, at both which places Tecumthe delivered speeches and at which all those gentlemen together with myself were present. If I could see you I could probably relate to you many particulars which would be serviceable in your interesting work. I have hastily written my statement and have not time to even transcribe it and correct errors in the composition. You, I hope however, will excuse its crude and indigested form. You can extract from it whatever may be of service to you.

I am very truly glad you are engaged in writing the Biography of Tecumthe—the name of so great and good a man ought not to be suffered to sink into oblivion.

I am very respectfully your friend,

STEPHEN RUDDELL

Benjm Drake, Esq.

ACCOUNT OF TECUMTHA

By STEPHEN RUDDELL

Tecumthe, as the Indians pronounced the name of the celebrated Tecumseh (or "the blazing comet," in English, from his mother's seeing a meteor shooting across the sky, on the evening of his birth) was born in the neighborhood of Old Chilicothe in the year 1768. He was of the Kispockoo[33] tribe of the Shawnee Indians. The Shawnees were divided like the Israelites, into twelve tribes and with the exception of the Maykocha[34] tribes, the chiefs owed their power and authority to their merit; but the tribe just mentioned had a king over them whose authority was hereditary. His father was a great war Chief and fell at the head of his tribe in the battle between the whites and Indians at the mouth of the Kenhaway. He was a man highly respected among the tribe both as a statesman and warrior. At his dying moment he called to him his oldest son a youth of twelve or thirteen years named Pepquannahek, or gun shot,

---

[33] Accepted spelling, Kispokotha.
[34] Accepted spelling, Makujay.

and strongly enjoined on him to preserve unsullied the dignity and honour of the family and directed him in future to lead forth to battle his younger brothers. The Mother of Tecumtheth was of one of the most respectable families in the Peckaway tribe of Shawnees.

They had five sons and one daughter, Papquannake, Tecumthe, Lolloway[35] the Prophet—the other three's names I cannot recollect. *The Prophet and two other boys were born at one birth.* The oldest was a great warrior and fell at the head of a war party which he had conducted to attack some fort in the south during Wayne's war. Agreeably to the instructions of his father at his death, he took upon himself the education of his brothers and used every means to instill into the mind of Tecumthe correct, manly and honourable principles leading him forth himself to battle and instructing him in warfare. He taught him to look with contempt upon everything that was mean. He used frequently to take Tecumthe and they alone would go and commit depredations on their enemies when they were mere boys.

I first became acquainted with Tecumthe at the age of twelve years and being the same age myself we became inseparable companions. Tecumthe was always remarkable from his boyhood up for the dignity and rectitude of his deportment. There was a certain something in his countenance and manner that always commanded respect and at the same time made those about him love him. During his boyhood he used to place himself at the head of the youngsters and divide them, when he would make them fight a sham battle in which he always distinguished himself by his activity, strength and skill.

He was a great hunter and, what was remarkable, would never, if he could avoid it, hunt in parties where women were. He was free-hearted and generous to excess —always ready to relieve the wants of others. Whenever he returned from a hunting expedition he would harangue his companions and made use of all his eloquence to instill

---

[35] Lo-waw-hi-way-si-ca. Generally known as Tenskwatawa, which name he adopted upon becoming a "Prophet."

into their minds honourable and humane sentiments. He rarely ever drank ardent spirits to excess. When inebriated he was widely different from other Indians—perfectly good-humoured and free from those savage ideas which distinguished his companions; and always reproving them for their folly. He was by no means savage in his nature, always expressed the greatest abhorrence when he heard or saw acts of cruelty or barbarity practiced.

From his earliest days he was remarkably easily awoke out of sleep. He was always on the alert and it was impossible to take him by surprise. He was always averse to taking prisoners in his warfare, but when prisoners fell into his hands he always treated them with as much humanity as if they had been in the hands of civilized people. No burning—no torturing—he never tolerated the practice of killing women and children. He was a man of great courage and conduct. Perfectly fearless of danger. He always inspired his companions with confidence and valour. He never evinced any great regard for the female sex—it was a custom among the Shawnees to marry as many wives as they pleased and to keep them as long as they pleased. Tecumthe had at different times a wife whom he did not keep long before he parted provoked. He had a Cherokee squaw who lived with him the longest of any. The women were very fond of him—much more than he was of them. He was a very jovial companion—fond of cracking his jokes, but his wit was never aimed to wound the feelings of his comrades.

The first engagement in which he particularly distinguished himself was in an attack on some boats coming down the Ohio, he being then about fifteen years old. The boats were taken and all the persons on board were killed. In the action Tecumthe behaved with great bravery and even left in the background some of the oldest and bravest warriors. In the action one prisoner, as well as I recollect, was taken—the Indians proceeded to burn him and after it had been done, Tecumthe, who had been a spectator expressed great abhorrence of the deed and finally it was concluded among them not to burn any more prisoners that should afterwards be taken, which was ever after strictly adhered to by him. The boats were owned by traders— number of persons on board not recollected. These boats were taken in the spring and in the fall they moved towards the south on an expedition against the whites. On the route to the south Tecumthe's horse fell with him and broke his thigh which confined him until the spring following, when the party headed by Tecumthe's oldest brother proceeded on their expedition. He was then able to walk with the assistance of crutches, his brother endeavoured to persuade him to remain behind but he could not be prevailed on to comply. They had several engagements with the whites in this expedition which kept them absent from home three years. Tecumthe always distinguished himself. It was in this expedition that his oldest brother fell in an attack on some fort, the name and situation of which I cannot now tell.[36] The party was chiefly composed of Cherokees—a few days before they attacked the fort this oldest brother or Gunshot harangued the party and told them that on such a day and such a time of the day they would arrive at the fort—that they would attack the fort in the morning and would succeed if they would persevere in the fight—that precisely at noon he would be shot through the centre of the forehead. When he related this the Indians endeavoured to persuade him to turn back, which he refused to do. The attack was commenced and as he predicted he received the shot in the head and fell saying that his father had fell gloriously in battle—that he considered it an honour to die in battle and that it was what he wished and did not wish to be buried at home like an old squaw, to which he preferred that the fowls of the air should pick his bones.

After his death the party was disheartened and in spite of all the exertions of Tecumthe the Cherokees left the ground—thus they failed in their attempt. Tecumthe then told the party that he would not go home until he had done something to show for his good conduct. He accordingly took with him a small party of eight or ten and a short time

---

[36] Chiksika was killed in an encounter with the whites on the Tennessee frontier, 1788 or '89.

after attacked a family, perhaps killed the man and took the woman and children prisoners. I cannot recollect any of the particulars of the other engagements which occurred on this expedition. He was three times attacked in the night in his encampment, but being remarkably watchful he was always ready for the enemy and they seldom gained any advantage. He always examined with great care the ground on which he encamped no matter whether in the neighborhood of the enemy or not, so that it was almost impossible to gain any advantage of him—during the expedition he was attacked on the edge of a cain brake; perhaps on the waters of Tennessee whilst dressing some meat, by a party of about thirty whites. He immediately ordered his small party to charge and leading on himself with the most determined bravery, he put the whole party to flight, two whites were killed. At the expiration of three years from the time he left home he returned—this was shortly after Harmar's defeat. He was not in St. Clair's defeat; being at that time on a hunting expedition and not having heard of the arrival of St. Clair.

In Wayne's battle, he took a conspicuous part, at least as much as the nature of the case would admit of. There he commanded a band of the Shawnees. At the time the Indians commenced retreating he together with two or three others rushed on a party of the whites that had a field piece in charge, drove the artillery men from their posts, cut loose the horses, mounted them and cleared themselves.

In April, 1793, a hunting party headed by Tecumthe were one night attacked by a company of men under Simon Kenton, the circumstances of which are as follows: In the day one of our party was out hunting up the horses and being discovered by Kenton's party was shot. They put forward on his tracks and on coming in sight of our camp, they discovered that we were unalarmed and after making all the observations they wished, they returned back some distance where they made their preparations for the attack. Tecumthe had laid down at night outside of the camp or tents, alongside of the pine where we had been gherking some venison through the day. In the night the attack was made by firing into the tents. Tecumthe sprang to his feet with his war club in his hand, a weapon which he invariably carried both in peace and war, hunting and in battle, and calling to me asked Big fish,[37] where are you? Here I am says I. Then do you charge on that side and I will charge on this with that he rushed on those on his side, knocked one in the head with his club and drove the rest back. I on my side met a man as I came out of the tent, whom I afterward found out to be Kenton himself. I fired on him but my gun having gotten a little wet through the day it blowed considerably and at last just blowed out the ball without injuring Kenton who had taken to his heels. I raised the Indian yell and called that they were running, upon which the rest of the Indians in the tent who had till now remained silent, sprang out and raising the war-whoop we run them off the ground. This took place on the waters, of the little Miami or Brush Creek. We had ten men including the one killed in the morning—they had twenty-eight men.

Tecumthe was particularly attached to the war club; it was a weapon which he said had been used by his forefathers. One of Kenton's party named McIntire, a resolute fellow, resolved to take a horse, and leaving the rest of his company, accordingly went to where our horses were feeding and carried one off. In the morning Tecumthe with four others followed after them and after going some distance they came to where McIntire had turned off the road. He had struck a fire and was cooking some victuals. They charged on him. McI. took to his heels; but after running some distance he discovered the Indians fast gaining on him, he faced about and presented his gun—two Indians that were somewhat in advance of Tecumthe sprang to trees; but he rushed right up to McIntire and made him prisoner. McIntire was brought back to camp and tied. We then concluded that we must retreat and requested the rest of the Indians to go out for the horses; but they being somewhat timid, Tecumthe proposed that he and myself should go out. On our return we found that the rest of the

---

[37]*Sinnanatha* or "Big Fish" was the name the Indians had given me.

Indians had killed McIntire, at which Tecumthe was very angry telling them that it was a cowardly act to kill a man who was tied and expressed in his strongest terms his disapprobation of their conduct.

In the spring before the battle with Wayne, Tecumthe was on a hunting expedition in the same neighbourhood where the action with Kenton took place. The party was composed of six or seven warriors. He was attacked by a scouting party of whites of between 20 or 30 men. In the fight one of Tecumthe's party, a white man named Joseph Ward who had been taken prisoner when a small boy during Dunmore's war and had been raised by the Indians, was killed. Tecumtha and his party were compelled to give ground after fighting desperately; but he made out to carry off Ward. His company deserted him during the battle. He then returned home; but not being pleased with an inactive life, he again went out to hunt and continued in that employment until the Indians gathered to give Wayne battle in the fall of '94.

He was not engaged in any other battle or skirmish after that with Wayne during my continuance with the Indians. He was pleased with the peace of Greenville—said that now he was happy—that he could pursue his hunting without danger. He had no children whilst I knew him. He was naturally eloquent—very fluent—graceful in his gesticulation but not in the habit of using many gestures. There was no violence—no vehemence in his mode of delivering his speeches. He always made a great impression on his audience. He was about five feet ten inches high, very well made, full of activity and professed a great strength.

I know of no peculiarity about him, that gained him popularity. His talents, rectitude of deportment and friendly disposition, commanded the respect and regard of all about him. In short I consider him a very great as well as a very good man, who, if he had enjoyed the advantages of a liberal education, would have done honour to any age or any nation.

[This account of Tecumtha is from Stephen Ruddell,

REBECCA GALLOWAY
When she was seventeen years of age, Tecumtha sought to win her hand

procured for me from him by William R. Graham. Ruddell lived at the time in Mipomi—a man of Veracity.

B. DRAKE.]

A PIONEER ROMANCE

Rebecca Galloway was past sixteen in 1807; of medium height; with blue eyes, auburn hair and fair, clear complexion. She was a thoughtful girl of the student type, and was well known all her life as a close reader with clear recollection of the texts of the many books she read. Her opportunity to obtain these books from the two sources before noted opened to her the only means then available for her education.

The portraitures given of the suitor, the girl and her home will add to the interest of their historic pioneer romance. With her father's permission to appeal to his daughter, Tecumtha declared his desire directly to Rebecca. It is impossible to think that she was not flattered with his dignified proposal, even though racial and other differences seemed to be insurmountable barriers to his desire. It was, nevertheless, a proposal—which came with unexpected directness, from a man whose qualities compelled admiration. The issue was met frankly by both. Much as she appreciated his proposal for her hand, and highly as she regarded him, it would be impossible for her to adapt herself to the life and limited environment of the women of his race. Polygamy, also a custom in his tribe then, was an impossible thought to her. On his part, he approached her objections in the only way left to him. He would make her his only wife, and would not expect the work usually required of Indian women. In another moon he would return for her answer.

The matter was not referred to again during his visit, nor did he hasten to depart. The usual agreeable relationship with the family was maintained as though no unusual incident had occurred. As Tecumtha departed from this visit, its true significance and portent was realized by the young girl and her family. They had heard in their own home from this Indian chief the first rumblings of the storm that was soon to break in the fury of battle. He had discussed the injustice of tribal treatment by the United States in which as little as one cent per acre was realized from the land treaties, and the refusal of the government to permit the Indian himself to sell his land to individual purchasers. He had discussed the disregard of the government for the overlapping tribal interests in Indian land treaties, and the ever-increasing tidal wave of white settlers pushing westward over the Alleghany Mountains. He had talked of the cloak of the white man's treaties, which too often covered the hand of the aggressor, and of the need of an Indian protective confederation to save his people from the inevitable losses which threatened them. The master of this impending storm of unrest had spoken and was to come again with the next moon for his answer.

As she watched his departure from the threshold of her father's home, it was not possible for her to foretell the portentous events of 1812-'13, which were rapidly approaching in the Northwest Territory, or to foreknow that the cost in human life would be great to his race and hers, or that the results to his nation would be further subordination and to hers the loss of an empire. Yet with the prescience by which many women have sensed the events of the future, she knew that this man bore within him a rising power, dangerous to her people and fateful to his own. Her thoughts continued to dwell on the possibility that this incident of love might, in some way, be made to change impending events—the fulfillment of which had seemed inevitable to her when she listened to his discussions with her father in their home. With woman's intuition, she had grasped their meaning, and feared their fulfillment. Foreordination was a strong doctrinal tenet of the Scotch Associate communion. Unconsciously it influenced the thought of its members in life's daily relations, but it very consciously influenced them in life's serious emergencies. Her thoughts turned to what might be done to stay the threatening storm she saw approaching. If she gave consent to his honorable suit, could the power of this unusual man be turned from war and enlisted in the arts of peace? The pioneers of the old Scotch Associate belief submitted all great questions affecting their life at the family altar. Through this source, they sought the interpretation of God's plan in their lives.

It must have been a notable moment when, after the customary singing of a psalm and reading from the Scriptures, this family knelt together in the girl's home and listened to their pastor's supplication that divine direction be given to the one who now needed her Master's hand to lead her through a difficult way. No further words referred to the girl's problem. With an admirable sense of appreciation of the position of this alien but distinguished suitor, she reserved her declarations for him, the one most nearly interested. The next moon waxed full, and with it the suitor came for his answer. The usual hospitality of the home was extended him, and accepted by him as it had been many times before.

Rebecca was always a wonderful character, but she was essentially feminine. In spite of its far-reaching possibilities, which she seemed to have realized, she could not resist this first romantic incident in her life. As the evening wore on, the girl suggested the near-by river and the birch-bark canoe he had given her. Thither they went, she to give, and he to receive her answer. Nowhere are the charms of a maiden so subtle as in a canoe, drifting in and out of the shadows of overhanging trees in the light of a full moon with a cloudless sky overhead. Always and ever a woman has the weapons of her defense in her own hands, so with a gentle candor which well became her, and in a setting which was matchless for the expression of life's greatest sentiment, she quietly gave him the answer he had come to learn. She would accept him if he would adopt her people's mode of life and dress. No expression of assent or dissent escaped him. His answer, when he took his departure, was that "he would return at the next full moon." Later taking up the calumet he had given her father, confirming the pact of peace and friendship between her family and his people, he said: "You and your family need have no fear from my race." The dread of harm which had haunted the family should Rebecca refuse to consider the noted chief's proposal, was now lifted. She had met a serious situation tactfully, and in the only way possible to her. The decision was now Tecumtha's.

Tradition is silent on the emotions of the problem which confronted him for the intervening month he chose to take before he gave his decision, but the length of time itself speaks eloquently of the struggle between the call of his heart and the call of his nation. His decision commands our admiration. *He gave his all to his own;* yet who may ever know if the phantom of love rode beside him to conference calls and battle-camps? Already, he was formulating plans of a great defensive confederacy of American Indians, and was preparing for his first journey south to organize it. Whether successful or not, future strife and war with the girl's race must have seemed even then inevitable to him. He made her a short visit at the appointed time, and with great dignity stated that "to do as she required would lose him the respect and leadership of his people." With that decision, he departed to begin at once the preparations which resulted in the last stand of the Shawnee nation at the Battle of the Thames, and all the intermediate and stirring events that cluster about the name of this notable man from 1808 until October 5, 1813.

Had Tecumtha accepted Rebecca Galloway's alternative, the events of 1810-'13 might have been averted. Her notable patriotism would then have found its best expression in directing his great abilities into the realm of peace-making statesmanship. At this time, there seems little doubt that a favorable adjustment of his nation's difficulties would have attended his efforts as a statesman instead of a warrior. His nation's need was a peace-making Tamanend. The fates gave it a warrior, Tecumtha.

One is tempted to romance with history's alternatives. The universal esteem and admiration Tecumtha commanded from leaders of his period leaves little doubt that, for him and his nation, under the inspiration of the girl for whose hand he was a suitor, the victories of peace would have been uniformly as great as were the irrevocable losses of war which his nation eventually was forced to endure.

BROTHERS BY BLOOD

Tecumtha—(Lo-waw-lu-way-si-ca)

and The Prophet—(Tenskwatawa)

The American Indians' powers of spiritual imagery centered in and about their "Great Spirit." The concept of his personal interest in the well-being of his red children has been noted in Tecumtha's own views, as expressed in the home of his host, James Galloway. These were, in a way, a confession of faith in the direction and care given by the Great Spirit to his red children, expressed in terms not beyond their primitive comprehension. At that period, the ancient Shawnee concepts were unmodified by contact with the more complex spiritual doctrines of their foes. That they so continued for some years is indicated by Tecumtha's answer to the protest of his friend, Stephen Ruddell: "The time of visions may be past so far as the white man is concerned, but not so for the Indian." Profound regret had been personally expressed to Tecumtha by this boyhood playmate and intimate friend, that he permitted himself to fall directly under the quasi-spiritual influence of the teachings and *visions* of his brother, "The Prophet."

The purposes of the Prophet's mission at Greenville, however, were set forth in favorable terms by the reports of the Shaker Committee—1805, and that of Governor Kirker's commission in 1807—consisting of General Worthington and General MacArthur, followed by Tecumtha's famous speech at Chillicothe in 1807. The Stephen Ruddell record taken from the Session Book of the old Cooper's Run Meeting-house, Kentucky, show a continued favorable attitude of the Shawnees to his missionary work as late as 1810-12.[38] The tenets the Prophet emphasized, both in language and by symbol, suggested such reforms as seem to

---

[38]See account of Stephen Ruddell in chapter, "Pioneer Stories."

us now to have been both needed and desired under the changed civil and economic condition that confronted the Shawnees and their allies after the Treaty of Greenville.

Tenskwatawa (Lo-waw-lu-way-si-ca—"one with open door"), known in our history as "The Prophet," died in 1834, in Shawnee Township, Wyandotte County, Kansas, and is buried there. From October 5, 1813, the date of the Battle of the Thames, in which he took part, until the date of his death, he received a pension from the British Government. His name is found on the roll of the *United Service Journal*, London. It thus appears that he, as well as his brother, Tecumtha, attained international recognition while yet living. Tenskwatawa was born a member of the Kispokotha clan of the Shawnee nation. This clan, according to ancient Shawnee law, furnished the nation's war chiefs and leaders. The historic office of Prophet, with its spiritual leadership, placed him in the latter class. The position of "Prophets," in the Shawnees' civil organization of that date, should not be confused with that of "Medicine Men," who, according to long-established Shawnee law, were taken, when available, from the Makujay clan. The Lebanon Shaker records, however, state that Tenskwatawa was first a doctor, and that the vision from the Great Spirit which was granted to him, and which led to his conversion, and later to the office of Prophet, came while in attendance on his people at Tawa, on the Auglaize River during some sort of an epidemic. His conversion seems to have been wholly esoteric.

The office of Prophet—spiritual leader—was a usual one among Indian tribes and nations in the Northwest Territory. The aged Prophet, Penegashega ("the change of feathers"), held this important and influential position for a long time prior to 1805, the year of his death. History does not relate whether succession in this office was by council designation or tribal election, or was, in a measure, self-assertive. Our historians have assumed the latter method was used by Tenskwatawa who, before this date, was known by his Indian name, Lo-waw-lu-way-si-ca. From the orderly way in which the Shawnees' civil organization is known to have functioned, his accession to this office may be accepted as having taken place in 1805 by consent of the council, which was the executive organization of his nation. After this date, he was known in Shawnee language as Tenskwatawa ("one with open mouth") and in English as "The Prophet." His personal abilities and characteristics, and his ministrations of the office of "Prophet" present such variants of description that study of the man and his purposes, at a time when prejudice has passed away, readily tend to further inquiries. These inquiries are quickened by the views taken by many writers, that the Prophet improved the opportunities of his position, under the abler direction of Tecumtha, to the advantage of the latter's career, and that these brothers operated together for the benefit of Tecumtha's Indian patriotic organization, a nation-wide confederation of his people for the preservation of their lands and homes. Drake's *Life of Tecumseh* gives the best summary of these various views, should the reader desire to pursue this study.

The Prophet's activity, in the beginning, was limited to the religious and moral betterment of his people. Their physical and civil condition, however, is known to have given serious concern to this leader. His methods of appeal were those of an Indian to Indians only and naturally were built on Indian psychology. His first propaganda, in 1805, was among the several Indian nations then residing on the Auglaize River. With few exceptions, and for reasons given later in this study, our leaders failed to grasp the values of this psychology, or to consider with sympathy the extremities these human beings were rapidly approaching.

The beginning of this reform movement, near Greenville, Ohio, occurred sometime during the year 1805; its end came at the Battle of Tippecanoe, November 7, 1811. It therefore functioned about six years.

President Jefferson set forth a humane sympathetic view of the Wabash Prophet's source of power and the reforms he advocated. He wrote to his successor, President Madison, early in his administration "as to the reforms the Prophet advocated; he had early reached the conclusion that this leader was visionary and enveloped in his race's antiquities; vainly endeavoring to lead back his brethren to the fancied beatitudes of their golden age." Elsewhere, these beatitudes are described as they actually occurred in the period of "the town of towns" during early Pennsylvania Shawnee history. This golden age was of short duration before the hand of civilization had laid hold on their young men and exacted a deplorable toll. From the beginning, there were sane and sensible Shawnee chiefs like Black Hoof and Little Turtle, who were not in sympathy with the Prophet's activities or with his declaration of divine revelation from the Great Spirit. This opposition became outspoken when large numbers of Indians, many from far distant tribes, made pilgrimages to the camp of the reformer, and departed converts to his pleas for the restoration of his people to the faith and the simple life of their forefathers.

In "Shaker Missions to the Shawnee Indians,"[39] Dr. J. P. MacLean quotes from the records of the Lebanon Society of Shakers, a reliable and authentic report of the status of the Prophet's reform movement in 1807, as observed by an authorized committee of this organization. This committee visited the Prophet's camp to observe the character of the reform work being done there, and to determine whether financial help and evangelical assistance would forward its progress. Their report, submitted after their return, gives an authentic basis from personal contact by which the purposes and methods of this primitive reform work may be judged. The three men composing the Shaker committee were David Darrow, Benjamin S. Youngs and Richard McNemar, the latter a well-educated Presbyterian minister, who had joined the Shaker Society after prominent leadership in the notable Kentucky and Tennessee revivals of 1800 and 1801. The committee reported the peaceful and spiritual character of Tenskwatawa's teaching, and noted the material poverty of his adherents, apparent during part, if not all, of the period of their Greenville residence. The report is a remarkable document. Its con-

[39] *Ohio Arch. and Hist. Quarterly*, 11:221-228.

clusions are at variance with much of the current history of that period, and are of unusual interest in a study of Northwestern Territory and early Ohio history. Short excerpts only can be given in this story. Interested readers, however, will be well repaid by a study of Dr. MacLean's Shaker articles in full as they appeared in the publication above noted.

A rare note of "wisdom and understanding" is found in the Lebanon Shakers' Report. This committee grasped the essential facts. The movement required a knowledge of Indian psychology, and they found that there was no English terminology by which they could attain to a proper understanding of the Shawnee language.

The committee's interpreter was George Blue Jacket, probably a son of Blue Jacket, the noted Shawnee chief. George had attended school, and spoke our language well, but met the same difficulty in translating the Prophet's addresses from Shawnee into English[40] that is noted by Thomas W. Alford, in translating into English his own Shawnee address on the re-celebration of "The Pact of Friendship and Peace," as told elsewhere in this story.[41] These difficulties are emphasized in Blue Jacket's case when it is known that Mr. Alford has had many years of experience as court interpreter, and also is competent in his English scholarship to surmount, as far as possible, the difficulties of interpreting the true Shawnee meaning in properly expressed English. Except the general sense of the Prophet's addresses, Blue Jacket frankly stated he was unable, from lack of suitable vocabulary, to translate them into proper English meaning. The Prophet spoke vehemently against Indian vices of that time. His race was to reform and put behind them the sins of witchcraft, poisoning, fighting, murder, beating their wives because they will not have children, stealing, lying, adultery and whisky-drinking. Special emphasis was laid on the latter vice, as destructive of every essential virtue of manhood. He like-

---

[40] *Ohio Arch. and Hist. Quarterly*, 11: p. 223.
[41] See pages 168-169.

wise declaimed against Indian women contracting interracial marriage, holding this to be one of the principal causes of their misfortunes. He advocated a return to their ancient custom of community of property and dress, and asserted the duty of all young Indians to love, honor, cherish, support and respect the aged and infirm fathers and mothers of their nation.

There is a striking analogy between Indian culture at its best and certain fundamentals of Greek and Roman culture. Both were built on the conception of the subordination of the individual to the community, and of the citizen to the state; each set the safety of the commonwealth as the supreme aim of conduct, above the safety of the individual, whether in this world or in the world to come. Trained from infancy in this unselfish ideal, each race devoted their lives to the public service and were ready to lay them down for the common good; or if they shrank from the supreme sacrifice, it never occurred to them that they acted otherwise than basely in preferring their personal existence to the interests of their country. These features were especially emphasized in American Indian culture. Cowardice, in the presence of danger threatening either himself, his family or his associates, was practically unknown; but when it did occur, the unfortunate man's name became anathema among his own people, as well as among all other Indians.

The committee's personal reaction after attending one of these meetings addressed by the Prophet is significant as an authentic record submitted by men competent to investigate the question in hand:

On this occasion, our feelings were like Jacob's when he cried out "surely the Lord is in this place, and I knew it not.... How dreadful is this place." ...

Although these poor Shawnees have had no particular instruction but what they received by the outpouring of the Spirit, yet in point of real light and understanding, as well as behavior, they shame the Christian world. Therefore, of that Spirit which hath wrought so great a change, the believers at Turtle Creek are not ashamed; yet they are far from wishing them to turn to the right hand or to the left, to form an external union with them or any other people. But they are willing that God should carry on His work among them without interruption, as He thinks proper."[12]

In conclusion, Dr. McLean states: "The records show that the Shakers desisted from any real efforts to promulgate their doctrines among the Indians. While they were well received, the evidence conveys the idea that the missionaries saw no opening for instructions after their manner."

That the Prophet and his followers were then pitifully poor is indicated by the committee's statement that: "The only meal we saw them eat, was a turkey, divided among thirty or forty, and the only relief we could afford them was ten dollars, for the purpose of buying corn."

Some time after the Shaker committee's visit, an unusual situation arose. A short, but active, campaign was inaugurated to wipe out the evil of witchcraft, against which the Prophet had been exhorting for three years. Details of conditions which led to this outbreak are meager and unsatisfactory. Whether this diabolical custom was adopted to counter the opposition of many of the Shawnee chiefs which, by this time, was open and persistent, or was due to certain superstitions in the Delaware and Wyandotte nations is not clear. It was probably an expression of the human obsession noted in other mass religious movements in history, as in the debacle at Salem, Massachusetts, where 55 suffered torture and 20 lost their lives; or later in the acute mass hysteria observed in the revival of 1801 in Kentucky; or the sectarian prejudices which marked the repeated mob violence against the Society of Shakers at Lebanon, Ohio. In connection with the Prophet's witchcraft outbreak, two incidents of sanity are outstanding: Tecumtha, Anthony Shane declared, opposed the witchcraft trials and executions with all his power. The other incident, which was spectacular and notably courageous, is quoted from Drake's *Life of Tecumseh*. It is regrettable

---
[42] *Ohio Arch. and Hist. Quarterly*, 11:228.

that the name of the young Indian concerned in it has not been preserved in history. He is worthy of the Indian salute:—"Ho-c-o-e!"—"This is a man"!

In quick succession, the Prophet had condemned to execution, either by tomahawk or the stake, Teteboxti, a Delaware chief, and his son-in-law, Chief Billy Patterson; the Wyandotte chief, Leatherlips; Dead chief; Coltos, an old woman, and Joshua, an old man. The wife of Teteboxti was arraigned, brought before the council, and condemned.

While preparations were making for her execution by fire, her brother, a youth of twenty years of age, suddenly started up, took her by the hand, and to the amazement of the council, led her out of the house. He soon returned, and exclaiming, "The devil has come among us" (alluding to the Prophet), "and we are killing each other," he reseated himself in the midst of the crowd. This bold step checked the wild frenzy of the Indians, put an end to these cruel scenes, and for a time greatly impaired the impostor's influence among the Delawares.[43]

The influence of the Prophet grew with the spreading of the news of his new gospel. Many Indians, some of whom came from great distances, returned to their homes, convinced that a new era for them was about to dawn. Larger parties from various sections began to visit the camp. Their number, amounting at one time to 400 Indians, alarmed the Greenville pioneer settlers. The governor was asked to remove them to a more isolated location, largely because an unfounded suspicion had become current that this movement of the Prophet was military rather than moral.

After several futile attempts to arrange a conference looking to some further agreement covering these misunderstandings, which were beginning to appear early in 1808, Captain Wells, commanding the military force at Fort Wayne, sent the well-known Indian half-breed interpreter, Anthony Shane, to Greenville with a communication to Tecumseh and the Prophet, stating that the government desired them to move their mission from Greenville to

---

[43]Drake, Benjamin. *Op. Cit.*, 89.

some point beyond the territorial boundaries established by the treaty of 1795, and to that end would give them aid, should they find they needed it. There is no record that this offer of assistance was accepted, although removal by the Prophet and his followers took place quietly and at once. This communication, which contained no reference to territory to which they might migrate, must have been a message full of foreboding to these Indians, whose commission to Governor Kirker only a year previous had given assurance of the peaceful purpose of the mission at Greenville. Their report was fully verified by that of the governor's own commission of distinguished men.[44] These two communications amounted to a joint report. They were free from disagreements, and were accepted in good faith at the time. It is noteworthy that four years of peace followed, in spite of conditions which became progressively unstable.[45] The uncertainties and hardships of the removal were met in part by the Pottawatomie and Kispokotha Indians, who offered land from their own reservation on the Tippecanoe River to the expelled mission. At this time it seems that other settlers in western Ohio associated the Prophet's mission at Greenville with Tecumtha's leadership. In fact, many pioneers had maintained from the mission's early location there in 1805 that Tecumtha, rather than the Prophet, was its real leader. It was six years later, however, in 1811, that the intricate play of cross-purposes drove Tecumtha reluctantly into an alliance with the English forces against the United States.

Study of this movement throughout its short history—1805 till the Battle of Tippecanoe—and of the means employed to accomplish its avowed purposes, fails to identify Tecumtha's characteristics in its management, except in such details as might be expected to become common view-

---

[44] General Thomas Worthington and General Duncan McArthur. (General Cass, though not a member, is mentioned as agreeing with the favorable report of the commission.)

[45] The presence of the mission had become objectionable at this time to settlers in the vicinity. Personal, and other relations including unfounded fears of another Indian uprising, caused increasing alarm and determination to find means to force the Prophet and his mission to "move on."

points between brothers, who were close in interests whenever critical periods arose in their tribal life. The Prophet's personal and leadership characteristics are, however, plainly apparent from the date of the Shaker committee's report, which is here considered reliable history of record. It aids us in understanding the period of hysteria on both sides, which preceded the Battle of Tippecanoe. Had Tecumtha been back from his southern journey in the interests of his Indian confederacy, this battle would not have occurred. He had promised General Harrison at the end of their conference in July, 1811, before he departed on this trip south, that no disturbance of the existing peaceful relations should occur during his absence, and at no time had he contemplated war with the 17 fires. That he subsequently took up arms against the United States was due largely to circumstances which could have been avoided or acceptably modified. Failure to secure the allegiance of the Osage nation and the silence of representatives of other western tribes present at the conference to hear his notable plea for Indian union, including war as a final alternative, practically defeated his plan, although it did not break his spirit. It was the Battle of Tippecanoe, fought without his knowledge, during his absence, and contrary to his assurances of peace to General Harrison, that closed all avenues of hope for a successful issue of his plans for a country-wide protective confederacy of his own people, similar to that of the 17 fires. The battle likewise closed the final avenues to the peaceful amalgamation of two races, between whom there should have existed no insurmountable differences. That two-thirds of the Shawnees migrated from the Little Miami Valley in 1779, rather than adopt an active anti-pioneer war policy, is an abiding historic testimony of the peace the Shawnees desired and its denial to them.

The open rupture with Tecumtha, when it came, was the final issue of a long series of misunderstandings and misapprehensions of the sort ever in the making between white and dark-skinned races. After twenty-five years' service in the educational interests of one of these races, and intimate and agreeable relations with many of its leading men, remembered as among life's well-appreciated experiences, the writer is in agreement with Miss Beatrice Grimshaw that, "there lies in the heart of every colored man, deep-seated, deep-rooted in the very elements of his being, a certain dark reserve toward the white," This was the status of the red man at the time of this story.

Important events in history, as those of November 6th, 1811, leading to the conflict of November 7th,[46] have occurred by reason of decisions not always sustained by the calmer verdicts of history. Failure to grasp the red man's psychology added great cost to the winning of the Northwest Territory. An uncalled-for wound of Tecumtha's dignity and pride probably cost us the allegiance of this notable Indian leader and his allies. After an invitation by the Governor of Indiana Territory to present personally his arguments on treaties and land encroachments to the President at Washington, General Harrison denied him the honor of such escort from his own nation as was benefitting his rank and position. The wound to his self-respect and prestige was unbearable, and the permission, when granted, was promptly ignored by Tecumtha. Other incidents, now quite easily discerned, make regrettable our failure to grasp the Indian's racial psychology and the fact of *his urgent need for help* before he could comprehend the radical changes in life we had forced him to accept.

During the period of the Prophet's activities, 1805-11, pioneer opposition had grown so bitter that mob violence was threatened against the peaceful Society of Shakers at Lebanon, Ohio, because they had sent a small amount of needed food to the Indians in the Prophet's mission at Greenville.

In 1806, after the Delawares' witchcraft delusions, General Harrison addressed a letter to the Indians denouncing the Prophet as false. An excerpt of this *very remarkable* address is taken from Drake's *Life of Tecumseh*. It follows:

But who is this pretended prophet, who dares to speak

---
[46] The Battle of Tippecanoe.

in the name of the Great Creator? Examine him. Is he more wise or virtuous than you are yourselves, that he should be selected to convey to you the orders of your God? Demand of him some proofs, at least, of his being the messenger of the Deity. If God has really employed him, he has doubtless authorized him to perform miracles, that he may be known and received as a prophet. If he is really a prophet, ask of him to cause the sun to stand still—the moon to alter its course—the rivers to cease to flow—or the dead to rise from their graves. If he does these things, you may then believe that he has been sent from God. He tells you that the Great Spirit commands you to punish with death, those who deal in magic; and that he is authorized to point them out. Wretched delusion! Is then, the Master of Life obliged to employ mortal man to punish those who offend him? Has he not the thunder and all the powers of nature at his command? and could he not sweep away from the earth a whole nation with one motion of his arm? My children! do not believe that the great and good Creator of mankind has directed you to destroy your own flesh; and do not doubt but that if you pursue this abominable wickedness, His vengeance will overtake and crush you.[47]

The Prophet's answer was so convincing to his followers, that his influence at once became established. He prophesied that, on a certain day, he would draw a curtain across the sun, and darken the earth. On that date, as the shadows of a total eclipse of the sun grew deeper, the Prophet stood in the midst of his followers, and declared, "Did I not prophesy truly?" Although, as assumed by historians, the Prophet *must have learned from some outside source*, the date of the eclipse, the advance knowledge enabled him to satisfy his followers completely, to General Harrison's discomfort. There is, however, no historical record that General Harrison had this advance knowledge, or, if so, that he had the wit to anticipate the only natural phenomenon available for the Prophet to use as a convincing answer to the impossible demands of his letter. After the eclipse, no further means employed against the Prophet's influence were effective till the conclusion of the Battle of Tippecanoe, November 7, 1811. Assuming that the Prophet

---

[47]Drake, Benjamin. *Op. Cit.*, 89-91.

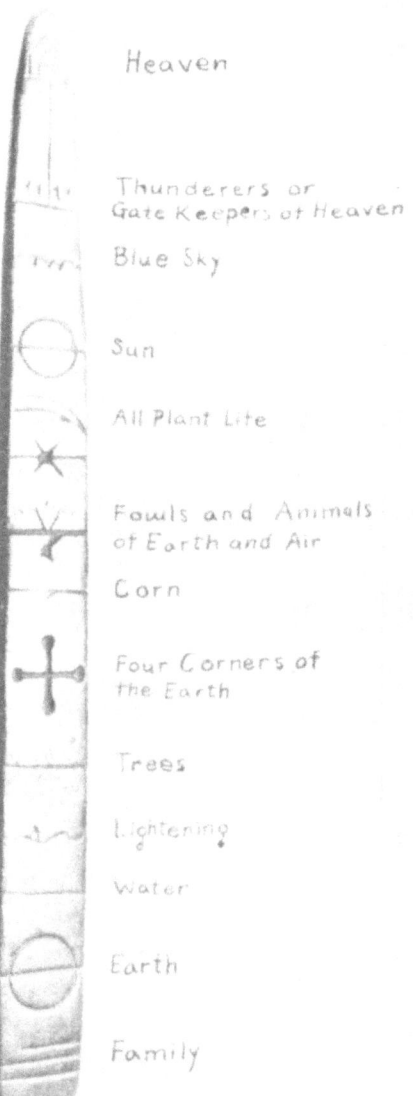

THE SACRED SLAB

may have possessed advance eclipse information, no advance knowledge was available to Tecumtha, on which to predicate his prophecy of the New Madrid earthquake, and its effect on the Cherokee village, Tuckhabatchee, on the Tallapoosa River.[48] Any conceivable percentage of chance for the fulfillment of this prophecy was microscopic. In seeking for an explanation of Tecumtha's prophetic accuracy in this instance, one is compelled to credit the belief that uses of subjective powers unknown to the white man have been available among the dark races for centuries past. Some of these forces, discussed in a story by Miss Beatrice Grimshaw, in the *Elks' Magazine*, have been known to the writer for many years.

No hope thereafter remained that Tecumtha's Indian confederation would be permitted to organize and function as a peace measure. Final determination on this point came with General Harrison's letter to the President, followed by his victory, November 11, 1811. That the great Indian of later days read the decrees of his enemy correctly, there can be no doubt. That he retained an open attitude for peace until finally forced to abandon it, is shown in the texts of his addresses subsequent to the Battle of Tippecanoe.

THE SACRED SLAB

In the Milford G. Chandler loan collection in the Museum of Anthropology, University of Michigan, is a slab of red cedar wood, $13\frac{1}{2}$ inches in length and three-eighths of an inch in maximum thickness, which is inscribed on one side with various characters. This piece was obtained by Mr. Chandler from the Winnebago Indians. According to them, the slab was given to the Winnebagos by the Shawnee Prophet (Tenskwatawa), and represents a prophecy made by him at a time when the Winnebagos were encamped with the Shawnees.

The following statement was obtained from Oliver LaMare, Winnebago informant:

---

[48]Drake, Benjamin. *Op. Cit.*, 144-145.

The story-sticks were made and given to war-bundle owners by the Shawnee Prophet. He only gave it to those who were sincere about life. It is said that he told those to whom he gave the sticks that at a time when the creation of things represented on the story-stick would be ignored and not kept secret that the end of the world would come to pass, that is to say, when the creation of the Great Spirit would lose the respect of the people.

Although the religious ideas of the Prophet were not largely Indian, "The Sacred Slab" seems aboriginal in its design and presents an interesting bit of symbolism.[49]

THE DEATH OF TECUMTHA

An Authentic Shawnee Statement

Shawnee tradition, Mr. Alford relates, has been transmitted with such fidelity to facts as to make it historically trustworthy. Concerning the death of Tecumtha at the Battle of the Thames, he states—as do our own histories—that Tecumtha entered this battle convinced that he would there lose his life. He divested himself of all clothing and insignia which might identify his body to the enemy, and dressed for the battle in plain tanned buckskins, frock shirt, leggins and moccasins. *He carried no arms or ornaments of any kind.* He fell in the thick of the fight, but his body was retrieved by his warriors, and later taken to a point well marked on the banks of a distant creek and buried there. After some years, a band of Shawnees who knew the burial location, journeyed to the grave to disinter the body and bear it to their western reservation for reinterment suitable to the greatest leader of their race. This

---

[49]It is not closely connected in the mind of the Shawnees' historian—an able student—with traditions that definitely connect it with the Prophet's mission work. In a letter, April 29. 1929, he writes:
I return you, herewith, "The Prophet's Slab" (photograph), which you so kindly sent me some time ago, and which I believe is genuine, as the Shawnees had a way of communicating and perpetuating ideas among other tribes by such means as this. I cannot interpret the markings on the slab, but I believe it would be a good thing to include it in your book.
(Signed) THOMAS W. ALFORD

party, selected because it knew the spot of the interment, found that the creek at flood times, had washed away all evidences of the great warrior's last resting-place.

This simple annal of the passing of his noted kinsman is worthy of Alford, the quiet and forceful historian who relates it. Many stories of imaginative incidents connected with Tecumtha's death have been written into American history. Drake records a number of these variants,[50] then leaves the reader to his own devices to find his way out of this historical copse. The same variations in historical imagination are noted in later works available from the files of the Congressional Library. None of these narratives approach, in historical value, the simple and accurate statement of Alford, historian and custodian of records, that Tecumtha, his kinsman, was killed at the Battle of the Thames. His body was retrieved by his warriors. Its identity was not discovered by his enemies. The location of his grave, though destroyed as such, by flood, remains a Shawnee secret. This is the entire story.

From Joseph N. Bourassa, born March 19, 1810, at Parravashe, now Bertrand, Michigan; and then residing near Topeka, Kansas:

Death of Tecumseh, Chau-be-nee, the Coal Burner, the uncle of Mr. Bourassa's mother (the same who is sometimes called Chambly) was a spy of Tecumseh—full of activity and endurance. He said, that in a council the day preceding the battle, Tecumseh said he was satisfied it would be useless to fight the Americans; that they would succeed; and as for himself he had it revealed to him that he shall fall in the impending fight tomorrow noon; but "am willing to go with my people, and will be guided by your wishes." That he loved his friends and people too well to see them sacrificed in an unequal contest, where no good would result from it— and that while he would dissuade them from engaging in the fight, he would nevertheless yield to their desires in the matter. That when he shd. fall, he urged them to retreat, as further fighting would be useless. The Indians insisted on fighting a last fight. In the fight, Tecumseh was among the foremost, and did as he counselled others, that

---
[50]Drake, Benjamin. *Op. Cit.*, 199-219.

when the Americans fired, they would fire too high, and *then* for the Indians to rush in.[51]

By 1840, the many partisans, noted in our own different stories, were engaged in acrimonious discussion as to the identity of Tecumtha's slayer. The leader of the Kentucky forces, which were a part of the wing which attacked the Indian section in which Tecumtha fought, was Colonel Richard M. Johnson, a member of Congress from Kentucky. He was candidate for Vice-President of the United States in 1840. A popular slogan of that campaign was:

"Humpsy Dumpsy,
    Col. Johnson killed Tecumseh."

Its jingle persists among the recollections of the present older generation. The following quotations, taken from the writings of Colonel William Stanley Hatch, bear directly on Tecumtha's death:

"Colonel Johnson informed me, and also stated in his campaign of 1840, that he did not pretend to say the Indian warrior he killed was Tecumseh. He was not acquainted with Tecumseh's personal appearance."[52] The description given by him of the warrior he killed did not fit Tecumseh, but did fit the known battle dress and personal appearance of a Winnebago chief who fought by Tecumseh's side. It may here be noted that the myth that Tecumseh "wore a ring in his nose" at the time of his death or at any time in his life, was a figment from the imagination of some one of the many historical writers of rumors in the period which followed. Those who personally and intimately knew the chief, and others who frequently came in contact with him, have left no such story. It was not his nation's habit to slit their noses, or to require it of their captives who behaved themselves. Even so refractory a captive as General Simon Kenton was not subjected to this indignity.

---

[51] Draper MSS., 23 S 165-169.
[52] Hatch, William S. *Op. Cit.*, 151.

TECUMTHA

*Speech of Colonel Richard M. Johnson
at Lafayette, Kentucky, October 17, 1840.*[53]

After the address of Mr. Hannegan, Col. Johnson proceeded:

... I suppose you want me to say something about the battle of the Thames. I had trained my men from the first to charge in column. They were the hunters of Kentucky. When I found we were going to have a battle I told my men, if any of them felt afraid to meet the enemy, to go back home and tell their mothers and sisters and I knowed they would soon send them back; for I never knowed a lady a coward in my life, (immense cheers). (Here a few sentences were lost, the close of which was) I intend to keep in with the Dutch and the Irish. Well, when we overtook the British, we found them on the Thames and it was as beautiful a river as ever flowed.

I said to General Harrison I had trained my men to charge in column and asked leave to bring on the attack. I knowed my men, they were the hunters of Kentucky:— they were the men that Pakenham boasted that he would give the beauty and the booty of New Orleans; and the ladies run to Old Hickory for protection, but Old Hickory and the hunters of Kentucky soon taught the British that they couldn't come in. (Cheers). General Harrison said to me, Colonel Johnson charge them, and I will go back and tell Governor Shelby and Cass and the rest of them; for there were several that had volunteered as General Harrison's aids, for we were all anxious to catch Proctor, but he was like the Captain I once heard of that when they were about coming into an engagement told his men that he knowed they would get whipped and how and they might as well give up, and as he was a little lame he would start a little while before the rest. He ran away anyhow, and we didn't catch him and I reckon it was well enough.

I wanted to catch Proctor, and I thought a good deal about what I should do with him. I wanted to bring him home that our people might look at him and see the monster that had been so cruel to our men when they fell into his hands; but my men were Kentuckians and I knowed if they got hold of Proctor they'd eat him up; for you know a Kentuckian is half man, half horse, half alligator (Cheers).

---

[53]From the Lafayette *Free Press*. Reported for the *Free Press*, by Benjamin Henkle, Esq. Reprinted from the Lexington *Intelligencer*.

There are so many Kentuckians here, I feel almost at home. I didn't know but the blood would become adulterated by comin' out here, but I find it doesn't, but that it grows higher and higher. (Cheers).

I had 1000 men in my regiment: I commanded 500 and my brother James 500. My brother James attacked the British and I attacked the Indians. (Here followed a long story about the nature of the ground on which the battle was fought and showing the great advantage our men had over the British). I had four brothers along with me and two young nephews, sons of my Brothers; one of them fourteen and the other sixteen years old and I had several cousins. In all I suppose I had about 20 blood-relations along.

When brother James charged through the British lines, they made no resistance at all. Brother James said it was less trouble to take them than to know what to do with them after they were taken. They seemed anxious to give up their arms,—one Irishman came to brother James and asked what to do with his arms, Brother James said he had never thought of that, but the Irishman said if your honor pleases we'll stack them, and brother James ordered them to do so. . . .

I asked General Harrison to give me leave to bring on the attack, (a voice from the crowd—"Where was General Harrison?" Hannegan,—"Don't answer him, Colonel, it is not a friend that asks the question.") I asked General Harrison to give me leave to bring on the attack and the General he told me to do so; and I went back to my men and told them if they were afraid to meet the enemy to go back; but they were Kentuckians, they were the hunters of Kentucky; I knowed them well; many of them were my neighbors and a good many of them had been Indian fighters. I knowed there was not a coward among the whole lot, and here I must make a political reflection:—Democrats are you afraid to meet the enemy, are there any cowards among you? I would recommend to the Democrats to fight as my regiment did. You have a great many things to fight against; the Whigs have told a great many lies. If I could get a vote for every lie they have told about Mr. Van Buren, I would be sure to be elected: one member of Congress has told you a great deal about the gold spoons that Mr. Van Buren has bought, and there they are, the same old spoons that I used to eat with in the time of Mr. Madison. That is one lie, so that is one vote I would get.

Well now I'll talk a little about myself again. It has been published in some of the papers that I was taken off the ground at the commencement of the action: this is not true; I never left the ground till the British was taken and Tecumseh killed: and as soon as it was known that Tecumseh was killed the fighting ceased.

I fought it out, but I was pretty badly wounded. I received one ball in my left leg which makes me limp a little, and I received another ball in my thigh which is there yet, and another in my arm which went in here and came out there, (holding it up and showing).

When I was about to bring on the attack some of my men would keep getting ahead of me, but I told them if they would only keep up with me I would lead them into danger enough.

I selected 20 men that I knowed I could depend on as a forlorn hope. I was determined that we wouldn't play at long taw with them any more; and I was determined that we would make short work of it; so we charged upon them in three columns two abreast, so that we had the advantage of them. They could only shoot at two of my men, while my men could shoot at their whole line; I placed the forlorn hope in advance of the rest, so that here was the charging columns, here was the forlorn hope, and where was I? right here in front. (Cheers). Well, we charged on the enemy and in five minutes 19 of the forlorn hope had fell from their horses killed or wounded or thrown from their saddles. Some of their horses wouldn't stand fire, but my grey mare that I rode, would stand a cannon-shot and never start in the least. I was afraid that my horse that I generally rode wouldn't stand fire and so I changed him before the battle commenced for my grey mare that I knowed could be depended upon, but it is very few animals that would stand fire as she would; and so 19 of the forlorn hope was very soon either cut down or thrown from their horses.

I told them to take it on foot, and so we fought on for a while, but I soon saw a large but likely-looking Indian who seemed to be a master-spirit among them. Some said it was Tecumseh. I cannot tell whether it was or not, but many of my friends think it was; but I could see that he was a master-spirit and I thought if I could get a fair chance at him, I would soon end the battle for he appeared to be the master-spirit amongst them.

I advanced toward him, but there was a fallen tree

between us, which I had to ride around before I could get within pistol-shot of him. I started to go round the tree top; my mare stumbled and fell to her knees for she had been wounded, but with some difficulty she rose again and started. I started on up the tree or log, and as I paced up the log, he paced down; but remember my pace was a walk for my mare could not go out of a walk. I let the Indian have the first fire. He fired and I received his shot in my arm the ball going in here and coming out here, but it did not disable me much for I run my arm through the bridle-rein: you know we often tie a knot in the rein anyhow, and so I just run my lame arm through the rein and when I came within pistol-shot I found he was flourishing his tomahawk, but before he got ready to throw his tomahaw I fired my pistol and shot him right through here, and his heels flew up and he came down like a tobacco hogshead. I never saw a man fall so heavy in my life. (Cheers). The fighting ceased immediately, except by General Thompson about a fourth of a mile off, and this was what may have misled Captain Davidson to suppose that I was taken off the ground early in the action. Captain Davidson claims that he fought on after I was taken off the ground and gained the victory: but I know he was mistaken, he may be honestly so, and I think it quite likely he is, but I suppose he claims that he is the hero of the Thames so that we have three heroes of the Thames and I'll give up my claim.

I shall now read to prove that I asked General Harrison to permit me to bring on the attack. It is so stated in General Robert McAfee's history. (The reading, however, was not done).

I planned the battle and asked General Harrison's leave to bring on the attack. General Harrison was not in the fight but was where I always thought he ought to have been, with the main army ready to lead on the battle in case I fell, and I think it is a good deal more to General Harrison's credit to be placed where I place him than where his friends wish to place him.

The first indirect evidence that Tecumtha was dead came from across the border in the spring of 1814, when it became certainly known that Lady Prevost, at the governor-general's residence, had given many mourning presents to Tecumtha's distinguished sister, Tecumapese. The status of information on this side of the border is further set out in Colonel Hatch's *History*.⁵⁴ Here again was illustrated that line of demarcation in the dark skinned races, past which even their best white friends are not permitted to go. The information sought was "none of the white man's business." Shawnee Indians, related Hatch, in 1837, after the Battle of the Thames and the second Greenville Conference in 1814, came in large numbers to Cincinnati for purposes of trading and obtaining supplies. They often numbered several hundred, and camped in the woodland north of the town. A number of men then resident in Cincinnati had been captives in their boyhood, and knew many of these Indians from a playmate and "pardner" standpoint. Intimate as this relation had been, these men were not able, at any time, to obtain from their Indian friends any information as to Tecumtha's death. Hatch relates further:—"No Indian I have seen, has with certainty known it."

Of the death of Tecumtha, General Harrison, the commander-in-chief of the American forces, remained in ignorance. No one but the Indians certainly knew of the great chief's passing. Those who know them, know that no personal danger to them could have prevented their retrieving their leader's body. This they promptly did almost under the lights of the fort. "It may be doubted," Eggleston wrote, "after close historical examination, whether anyone ever did know who shot the chief. The Americans who saw him shot did not know him from any other plainly dressed Indian, and the Indians who saw him fall could not identify the slayer." That his death was not certainly known in the army for a long time, is finally established beyond all doubt by Dr. David I. Bushnell, Jr., of the Smithsonian Institution, who has contributed for this narrative, with his own imprimatur, a copy of the priceless historic letter of General William Henry Harrison—April 9, 1834—to Colonel John O'Fallon of St. Louis:

Mch. 13, 1928.

My dear Dr. Galloway:
It affords me great pleasure to send you a copy of the

---

⁵⁴Hatch, William S. *Loc. Cit.*

letter written by Gen. Harrison, concerning the death of Tecumseh. It is an exact copy, spelling and punctuation the same. Use the letter as you desire.

The original is so closely written, the ink so spread, that a photograph when reduced to page size would be quite useless, therefore, I am sending this copy.

I believe you will find this to be of considerable interest. It certainly covers the various details which you mentioned, and may offer other clues.

Very truly,
(Signed) D. I. BUSHNELL, JR.

"North Bend 9th April 1834

"Dear Colonel

"A most vilanous attack has been made upon me in a paper recently established at Washington City for the support of Col Johnsons pretentions to the presidency, titled The American Mechanic. It seems in a history of the late War published in London the Author expressed his surprise that I had not mentioned that Tecumthe was killed in the battle of the Thames & by the hand of Col Johnson. Upon this text the writer in that paper of the 29th ult. comments upon me in no very marked terms. The article was sent to me by my friend Genl Tipton of the Senate who advises me or some one to reply to it. Fearful that I might have forgotten some of the facts I determined to write to you, Col Todd & Major Chambers to see whether our recollections agree.

"In the course of the evening after the action I learnt that there was a French Man amongst the prisoners who asserted that Tecumthe was killed. Either that eve or in the morning I went to see this man (who was woonded & soon after died) & he said that he was mortally woonded & I think that he was taken off by the Indians. In the course of the following evg I went to examine a body which I understood some persons supposed was T— Commdr Perry & several others (perhaps yourself went with me). We found the body alluded to naked & having some strips of skin taken off the back. The face was so swollen that altho I thought it was either T. or a Potowatemie chief whom I had been accustomed to see with him yet I could not positively say which it was or indeed whether it was either or not. I would not have recourse to any of the British to determine that point because of the mutilation above mentioned. I do not recollect whether it was at

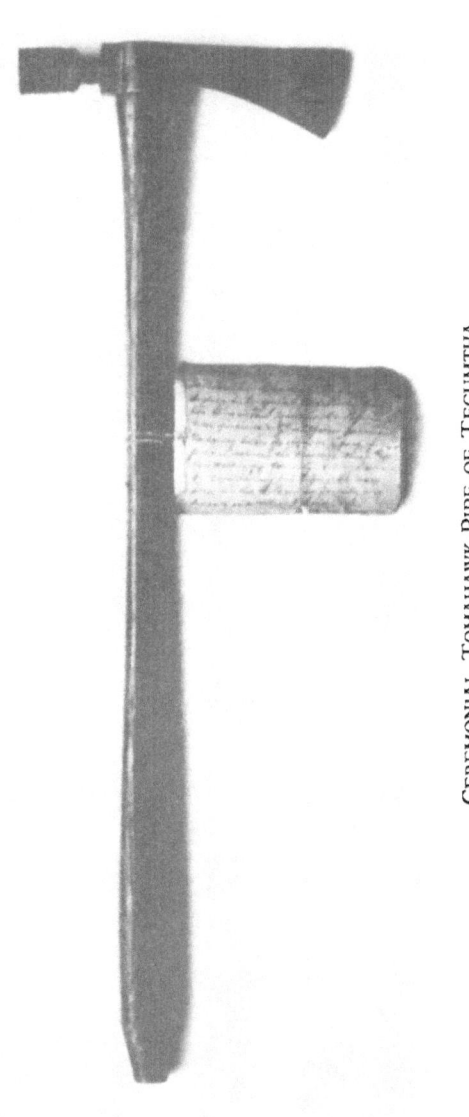

CEREMONIAL TOMAHAWK-PIPE OF TECUMTHA

Used in celebrating the Pact of Peace and Friendship between the Shawnee Indians and James Galloway, Sr., and his family, in 1797. Used again in 1926 at the ceremony of the renewal of this pact. Now in the Museum of the Ohio State Archaeological and Historical Society

TECUMTHA

Detroit or after we went to the Niagara frontier that I learnt that the Hostile Indians acknowledged that T. was killed & that they had returned to the Moravian Towns to bury him. The British writer asserts that the body of T. was recognised by Cmdr Perry & other American officers who knew him well and by the British officers. Now there was not an officer nor man in our army who had ever seen T-e in their lives but myself. The British officers were removed in the morning of the 8th to a house some distance below & none of these to my knowledge with the exception of two who were permitted to come to the camp to search the packmen of their Army for their baggage which they had plundered. When I went to visit Col Johnson soon after the return of the troops to the encampment he told me that he had killed one of the Indians who had assailed him. But he at that time did not dream of its being T--e. He J— knew no more of T-e than the latter did of him. It was not for a long time after the action that I heard that it was supposed that Johnson had killed T--e. When I did hear it I considered it very probable from the circumstance that Jn had told me that he had killed an Indian that it was the Chief. Altho I also heard that others of the Corps had laid claim to the honour. Col Todd informed me in a letter some time ago that the majority of the Corps assigned the honour to a man of the name of King of Lincoln.

"Until Johnson told me that he had been wounded by the Indians I did not know that he had come in contact with them for it was not my intention that he should. I did not mention the death of T-e in my official letter because of its uncertainty. I could not of course say that J- had killed him.

"Will you be good enough my dear Col to write to me immediately upon the recpt of this & give me your recollection of the points above mentioned. Even if I had known T-e was killed I could not say that it was even by one of Johnsons Corps because the Infantry on the left were also engaged with the Indians.

I wrote to you 8 or 10 days ago
In haste your friend
W. H. HARRISON"

To Colonel John O'Fallon,
St. Louis, Mo.

OLD CHILLICOTHE

"IF A MAN DIE, SHALL HE LIVE AGAIN?"

*The Shawnee legend that Tecumtha will live
again and come to them*

From a time so far distant that it fades into the shadows of antiquity, the heart of man has looked upward as it cried out, "If a man die, shall he live again?" The answer, which seems the same in every age, expresses the universal longing of the human host—*To live!* In the hearts of mankind, the heroes of their own races dwell on Olympus, and there await the hour of a triumphant return to restore the lost fortunes of their own kind. Such a legend gathers about Tecumtha, the lost hero of the Shawnee race. It is, however, unusual, as tradition places its origin before the hour of the battle in which he lost his life.

The Shawnees relate that Tecumtha divested himself of all insignia of his rank before the battle of the Thames so that, after his death, which he foretold, the enemy would not recognize his body and prevent its recovery by his own warriors. He took the ramrod from his own gun and gave it to a party of his own men, instructing them that when they saw him fall, they should fight their way to where he lay and strike his body four times with it. He would then arise and, with his life renewed and charmed against further harm, would lead them to victory. History relates that he was seen and heard in the thick of the fight, leading his men and encouraging them with his commands, and that the Indian retreat became precipitous when their commander's voice remained silent and his form was no longer to be seen. The warriors, charged with his command to reach his body and strike it, were unable to reach it. Their failure to do so and its unexpected consequences demoralized the entire Indian contingents of Proctor's army. His death and failure to return bearing a charmed life, was quickly known by every Indian in this battle, and without awaiting its issue, which was at that moment holding well for them, they fled almost in panic. The power of mass psychology seized them to their quick undoing. The tradition of what is yet to come is a living expectation—one of the nation's most sacred traditions. "Tecumtha will come again!" In that hour, there will be *"nakude-fanwi udawa,"* or "one town of towns," as fulfilled once in the ancient Allegheny country. This "second coming," the fulfillment of another "town of towns," will be in the future when it pleases the Great Spirit. It will mark the end of strife, wars and contentions among all Indian tribes. Then the celebration will consummate all that the Great Spirit intends for his red children. It will begin in the spring, and continue without ceasing, from tribe to tribe, until the season closes. The sign of this will be another star appearing and passing across the sky, as it did at the time of Tecumtha's birth, and Tecumtha will again be born under the same circumstances, to lead his people to this future "one town of towns" for all the Indians—the Indian Valhalla.

"If a man die—shall he live again?"

THE DEDICATION OF TECUMTHA'S BIRTHPLACE

In the presence of the Regents of Catharine Greene, George Slagle and Cedar Cliff Chapters of the Daughters of the American Revolution, all of Greene County, Ohio, and their assembled friends, Thomas Wildcat Alford, great-grandson of Tecumtha, designated the birthplace of his great ancestor, Tecumtha, at the place where the Shawnees located it, and gave the location to the records of this patriotic society on September 4th, 1928. His address given on this historic occasion was as follows:

Regents of the Daughters of the American Revolution and friends: In honor of the location, according to Shawnee history, of the birthplace of my people's greatest statesman and leader, I am able to state for your records that there is no dispute among our nation as to the birthplace of Tecumtha being here at these springs where we now stand. This ravine, with its fertile valley and the hills surrounding it, the fine spring which we remember, and this distance of a few arrow-flights from our ancient village of Old Chillicothe which at first was Pecuwe—Peccaway or Piqua—and its direction toward the mid-morning sun from the village, are all in agreement with our tradition and history of our leader Tecumtha's birthplace.

Our way of handling history is from mouth to ear. We have no system of dates as you have. We date any important event in our history as so many moons before or after some notable or unusual occurrence. In that way we get our records in mind. Also, in reference to the lay of a river or a peculiar elevation of land, we keep in memory everything in nature of that kind for the benefit of our traditions and history. We have many things in our traditions that have never been written. I shall, here, speak to you about an ancient one concerned with my people and yours.

Back about the time of, or just before, the Revolutionary War, there was great agitation among the Shawnees as to what was best to do to preserve our nation from being destroyed. This agitation lasted a number of years. Meesawmi, or the essence of our religion, grew out of this agitation. Everything of importance that took place was done in accordance with it.

Part of our chiefs gave counsel that "we had better make peace with the white people, as they are outnumbering us and increasing fast. It seems God is with them. Let us make peace with them and be always in peace with them." The other part, consisting mostly of warriors, said, "No! Let us not make peace with the white people. Let us fight them until they destroy every one of us." Discussions were held for several years, until finally a division occurred which still exists among us. The Shawnee division is at Oklahoma. The other division incorporated themselves into the Cherokee nation, one of the five civilized tribes of today, living 65 miles northeast of Shawnee, Oklahoma, around Tulsa and Vinita.

In order to find out the best thing to do to preserve the Shawnee nation, secret councils were held in the temple or council-house. Two clans, the Kispokotha and Peckuwe, have always been closely allied. They had their councilhouse at Old Chillicothe where many great councils of the allied nations were held in times past. At these meetings, they discussed a great deal about what to do to preserve their nation. In order to be near this temple, *Msikumequa*, the chief, Pucksinwa, Tecumtha's father, and my great-great-grandfather, moved his clan, the Kispokotha, from the plains of the Scioto River to Old Chillicothe in 1768. On the way, Tecumtha was born near these large springs distant from Old Chillicothe about as many arrow-flights as the fingers of both hands, and in direction from Old Chillicothe towards the mid-morning sun. A temporary hut was put up, and there they stopped for the night. While the women were around waiting on Methotase, mother of Tecumtha, a brilliant light flashed across the sky, and they saw an immense star. They called it "Panther." It was a spirit passing over to the south where it sought a deep hole for sleep. Every night it passes somewhere on the earth to go to that home in the south. I presume that is what is called his (Tecumtha's) *umsoma*. While the star was passing, the women were excited about it. "One passed across," they went in and told Methotase. Tecumtha was born, and was given this name which, in our language, means "passing across" and "Panther."

I have been over this country once before, but the lay of the land and hills, and the great spring, all near to our Old Chillicothe, indicate that, without a doubt, this is the place where our traditions say Tecumtha was born. This location near Old Chillicothe indicates it is the exact place. I am glad to say that I have seen it with my own eyes, and I will now have a better idea of it to tell my people when I get home.

The ceremonies at this preliminary marking were unusual. Following a high tribute to the character and career of Tecumtha by Judge James Johnson, former member of the Ohio Supreme Court, Mr. William Henry Harrison, a direct descendant of the Virginia Harrison family of General William Henry Harrison, Tecumtha's foe and conqueror, prepared the ground for the placing of a small commemorative flag as a temporary site mark. The flag was presented to Thomas Wildcat Alford, the great-grandson of Tecumtha, by Mrs. Frank A. Jackson, Regent of Catharine Greene Chapter, Daughters of the American Revolution, and by him set in the place prepared for it by General Harrison's kinsman. The regents of the three Greene County Chapters of the Daughters of the American Revolution, Mrs. Frank Jackson, presiding, Mrs. Charles Erwin and Mrs. W. W. Johnson, with the past regents and other Daughters present, then recited "The Pledge to the Flag," completing, with this ceremony, a cycle of 115 years following the death, at the Battle of the Thames, of America's greatest Indian statesman and leader, and 160 years following his birth by the great spring, which is now marked as the place of his birth.

THE PACT OF PEACE AND FRIENDSHIP, 1797

Outlines of the story of Tecumtha's courtship of Rebecca Galloway, and a picture of the Galloway chair are given in Howe's *History of Ohio*.[55] The courtship—a notable incident in Ohio pioneer history—has been referred to by other writers of early date. Details of the story, as one of the interesting events in her own history, were related by Rebecca Galloway to her descendants at various times. Tecumtha's visits to the new pioneer home began soon after the settlement of James Galloway and his family near Old Chillicothe in 1797. Rebecca was then a little girl past six years old. The new pioneer home of her father and its strange environments, with the large Indian village nearby, caused her early concern and fear, and she related that she would frequently run back to the home, and hide herself under the bed, or in the loft of the cabin, when Tecumtha and the other Indians began to come to her father's home. The Galloway chair, shown in Howe's *History* and reproduced in this volume, was the guest-chair of the household.[56] This distinguished visitor usually sat in it during his frequent visits there.

In the first pioneer cabin of James Galloway, Sr., in 1797, a notable and unusual event occurred, expressing the good-will of the Shawnee Indians to their new white neighbor and his family. In it, Tecumtha used his own ceremonial tomahawk-pipe, which was filled with kinnikinick, and smoked by him and his host, after which the handle was touched by the other members of the family in the order of their ages. This act was emblematic of the purposes of the compact. After the ceremonial this towahawk-pipe was presented by Tecumtha to his host as a token of their inviol-

---
[55] Howe, Henry. Op. Cit., 1:706.
[56] Now in the Museum of the Ohio Arch. and Hist. Society.

TECUMTHA

able agreement, and has been kept by each generation of the Galloway family as a priceless historic possession. It passed by will to the writer in 1914.[57]

THE RENEWAL OF THE PACT OF PEACE, 1926

In September, 1926, the writer was the guest at Shawnee, Oklahoma, of Thomas Wildcat Alford and his family. Mr. Alford is a great-grandson of Tecumtha, and his guest, a great-grandson of James Galloway, Sr. The group picture of this family and their guest, taken on the lawn of his home, shows Mr. Alford holding his distinguished ancestor's tomahawk-pipe. The taking of this picture had been preceded by a renewal of the pact entered into 129 years before. The tomahawk-pipe was filled with tobacco, and then relit by Mr. Alford. The ceremonial of 1797 was then reenacted in the Shawnee language by his host and his family and their guest. This ceremony, coming from out the distant past, and again entered into by those who are blood descendants of the same relation to the first enactors, was epochal to those who took part, and was as though surrounded by the approving spirits.[58]

REMARKS AT THE RENEWAL OF THE PACT OF FRIENDSHIP AND PEACE

Made in Shawnee language, September, 1926, by Thomas Wildcat Alford

Ne tabawa tfwi gikvtu gita neswrpitvgi gita jrkvtfwi, mahdrcimowa si wihgrnadewa macimi grmrnelafewa macdwrdeki msi msi ki mahsomfanv, Tikvmfa, macimi wihgrnvli James Galloway si wefoli betiga mvivgi yadrlici utqi-kvhi. Hina gahtv lr Srwvnu yrsvyegi u tasi fvgifwrli ki gahgirmanv, Tikumfa, vlv-yolumv u daghrkvni uqrkvnvli macimi u tasi daphrli wihgrnvli, welv uci macimi wecigamu

---

[57]Now in the Museum of the Ohio Arch. and Hist. Society.

[58]At this event, Dr. Galloway was given a Shawnee name. His visit with Mr. Alford was concerned with obtaining the Shawnee history of the Old Chillicothe period for more permanent record, and for presenting Shawnee historical viewpoints, which have not been consulted and recorded by our own historians.

yasi Srwvnwvnki bonv-mvwr-wrci uwasi tahawa takusiyawi lanvwahi wvhsi grmrne si lanvwawemr-wrci nihi; chena nili uwasi wihgrnvli, James Galloway li, weci-gamoli nili yatfwi kvmigi-filici. Mvtv-lrqv puskunota yomv wihgrnadewa brlu hinugi.

Huwa ini uwasi-nrqvtwi macimi uwas-fanwi yasi mrwvtusgr-ivqa inugi wvhsi nughi-nvmv-wvqa yomv wihgrnadewa nauhalvqa, W. A. Galloway, u mvyrwi odosrkvnvli nivhgi James Galloway, macimi vwvqa inugi grsagigi vlv-yrmv inv wihgrnadewi uqrkv pvivh nemrwrci u laciwrgi qelrni nihki neswi ki gahgirmanrki, yasi inugi pvh nemvgi ni lacigi yalvhfvme-ivqa.

Wahi, waciganvhi, n'uqrwafwv yrmv uqrkv yalvhfvme-ivqa, macimi yalvhfvmeci nauhalvqa, W. A. Galloway, macimi yalvhfvme-lici u cvjrlvhku-mvwhi nihki neswi niahkvki ki gahgirmanrki, macimi vlv-nihki ki mahsomfanrki mtaqi-laneki bami sgipv-grnqagrpvwicki gahcitvwvh docki kit vlvwewanv lr mtaku-mesihgi macimi iniv waciganvhi, huwa ni tapvsvuwa, macimi ni weci-mu jrivhgi ki sqe-lanvwa-manv, yasi uwa nuhginvmvwvqa yomv mahdrcimowa si wihgrnadewa macimi grmrnelafewa ki nvuhademanv; macimi srpwi welv jrivhgi nihi yavqalamafici, yasfado-wrci iuhkumv ki gahgirma-nrki sahkvmikv; chena uwa ni fvgifwv yrmv uqrkv (cahi mvtv ki bonrpa gilaginikv) macimi ni tah melv nhihtv, gcimvyrni ki drnfanv, nyawana utvhpvmrli, walr u pahsanrli, noci brluhi gcivlikv yatfwi gikvdo-witv; noci ugiwrli macimi nelv, jrivhki ini ivskv si lvweki; uwa chena ki nvuhademanv Dr. W. A. Galloway ivskv ini inv si lvwi vnkuci.

Huwa galv patagi ni tah bonv yrmv wihgrnadewi daghrkvniuqr kv u lacigi ki nvuhademanv ya-bonr-wrci ki gahgirma-nrki sahkvmi kv tv hvpici inugi yoci.

In giving a translation of the Pact from Shawnee to English, Mr. Alford adds the following note of explanation:

> It is difficult to convey the full sense of some Shawnee words into English sense, and vice versa; to say nothing of idioms of language which cannot be translated word for word. It is also hard to transmit sense from Shawnee standpoint into English, and vice versa; owing perhaps to

(Front row, seated, from left to right) Dr. W. A. Galloway, Na-nvhkunvkv, pronounced, Nay-nah-ko-nah-kah, meaning, "One that catches." Thomas W. Alford, Ganwrpiahsikv, pronounced, Gay-nwaw-piah-si-kah, meaning, "One who strings out long." Fannie T. Alford, Halskunapiahsi, pronounced, Hay-lay-ko-nay-piah-si, meaning, "One was once in water." (Her grand-daughter on her lap) Rosalyn Marie Stacey, Nvtvwrmiahsi, pronounced, Nah-tah-wawmiah-si, meaning, "One hunting a path." Martha Alford, Wedrkvmsi, pronounced, We-daw-com-si, meaning, "One also in wave (of water)." Ruth Alford, Mosvtvwrmishsi, pronounced, Mo-sah-tah-waw-mish-si, meaning, "Always on the way (or path)."

(Back row, standing, from left to right) Rachel Alford, Ufabrmiahsi, pronounced, O - they - haw - miah-si, meaning, "One on clean way (or path)." Thomas W. Alford, Jr., Negrmihsimu, pronounced, Ne - kaw - nih - si-mo, meaning, "One first to say (or voicing ahead)." Pauline Alford, Wesigalamv, pronounced, We-si-gay-lay-mah, meaning, "Thinks him (or her) great." Eugene Alford, Brmihsimu, pronounced, Baw-mih-si-mo, meaning, "Voicing about." Opal Alford, wife of Thomas W. Alford, Jr., who has no Shawnee name.

THOMAS WILDCAT ALFORD AND FAMILY, AND THE AUTHOR

Taken at Shawnee, Oklahoma, after the renewal of the "Pact of Peace," in 1926

TECUMTHA

the fact that the Shawnees view and conceive things from a primitive standpoint; and their words change into many forms to conform with the sense intended. Sometimes one Shawnee word takes several English words to express it, and again the reverse is the case.

I have done the best I could to transmit all the sense in the meaning of my remarks in the Shawnee language made at the Renewal, which are as follows:

THE TRANSLATION

One hundred and twenty-nine years ago, a Pact of Friendship and Peace was made between our great-grandfather, Tecumtha, and his friend James Galloway, Sr., in the new log-cabin home of his friend. In accordance with an ancient custom among the Shawnees, our ancestor lighted this his tomahawk-pipe, and so presented to his friend, for himself, and with expression that the Shawnees had good feelings (good heart) for the white people, that they desired to live in peace with them; and his good friend, James Galloway, Sr., did the same for himself and for his entire family. This Friendship was never broken.

It is fitting and becoming, as we are now gathered today, to renew this Friendship to our visitor, William Albert Galloway, and to use now the same Pipe of Friendship, which our two ancestors held in their hands, as I hold it now in my hands before us.

Let me, therefore, fill this Pipe in our presence, and in the presence of our visitor, Dr. Galloway; and in the presence of the spirits of our two departed ancestors; and of these, our grandfather's tree-men standing with green hairs, guardians of our hunting-ground of the forest; and declare, which I now do, that this Pact of Friendship and Peace is renewed to our visitor and guest on the part of ourselves, and voicing all our generation of Shawnees; and through him to his dear ones, as established by those our ancestors long ago; and now I light it (alas, we have no kinnikinick) and present it first to our youngest daughter, who draws four times or touches it; thence on to the oldest; thence to their mother and myself, who all do likewise; then to our visitor and guest, Dr. Galloway, who does accordingly.

I now place this Tomahawk-pipe of Friendship in the hands of our guest where it will be henceforth, as placed by our ancestors long ago.

SHAWNEE DOMESTIC AND TRIBAL LIFE

Sketches from Old Chillicothe and Later Periods, in Manuscripts of Thomas W. Alford

VALUABLE contributions to Shawnee Indian history have been prepared for this volume by Thomas Wildcat Alford, Keeper of Records of his nation. These narratives describe the building of their homes; the cultivation and uses of Indian corn (maize); the training and parental direction given to the Shawnee boy and girl in the "Wegiwas," the family home, known to us as the "Wigwam." In another work of great spiritual value, to which years of studious devotion was given, Alford has also preserved the language of his people in the translation from the King James' Version of "The Four Gospels of Our Lord Jesus Christ," into the Shawnee Indian language in 1929.

These and other contributions place us under obligation to him for records, preserved to history, which otherwise would soon have passed into the realm of uncertain tradition. It will be appreciated by students familiar with the difficulties of white historians, in obtaining the facts connected with Indian history from Indian sources, that this history is from the pen of an Indian, whose position as historian of his nation is official, and whose education and experience are equal to the important task of preserving it in correct detail in his narratives, free from conclusions drawn from casual information, imaginative descriptions, and poor translations. They may, therefore, be accepted as narratives of fact from that section of interesting American racial history, of which Alford is still a living part.

The negative psychology which has characterized the American Indian's attitude toward the historical narratives that concerned him, especially in the interrelated events of his own history with ours, is here, as in other parts of this book, given release in approved narration, or in portions written by the Indian historian himself. This change of attitude was due to the belief that the time had arrived in their co-relations with the civilization, of which they have now become a more active part, when their own historical connections to the past, as preserved in their traditions, should become a part of their country's history.

BOYS' AND GIRLS' NAMES AND GAMES

When I was ten days old, I was given a name, in accordance with the custom of our people. Some friend of the family conferred my name upon me (the conferrer, in most cases, was an old person) and I thereupon belonged to the same *Umsoma* as the person who named me. The name given me was Gay-nwaw-piah-si-ka ("one of long following, or file," as the leader of a drove of wild horses) which was soon shortened to Gay-nwah, for the same reason that Thomas is shortened to Tom. No surname was used among the Shawnees.

If I had been a girl, I would have waited two days longer, before I received my name, which would, in all probability, have been the same with the last syllable left off to denote gender. It would have been the same, if the same *Umsoma* had been desired to be represented in the name, for a child is classed with the person who names him, and is considered to be under the same kind providence, or care. This clan division is the occasion of strong partisanship, and much pleasant rivalry among the Shawnees. It is simply a social division, and should not be confused with the real clanship of the tribe, which determines the chieftainship, and in fact the very existence of the tribe organization, and is fully explained in another chapter.

I was never told anything that would indicate that I was different from other little Indian babies. Boys were usually more desired in Indian families than were girls, and I suppose that, as I was the first boy born to my parents, they were very proud of me, and gave me, perhaps, a little more attention than was usually accorded a baby. I know that my parents were considerably above the average in intelligence, and gave their children more care than many of our people gave to theirs.

My mother carried me on her back, strapped securely to a board called a *tkithoway,* as did other Indian mothers of that time. This *tkithoway* was carved and ornamented according to the taste of the parents, even as a baby carriage of today is indicative, often, of the pride and prosperity of the parents. Indian mothers carried their babies on their backs for several reasons; the first reason was the safety of the child. Wild animals often invaded the settlements, and it would not have been safe to leave a young child unprotected in the crude cabins, or wigwams, of those days; then the mother's work often took her away from her home for hours, and she generally had some burden to carry besides her child, as she went about her daily tasks. With the child securely strapped to its *tkithoway,* and that swung on her back, her arms were free for the work to be done; to carry utensils for work, a jug of water, or whatever the burden might be. Another reason for strapping the child to a *tkithoway* was to make the little back grow straight and strong; then, too, the little head was bound closely to the flat surface to make it grow flat, so that when the child reached maturity, there would be a flat spot on the back of its head where a plate would fit, to which would be attached an eagle feather, the desired head-dress of a Shawnee brave.

Indian children of those days were as healthy as little animals, and even in play did those things that strengthened their muscles and developed their bodies. Running, swimming and jumping were matters of course with us, and the older men encouraged boys to shoot with bows and arrows, and to practice those things that developed accuracy and skill in hunting.

A favorite game when a group of boys played together was one that taught skill in shooting at moving objects. A hoop was made out of a wild grape-vine bent around until the ends met and lapped a little, and tied securely with strips of bark. It was then woven closely with bark, making a thick, strong and perfectly smooth hoop. The group

SHAWNEE CUSTOMS

of boys "chose sides," even as white boys do in playing games, and stood in lines facing each other. One party rolled the hoop along the ground towards the opposite party of boys, who shot at it with their bows and arrows as it passed along. The boy whose arrow stuck into the hoop was the winner; and then those of the opposing side stuck their arrows into the ground, and the winner tossed the hoop flatwise to the row of arrows to knock them down, and as many as he succeeded in knocking down, became his own. This game was something like the game of "keeps" I see small boys playing today with marbles.

Then we had a game we played with smooth round stones; and we sometimes found peach-stones that we whittled into balls, that we played with after the manner of marbles. We played ball, too, but the game was not played as boys of today play baseball. All the games we played developed strength and resourcefulness. We had no toys but those we made ourselves, as I have described. We wrestled and rode the ponies, fished and hunted, and set traps for birds and rabbits.

Indian girls were never allowed to play with the boys. In fact, from the time little boys learned to walk, they felt a sense of superiority to their sisters, and a boy who played with girls, or who would have done so, was a subject for ridicule. Little girls played much the same as little girls play today, imitating their mothers, I suppose, making mud cakes, and especially learning to mold vessels of clay. They "kept house" and mothered the smaller children, just as I have seen my own little girls doing in recent years.[1]

HOMES AND FAMILY LIFE

It must be remembered, that our people lived principally on game and corn, and that hunting formed the principal

---

[1] This authoritative history of Shawnee tribal or home life, coming from first sources, will be fully appreciated by all students of Shawnee sociology. Much of it has heretofore been a closed book. It will be welcomed into the records of American history.

occupation of the men. The women of the tribe, with few exceptions, did most of the real labor, such as the planting and cultivation of corn, dressing game, and even of building our wegiwas or houses. The term teepee, as we understood it, was used by naked or plains Indians of the West, as distinguished from timber, or woods Indians from the East. A teepee is a movable tent of hides, rush mats, or cloth in a conical shape, held up by poles brought together at the top and tied securely together. The wegiwa, or wigwam was fixed and not removable, and made in square form or oblong, like the house of bark or hides with vertical walls and sloping roofs.

In building a wegiwa the bark was obtained by first severing it from the body of a tree as it stood, mostly from elm and birch, with an axe, or some other sharp implement, around the bottom as well as above as high as could be reached; then disjoining it from the top cut, clear down to the lower cut. Into the opening thus made was inserted a flat wedge-shaped end of a hard seasoned stick, prepared for this purpose, and pried open into a whole sheet of bark. This was easily accomplished in spring and summer when trees were in sap. Then the bark was laid flat on level ground with flesh side under and weighted down with small logs, and allowed to dry to a certain extent, but used while still soft and pliable.

The poles were cut of straight young trees, and set into the ground at regular distances apart, outlining the size desired for a wegiwa. All bark was peeled off the poles to keep worms from working in them. Two of these poles, with a fork at the top of each, were set opposite each other at each end, and at exactly half way through the width of the wegiwa, and tied securely thereon with strips of tough bark. This formed the top comb of the roof, to which the rest of the poles were bent at a suitable height of the walls, and secured there with strips of bark. Then upon, and across these, were laid other poles, at certain regular distances, from the top comb, down the slope to the end of the roof, and on down the sides, to form walls. Upon these cross-poles were laid the sheets of bark to close the roof and walls, held firmly in place by other poles laid on the outside of the bark, and tied by strips of bark to the poles within.

These wegiwas were waterproof, and afforded far more comfort in extremely cold weather than one would think, for there was a skill in their construction that was the cause of much friendly rivalry. Constructed as they were without the use of saw, hammer or nails, they mutely testified to the neatness and pride of their owners and builders, even as do the homes of the working people of any community today.

Some of our people made their beds in somewhat the same manner, by driving four forked sticks into the ground, and upon these were laid two long poles, that were a support to shorter poles laid crosswise, and all securely tied, making a firm smooth support for bedding. Others not so industrious merely spread their bedding upon brush laid on the floor of their wegiwas.

Moving, then, was a simple matter, as wegiwas or cabins could be built easily in a few days, and were abandoned with little concern. We had little in the way of household effects; a few clothes, buffalo robes, blankets, cooking vessels and the crude utensils and implements used in carrying on the work about the camps.

Our moving, too, was a prolonged journey, for we often camped in a locality for weeks, or even months, waiting for floods to subside, or for one reason or another that suited the fancy of the leaders of our people. There was no cause for hurry, no business awaited our men's attention. Sometimes a crop of corn was planted and harvested before the journey was resumed. There were very few wagons, and the family effects were tied in bundles and strapped on the backs of the horses, or carried by the women through woods and over mountains and hills and boggy swamps. Streams were forded, or when too deep and swift for that, rafts were made.

The women also cared for the ailments of the tribe, whether on hunting migrations, or back in the home village.

They were skillful in setting fractured bones. At one time I was thrown from a wild pony I was riding. My arm was broken! I felt no pain just at first, but as I took hold of it with my other hand, it began to pain me, and I was scared frantic. I made the woods ring with my howls, as I hurried home to mother. She shamed me for making such a noise, appealed to my manhood to endure the pain quietly, while she was hurriedly examining my arm. Then she made me as comfortable as she could, while she hastened to prepare a bandage, for which she was known to be very skillful. Going to a creek near the house, she took a limb about the size of my arm from an elm-tree. Then she very dexterously slipped the bark from the limb, and placed it about my broken arm. She pulled the bone into place, adjusted it carefully, and bound the bark comfortably loose about it, with a dexterity that is seldom used except by skilled surgeons. I was kept quiet, given plenty of cold water until the fever had passed, and in due time my arm was perfectly healed.

Like other Shawnee women, she had a knowledge of medicinal plants and their uses in sickness, which was rare among us. Many of the favorite botanical remedies used by white doctors now were well known to the Indians and first used by them, even before the "pale-face" came to the great Northwestern Territory.

It was about the year 1868 that my father and mother, with the other members of their tribe, returned to the country then known as the Indian Territory, and were told to select their permanent homes. For eight years they had wandered from place to place with no settled home, but their family had increased. Often we had slept on the ground, with no roof to shelter us, yet our family life had gone on. On our hunting trips or migrations, the care and training of the children was given as much thought as when we were living happily in an established community. I believe many people will be surprised to hear that Indian parents realized just as much responsibility for the training of their young as any other race of people.

RELIGION AND MORALS

In matters of religion, Indians were considered heathen, but we were not pagans; we believed in the existence of a SUPREME BEING, whom we designated as MONETO, who ruled the universe (*yalakuquakumigigi*), dispensing blessings and favors to those who earned his good-will, and bringing unspeakable sorrow to those whose conduct merited his displeasure. The Great Spirit is spoken of in the personal neuter gender (although the pronoun "he" is used), because there is no masculine or feminine gender in the Shawnee language. Men and women are spoken of as of the same gender, and only the name of the individual contains the discrimination. Personal pronouns are neither masculine nor feminine, and most of them are mere affixes to other words.

The Great Spirit, or ruler of destinies, was believed to be a grandmother, who was constantly weaving an immense net, which was called a *Skemotah,* and it was our belief that when the great net was finished, it would be lowered to the earth, and all who had proven themselves by their actions to be worthy of the better world—the happy hunting ground—would be gathered into its folds—and the world would then come to an end. Some horrible fate awaited those who were left. We were always taught that good conduct would earn a reward, and that evil conduct would bring sorrow. We had our own religious beliefs and convictions. Our standards were just as rigid as the laws of any other people, but force was seldom used to obtain good conduct. One point that I want to emphasize, and make strong and clear, is that among primitive Shawnee Indians, morality was a fixed law, but *each person was his own judge.* From early childhood this principle was instilled into our minds, and deceitfulneess was a crime of itself. We lived according to our own standards and principles, not for what others might think of us. Absolute honesty towards each other was the basis of character. Apparently, without that which the white race considers "good breeding," there were standards and rules of conduct that were followed scrupulously. Utterly without those commonly known to society, we, or I should say they, observed certain forms that were inflexible, and followed by even the most ignorant of our people, chief among them being consideration of the rights of others. They had never heard of the "Golden Rule," but it might be considered the foundation of all their intercourse. They expressed it in their language in the following form:

Tagi nsi walr mvci-lutvwi mr-pvyaci-grlahkv, xvga mvtv inv gi mvci-lutvwx, gi mvci-ludr-geiv gelv. Walv uwas-panvsi inv, waciganv-hi gi gol-utvwv u kvgesakv-namv manwi-lanvwawewa yasi golutv-mvni geyrgi.

Tagi bemi-lutvwi walr segalami mr-pvyaci-grlahkv, xvga mvtv inv gi bemi-lutvwv, gi bemi-ludr-geiv gelv. Wakv vhqualami inv, xvga nahfrpi Monetu ut vhqualamrli nili yasi vhqalamahgi gelv! And so on.

The translation of which is as follows:

Do not kill or injure your neighbor, for it is not him that you injure, you injure yourself. But do good to him, therefore add to his days of happiness as you add to your own.

Do not wrong or hate your neighbor, for it is not him that you wrong, you wrong yourself. But love him, for Moneto loves him also as he loves you.

In this form—giving a reason why one should not do this wrong or that wrong—is a sort of boomerang to the evil-doer. If this spirit was lacking in their intercourse with other races, who can say that it was not justified? If cunning and deception were resorted to in the dealings with the white people, it was pitted against a wisdom that the red man felt powerless to cope with on a common ground.

The Shawnees had no officers, no jails; but misdeeds did not go unpunished. Punishments were of many kinds, and were determined by the gravity of the offence. Our chief's word was law and any persistent refusal to obey the unwritten code of honorable conduct was punishable by severe flogging, or even by death. Any one refusing to take his punishment like a man was ostracized from his tribe, to which death was preferable. Nor were the women of our tribe free from the law. The most heinous crime of which a woman could be convicted was that which we called *pockvano-madee-way*—gossip about people.

If some of our beliefs were based on superstition, it must be acknowledged that they are not unlike the teachings of Christianity. The main point of difference is that our people believed *they only were responsible for their conduct towards their own race*. To others they owed nothing, *except to return in kind the treatment they received*.

EDUCATION

The training of the young, then, formed an important part in the life-work of our people, and was not neglected, even though the family had no fixed place of abode, nor established household regulations. In fact, I believe that the men of our race take a greater interest in the training of their sons than do the white people with whom I have been associated; for the white men generally leave the moral training of their children to their wives; while pride of offspring is one of the strongest factors in the lives of our people.

All of our lessons were learned from our elders. All of our histories, traditions and codes, were passed from one generation to another by word of mouth, and always accurately memorized and translated. We had no books, no printed rules; our memories must be kept clear and accurate; we must be taught keenness of observation, and above all, taught to be absolute master of ourselves.

Every father was a teacher of his sons, every mother sought to instil into her daughter's mind those things considered essential for her to know; nothing was left to a public teacher, or to chance. To begin with, children were taught respect for their elders, which virtually means respect for authority. Not only their own parents, but all who were beginning to show an advance in years assumed some degree of importance and authority.

It is often remarked that Indians take to institutional training better than white people; make better soldiers; better subjects for discipline; and it is true. Indian parents give few commands, because they are advocates of freedom of character, and children are seldom punished. But obedience is exacted from the beginning. A few words of praise from a parent or an elder is regarded as the highest award or prize that could be given for good conduct.

Our people appreciated superior wisdom of any kind, but naturally they thought more of that wisdom that formed the background of our own racial life. A knowledge of warfare, of history, and of nature, and the habits of wild creatures; an acquaintance with trees and all wild plants, wild fruits and their use; to be able to judge of weather; to foretell what seasons would be and to recall those past, this constituted a well rounded education for our men.

All these things called for a good memory, keen observation and close application. Endurance and self-control were taught so rigidly that those qualities became natural with us. It was a proud and happy day when an Indian boy realized that his father considered him old enough to begin actual training.

TRIBAL GOVERNMENT

To fully understand the divisions in the Shawnee tribe, and the functioning of its different bodies, as well as the government of the tribe, one must be familiar with the different clan divisions, and the general history of our people. It must be borne in mind, too, that a tribe means the whole body of a nation or people, while a clan represents the different groups or divisions that constitute the governing body. In fact the clans form a government that is somewhat like our national government. The principal chief corresponds to the President of the United States, and the other chiefs correspond to the governors of the different states, or the heads of the different departments of government.

SHAWNEE CUSTOMS

Originally there were five clans that made up the Shawnee tribe or nation, the names of which are preserved in colonial history, the Cha-lah-gaw-tha (generally known as Chillicothe), the Tha-wegi-la, the Pec-ku-we, the Kis-po-ko-tha, the May-ku-jay. Each clan has a certain office or duty to perform for the whole tribe; for instance, the Peckuwe clan, or its chief, has charge of the maintenance of order or duty, and looks after the celebrations of things pertaining to our religion or faith; the Kispokotha clan has charge of matters pertaining to warfare, the preparation and training of warriors; the Maykujay has charge of things pertaining to health, medicine and food. But the two powerful clans, the Thawegila and the Chalahgawtha, have charge of things political and all matters that affect the tribe as a whole. They are equal in power, and from one of them the principal chief must come, because of the *Mee-saw-mi*, which is the potency of life. The chiefs of the other clans are subordinate to the principal chief in all matters of great import to the tribe, but their chief is independent, an authority in the matters pertaining to his own jurisdiction.

The Thawegila, Peckuwe and Kispokotha clans have always been closely related, while the Chalahgawtha and Maykujay clans stood together, and while there might be slight dissensions and perhaps jealousies at times among the different clans, as a whole the Shawnee people have stood together and held the same ideas and traditions. When the clans were separated, they maintained communication and held council together whenever questions of importance affected them as a people.

[Eventually the three clans mentioned separated from the Chalahgawthas and the Maykujays and migrated to Spanish Territory in the spring of 1779. They resided there for a number of years on a Spanish land grant. Later they moved to Old Mexico, later the State of Texas, and finally to Indian Territory—now Oklahoma—where they now reside. This section of the nation is known as "The Absentee Shawnees." The segregation, as noted elsewhere, was due to different views of their nation's policy, and occurred after some years of formal consideration in meetings at Old Chillicothe. Those of the nation who favored peace with the white invader of their country, and adoption of his methods of life, emigrated West. Those stayed who were in favor of war till the last Shawnee should fall in battle.

There are other notable instances in the history of the Shawnee nation when a positive stand was taken on the questions affecting their best interests. One of these decisions on a question which seriously affected both their tribal and personal lives was definitely dealt with after serious consideration in their council. Alford relates this history, which may be verified if the reader desires to do so.]

It is permissible here to digress a little, to note the fact that the Shawnee Indians were the first body of people to advocate prohibition. According to colonial records of Pennsylvania, they first took action on April 24th, 1733, requesting Governor Gordon that "firm orders be sent" to "break into pieces all kegs of rum brought into their town." And on May 1st, of the following year, they dictated a letter to the governor and his council, asking that no trader be allowed to bring more than thirty gallons of rum in a year into their territory, and added that if more was brought they "would stave his kegs, and seize his goods."

Four years later, on March 20th, they reported to the council of Pennsylvania that after holding a council, they concluded "to leave off drinking four years. That they had staved, and spilled, all the liquor in their towns, belonging to both whites and Indians, which consisted of about 40 gallons, thrown into the streets." This report was accompanied by a pledge signed by 98 Shawnees and two traders, agreeing that all liquors be spilled; that four men were appointed in each town to see that no rum be brought for the term of four years.

Our chiefs and rulers maintained a dignity and a courtesy towards each other, even in their most intimate association, that I found painfully lacking in the intercourse of many of the white men with whom I have been thrown.

GUEST CHAIR OF THE PIONEER GALLOWAY HOME
Tecumtha sat in this chair during his frequent visits in the Galloway home. The chair is now in the Ohio State Museum

Believing that all natural things were sacred, there were no cheap or ribald jokes about the functions of nature.

It is a little difficult to explain the supremacy of the ruling class of the Shawnees. Although we were absolutely democratic, believing that all men (all Shawnee men) were born equal, we accorded to our leaders, our chiefs, an aristocracy that was spontaneous. There was no vacillating between different leaders. Once a man established his reputation for bravery, for wisdom and discretion, he became an object of admiration and confidence, for those qualities could not be assumed, they must be born.

Shawnee men were absolutely honest with each other. Whatever cunning or deceit they might practice toward others, they looked upon as permissible, even as some white men maintain that "business is business, you know," when trying to explain some of their transactions. Among Shawnee Indians this shade of dishonesty does not exist, or if it does exist, it is looked upon as a heinous crime.

FOOD AND ITS PREPARATION

The Shawnees developed varieties of corn, suitable for different food dishes.[2] They were also skillful in preserving and preparing it for family use. This and other food information is here given.

As corn (rightly called Indian corn) was our staple food, it may be interesting to note some of the methods of preparing it, for it was used in many ways besides that of making bread.

When I was a child, corn was planted and cultivated

---

[2] Varieties of Old Chillicothe grown corn are yet preserved among the Shawnees. A flint corn, with solid good sized kernels and opaque pearl-colored hull, was used for hominy. A corn with a white appearing hull, deep or narrow grain, a soft flour-like white kernel and small cob, was used for bread flour. A large medium hard grain variety was used for corn meal. There was also a quick maturing small-eared corn for early roasting ears and succotash. All varieties were white. An attempt to acclimate them here again, in 1927, was unsuccessful.

by the women and girls of the family in most Indian homes. But some of the more industrious and energetic of the men helped their women, until gradually the practice became general, and was finally taken over, as it should have been long before it was.

As we had practically no storerooms, no cribs to hold our corn, because of the migratory habits of our people, it took a great deal of ingenuity to keep a supply from one year's crop until another could be grown and harvested. The usual method was that of stripping back the husks or shucks of the corn without breaking them off, and braiding them together securely, in long ropes, with the ears dangling. These ropes were hung inside the cabins, or wegiwas, high up against the roof, when the family had no other storehouse. Very few families raised enough corn to feed their horses over winter, but there was always an abundance of hay, which, with other growth, kept the animals in good condition.

One favorite dish made from roasting-ears was called *weskupimi*, and was prepared in the following manner: a ditch or trench was dug about one foot deep, piling the soil removed at each end of the ditch to serve as a support for two long poles of green wood, laid lengthwise of the trench. But before the poles were laid across the trench, hickory logs were burned in the trench, until there was a bed of glowing, red-hot coals. Then ears of corn that had been carefully husked and trimmed of faulty spots, were placed on end on the ground, a row on each side of the trench, with the tips resting against the green poles, and roasted. They were watched carefully and turned often, so that the milk of the corn was cooked, and the grains were toasted a delicate brown. After they were thoroughly roasted and cooled, the grains were broken from the cob with a blade made of bone, or a dull knife, and dried in the sun. It was then stored for winter use.

When eaten this corn was cooked in water; sometimes meat was added and, properly seasoned, it was a delicious food. The rich flavor imparted by the hickory coals was especially liked.

Another way of preserving fresh corn with its peculiarly delightful flavor, was by grating it from the cob, making a soft, milky mush, which was then poured into an iron oven or baking kettle with a close-fitting lid, and baked very slowly and carefully, until it became a solid cake. This was called *nepanwi-takuwha* (production bread), and when eaten it was prepared much as we prepare commercial cereals now.

There were other ways of preparing corn for food after it had become ripe and dry on the stalk. One of the most favored was called *takuwha-ñepi* (bread water) by the Shawnees, and *afke,* or *sofke* by the Muskogee Indians, who must have taught it to the Shawnees, for we call it *sofke* generally, and that is a Muskogee word. In this preparation the flinty variety of corn was used. The corn was brayed or pounded in a deep mortar with a pestle, until the skin covering the grain was broken and separated from the kernels, which were then taken out into a broad, shallow, woven basket, called a *lawasqahthika* (wafter), and wafted in the open air until cleaned of all skins of chaff. It was then boiled in water until the kernels were thoroughly cooked and it became a heavy whitish fluid. Then more water was added, and a small quantity of seeping fluid (made by letting water seep through clean wood ashes), was added to the corn mixture. All was then poured into a large wooden vessel and covered. This was set away until it fermented, then it was ready for use, and would keep indefinitely. It had a most pleasing taste, somewhat like a sweet-pickle, and was constantly kept on hand in an established hospitable Indian home, and always offered to visitors.

Another way of preparing ripe corn of the soft starchy variety was somewhat like hominy. The grains were boiled in water mixed with clean wood ashes, until the skins would slip from the grains. Then the corn was washed in clear water, until thoroughly free of skins or husks. It was then cooked in a kettle, well seasoned, sometimes with meat, until very tender. This was called *suhdaywali* (swelled grains).

Another great delicacy that my mother often prepared

was made of the flinty variety called *osahsawbo*. It was made in the same manner as *takuwhaw-nepi* mentioned above, except that the seeping fluid was left out, and it was not allowed to ferment; but instead pecans, walnuts, or hickory nuts were pounded and added, and all cooked together. It was a delicious food and one that we especially enjoyed—nothing equal to it.

As for our daily bread, our Indian women brayed or pounded ripe corn, of the soft starchy variety, in a mortar until fine. It was then sifted through a sieve, the coarser parts being returned to the mortar, and pounded again, until it became a fine meal, or flour. This was made into a dough with water, sometimes mixed with wheat flour and baked in the iron kettle or deep oven with fitted lids, on which coals were laid. Sometimes the cakes of dough were wrapped in clean corn-husks (several layers, moistened) and baked in hot ashes until thoroughly done. The delightful flavor of bread baked this way can not be described, and is known only to a few experienced campers.

Another way of preparing corn-meal was called *golthawali* (emergency meal). This meal might be kept indefinitely, if kept dry, and was prepared in the same way as the other meal, except that the grains of corn were thoroughly parched before being made into meal. This form of corn-meal was always kept by our people for use in any emergency, such as a sudden journey. It was an emergency ration of the warrior or the hunter, who never made a journey without some of this food. It was carried in a little bag inside a larger bag of buckskin, and was very much condensed. A small quantity stirred into a cup of water made not only a good drink, but a nourishing meal in itself, and would sustain one for many days in an emergency when no other food could be found.

There was also a kind of bread called *skepulhawna* (blue biscuit) made from this meal. A small quantity of a peculiar kind of ashes was put into the meal, as is done with soda these days, and with water the meal was made into a heavy dough of a bluish color. It was moulded by hand into a sort of three-cornered biscuit that was dropped into a kettle of boiling water. When thoroughly cooked these biscuits had a pleasing flavor entirely their own. They were very solid, and of a deep blue color, and were sometimes dried and kept for future use, being re-boiled when needed. The ashes referred to were made by burning matured bean husks on a flat rock. They produced a pure white ash, that was stored in bags by our women and kept as we now keep soda.

At this point it may be interesting to note how our mothers made their sieves and other baskets used for culinary purposes, for it was done with a skill that is now a lost art. They obtained their material by cutting down a hackberry, or false elm-tree, of the size they wanted. A section of the tree-trunk clear of any defects was chosen and carefully barked the desired length. The trunk of the tree was then pounded, gently but firmly and thoroughly, with the flat edge of an ax; every fraction of the surface receiving its gentle beating, until the layers of wood that represented the different years' growth became loosened, so they could be peeled from the trunk in narrow, uniform strips. These were woven so closely they would hold water. Some were woven to be used for sifters of meal, and others to grade grains of corn, letting all under a certain size pass through. Marvelous, the ingenuity of those women! It was an arduous task, but baskets once made could be used a long time. However, one of the commodities most eagerly sought after from the Indian traders was a white man's sifter.

As to other foods, we had many kinds of game in the olden time, but as the years passed, and the country became more populous, of course the game dwindled more and more, until a squirrel or an opossum became a rarity. Fish, too, that used to be plentiful in my boyhood in the streams of the country, are a thing of the past, except for an occasional lucky day, when a pitifully small string can be caught. And I want to say that for fine cooking of meat, the women of my boyhood time had the best of it over the modern methods. Meat broiled over an open bed of coals has a juicy tenderness that cannot be equaled in the finest kitchens. A duck or squirrel wrapped in wet corn-husks and baked or roasted in hot ashes cannot be surpassed.

We had also an abundance of wild fruits—strawberries, dew-berries, blackberries, plums, cherries and grapes. Papaws were abundant in some localities and were a very delicious fruit when fully ripe. I believe they belong to the banana family. Even the lowly persimmon was not despised, for there were several ways of using them. As a general thing we only used fruit when fresh, and that just picked seldom cooked. Our mothers had no preservatives to keep fruit, nor any cans to keep it fresh, yet those fruits that could be easily dried were collected, dried and stored for use during the long winter. For instance, the humble persimmon was carefully cured and highly valued as a food. From it was made a cake that resembled a date cake of the present day, which was called *muchahseeminitakuwha* (persimmon cake). This fruit is very rich in sugar and, when freed of seed and a kind of fibrous core that gives it a puckery taste, it is very pleasant to taste. When so treated, the remaining pulp was kneaded into oblong cakes of a uniform size and thoroughly dried in the sun. When needed for use, it was freshened by steaming in hot water, or it was very palatable eaten dry. Other fruits, such as plums and berries, were similarly prepared for drying, some slightly baked before being dried.

There was a favorite dish that mother used to make, called *psgibhaw* (sour food, a misnomer), that was delightful to my sense of taste. It is made of wild grapes that are first slightly scaled, so that the thick, rich juice can be pressed from the grapes. The juice is then heated, and while boiling, dumplings are dropped into it and sugar added if we had it.

Sugar and syrup were made from sugar-maple, but when our people were not in the country where sugar-maple grew, they substituted soft maple, box-elder, and even hickory for it, though, of course, the product was not so good. My parents used to talk about the olden times when a great number of our people would gather together during the season when the sap was flowing, and work together making their sugar and syrup. Of course, that was before they came to the Indian Territory, for real sugar-maple does not grow in this part of the country.

As I look back over the years and recall the hardships and privations endured by our people, my heart aches with pity, then swells with pride, when I think how nobly they combatted the odds that were against them. Our mothers knew nothing of a balanced diet, they had never heard of calories or vitamines, they had no markets to supply delicacies and out-of-season vegetables. They must rely on their own industry and skill to provide food for their families, yet they did that with never a complaint, and with a cheerfulness that should be an inspiration to the present generation. Little Indian children of that day and time were as healthy and generally as happy as little animals. It remained for civilization and the white man's system of living to make invalids of a large number of our people.

CEREMONIALS AND RECORDS OF TIME

As our people had no almanacs or calendars, records of time were kept only in memory, but even to me it is a wonder how accurately they knew or could calculate the happenings of the seasons. Today, I cannot tell the season more correctly than could my father, or mother, reckoning by the moon and the signs of nature. Thirteen moons made a year, and dates were kept by fulling or waning of the moon; the position of the sun being used in the same way. Dawn and dusk, sunrise and sunset, and when the sun was high in the sky, were significant hours to be observed.

Certain stages of the moon were to be observed in almost every work that was undertaken, and in this I have seen similarity in the white race, since some superstitious persons insist upon planting potatoes, or other seeds, only in certain periods of the moon. I have known white people who would not make soap, or clapboards for roofing their cabins, except before the moon reached its full, believing that if they did so, the soap would all shrink away, and the clapboards would curl up at their loose ends on the roof.

One of the most sacred rites of our people was called the Bread Dance (*Takuwhaw-nagaway*), and I am glad to say that it is one of the customs of our fathers that is still followed, though not with the sincerity and faith that characterized those I remember in my childhood and youth. The Shawnees believed that before they planted a crop, or started the work of a new year (the latter began with the advent of spring and not by the white man's calendar), they should hold this Bread Dance, when the Great Spirit would be implored to bless the people, and give them a bounteous crop, and a peaceful and prosperous year. Contrary to the white man's idea of religion, the Shawnees believed that in order to obtain a blessing they should show a merry spirit, and a contented countenance. Therefore, when we sought a blessing, it required an occasion when all were gay and cheerful, and we looked forward to the spring Bread Dance as to our most festive occasion. Really the Bread Dance opened the rejoicing and festivities of the spring and summer, when all nature seems to be happy, and not until after this important ceremony would any one venture to plant a crop, or start any important undertaking.

The time for the Bread Dance was determined as follows: Early in the spring when the buds began to swell on the trees, the birds began to sing and chatter, and the wild ducks and geese to depart for their northern homes, the air became warm; and soft winds blew from the south, the sun rose earlier, and the days grew longer. Observing all these evidences of the passing of winter, the people began to make preparations for their festival of Bread Dance. *But the dance could not be held until after the full of the moon.* As the Bread Dance is considered a religious rite the preparations for the dance and festival are under the supervision of the chief of the Peckuwe clan who, by virtue of clan, had charge of all matters pertaining to the Shawnee religion or relating to the Great Spirit. There are two standing committees, one of twelve men, and the other of twelve women. These committees are appointed by the chief for life or during good behavior. Each group has a leader who was appointed by the chief.

Here again we see a vast difference between the

customs of the white people and our race. Only young people generally dance, among the whites, while the presence of the very old members of our tribe is desired at our dances to lend dignity and honor to the occasion.

The committees are designated *Naynahowaychki* (preparation utterers), or *May-yaw-wa-thech-ki* (those in line by birth). When the proper time arrives, and is recognized by all the people, the chief assembles both of the committees and makes his appointments to fill vacancies if any exist.[3] He informs them that the time has arrived in which to perform their duties to their people and to the Great Spirit. Very solemnly he repeats to them the tradition connected with the festival, the dance, and its proper observance. He sets a date for the twelve men to begin their hunt for the game required for the feast. Only certain kinds of game should be used for this feast, namely, deer, wild turkey, quail or grouse and squirrel.

After all the instructions are patiently given to the committees, the chief opens a ball game that is peculiar to this event, in which the men play against the women, and all the people that so desire may take part. Whichever side loses, provides the wood for the fires at the Bread Dance. As the grounds are lighted by bonfires at the time of the dance, the preparation of the wood for the event is no small matter, but whichever side loses the ball game, cheerfully and merrily undertakes this necessary part of the preparation.

The twelve men begin at once to get ready for the hunt. They set out prepared for a three-days' trip, not forgetting to take along some of the parched meal which is always carried by hunters as an emergency ration. Those who are to procure the wood make sure there is enough to provide for the cooking of the game, and for bonfires which illuminate the dance grounds for as many nights as they expect to continue the frolic. All the people gather at the designated place and camp, awaiting the hunters, who return on the third day at sunrise. They are relieved of their game at the

---

[3] Nancy and Nellie, two of Mr. Alford's sisters, are members of the women's committee, today. Nancy, the elder, is leader of her group.

dance ground by the women's committee, who prepare and put it to cook.

After they are relieved of their game and all the people are gathered at the place for the dance, the twelve hunters enter at once into the dance, in single file, the leader at the head of the line. Four songs are sung by the singers, who sit at the west side of the dance ground and beat on drums as they sing, in a rhythmic, monotonous strain. The men move in solemn, graceful, slow movements in a circle. When four songs sacred to the occasion are sung, the dance is ended for the time being, and breakfast is brought to the twelve hunters. The people wait quietly for the next part of the dance.

When the game is all cooked and a great quantity of bread prepared in several different ways, it all is brought and laid on a clean white cloth in the center of the dance ground, and carefully covered over with another white cloth. Then all the people gather round it, and a prayer is offered by a man versed in the ancient customs and forms as handed down from one generation to another, by word of mouth, from time immemorial. He is generally an orator. He asks the Great Spirit for fruitfulness for the coming season; that they may be given an abundant crop of corn and beans and pumpkins, and for the general welfare of the people; for success in their undertakings, and voices an eloquent prayer for an increase of game. He thanks Him for the success of the hunters during the winter, and for all the good things that have come to them during their whole lives.

After this prayer or declamation, for it is usually a wonderful piece of oratory, the serious side of the occasion is over, and the people begin the dance proper, which is as follows: The women congregate in compact form in front of the singers, who continue to sing as they beat a rhythmic, weird music on their tom-toms. The women sing with them, and move with a slight swaying motion of the body, right and left. At certain places in the song, a phrase is rendered ridiculing the weakness of human nature. This phrase, when sung by the men, is directed against the women, and when sung by the women, is directed against the men. In spite of the reticence practiced, exclamations can usually be heard in the crowd that shows their sympathy with the singers. The women in the crowd would exclaim, "The women conquer," or the men would cry out, "The men have conquered," showing a pleasant, friendly rivalry or partisanship between the sexes.

After this dance comes the dance around the ring by the two committees mentioned before. Twelve men dance inside the circle, and the twelve women dance outside, each side being led by its appointed leader. In this dance all of the people may take part, but they must follow the committee, and under no circumstances must one break into or enter the file. This dance continues at intervals during the day, until late in the afternoon, when all partake of the feast. The men of the committee distribute the bread and the women the meat.

At dusk the frolic dance begins and is continued all night. When men and women dance together, as they sometimes do, it is not as partners, as white people do, but one behind the other. The dance usually closes at sunrise, when each family departs for home, tired but usually happy and full of hope, and a glorified feeling of having appeased the Great Spirit. The dances that follow the Bread Dance, such as the Green Corn Dance and many others, are for frolic and fun. Each has its own set of songs and customs, but they are not considered obligatory. The Bread Dance is and always was observed strictly according to the accepted custom. In the olden times corn was never planted until after the Bread Dance, and as full moon sometimes appeared late, then the corn was accordingly planted late, which often resulted in a short crop, despite the eloquent prayer of the master of ceremonies at the dance.

In some dances—frolic dances—the men and women join hands to form a circle, but not side by side as white people do. The man holds his hand behind him, and it is taken by the woman, with a handkerchief in her hand. She in turn holds her hand out behind her, to be taken by another man. In this dance the young woman is permitted to select the brave she wishes to dance with, by simply taking her place behind him.

The Shawnee young people of today seem to have adopted the white man's way of courtship, as they have his way of marriage. I believe the young women rather like to be talked to about love, and are not so willing to take that emotion for granted.

Another sport that was much enjoyed by our people, was a ball game which was played by both men and women early in the summer. But after the month of June, as we counted the season, the ball game closed, with a pretty ceremony that put the ball away until after the Bread Dance of the next spring. (See Judge Burnet's description in his *Northwestern Territory*.)[4]

All the rules and ceremonies were known to all the people, and they were respected and observed, kept sacred and inviolate.

About the middle of August the chief of the Kispoko, or Kispokotha, clan, who has charge of all things pertaining to war, holds a war dance. We call this *Ilani-wagaway* (man dance or brave dance). This may be followed by other war-dances, for frolic only, until the end of the season.

About the end of September, the dance is held which closes the season for dances until the next spring. This is similar to the early spring Bread Dance, except that it takes the form of a thanksgiving ceremony, when a prayer of gratitude is offered to the Great Spirit, and a petition for an abundant game season.

SOCIAL LIFE OF THE SHAWNEES

It is a little difficult to describe the social life of the Shawnees of fifty years ago, though contrary to prevalent notions, the Indians were given to much sociability among themselves. They were after all just human beings with all

---

[4] Burnet, Jacob. *Op. Cit.* Pt. 2, v. 1:57-58.

the human desires for comradeship and congenial association with their fellow-beings. The greatest difference that I have found in the social life of the two races—Indians and white people— is the deference paid to age, and in the association of the sexes. In all our gatherings and in our home life, the older people "had the floor," so to speak. They were given the consideration and deference of the younger people, and their counsel was listened to with respect.

We were taught so thoroughly to guard our expressions, to control our passions, that it became a second nature; perhaps I might even leave out the "second." So complete was this control that an Indian's face has been likened to a mask.

But to return to the subject of social life. Consider that we had no newspapers to disseminate the doings of our people or the news of the world at large; there were no shows, no places of public amusement, and there was comparative leisure for the enjoyment of such things, because the simple life we lived did not demand continual effort to provide necessities. Hence visiting was much enjoyed. There was little strain on hospitality, for a visitor usually contributed something to the larder of the host, and sleeping quarters meant simply a shelter from the elements.

The men enjoyed hunting together. Parties would go out together and hunt during the day, and sit about their campfires at night and talk. The national history was a subject that was ever new and interesting, the traditions often being embellished by the lively imagination of the speaker. The stories relative to one's *Umsoma*, or against the *Umsoma* of the other parties present, was one phase of story-telling that gave vent to the wit and humor of the narrator. (The *Umsoma* is a purely social classification, largely determined by the clan into which one is born or adopted.)[5]

The Shawnee language is peculiar in that it contains few or no idioms and does not lend itself to light and familiar speech, but it is effective in oratory and in dignified

---

[5] For discussion of the *Umsoma*, see last section of chapter, "Indian Stories."

speech. Our belief that all nature was animate, sympathetic and responsive gave color to the speeches of our chiefs. When the warrior Tecumtha made his famous speeches in behalf of the confederacy of the different tribes of Indians, his references to Mother Nature were considered merely poetical, but in reality they voiced the sincere belief of his people. On one occasion he cried, "The very trees of the forest drop tears of pity upon us as we walk beneath them," which only illustrates that feeling of actual kinship that existed in his mind.

When I was a child we had a distant relative, *Maygilawfani*, who visited us occasionally. He was a good story-teller and when he was with us, our neighbors would gather to hear him talk, and we would sit about the fire and listen for hours. For him mother would always prepare *Osahsawpo* (corn and nuts prepared together), which was his favorite dish.

There were no courtships among our young people as there are today. Usually marriages were arranged between the parents. The parents of a son, seeing a maiden whom they considered would make a fit wife for him, would approach her parents with a proposal for their son. Either party could object, in which case there was no compulsion, but as the parents were more particular than the young people, usually their wishes were considered in this matter.

However, young people did sometimes arrange matters for themselves. For instance: should a maiden like the looks or the manner of a young brave, she might seek a place beside (or behind) him in the dance. If she especially liked him, when he reached his hand back (he never turned his head) when forming the circle, she might give him her naked hand, but if she was not particularly desirous of encouraging his attentions she always held a handkerchief between her hand and his. The naked hand given in a dance, therefore, denoted a willingness to be regarded as a future mate. Then the young man could, if he desired, make further advances. This he did in a very dignified manner. There were no gushing speeches, no protestations of affection, no promises, but a perfect understanding resulted from the few quietly spoken words, the glances, perhaps a handclasp. Yet I believe there was just as much sincere affection between men and women of our race as in any other. Having arrived at such an understanding, the two announced their intentions to their respective families and took up their lives together. Usually there was a period of feasting, each family contributing to the good cheer, and all the intimate friends enjoying the occasion. There was no ceremony, but neither were there any divorce courts. Once in a great while a man would desert his wife, but it was not regarded as the proper thing to do, and with us public opinion or the opinion of our friends made our social life.

There were no positive laws forbidding polygamy, but it was seldom practiced, and was frowned upon by our people with just as much condemnation as do the white people of today resent the intrusion of such a social error (considered from a social standpoint). Our laws did not forbid a man having two wives, but our social system did not approve of such a situation, hence it was avoided. An Indian cannot endure to be ostracised by his people. It may be interesting to note right here, that when the Indian Territory opened for settlement, and old tribal laws gave way to state and government statutes, there was found only one man among the Shawnees who had two wives.

Shawnee men have always worn their hair trimmed short to near their shoulders. They never braid it as other Indians do. We boys wore our hair trimmed short to near the shoulders, very much as the girls of today wear their hair bobbed. But the girls wore their hair long and braided.

We had no hats, but sometimes wore caps made of the skin of a wildcat, a coon or a beaver, with bunches of feathers puffed or stripped from the stem to look like a fine plume, placed on the top of the cap.

Sometimes the girls and women wore a handkerchief tied about their heads, and they often went bare-headed. They wore long dresses of calico or linsey, with skirts gathered full about the waist.

THE PASSING OF A LOVED MOTHER

I was nine years old when my mother died. She had been ailing for several days, and we children knew that there was something unusually wrong with her, but we were not allowed to go into the cabin where she lay. Father told us she was *ahquiloky* (ill). Some of the neighbor women were with her, and a medicine-man from Little River came to see her. A great sadness seemed to hover over the earth. It was only a few days, probably four or five, when as I passed the door one day, I saw that she was carefully covered over, and all the women were silently weeping. Soon father came to where we children were sitting gloomily alone, and told us that our mother *ahsanwah*, vanished or disappeared, an expression that is always applied to the death of a person. A great many people came to the house. Everything was done in an orderly way, and very quietly. There were no noisy protestations of grief. Just a little way from the house a grave was dug, and at the appointed time four men carried the body to the grave, by straps placed beneath it, and lowered it into the grave. After the body was placed in the grave, a silent procession formed at the house, with father at the head, we children next, then relatives and friends.

Between the house and the grave an elderly man stood holding open in his hand a small buckskin bag, which contained sacred tobacco, always used for such occasions. As the procession passed him, each person dipped his thumb and forefinger into the bag, taking a small bit of the sacred tobacco, holding it thus as he passed around the grave, from the foot to the head; there he would slightly stoop while he dropped the tobacco into the grave. (This tobacco is not used in smoking. It is rare and scarce and is found only near Canada where it is indigenous.) The procession continued, until all had passed by the open grave, and returned to the house. Lastly came the elderly man who knelt at the side of the grave. Holding a bit of the tobacco over the grave he made remarks: First, he called the deceased by name, and gave his relation to her, then addressing her he said in effect that she should not allow the sorrow of her children and other relatives to hinder her in her journey to that world beyond, but should go serenely and happily as was intended by *Kuhkoomtheynah*, our Grandmother, or Great Spirit. Then, after dropping a bit of the tobacco into the grave, he continued that it was true her children and relatives were full of sorrow, for that was *wachitah* ("natural;" really this word meant "intended"), but their sorrow would soon be wiped out by the goodness of *Kuhkoomtheynah*. The love they had for her should make her happier in the land to which she was going, and still happier would be their meeting when they joined in the next world, the happy hunting-ground. The man then finished dropping the tobacco into the grave, which was covered by the men who carried the body.

Although outwardly we were calm, our hearts were torn with grief as deep and as sincere as ever children felt for their parents. Some of our neighbors remained with us to cheer us. The women cleaned our cabin and swept our yard and stayed with us until the fourth day, when every one bathed, even our hair, and changed into clean clothing, and a ceremony of cheer was held for father and for us, in which we were advised to lay aside our grief and be happy, for so our departed loved one would want us to do.

This rite of cheer that followed the burial of my mother was used by the Shawnees for all cases of death, only being a little different when a mother with children loses her husband by death. The custom is then as follows:

For the first day after the burial of her husband, a widow is allowed to give way to her grief; then she is advised to choose a man for the sake of her children and herself to take the place of the departed one, to rest herself with sleep, and to take food for the ordeal that is before her. On the third night her friends gather about her, and a cheerful night is passed. The men and women all assume a lively manner and tell stories of the bravery of their men and interesting legends and even jokes, to keep her interested and awake. A preparation of herbs and cold water is prepared and cloths dipped into it are used by the women to wipe her face to keep her fresh and awake.

OLD CHILLICOTHE

As the sun begins to rise, an elderly man, some relative or intimate friend, takes a position at the back of the widow's seat and addresses her after this manner: "My daughter, your husband has vanished, and has left you alone, with your little children. He was a good man" (there follows a long list of his good qualities), "but he is gone. It is not right that you should grieve for him, for he would not have it so. It is right that you should select some man to take his place, and be a father to your little children." He then calls upon her to select the man whom she would like to take his place. If she selects one, then the friends depart, and the two are left alone together, and that little ceremony of cheer was looked upon as a marriage ceremony.

If the widow did not select a mate then, the usual order of selection was used, which was simply the desire expressed by two people to take up the duties of life and of raising a family together. No ceremony was necessary.

Mourning Song of the Shawnees

My boy has gone, my boy has gone
To the happy hunting ground.
He waits for me, he waits for me
Where bear and deer abound.

My boy has gone, my boy has gone
To the happy hunting grounds.
He beckons me, he beckons me
To the land where game abounds.

I hear his call, I hear his call
From the hunter's lodge beyond.

Mother, I await your coming
My teepee awaits for thee,
Deer and turkeys are running,
The land is fresh and free.

Come, Mother dear, I wait for thee,
There is no fear with Manitou.

SHAWNEE CUSTOMS

Shawnee Sunrise Love Song

(Girl)   My teepee door is open wide,
I wait alone, alone for you.
The morning sun will never hide
Your smile so true, from your Indian bride.
Hasten along the forest trail.
No more alone, with me abide.

(Brave) I come! I come! My heart is won.
The trail is plain, your heart is true.
Sunrise is here. I come to you.

(Girl)   O lover, brave, I give to you
My heart, my hand, and now renew
My vow to serve and care for you.
The sun shines bright with morning light.

(Brave) In the morning light
My Shawnee bride
Stands by my side.

(Both at teepee door)
Great Spirit, guide us on our way.
The sun shines bright,
'Tis our wedding day, our wedding day.

PIONEER RECORDS OF SHAWNEE CUSTOMS

An interesting story of the allegorical rechoosing of mates harks back to a date some years before the Northwest Territory pioneer period, and is gleaned from the *Journal* of Christopher Gist, surveyor and scout of that interesting period centering about 1750. This was twenty-five years prior to the visit of Captain Bullitt to Old Chillicothe on the Little Miami River. He also was a Virginia surveyor who, for the purpose of establishing friendly relations with the Shawnee Indians before beginning his work south of the Ohio River in their hunting-grounds, left his surveying party encamped on the south banks of the Ohio, and journeyed alone to Old Chillicothe. He approached the village unannounced, was well received by the Shawnee chiefs, and gained their consent to survey ground for settle-

ment on the south side of the river. At that time—1774—
territory that is now Kentucky still remained the favorite
hunting-ground of the Shawnees, though it lay beyond their
south boundary line (the Ohio River) as established by the
first Fort Stanwix Treaty in 1768. The acquisition of land
seems then to have been an open sesame for family and
personal position and influence, and was a type of specula-
tive wealth much sought after. Later, extensive acreage in
Kentucky and between the waters of the Little Miami and
Scioto Rivers in Ohio, was reserved by Virginia and deeded
to her soldiers of the Revolution as compensation for their
military services.

    In Christopher Gist's *Journal* of 1751, written while he
was on a land exploring journey into the Northwestern
Territory in the interest of the agents of the Ohio Company,
narratives are found which give a first view of the Shawnees, who dwelt at the mouth of the Scioto River and were
in direct contact with the early French trading-posts. At
this point, Gist found a settlement of "40 houses on the
south banks of the Ohio River and 100 on the north banks."
On the north side, the settlement's community center was a
council-house, 90 feet long and tightly roofed with bark.
There was also a large French trading-post, which had been
established there for a number of years. Gist approached
the village on Tuesday, January 29, 1751. His exploring
party fired their flintlock guns to announce themselves.
They were answered by the traders who met them and
rowed them across the river in canoes to the principal part
of the village on the north banks. This part of the village
centered itself about the council-house. It was there that
Gist records his observation of a ceremonial which celebrated an unusual custom in Indian domestic life. The
"courtship story," though probably apocryphal, is interesting as one procedure of early Indian courtship negotiations.
The marriage following a successful courtship was not
ceremonial. It was entered into by personal agreement of
the contracting parties, and their departure from the
bride's teepee to one erected by the groom, or, at times, by
the simpler method of the groom taking up his residence in
the home of his new bride, when agreeable to her family—

an alternative which in our present advanced civilization seems not to be wholly objectionable to the groom. The chiefs, however, permitted no warrior to marry till he had proved to their satisfaction that he had attained sufficient skill as a hunter to provide game and furs for the new establishment.

But let Gist tell his own story:

> In the evening a proper official made a public proclamation, that all the Indian marriages were dissolved, and a public feast was to be held for the three succeeding days, in which the women, as their custom was, were to choose again their husbands. The next morning early the Indians breakfasted, and after, spent the day dancing until the evening; when a plentiful feast was prepared. After feasting, they spent the night in dancing. The same way they spent the next two days until the evening. The men danced by themselves, and then the women in turns, around fires, in the form of the figure eight, about sixty or seventy of them at a time. The women, the whole time they danced, sung a song in their language, the chorus of which was,
>
>> "I am not afraid of my husband,
>> I will choose what man I please."
>
> The third day, in the evening, the men, being about one hundred in number, danced in a long string, following one another, sometimes in a long row, at other times in a figure eight, quite around the fort, and in and out of the long house where they held their council, the women standing together as the men danced by them. As any of the women liked a man passing by, she stepped in and joined in the dance, taking hold of the man's shroud or blanket, whom she chose, and then continued in the dance until the rest of the women stepped in and made their choice in the same manner, after which the dance ended, and the new order of domestic relations was established.

A close search of Shawnee literature and tradition has failed to verify this procedure as a custom of this nation. On the other hand, their marital and domestic habits have been described by a number of writers who were captives, as essentially monogamous, with devoted and faithful relations existing during married life. The story, therefore, seems apocryphal, though coming from Gist, and is gleaned more as an oddity than as the relation of a racial characteristic.

INDIAN BURIAL OF BLACK HOOF

at Wapakoneta, Ohio, 1831

Black Hoof was the last of the noted Shawnee chiefs to be buried in Ohio. At the time of his death, 1831, he was 105 years old. He was equally noted as a warrior and as a peace leader. For many years before his death, he enjoyed the confidence of the white settlers in the Miami valleys. His burial, as described by the Rev. Henry Harvey, the Quaker missionary, is an authentic story of the burial ceremonies accorded to this noted chief by his own people:

On arriving at the residence of the deceased chief, on the day the funeral was to take place, we found the corpse wrapped in a clean, new Indian blanket, and a large quantity of fine new goods, such as calico, belts, ribbons, etc., around and about the corpse, which was laid upon a new, clean slab prepared for the purpose, his gun, tomahawk, knife, and pipe lying by his side. All the Indians present, and there was a large number of them, had their clothes hanging loose around them, their hair also down about their shoulders in the loosest manner, many of them having their faces painted in the ancient Indian style. All the men were smoking, all classes seated near where their ancient, beloved, and faithful chief was laid. He who had been their leader and counselor in peace and war was lying lifeless there before them. They had their eyes set on him in solemn silence—not one word was spoken for hours in that large concourse of people—all felt their bereavement in the loss of him—tears were to be seen in every eye. No one could distinguish between his own children (a number of whom were present) and others; all grieved alike the departure of the great chief; no affectation, but real, heartfelt grief, as of a group of children for the loss of an only parent, and no one left to look up to.

In the yard, in front of the cabin was a very large quantity of meat from wild animals, such as deer, turkeys, etc., the spoil of a two days' hunt by young men selected for that express purpose. Twenty deer were killed, beside a large number of turkeys and what smaller wild animals they considered fit to eat—no tame animal or fowl was suffered to be eaten on that occasion, though there was a large quantity of bread prepared. All this vast amount of provision lay in one pile; stacked handsomely together, and carefully guarded by boys, so nothing should molest it. Although the Indians on ordinary occasions always have a large number of dogs with them at their gatherings, here was scarcely one to be seen. At the arrival of the time to proceed to the grave with the corpse, a few of the choice young men (provided for deceased), arranged the clothing about the body, took four large straps, and placing them under it, one taking hold of each end, started off directly to the place of its final rest. No child was taken along in the procession; my wife had her babe with her; when about starting, an Indian woman offered to keep it for her, which she did, as they feared it might make a noise. The children of the deceased proceeded next the corpse, then the head chief, who was to succeed the Black Hoof in that office, then the other chiefs in succession, then ourselves, and after us, came the whole company.

On arriving at the grave, they all gathered round in a group. The grave was about three-and-a-half feet deep—at the bottom a split puncheon was placed, and one set on the edge at each side, about ten inches wide; the corpse was let down, the clothing of the deceased, which he last wore when in health, laid on his body; his old moccasins were cut in pieces and placed with the rest, but no weapon was put in; then another puncheon was laid over him. This being done, John Perry, head chief, took some small seeds from a cloth, and, commencing at the head of the grave, walked carefully around it, sprinkling them all over it as he went; this done, he set off on the path directly to the house, and in this was followed by all present, except three men, who remained to close the grave. After this was finished, the men went toward the creek, and in about half an hour returned to the house. On their return, the smoking and conversation commenced.

When the company started from the grave, they moved in single file, one after another, not one looking back. On the arrival of those who had filled up the grave, I observed them to commence conversation. I inquired of Henry Clay, one of them, and also a chief, what they went to the water for?

He replied that as I was their friend, he would tell me;

it was to purify themselves by puking, and washing their bodies.

As soon as all had smoked in the company, they commenced their feast, but it being now late in the day, they pleaded with us to remain and partake with them, still we were compelled to leave for home, which was about ten miles.

We attended on this occasion, at the particular request of the chiefs, and I can say truly, that this was altogether the most solemn and orderly funeral I have ever attended; and was said to be conducted entirely after their ancient Indian style. We were the only white people present.

The Shawnees were in a great strait about the time their great chief was taken from them. He, who was the bearer of the remarkable letter of Thomas Jefferson, in 1802, to his people; had visited Washington City and Philadelphia on that occasion; had lived to hear the demand again made for their land; but before that act was consummated, he was gathered to his fathers in Heaven.[6]

To this most interesting story, is added the following quotation from a letter dated December 10, 1928, to Dr. W. A. Galloway, from Thomas W. Alford:

You asked, in one of your former letters, about the funeral ceremony of Black Hoof, in 1831. Henry Harvey, who was present, being invited by the Shawnees, gave a complete narrative—the most complete I ever saw in print —in his *History of the Shawnee Indians*. The only mistake he made was in saying that the Indians used some kind of seeds which they deposited in the grave. It was not seeds, but it was the *Nilvhfamv*, or sacred tobacco, which they deposited.

---

[6]Harvey, Henry. *Hist. of the Shawnee Indians*, 186-189.

PIONEER STORIES WHICH MUST NOT BE FORGOTTEN

IT WILL interest the reader to know that *Pioneer History*[1] from which several "Pioneer Stories Which Must Not Be Forgotten" have been drawn, was written by an Ohio physician who found time in 1848, while engaged in the duties of his profession, to prepare many evidences of the pleasure historical narration gives to a writer who indulges in it as an avocation. Those who may endeavor to visualize his environment will appreciate the many sources, unavailable now, which contributed points of contact with the stirring events and interesting personnel of his day. The stories of *Old Chillicothe* which were written during periods of busy medical practice, have furnished recreation and renewed vision for the serious problems attending a physician's vocation. The compensation therefore has been ample, and the reward already has been received in the happiness brought to Indian friends whom our historians have failed to consult for their viewpoint of history, in which they were as intimately concerned as we.

For the early writer, however, there were experiences and inspirations, and also hardships, that cannot be approximated in the professional life of the writer. There were the long horseback rides with the intimate and almost human companionship of a favorite saddle-horse, through wonderlands of forest and stream peopled with interesting bird and wild animal life. There was the trail with its profusion of native flowers, rich in colors that blend into purple. This basic color, so pleasing to the eye, may easily be seen in the landscape during the early springtime. Then the kingdom of the clouds and sky with its sunsets, and for him very often a sunrise as well; and the subtle powers of night with starlit canopy, from which may be drawn

---

[1] Hildreth, Samuel P. *Pioneer History*.

strength of spirit and quietude of mind, *if one but looks up from the saddle*. And then, the blessing of the most valued pioneer associate—the "family doctor." May I liken this last relationship to the warm rains of the pioneer June, which released and filled the forest with the exquisite aroma of the "sweet knot"? The family doctor and the forest have gone, and the other may never be expected to return.

Stories of pioneer life center largely about the transactions of men. We read them, too often forgetful that women bravely shared every circumstance of human experience that this period developed. The pioneer wife of the Northwestern Territory was as brave and venturesome as her husband. She stood with him and, without hesitation, faced the genuine and stirring experiences that fell to his lot; or if a daughter of the household, she shared her family's fortunes until her own became assured. Lack of historical appreciation has caused us to read into her life a poverty of compensation which did not exist. We think of her as possessing masculine characteristics developed to meet the isolation of her environment, or as a more rugged example of her sex's possibilities when compelled to endure hardship in a situation of danger, that held for her a continuous battle for food, raiment, shelter and the right to live. In a way this was true, but she met those problems without loss of the womanly qualities from which the world has always drawn its best inspirations and its most compelling incentives. In the midst of every danger, hardship, privation and sacrifice of the Northwestern Territory pioneer period, she easily retained those salient graces which always compel man's admiration and assure his progress.

In the introduction to his *History and Stories of Nebraska*, Dr. Sheldon defines the value of pioneer stories and place-tales in the history of a country. The paragraph here quoted is unequaled in American literature for clear definition:

Stories are the harp-strings of history, transforming the past into melody and rhythm. The best stories live forever in the human mind. They greet us in the Latin, Teutonic and Celtic tongues, surprise us in the ancient Greek,

Arabic and Hindoo literature, and astonish us in the rude tales of primitive peoples who have no written language. The demand for a good story is as wide and as unsatisfied as human longing, the search for a new one as difficult and elusive as the discovery of a new element in nature. Stories are the inspiration of patriotism and of home virtues. No land is loved without its place-tales, and no nation became great without the lift of noble examples and ideals in the stories of its common people. Every hill and mountain must find its hero, every vale and prairie its legend, ere it becomes invested with living human interest. With the flight of years, the deeds of pioneers in a new land are transformed into the hero tales and place-legends of the later generations. It is well that in the process what is brave, generous and strong survives; what is common, mean and trivial perishes.[2]

GENERAL THOMAS WORTHINGTON

The pioneer village of Chillicothe, Northwest Territory, first known as Massiesville, to which General Thomas Worthington and his family removed from Virginia in 1798, was a small log-cabin settlement, typical of the best immigrant centers of the period. The rich bottom land of the Scioto River and the rolling terrain near which the village was located, had already attracted a considerable number of settlers. Some Virginia Revolutionary soldiers who were entitled to free land allotments—according to rank in service—had already located between the Scioto and Little Miami Rivers. Among those entitled by rank to large allotments in this Virginia Military Reservation between these two rivers, was General Darke, guardian of Thomas Worthington, an orphaned neighbor boy. Unable to locate and survey his lands because of age and the hardships of the journey, General Darke delegated this duty to his ward, and subsequently sold the land to him. The opportunity this survey gave young Worthington to examine the quality of the land he had located for his guardian, determined him to dispose of his estate in Virginia and establish his permanent home at Chillicothe. Following his return to Vir-

---

[2]Sheldon, Addison E. *History and Stories of Nebraska.*

ginia and the disposal of all of his interests there, he prepared at once for the comfortable transfer of his family and a number of former slaves to their new abode. With him and his accomplished wife came his brother, Richard Worthington, his sister and her husband, Dr. Edward Tiffin, Ohio's first governor.

The Ordinance of 1787, which prohibited human slavery in the Northwest Territory, gave General Worthington the opportunity he desired to manumit his slaves before he migrated, and to bring them with him as freed men. Emancipation in Virginia at that period required, also, the provision of a suitable home for the freedman. A few of them who declined emancipation and elected to remain in Virginia, were given opportunity to select their own masters. The others who came with the family settled in and near Chillicothe, where General and Mrs. Worthington could give them such personal aid and assistance as they needed while adapting themselves to a new life in a new country.

It was a memorable day, April 17, 1798, when the long journey by land and river was ended, and the little log-built village of Chillicothe on the Scioto River presented itself before their eyes. There was great rejoicing, for it marked the end of an arduous journey to the place of their choice, where new homes were to be established permanently, and their remaining years were to be spent.

Following the building of a number of homes for those who came with him, General Worthington began the erection of "Adena," his own home, in 1807, and finished it for occupancy in 1811. To a friendly inquiry as to why he had built so elaborate a home, he replied: "That Mrs. Worthington and I may be able to entertain our friends as we did in our old Virginia manor-house." Its subsequent guest-list included many of the country's distinguished men and women, and also the names of some of the more noted Indian chiefs of the Northwest Territory. A distinguished guest, Governor Clinton, on his departure, designated Adena as "the abode of hospitality, both genuine and elegant."

GEN. THOMAS WORTHINGTON   MRS. THOMAS WORTHINGTON

GIFT OF THE GREENVILLE INDIAN COMMISSION TO
GENERAL AND MRS. WORTHINGTON

During its conference with Governor Lucas at Chillicothe, Ross County, Ohio, in 1807, the Indian commissioners were entertained by the Worthingtons at their home, "Adena." The commission was composed of Tecumtha, Blue Jacket, Roundhead, the Panther, and their interpreter, Stephen Ruddell, Tecumtha's beloved adopted brother

PIONEER STORIES

General Worthington's rise to power and position was rapid and continuous until his demise at the early age of fifty-four. In 1798, the year of his arrival at Chillicothe, he was appointed major of militia and deputy surveyor-general of the Northwest Territory. He was later elected a member of the first Ohio Constitutional Convention; Ohio's first United States senator, and in 1814, her fourth governor. In his long service to the State and Nation, he was a wise and constructive statesman, and a leader in that coterie of remarkable men whose service in the early years of Ohio's organization should more often be recalled and more signally honored.

General Worthington's interests were largely, if not entirely, in land investments. Close contact with the immigrants then seeking new homes in the Northwest Territory led him quickly to see the hardships imposed on them by the Ordinance which required the purchase of not less than a section (640 acres) of land for bona fide settlements. At his own expense, he spent the winter of 1800 at Philadelphia, and presented to Congress a plan to reduce this acreage from 640 to 160 acres. The final acceptance of this plan resulted in the more rapid settlement of the Northwest Territory with desirable pioneers. During Worthington's stay in Philadelphia, he searched every nursery for varieties of fruit-trees, grapes, roses and shrubbery. These were sent to "Adena" and grown there. Following his election as governor, he established the beginning of Ohio's Agricultural Department. Unable to obtain the services of men experienced in the growth and care of fruit-trees and vineyards, he indentured several skilled horticulturists from Amsterdam. His influence was for the educational betterment of Ohio.

General Worthington was scarcely of legal age when elected to the United States Senate in 1803. Public works built and maintained by the Federal Government were then a new concept. His own state was urgently needing outlets for trans-Alleghany markets and for their return shipments. As senator, he directed his energy to the problem of highways from the seaboard to the Mississippi River.

He was successful in securing the passage of a bill which marked the beginning of our present elaborate state and national highway system, in the extension of the old Cumberland Road, which became the first trans-Alleghany highway from Baltimore and Washington to St. Louis. After his service as governor, General Worthington, still recognizing the need of transportation to develop the resources of the state, reentered the Ohio legislature to secure "bills drawn by himself which would lead to the construction of the Ohio Canal." Upon the completion of its survey, he invited Governor Clinton, of New York, himself a leading proponent of canal building, to join with him in the breaking of ground for the canal. The elaborate ceremony took place near Newark, Ohio, July 4th, 1825. Governor Clinton and his staff remained for some days, as guests of "Adena."

With these evidences of far-sighted statesmanship, there occurred in the War of 1812-'13—"Madison's War"—an act of personal, if not reckless bravery, which demonstrated his courage. The war brought great anxiety and hardships to the settlers in Ohio. As the fighting settled about Fort Meigs, it became apparent that, if it fell, the English could repossess Ohio, if not regain the entire Northwest. General Harrison and his little army in the fort were about the only military forces available to prevent this threatening disaster. Reports were current that want of provisions might compel Harrison to surrender if the fight were prolonged. Realizing Ohio's danger, General Worthington resolved at all hazards to communicate with the beleaguered forces. Disguised as Indians, he and Major Oliver, with Logan, a trusted Indian friend, reached the fort without suspicion of their identity. By means of a letter carefully wrapped about an arrow, and shot into the fort, they got word to General Harrison that speedy relief would reach him. The three men then made their retreat without discovery. Capture would have meant the stake. It was a daring, but successful adventure, calling for the highest quality of courage.

This hazardous adventure was one of the dramatic incidents of the siege of Fort Meigs. No intimation of their purpose was given by any of the men who participated in the undertaking. The unexplained absence of the master of "Adena" led quickly to the conviction that he had been killed, leaving no clew as to how or where to make search. The return of the three to Chillicothe, with the story of their success, caused great public rejoicing, "Adena" rejoicing as never before nor since.

THE HISTORIC BANQUET AT ADENA, 1807

"Adena," the historic Worthington home, is located on a commanding range of hills west of Chillicothe. It looks across to Mount Logan, from which the face of the Great Seal of Ohio was designed. It overlooks the Scioto Valley, a terrain favored alike by mound-builders, the Indians and ourselves.

The story of this banquet harks back to the time of Tecumtha and his brother, Tenskwatawa, "the Prophet." The presence of a large number of Indians drawn by the Prophet's mission to Greenville in 1807, caused increasing alarm among Ohio settlers in the central and western part of the state. After mobilizing several companies of the Ohio Militia (organized under the Ordinance of 1784), Governor Kirker dispatched General Thomas Worthington and General Duncan MacArthur to Greenville. They bore a peace-message to the Indians, and were instructed to obtain from Tecumtha and the Prophet the status of the activity there, and its purposes. The commissioners left Chillicothe, then the capital of Ohio, on September 8, 1807, and arrived at Greenville on September 16th. Their journey was unattended and without incident. They were cordially received and treated during their visit, and invited to attend a large Indian council about to be held at the settlement. On their return journey, they were accompanied by an Indian commission of four, Tecumtha, Blue Jacket, Roundhead and the Panther, with Stephen Ruddell as interpreter. They had been appointed by the council at Greenville to wait on the governor, and assure him of the peaceful purposes of the Prophet's mission.

The report submitted to Governor Kirker by his commission was entirely favorable to the Prophet's cause. They found no evidence that it was a covert war movement. A few days after they arrived at Chillicothe, a record-breaking mass meeting was held. It was addressed by Tecumtha, and presided over by Governor Kirker. The address was able, magnetic and convincing. The pioneer unrest and fear of Indian hostilities was set at rest. Tecumtha's assurances that his people desired to live in peace with their white brothers were accepted. To that end, the Prophet's mission work—a labor of love—was teaching better moral preparation and better understanding of the new conditions that confronted his race after the Treaty of Greenville. The magnetic oratory of the great Indian patriot won. Hundreds of men who listened with close attention to this historic address departed to their homes, relieved of their fears that another Indian war was impending. Governor Kirker discharged the militia he had mobilized as a precautionary measure. Hospitable entertainment was shown the Indian commissioners on all sides during their short stay. General and Mrs. Worthington, who had opened the doors of "Adena" to Tecumtha and his associates, gave a reception in their honor on the eve of their departure for Greenville. The banquet, after the fashion of that day, was elaborate and bountiful. It was the age of "the pyramid table." In the serving of coffee, one of the chiefs was overlooked. From the Indian viewpoint, such an individual omission at a friendly feast opened a fine field for Indian banter of the "coffeeless chief" by the other Indians. This custom is explained in Alford's notes on the Shawnee's *"Umsoma."* The situation naturally grew tense to the other guests who could have no knowledge of the *"Umsoma."* Tecumtha quickly exercised his good offices, to the great relief of his hostess' embarrassment. The neglected chief was served gospel measures of coffee, poured by her own hands, and was honored for the remaining hours of the reception with her personal attention. Alford's comment, on reading this story, adds much to its historical value. He writes:

Referring to . . . this banquet, in the serving of coffee on that occasion, one of the chiefs was overlooked. It, of course, appears to the whites that the Indians took this omission as an intended affront, but they did not. From the Indian viewpoint, it was a joke, undoubtedly, and was thrust against the chief by the opposite division of the *Umsoma*, which has been described elsewhere. Of course, it was his duty to defend his *Umsoma* by defending himself and others present on this occasion. Of course, 'the situation grew tense,' to the whites not knowing the *Umsoma*, the real cause of all this wrangle, until Tecumseh noticed the feeling of the whites, and exercised his good offices. That which followed was quantities of coffee, and I have no doubt these quantities of extra coffee was another great joke followed up after they returned to Greenville. I could not help laughing when I read about the chief, knowing what followed.

General Worthington's daughter has written that four Indian commissioners accompanied her father on his journey home after he had finished his peace mission at Greenville. They, with Stephen Ruddell, the interpreter, were entertained at "Adena" while they remained in Chillicothe. "We were all," she wrote, "strictly charged to take no notice of their eccentricities and to manifest no displeasure at any accident; and Ruddell informed us that our savage guests departed well-pleased with their entertainment."[3]

---

[3]Tecumtha and Blue Jacket were well known in the history of the period. The other members of the commission, Roundhead and the Panther, were not so prominent as chiefs or leaders, though they contributed materially to stirring Indian history of their time.

Roundhead was a noted Wyandotte chief held in high esteem by Tecumtha. His Indian name was Stiahta, and he was well known during the period between 1807 and 1818. He probably lost his life in the battle of the Thames. General Proctor, in a letter dated October 23, 1813, states that "the Indian cause and ours experienced a serious loss in the death of Roundhead."

"The Panther" is not found among the signers of regional treaties, or in the pioneer history of the period. The high standing of Tecumtha, Blue Jacket and Roundhead, as chiefs and leaders in Indian affairs, would preclude the appointment of a fourth member of the commission of unimportant tribal record or rank.

Alford's explanation of variations in titular designations and

OLD CHILLICOTHE

It will be noted by students that no course of the trail from Greenville to Chillicothe (Ross County), as traveled by this commission is given. In his oration, during the first celebration of the centennial of this battle, in 1880, Thomas F. McGraw, generally considered a very able Clark County historian, notes that no evidences of a trail out of the village (other than the one to and from "Old Chillicothe," now Oldtown, Greene County), have been found, "though we know there must have been one."[4] This is not necessarily so, since Old Piqua was a terminal territory village, both as occupied by the Miami Indians, and after their expulsion by the Shawnees. Prof. William C. Mills, in speaking of Ohio Indian trails, shows the trail from Greenville to Chillicothe to have passed through St. Mary's, Urbana, Springfield and on to Chillicothe, without deviations. Prisoners of that

---

treaty signatures of individual chiefs, is helpful in tracing identity of this sachem. Dr. Hewitt of the United States Bureau of Ethnology, whose knowledge and insight into Indian history and ethics is broadened by ties of racial descent, has suggested the probable identity of Panther as that of *Machinqwe-Pushis*, or "The Large Cat," who was sachem of the Unami, a tribe allied with the Delawares, and was a chief of influence and importance. He signed the treaty of the Shawnee chiefs and warriors with the United States in 1786 as, "The Big Cat of the Delawares." Dr. Hewitt's explanations of "Erie" and "Fat-Face" are of interest, since they are drawn from personal study of Indian variation in designations. Word-sentence expressions were characteristic of the Algonquin language and, as in the case of "The Panther," present interesting possibilities of derivative terminology.

"Erie" is a Wyandotte word for Panther. It means "Long-Tail." The Big Wild Cat, a fierce and dangerous forest feline of the period, was called "Fat Face" by the Indians. This name was suggested by the heavy bushy hair, standing out from its wide malar bones. Narrow and rather long upper and lower maxillae gave prominence to this animal's fat-face appearance.

"Panther" was a terminal name, suggested with interesting derivations, by any one of which he could have been identified by his own people as "The Long Tail Large Cat"; "The Big Cat with the Long Tail"; "The Panther" and "Erie", following the Indian custom of personal designation by some familiar animal name. Machinqwe-Pushis could have had an easy ascent through some event or some fancied characteristic to "The Panther." In the word-sentence designations of the Indian, the shorter terminology for "The Long Tail Large Cat" appears as "The Big Cat" of the Delawares in the treaty signature of 1786, and "The Panther" of our story. "Of the Delawares" was not a part of his name, but was a tribal designation.

[4] Springfield *Gazette*, August 9, 1880.

period do not mention trails. If this commission kept to the trail, it could never be nearer Old Piqua than Springfield. The denseness of the forest copse then, as even now shown in small wood enclosures, precluded any chopping of new lines of travel in place of one already opened and used. The frequent use by our historians of "Chillicothe" in connection with Tecumtha's birth, and their lax use of location prefixes or suffixes, indicates the close associations of the man with towns or a town of that designation, and also the scarcity of details of value in dependable narratives of that period, as they come to us now. The same may be said of maps made by cartographers fifty years after events. "Somebody said fifty, so we will mark it down that way," seems to have been the plan of the map-maker.

THE STORY OF JOSIAH HUNT

In the description of Simon Kenton's run of the gantlet, the narrative notes the admiration of the Shawnees for the white man who could beat them at their own game. A short excerpt taken from the papers of the late Judge Thomas Coke Wright, Greene County's early and able historian, quoted by Howe, is here given of Josiah Hunt, the Northwestern Territory's greatest hunter during the period covered by this story. He was *not* one of the notable white prisoners at Old Chillicothe, although the desire to capture him or get his scalp became the business of the craftiest warriors of the Cha-lah-kaw-tha clan. For a number of years, he was a resident of what is now Greene County, Ohio.

He was one of Wayne's legion and was in the battle of Fallen Timbers, August 20, 1794. . . . In the winter of 1793, while the army lay at Greenville, he was employed to supply the officers' tables with game, and in consequence was relieved from all garrison duty, and was permitted to leave or enter the fort whenever he chose. . . . To keep from freezing to death, it was necessary to have a fire, but to show a light in an enemy's country was to invite certain destruction. To avoid this danger, he dug a hole in the ground with his tomahawk, about the size and depth of a hat crown. Having prepared it properly, he procured some *roth* (thick white oak bark from a dead tree, which will retain a strong heat when covered with its ashes). Kindling a fire from flint and steel at the bottom of his "coal pit," as he termed it, the bark was severed into strips and placed in layers crosswise, until the pit was full. After it was sufficiently ignited, it was covered over with dirt, with the exception of two air-holes in the margin, which could be opened or closed at pleasure. Spreading down a layer of bark or brush to keep him off the cold ground, he sat down with the "coal pit" between his legs, enveloped himself in his blanket, and slept cat-dozes in an upright position. If his fire became too much smothered, he would freshen it up by blowing into one of the airholes. He declared he could make himself sweat whenever he chose. The snapping of a dry twig was sufficient to awaken him, when, uncovering his head, he keenly scrutinized in the darkness and gloom around—his right hand on his trusty rifle "ready for the mischance of the hour."

At daylight, he commenced hunting, proceeding slowly and with extreme caution, looking for game and watching for Indians at the same time. When he found a deer, previous to shooting it, he put a bullet in his mouth, ready for reloading his gun with all possible dispatch, which he did before moving from the spot, casting searching glances in every direction for Indians. Cautiously approaching the deer after he had shot it, he dragged it to a tree and commenced the process of skinning with his back towards the tree and his rifle leaning against it, within reach of his right hand. And so with his rear protected by the tree, he would skin a short time, then straighten up and scan in every direction to see if the report of his rifle had brought an Indian in his vicinity, then apply himself to skinning again. If he heard a stick break, or the slightest noise indicating the proximity of animal life, he clutched his rifle instantly and was on the alert, prepared for any emergency.

Having skinned and cut up the animal, the quarters were packed in the hide, so arranged as to be slung on his back like a knapsack, with which he wended his way to the fort. If the deer was killed far from the garrison, he only brought in the fore-quarters. One day he got within gunshot of three Indians, unperceived by them. He was on a ridge and they in a hollow. He took aim at the foremost one and waited some time for a chance for two to range against each other, intending, if they got in that position, to shoot two and take his chance with the other in single combat. But they continued marching in Indian file, and though he could have killed either of them, the other two would have made the odds against him too great, so he let them pass unmolested. Amidst all the danger to which he was constantly exposed, he passed unharmed.

Owing to the constant and powerful exercise of the faculties, his ability to hear and discriminate sounds was wonderfully increased, and his perceptive faculties much enlarged. He made $70.00 that winter by hunting, over and above his pay as a soldier. This was a large sum of extra money for a man to earn during that period of government service.

At the treaty of Greenville, in 1795, the Indians seemed to consider Hunt as next in greatness to Wayne himself. They inquired for him, crowded round him, and were loud and earnest in their praises and compliments: "Great man, Captain Hunt—great warrior—good hunting man; Indian no can kill!" They informed him that some of their bravest and most cunning warriors had often set out expressly to kill him. They knew how he made his secret camp-fire, the ingenuity of which excited their admiration. The parties in quest of him had often seen him—could describe the dress he wore, and his cap, which was made of a raccoon's skin with the tail hanging down behind, the front turned up and ornamented with three brass rings. The scalp of such a great hunter and warrior they considered to be an invaluable trophy. Yet they never could catch him off his guard —never get within shooting distance, without being discovered and exposed to his death-dealing rifle.[5]

THE CENTINEL AND *THE MAXWELL CODE*

The *Centinel of the Northwestern Territory* was the first newspaper published in the Territory. Its editor and proprietor, William Maxwell, was the second postmaster of Cincinnati. It is interesting to read in Burnet's *Notes on the Northwestern Territory*, that "at a legislative session held at Cincinnati in 1795, they prepared a code of laws adopted from the statutes of the original states, which superseded the chief part of those they had previously en-

---

[5] Howe, Henry. *Op. Cit.* 1847, 2:698-700.

acted."[6]   Only one copy of the *"Centinel of the Northwestern Territory,"* containing the minutes in full of the first Territorial legislature, is known to be in existence. The legislature consisted of Governor Arthur St. Clair, Judge John Cleves Symmes, Judge George Turner, and General Rufus Putnam (who could not be present).

This body of laws was printed at Cincinnati by William Maxwell in 1795, from which circumstance it was called the *Maxwell Code*. It was the first job of printing done in the Northwestern Territory, and the book should be preserved as a specimen of the printer's art in the western country at that period. All the laws previously passed had from necessity been printed at Philadelphia, because there was no printing office in the territory before this date —1795. The *Maxwell Code* was so full and complete that but one short legislative session was held thereafter, in 1798, at which a few additional laws were adopted; after that date, the statutes of the Territory underwent no alteration till the first session of the general assembly, held under the second grade of government, in 1799.

The first issue of the *Centinel of the Northwestern Territory*, printed by Maxwell, Saturday, November 9th, 1793, was a small four-page issue, 9¾ inches by 12¼ inches over all, with a type mat 8½ inches by 10¼ inches; printed on browny-white rag paper, with type that was characteristic of the period when circumflexes and double letters were in vogue. There is no record of the number of first copies printed for subscribers and complimentary distribution— its subscription list, unfortunately, was lost. On the *third page*, however, printer Maxwell, with prophetic vision of the advertising policy of subsequent Northwestern Territory journalists, disclosed his own confidence in newspaper advertising—in large italics—as follows:

Subscribers to this paper will please to call at the office for it, as there has been a subscription-paper mislaid, and the names of a number of subscribers (are) not yet known to the printer.

---

[6]From *Ohio Arch. and Hist. Quarterly.* v. 30:17, 28.

This and two others in the same issue were the first newspaper advertisements in the Northwestern Territory. The others are found on the *fourth page*: One of A. Adgate and Company, Pittsburgh, cards and general merchandise; and the other of Job Gard, a reward of four dollars for a lost parchment pocket-book.

Among the articles of this first issue are a three and a half column story of "The Monk" by Sterne, and three columns of foreign and domestic news. Under the heading, "Foreign Intelligence," the date of the correspondence was July 15, 1793. The correspondence from the states bore the dates: Portland, August 24; New York, September 4; Philadelphia, September 4; Fredericksburg, October 3. Under date of Cincinnati, November 9, a column article describes the Indian attack on General Wayne's provision and supply wagon train by a band of Little Turtle's braves, seven miles beyond Fort St. Clair. Two commanding officers, Lieutenant Lowrie and Ensign Boyd and thirteen non-commissioned officers and privates were killed. Seventy horses were driven off by the Indians, but the supplies and wagons were left undisturbed. This article is a valuable historical reference.

The fourth page, in addition to the Gard and Adgate advertisements, contains a column poem, "In Imitation of Watts, Indian Philosopher," and a column and a half contributed article criticising land court decisions and signed by "Manlius."[7]

Across the foot of the fourth page the publisher adds this business statement:—"Cincinnati: Printed by W. Maxwell, at the corner of Front and Sycamore Streets, where Subscriptions, Essays, Advertisements, etc., are thankfully received, and printing in general performed, with accuracy and dispatch."

At this date—1793—the frontier town of Cincinnati consisted of about a dozen log cabins, three or four frame houses, and Fort Washington. The *Centinel* office was in a

---

[7] Pseudonym of Christopher Gore, Governor of Massachusetts, 1809-1814.

single log-cabin room, facing the north landing bank of the Ohio River at Front and Sycamore Streets, "the best location in the city."

The *Centinel's* name, observes Nelson and Runko's *History of Cincinnati*, was particularly appropriate, since Fort Washington was virtually the gateway through which the early pioneers seeking homes in the domain beyond had to pass. A "Centinel," therefore, on the outer limits, to signalize danger or proclaim safety, was of transcendent importance to those who were starting out to lay the foundations of what proved to be a mighty empire. Likewise the challenge of its motto—"Open to all parties, but influenced by none," was characteristic of this "Scotch editor," as he was known in his active and useful life from 1803 to 1809 in Greene County, Ohio.

William Maxwell's plans to publish a newspaper in the Northwestern Territory were well matured before he left New Jersey. His editorial in the first issue of the *Centinel* states that this was his principal object in removing to Cincinnati. He was evidently an experienced compositor and printer before 1793, for he purchased and brought with him type, paper, ink and a Franklin-Ramage hand press, an outfit as complete for his purposes as the state of the printing art of his period could furnish. He brought this publishing outfit overland from New Jersey to Fort Pitt, and by boat from that point to Cincinnati.

In the summer of 1796 William Maxwell sold the *Centinel* to Edmund Freeman. There is no record of the price received for it. It continued a Cincinnati publication, but its new owner changed the name to "Freeman's Journal." In 1800, Freeman removed the plant to Chillicothe, and merged it with the Chillicothe *Gazette*. This paper later became the *Scioto Gazette* and is, therefore, the oldest newspaper of continuous issue in the Northwest Territory.

No further records of Maxwell's activities as editor and printer appear after the sale of the *Centinel* to Freeman. His newspaper connections and his services to the legislative council of 1795, no doubt, aided him in obtaining his appointment as the second postmaster of Cincinnati.

(At left)

TITLE PAGE OF THE
MAXWELL CODE

The first book printed in the
Northwest Territory. Published at
Cincinnati, 1796

(At right)

FIRST NEWSPAPER NORTH
OF THE OHIO

A page from the "Centinel of the
Northwestern Territory," issue of
August 22, 1795.
William Maxwell, editor

PIONEER STORIES

All records of dates of postal appointments previous to 1812 were destroyed by fire during the British invasion of Washington. Approximate dates of appointments, however, are obtained from the quarterly returns of the postmaster to the auditor of the Post Office Department, records which escaped during the invasion.

The first quarterly return of Abner N. Dunn, first postmaster of Cincinnati, was filed October 1st, 1794; that of William Maxwell, second postmaster, was filed January 1st, 1796; that of Daniel Mayo, third postmaster, was filed July 1st, 1797. These returns show Maxwell to have held this office about one and one-half years and that his successor, Mayo, was appointed sometime during the second quarter—April 1st to July 1st—of 1797.

Further note of Maxwell's public activities is found in Hamilton County records of 1803. He was elected a member of the House of Representatives from that county to the first General Assembly which convened at Chillicothe, on March 1st of that year.

Judge Maxwell's first Greene County land purchase, previous to his removal from Cincinnati, amounted to 332 acres. He subsequently added 683 acres by purchase—in all 1015 acres. The west boundary-line of this land ran with the east bank of the Little Miami River; consequently, all of it lay within the Virginia Military Reservation. The Maxwell lands, in 1850, were joined on their south border by those of Wm. Cooper Howells, where his "New Leaf Mill" was located, a name and location later made famous by his son, William Dean Howells, in his novel of the same title.

Of their journey north from Cincinnati to their new home on the Little Miami River, Mrs. Nancy Maxwell White states in her notable interview given in 1868 to Editor Hamin, that Judge Maxwell, with the family consisting of herself, a son and daughter, came north to Dayton, Ohio. Finding no trail east from the little settlement of Dayton, to Alpha, a point of early Greene County settlement, one and a half miles northwest of his lands, he hired some Revolutionary soldiers who were out of work to cut a way through the forest between these points. This trail is the present Dayton and Xenia Highway, State Route 11. From Alpha the path was cut through the copse of the Little Miami River bottoms at Indian Riffle, beyond which lay his lands. So inaccurate were many of the survey lines of that period that he built his cabin one-half mile distant from the north boundary line of his original purchase. He subsequently bought this adjoining land—683 acres—and continued his residence there. Mr. C. B. Galbreath, secretary and editor of the Ohio Archaeological and Historical Society, has a photograph of this cabin, taken by himself thirty years ago. With his permanent residence located in Greene County, Judge Maxwell became a most active and useful citizen, and continued in public service until his death in 1809. By act of the legislature, he was appointed one of three associate judges of Greene County, April 6, 1803. He resigned this office on September 3rd, 1803, and accepted the appointment of sheriff in place of Captain Nathan Lamme, of Bellbrook, who had resigned to give his entire attention to the large tract of land he then owned in Greene County.

Mr. Galbreath, who was deeply interested in Maxwell history, notes in a letter to the writer, August 12, 1929:

I have just found in our archives, among the state papers of Governor Tiffin, William Maxwell's letter of resignation as associate judge for Greene County. The letter reads as follows:

Greene County,
September 3, 1803

Edward Tiffin, Esq.
Governor of the State of Ohio.
Sir:

You will please to except my resignation as Associate Judge as I shall consider myself not entitled to act in that office from and after date hereof.
I am, sir, with much esteem, etc. etc.

W. Maxwell

Edward Tiffin, Esq.
P. S. I take liberty in recommending Andrew Reed, Esq. or Mr. William MacFarland, either of whom would be a

proper person to fill the vacancy occasioned by my resignation.—W. M.

A note by Tiffin on the back of this letter indicates that the governor made an appointment. The note reads as follows:

Accepted September 20, and Mr. Reed, Esq. apointed September 24, 1803, to the meeting of the Legislature.

The Legislature met December 5, 1803, but judges were not elected until February 16, 1804. I assume that Maxwell resigned because he had been chosen Sheriff of Greene County. This would seem to indicate pretty accurately the date at which he became Sheriff.

Sincerely yours,
(signed) C. B. GALBREATH
Secretary

P. S. The "except" in Maxwell's resignation shows that he could make a mistake in spelling even when writing to the Governor of Ohio.—C. B. G.

Maxwell served as sheriff of Greene County until 1807. He took great interest in the state militia operating, then, under the Ordinance of 1787, and from 1805 to 1809 held the rank of major. Dill's *History of Greene County, Ohio*, 1881, notes a military court of inquiry held at the house of Peter Borders, Alpha, Ohio, by the officers of the first battalion, second regiment, third brigade of the first division of the Ohio State Militia, on Tuesday, June 11, 1805. The officers present were Lieutenant Colonel Benjamin Whiteman, Major William Maxwell and others. This is the earliest Greene County reference to Judge Maxwell's military activities. This militia was organized and carried on under the Ordinance of 1787. The law was repealed in Ohio in 1844.

During his term as sheriff in 1806, the most famous fight in Greene County militia history took place. Fights between the champions of various companies or sections were often staged after spring and fall musters, held on the county drill-grounds at Oldtown, known earlier as Old Chillicothe. This fight was between Aaron Beal and Ben Kiser, both notable in their line. A number of partisans were soon drawn into it. Major Maxwell, with several deputies, endeavored to stop it at the expense of blackened eyes, broken ribs and bleeding noses for all of them. Court echoes of this fight were heard for a number of years after the event. One hundred and twenty-five years have come and gone since it occurred, yet it is still remembered as a folklore tale.

The history of Judge Maxwell, father of journalism in the Northwest Territory, would be incomplete without reference to his wife, Nancy Robbins, by whose deft hands the first issue of the *Maxwell Code* was bound, one of many instances in her remarkable career of the assistance and inspiration she gave to her husband.

A few years after Judge Maxwell's death in 1809, she was married to John White. At the age of one hundred and eight as Mrs. Nancy White, nee Robbins, she gave to P. S. Hamin, editor of the Lafayette *Journal*, the story of her remarkable life. She was born where Wheeling, West Virginia, now stands, in 1761. Her father was killed and scalped near this frontier fort, at Grave Creek, and she barely escaped capture before reaching the fort. Nancy Robbins volunteered with Elizabeth Zane, when the besieged ran short of powder, to try to get the powder which was in a cabin outside of the Grave Creek fort. This incident is famous in American Indian warfare. "Betty" Zane was chosen for this almost hopeless venture, and succeeded not only in getting the powder, but in writing her name and the incident into American history. Nancy Robbins was denied this chance for fame, she states, because she was rapid and skillful in moulding bullets, and could thus relieve a man for defense of the besieged fort. After the siege, she and her mother, with several other families, embarked on a flatboat for Cincinnati, where the mother was engaged by Ebenezer, Betty's brother, as housekeeper, and afterwards married him. Nancy Robbins thus became a member of the Zane family and Betty Zane's companion. Nancy was soon married to Colonel Maxwell of the log-cabin town of Cincinnati, and joined in her husband's work as editor, printer and publisher of the *Centinel*.

Her story of their home and publishing-place differs

from that given in Nelson and Runko's *History of Cincinnati and Hamilton County*. She states that "they owned forty acres of ground along the hill where Fifth Street is now located, and built upon it a two-story frame dwelling-house, in which was his printing-office also." In her interview she refers to her husband as "Colonel," indicating a possible military title before he came to Cincinnati.

She relates that, "after a few years, Colonel Maxwell, imbued with a pioneer spirit, disposed of his property in Cincinnati, removing with his family to Greene County and purchasing five hundred acres of land, on which he began the stock-growing business." This was about the year 1800. Her description of the new home is interesting, and likewise valuable, since it corroborates certain important dates in Greene County Indian history. The log cabin which Colonel Maxwell built, on a mistaken location, was their home for a number of years. It had a front door opening, but no door; a quilt hung up answered this purpose. During Colonel Maxwell's frequent absences she, with their two children, slept in the loft, so that the Indians, still resident at that time in a very large village near the present site of Oldtown, would think the house was empty if they came there at night. From this interview, it is gathered that Colonel Maxwell purchased his five hundred acres of farm land, rather than "located it" as a soldier claim. This throws into further confusion the efforts that have been made to establish the Maxwell Revolutionary War record.

After the death of her second husband, John White, Nancy Robbins Maxwell White removed with her relatives from Greene County to Sidell Township, Vermilion County, Illinois, where she died November 9, 1868, aged about one hundred and eight. Her remains are interred in the village cemetery of that locality. In the closing paragraph of this unusual interview with her, Editor Hamin has recorded a tribute to this remarkable woman, without parallel in American history. It is here resurrected that it may henceforth live in the annals of eloquent tributes to American heroines:

Perhaps no other pioneer woman of the west or, in

fact, the country, lived to see such magnificent changes, such a revolution on the face of the continent, as did our heroine. She was in the flush of womanhood when the Revolutionary year of 1776 sprung a new nation and era for mankind. She was a heroine in Virginia when "out west" meant Albany, New York. She lived to the time when her countrymen had peopled the last margin line along the Pacific Ocean, and there is no longer an "outwest." She was born during the high tide of our Indian wars, when Washington was a subordinate officer of the British crown, and she died while Sheridan was persecuting the mere Indian remnants of these once multitudinous races. At her birth, Cincinnati was nameless, and Ohio was a rank wilderness, and without the signs of progressing civilization, as were many regions east of us. She heard the slogan of war which rolled and swelled over the thirteen colonies, saw the settlers hasten to war, was thrilled and saddened with success and reverses of the struggle, and joined the loyal chorus which freedmen sent from their wilderness homes when England acknowledged the independence of the Colonies. She saw the veterans of '76 grow old and fade away from earth. She lived while they were having their locks silvered and their forms bowed by Time's destroying touch. She remained until they were quite all gone from earth. She still lived when their children became old and their children became the armed legions which struck freedom's second blow. She saw the forests of Ohio disappear before the sturdy pioneer race of yeomanry, saw cities, towns, railroads, colleges, asylums and schools multiply in this same territory, which once she saw under Indian rule. Eighty-five years after '76 she was among us, and urged men to strike for the preservation of the Union, which she saw formed far back among occurrences of a past century. She again bore her part in freedom's struggle, and still lived when the resplendent sun of Union Victory rose and shone over a whole free land.

  She died, but not till it became known to her that the triumph of Union was complete and her requiem was the jubilant note of victory over the last enemy to the universal Union, Liberty and Freedom cause, and while they swelled forth on the Atlantic coast, were caught up and reechoed beyond the Alleghanies; and when in mid-nation the reverbations from the east met the triumphant song from the mighty west, Nancy Robbins, our heroine, bowed her head and passed away, wept, revered, lamented.

It was this gentle woman, his wife, who stood by the side of William Maxwell, aided and inspired him in all his Northwestern Territory career, and remained nearly sixty years after his departure to see the little Ramage hand-press she helped to operate at times, grow until the production of its successors could not be measured.

William Maxwell's remains rest on a beautiful hill of his farm, facing one of the many comely valleys of the Little Miami River. This hill, his favorite resort when living, became by his own direction in 1809, his final resting-place.

New and interesting incidents in the personal life of William Maxwell, first editor in the Northwestern Territory, 1793, have lately become available from the papers of Nancy Robbins Maxwell, his wife, and Jacob Haines, his neighbor, who were appointed administrators of his estate. Among the numerous papers in the estate's settlement, those which invoice the equipment used by Judge Maxwell in operating his large stock farm are interesting, since they indicate his business activities at the time of his demise. Other appraisals furnish interesting and suggestive points of contact with prominent pioneers of Cincinnati and the Little Miami Valley from 1793 to 1809.

The bill of earliest date—August 7, 1792—presented to the administrators of the estate, was filed by James Cowper of Christiana Bridge, Delaware, administrator of the estate of Solomon Maxwell. Twenty-four items that make up this bill consist mostly of household articles. Apparently this purchase was for anticipated needs in far-off Cincinnati, to which Editor Maxwell was preparing to emigrate with his printing and publishing outfit. The purchase amounted to £ 72 0 s. 10½ d. There are no credit entries on the bill, but an administrator's note on the back acknowledges payment in full for $86.72, November 21, 1810. This bill was probably adjusted on the values of the currency at the dates of purchase and payment.

All that is known of Judge Maxwell's illness and the date of his death is obtained from the service bill of Dr. T. Baird, the attending physician: "1809, Sept. 8th and 9th,

To sundries, medicines and attendance, $8.75, (signed) T. Baird." The bill indicates that the usual personal care given by the old-time family physician, was given by good Doctor Baird, and that the end came on September 9, 1809, after only two days' illness. The making of the pioneer's coffin by a friend or neighbor carpenter helps us to visualize the mutual dependence that everywhere marked the lives of Northwestern Territory settlers. Coffins of the period were made to measure, usually at the home of the deceased, of oak, ash or poplar boards, well dressed and securely put together. This was the "wooden overcoat" occasionally referred to in pioneer history, and was, for a while, at least, the simple habiliment used alike for rich and poor in the interments of that period. Under date of January 10, 1811, is the following: "Received of Jacob Haines, six dollars for the making of a cofin for William Maxwell, (signed) George Hittle."

On the day following Judge Maxwell's death, extra supplies were purchased for the funeral period, when all who came were served a substantial luncheon, following the minister's services, and before the interment. This custom was an expression of the generous hospitality of the pioneer period, and also a necessity. Distances were long, and connections were by forest trails only. The crossing of streams at fords was on horseback. There were few nearby taverns to furnish food and lodging. Prominent men rode long distances to the funerals of their friends. The luncheon, for these reasons, became a part of the funeral services of the period. Ample provision was made for it, and nearby women assisted in the preparations.

"William Maxwell, Dcd.   To David Davis, Dr.
  To 1 Lb coffee   .50
  ½ Lb Imperial tea @ 2.75   1.37½
12th To 2 Prs Hinges @ 37½   .75
  1 Pr silk hose   3.50"

This bill, paid December 1, 1809, indicates that our distinguished Northwestern Territory editor and citizen was laid away in silk hose—possibly also in the uniform of his rank, major in the Ohio militia.

PIONEER STORIES

Following the burial of Judge Maxwell, Nancy Maxwell, his wife, and Jacob Haines, his neighbor, qualified on September 26, 1809, as administrators, by the execution of a bond for $6,000.00 to James Galloway,[8] treasurer of Greene County. This bond was acknowledged in the presence of Josiah Grover, and signed by

	her	
Nancy	X Maxwell	(Seal)
	mark	
Jacob Haines		(Seal)
Jacob Smith		(Seal)
David Hanse		(Seal)
	his	
Peter	X Borders	(Seal)
	mark	

The names of all signers are well known in Greene County pioneer history. It is interesting to note that Nancy Maxwell, inspiring heroine of William Maxwell's life and work, did not write her own name. This revelation in no way detracts from the glorious record she left of a century of service to her country, and to those she loved.

The several deeds and filed tax-receipts show the total amount of land owned by William Maxwell, at his death, to have been 1863.56 acres. The largest single obligation of Judge Maxwell, which was not large considering his activities as a stock man, was $1000 owed to Moses Maxwell of Hamilton County, Ohio. No information is available as to the existing relationship, if any, of these two Maxwells. Under agreement signed by both, and witnessed by their seals, this debt was to be satisfied by William Maxwell, transferring to Moses, at a future date, a quarter section (160 acres) of good land, and a horse worth $50.00. The records showed that the obligation, or what remained of it, was settled by Jacob Haines, one of the administrators, on August 11, 1810, for $401.94. What the conditions were that changed the character of the payment from the original agreement is not stated, but it was, no doubt, satisfactory to both interests.

---

[8]Great-grandfather of the author.

The itemized appraisement of the personal property of the estate is interesting. The long list of bills and accounts receivable contained such well-known names, with considerable amounts due, as William McMillan, James Collier, Samuel Martin, Joseph C. Vance, John G. Gano and Greene County. The sum of the 62 accounts listed amounted to $4,181.65, a large amount for that period. Among the interesting items in the appraisal of personal property which was made October 23, 1809, were:

1 sword, $25.00; sundry articles of clothing, $30.00; 1 man's saddle, $12.00; 2 Testaments and 1 spelling book, 75c; 1 case of razors and hone, $1.50; 1 copper still, $118.00; 1 copper still, $75.00.

The total number of items returned by the three well-known appraisers were 80, and the amount $1,537.28.

The public sale of this personal property was held on October 26, 1809, at the Maxwell farm. John Haines was clerk of the sale and receipted for his fee, $2.00, therefor. Simon Shover, the auctioneer, receipted for $5.00, his charge for "two days' crying a sale." Notices published in a Dayton newspaper owned by Disbrard & McClure, and amounting to $1.25, are found in the administrators' accounts. The total amount realized and the purchasers' names, filed by the clerk of the sale, amounted to $1,104.09½, a large amount of money for that period.

The widow, Mrs. Maxwell, elected to take various items amounting to $413.69½. The total of the sale, with the widow's set-off, amounted to $1,517.79, a sum within $19.49 of the appraisers' invoice.

WILLIAM SMALLEY

Scout—Pilot—Master Sharpshooter

History of record is not in full agreement as to details of men who were sent, after St. Clair's disaster, on peace missions to the Auglaize country. Since these narratives are confusing, William Smalley's will be given as it was received from him by his daughter, Prudence Smalley Stump, and, by her told many times to her grandson, Fremont Miars, who is a well-known and reliable resident of Spring Valley, Ohio.

Smalley was born near Trenton, New Jersey, about 1790. When five years old, his parents moved to Fort Pitt where, under the protection of the guns of the fort, his father cleared land for the family home. While so occupied, he was killed during a surprise attack by a band of Delaware Indians, and William, who was with his father, was taken captive, and was taken by the Indians to their village on the Maumee River. There he successfully "ran the gantlet," and was adopted by one of the chiefs, who had recently lost a son. This chief was recollected to be either Captain Pipe, Wingynuim or Killbuck. The boy remained a prisoner for five years and seven months, and during this period he wandered with the hunting parties of the Delawares all over the country east of the Mississippi River. One winter was spent in Canada without adequate provision for food. The heavy snows prevented hunting, and the entire party faced death by starvation. They were saved when, by chance, they found a herd of a dozen deer, which had become snowbound and were unable to move from the small ring they had tramped down while the storm piled up impassable drifts about them. The deer were killed and removed to the camp where, after the first feast, a young Indian, much larger and stronger than Smalley, and who seemed to have a spite against him, struck him a stinging blow in the face. Smalley grasped a knife from an Indian who was standing nearby, and chased his foe well into the woods, but he could not catch him. When he returned, the other Indians laughed, patted him on the back, and called him "heap brave." There they named him "White Warrior," and he is so known in the tribe to this day. He was with the Delawares when Colonel Crawford was captured, and saw him burned at the stake. He was at the siege of Fort Henry, where Simon Girty was commander, and saw the hollow log they prepared as a cannon blown to fragments when it was fired. A number of Indians standing about were wounded, and some were killed. His escape from captivity was aided by a young Indian friend, who accompanied him on a long hunt during the spring hunting season. Equipped with camping outfits and ponies for transportation, they finally reached the Monongahela River, where Smalley, presumably, was captured by the whites, and the friendly Indian returned to the Maumee settlements with that explanation of the "White Warrior's" loss. Smalley then settled down and was married. Three children blessed this union. He then journeyed west to Fort Washington, where he helped build the first cabins on the site of Cincinnati, and was joined by his wife and children. They, with several others, floated down the Ohio River from Pittsburgh to Fort Washington in a large dugout canoe.

Shortly after St. Clair's defeat, President Washington commissioned Colonel Trueman and Major Lynch to repair to the Miami village, bearing a flag of truce and friendly messages of peace. A copy of the President's message carried by them, is found in *Western Annals*,[9] and is a document of great interest. Smalley, by reason of his captivity, had come to know all the territory the commission would traverse. He spoke the Shawnee and Delaware languages, also French, which he had learned from the French traders, so was chosen to conduct the commissioners. All went well as they approached the Auglaize country. There they met a hunting party of three Indians, who demanded to know why they were there. Smalley replied: "To make peace, to buy your lands, and to have no more war." The Indians seemed well pleased and promised to guide them to the Miami town. It was night when they met the Indians, and they agreed to camp together. The peace commissioners were well equipped with guns, horses and supplies. Smalley warned both men not to sleep, as these Indians were treacherous and should not be trusted. They stacked their guns, all of which were empty except Smalley's, and lay down for the night, an Indian and a white man, alternately. Smalley lay down with his loaded gun beside him. The young Indian asked Smalley if he might examine his fine gun—the camp fire was giving a good light. Smalley,

---

[9] Perkins, James H. *Western Annals*, 378-379.

knowing that it would not do to show any fear or distrust, consented. The Indian, promising that no harm would be done, took the gun, examined it, and admired it very much. Smalley turned about to look at Trueman and Lynch, and the Indian quickly raised and fired the gun at him. The bullet barely missed Smalley's head. With the report, the other two Indians sprang to their feet. One stabbed Colonel Trueman, and the other tomahawked Major Lynch. They scalped both dead officers, and seized all the equipment and personal possessions of the two murdered peace commissioners. They then journeyed to the Maumee town the next day, and presented the booty to the Chief Buckongahelas with the story of the capture. Smalley, who was permitted to go with them, states that this great chief savagely rebuked the Indians for this atrocity, but showed him great consideration, and provided him with a guard that no further harm should come to him. However, the hour of Smalley's trial approached. He was in the midst of the tribe which had adopted him in boyhood, and had given him the name of "White Warrior." He was placed on a stump and required to answer all questions, covering the years of his absence without return. To their question if he was married, he answered "No." His Indian questioner replied, "Yes, but we know you are, and have three children." Smalley replied, "I was married, but I didn't like the squaw, and I sent her back to her people, who also took the children." This being the Indian custom of final separation, his answer was considered perfect by his audience, and amid much hilarity, Smalley found himself restored to his Indian home and name. His second period of captivity now commenced, and lasted one and one-half years. He was later sent by the tribe, as its representative, to a post which he thought near the present site of Cleveland, and there helped to dictate the terms of a treaty, after which he returned to Fort Washington.

Wayne was then—1793—at "Camp Hobson's Choice," where he drilled his legion in Indian methods of warfare, as directed by Washington. Both at his camp and Legionville, drilling was uninterrupted during the two years' preparation preceding the Battle of Fallen Timbers. Individual marksmanship, one of Washington's explicit directions, was especially featured, as was Wayne's own favorite method of attack—close fighting with the bayonet and sword. Wayne recognized the value of Smalley, who was well acquainted, through years of captivity, with the enemy's territory and methods of warfare, and who had also been with Harmar and St. Clair in their disastrous campaigns. He quickly called him into active service again, appointed him guide, and gave him command of sharpshooters. At this point, the movement north to Fort Jefferson of a part of Wayne's force, directed by Smalley, becomes of much interest to Clermont and Warren County history. Smalley's narrative to his daughter, Prudence Smalley Stump, and by her to her grandson, Fremont Miars, states that: He led the "van" of Wayne's army past Fort Washington and Columbia. There was a settlement of Shawnees in Clermont County, and an open used way—the Bullskin Trace—which was their north and south trail from Bullskin Creek on the Ohio River, to all the north and northwest Indian settlements. This trace touched the present sites of Felicity, Bethel, Williamsburg, Dickey's Tavern, Slab's Camp, Edenton, Edwards' Schoolhouse, Clarksville, Harveysburg, New Burlington, Xenia, Old Chillicothe (Oldtown), Yellow Springs, Springfield, Urbana and on to Detroit. It is of interest, here, to note that the first Ohio legislature, by enactment February 7, 1804, established this trace as "the Xenia State Road." It is now a hard surfaced highway from Xenia north to Detroit, and from Williamsburg, south to the Atlantic and Pacific highway along the Ohio River.

Reference to Drake's "Map of the Miami Country," 1815, shows a trail from Cincinnati, past Fort Washington and Columbia, which skirted the north bank of the Ohio River to Big Indian Creek. From that point, four trails are marked, three of which connect with the Bullskin Trace: one to Williamsburg; another to Denhamstown—now Bethel; a third crosses the Bullskin Trace and ends at the Ohio River opposite Augusta, Kentucky; and the fourth, a short trace, ends at Nevil. Either of two of these trails from Big Indian Creek to the Bullskin Trace would have placed Smalley's "van" in position to clear the country of hostile Indians resident in Clermont County as it marched north to Harveysburg, and thence detoured west five miles to Camp Run at Waynesville, which is marked Waynesburg on General Rufus Putnam's Map of Ohio, 1804.

An interesting story, transmitted by Prudence Smalley Stump, concerns her father's life after the Battle of Fallen Timbers. He returned home and purchased 1000 acres of rich land on Todd's Fork at Clarksville. Five hundred acres were purchased from General Lytle, and 500 from Governor MacArthur. On this land, purchased in 1796 or 1797, Smalley erected a flour-mill, and a residence near by. On one occasion, his skill as a sharpshooter was well exercised. He had a log foot-bridge across the mill-race near the mill's office. Hearing a great commotion there, he ran to his office where he kept his rifle, and, looking out, saw that a bear and a catamount had met in the middle of the foot bridge, and were disputing the right of way. Smalley seized his rifle, which was loaded, and shot the catamount first. Then he reloaded and shot the slower moving bear. Both animals were killed, and dropped off the foot-bridge into the mill-race.

Years afterwards, when the "White Warrior" had passed into the Great Beyond, and the mill and residence had passed into other hands, the owner decided to remodel the residence. His carpenters were busy at this work, when a band of Indians on their way to Washington, D. C., stopped and camped near by. When they saw the remodeling work, they hastened to ask the owner if he had obtained the consent of "White Warrior" to remodel the house. Upon being told that he had not, the Indians became so demonstrative in their denunciations that the owner sought refuge among the carpenters, fearing for his safety. It is a strange story, but to one who knows the reverence of the Indian for the spirit of his beloved dead, there can be no doubt of the grief they felt, and the protest they voiced at the changes in the home of their adopted brother, the "White Warrior."

After the sale of his Clarksville interests, Smalley

joined his children, who had settled in Vermilion County, Illinois, and lived with them until his death in 1833. His final years were not impoverished, as related in Howe's *History*. He distributed his estate among his children, but retained enough to provide all the comforts of life for himself. He is buried at Higginsville, Illinois.

THE CAMP AT WAYNESVILLE (WAYNESBURG)

Interesting unrecorded history is connected with the various movements of General Wayne's army on its march from "Fort Hobson's Choice" to the battle-field at Fallen Timbers. Tradition has preserved this, in part, by narratives gathered from points of contact near enough to the events of that hour to lend authority to their recital. The traditions of William Smalley and General Charles Scott, and the camp site they both occupied at Camp Run, a mile south of Waynesville,[10] have only one intermediary between the men who made this history, and those who related it. It was an ideal location for defense encampment. Sentinel hills protected it from enemy approach, and a nearby spring, running strong at the present time into a stone trough on the road side of Route No. 47, furnished clear, cold water in abundance for every need of a large camp of men and animals. The adjacent Little Miami River bottoms were perfect terrain for military purposes. From the presence of one or both of these detachments of Wayne's army, the attractive village of Waynesville and Wayne Township derived their names.

William Smalley's occupation of the Waynesville camp with a deploy force preceded that of General Scott with his force of 1100 Kentucky mounted militia; the objective of each was Wayne at Fort Jefferson. Smalley's traditional line of march with the "van" had a military reason for its detour from Wayne's main line of march, which led from "Camp Hobson's Choice" via Fort Hamilton to Fort Jefferson, its temporary objective. An old and very consider-

---
[10] Waynesburg on General Rufus Putnam's Map of Ohio, 1804.

able settlement of Shawnee Indians was located in territory north of the present site of Williamsburg, Clermont County. The Bullskin Trace was the Indian trail north, for this territory, to Old Chillicothe on the Little Miami River. It connected there with the Winchester Trace, leading northwest to Peckaway (Piqua) on Mad River, and on to the Miami villages on the Auglaize. This hostile settlement, though not large, could not be left in the army's rear. The damage a few determined Shawnee warriors could inflict, if left there undisturbed, could and probably would have been considerable, as the garrison at Fort Washington was not large enough to be protective. Therein lies the reason for the "van's" line of march. There is tradition—now becoming history—that these advance troops engaged the Shawnees in battle at Evans' farm, West Woodville, Ohio. Howitzer number six balls and rusted bayonets have been found at this place, and Smalley's "van" is known to have carried a small howitzer. It was necessary military precaution to force these Shawnees to retreat to the Miami settlements. Smalley's "van" seems to have done this, then marched on north by the Bullskin Trace. Having passed the present locations of Dickey's Tavern, Slab's Camp and Edenton before the fight, the trail's course led past Edwards' School House, Clarksville and Harveysburg. At this latter point, the terrain is high and bog-free. Here, Smalley turned his march to a course pointing northwest towards Greenville. A march of a few miles brought him to the now noted camp site at Waynesville, where his narrative states he rested his command a day and a night, by which time all stragglers had reached camp.

THE SCOTT ENCAMPMENT

The following well-written traditional history is from the pen of the late George T. O'Neall. Omitting the narrator's introductory paragraphs, those here following will be found to be pertinent and to the point.[11]

---

[11] *The Miami Gazette*, March 16, 1927. Reprinted by permission.

We once asked an old gentleman, who had few superiors in either written or traditional history, if Wayne's army was at Waynesville. His reply was, "No, not Wayne's army proper, but an army of mounted Kentuckians marching to reinforce the army at Greenville, did pass by where Waynesville now is, and camped there."

In 1810 an old Kentucky pioneer, who had been a companion of Boone, and had fought with him at the Battle of the Blue Licks in 1782, was visiting a relative who lived at that time on the east side of the river. During the first evening of his stay, in conversation with one of the younger members of the family he said: "Seventeen years ago the past summer, I was here with General Charles Scott on our way to Greenville, and we camped in this neighborhood several days. We stayed on this (the east) side of the river one night, and then moved to the other side and camped in the bottom alongside of a large run which puts into the river from the west (Camp Run), near Waynesville's south corporate line."

Our informant has told us that the following morning the old gentleman expressed a desire to visit his old camp-ground, and that several members of the family went with him. He located the camp on the east side of the river, on a plateau between the foot of the hill and the railroad on the farm once owned by the Kelly sisters. While the party was listlessly strolling over the ground, the foot of one of them struck some metallic substance which, on being thrown from beneath the covering of leaves, proved to be an old cavalry sword which had been lost by some member of the camping-party seventeen years before. He stated that the army had remained in camp here one night, and the next morning they crossed the river, and camped on the run near where the power-house now stands. Here they remained in camp several days, and from this place moved directly to Greenville, marching across the corner of Greene County in Sugar Creek township, and making their first camp one mile north of Centerville in Montgomery County.

Here our tradition ends, and we must look to recorded history to tell us who our wandering detached troopers were.

In the summer of 1793, General Knox, secretary of war, called on Governor Shelby, of Kentucky, for volunteers to join Wayne in his campaign against the Miami

Indians, and in compliance with his request, General Charles Scott, with 1000 mounted men, marched from Lexington, and joined the army near Fort Jefferson on the 15th of October, 1793.[12] Owing to the lateness of the season, they were discharged, and returned home, while Wayne proceeded to build Fort Greenville, and to prepare himself more fully for battle.

In the succeeding summer, the Kentucky volunteers were again called out, and on the 26th of July, General Scott, with 1100 men, joined Wayne at Greenville, and on the 28th day, the army moved against the Miami villages.[13]

On the 20th day of August, the Battle of the Fallen Timbers was fought, and on the 12th day of October, General Scott marched for Greenville to be mustered out of service. Marshall[14] places Scott's forces at 1600 then, but the weight of authority seems to fix the number at 1100. The archives of the War Department have no record of the route of the line of march taken by General Scott from Kentucky to Fort Jefferson.

McBride, above quoted, states that General Scott, with 1000 mounted Kentucky militia, marched from Lexington, Kentucky.[15] This was the first volunteer reinforcement for Wayne, in event strenuous efforts by the government at Washington should fail to effect a compromise peace with the Indians. Considering the large number of horsemen and the neecessary camp impedimenta, it is probable that General Scott would take the route out of Lexington, most suitable for easy and rapid transportation of men and supplies. The great Buffalo Trace from Lexington to Maysville was, at that time, a well-beaten trail, 200 feet wide in places, and otherwise well adapted for cavalry movement.

At Washington—Kenton's town—four miles from Maysville, a tangent trace followed the highlands south of the Ohio River to Augusta, Kentucky, where it crossed and

---

[12]McBride, James. *Op. Cit.*, 1:225.
[13]*Amer. Pioneer*. 1:315.
[14]Marshall, Humphrey. *History of Kentucky*, 2:136.
[15]McBride, James. *Op. Cit.*, 2:137.

joined the Bullskin Trace (see Drake's Map, 1815). This well-marked trace would lead him near the site of Waynesville, Ohio, to Camp Run. From this point, the terrain, for cavalry transport, was excellent all the way to Fort Jefferson. .This route, at that time, was safe from Indian attacks. A Wayne force, guided by William Smalley, had already driven the southern Shawnees of the Little Miami country, on north to points where they were massing their forces for war.

Students of pioneer history are aware of the conflicting data found in state papers and other documents, on events connected with much of our important pioneer history. The *Draper MSS.* confuse certain events of their time, rather than clear our historical vision. It will be noted by the critical reader that William Smalley named Colonel Trueman and Major Lynch as President Washington's peace commission, which he accompanied as guide, and which met such a tragic and unexpected fate.[16] The probity of William Smalley was always unquestioned. Although it is not known why Major Lynch joined this unfortunate commission, on William Smalley's statement the reader may feel safe in accepting it as a fact. As an illustration of the complexity facing the present day narrator of pioneer events, the following note is quoted from *Western Annals*:[17]

The statements in relation to Trueman afford a curious example of the uncertainty in matters of detail of even our late western history. Marshall[18] and Butler[19] say that he was sent by Wilkinson, whereas he was sent by the Federal government; Atwater[20] says he was sent by Wayne; Judge Burnet[21] says he was sent by Harmar, soon after his defeat, at least eighteen months before Wayne was appointed to command; but his instructions, above referred to, are dated April 3d, 1792. The most perplexing account, however, is

---

[16] See pages 234-235.
[17] Perkins, James H. *Op. cit.*, 381-382 (note).
[18] Marshall, Humphrey. *Op. cit.*, 2:42.
[19] Butler, Mann. *History of the Commonwealth of Kentucky*, 219.
[20] Atwater, Caleb. *History of Ohio*, 145.
[21] Burnet, Jacob. *Op. cit.*, 30, note.

that given by William May, and contained in the *American State Papers*,[22] who states that he, May, left Fort Hamilton, on or about *the 13th of April*, "to follow on the trail of Trueman, who, with a French baker and another man, were sent as a flag to the Indians:" further on he says, that on the 7th day he "discovered Trueman and the two other men lying dead, scalped and stripped." He afterwards gives a particular account of Trueman's death, which account he received from an Indian. This statement appears suspicious, from the fact that General Knox wrote Trueman as late as the 22d of May, (American State Papers[23]) and also from the fact that news of his death first reached Vincennes, June 28th, (American State Papers[24]) as well as from the circumstance that May left in pursuit of Trueman only ten days after the date of his (Trueman's) instructions at Philadelphia. The whole mystery, however, is cleared up by reading in May's affidavit, "Freeman" for "Trueman"; Freeman left for Washington, April 7th; April 10th, Wilkinson wrote Armstrong to order May to desert, so as to acquire information from the Indians;[25] and on or about the 13th, he did so, and on Harmar's trace, which Freeman had been instructed to follow, found his body.

Kentucky, like Virginia, was displeased with Washington's choice of Wayne for commanding general. This first Scott expedition, which reached Fort Jefferson on October 15, 1793, returned home after seeing Wayne's preparatory work with much more confidence in his ability than they previously had. On the second call, a larger number of mounted militiamen responded. Scott reached Fort Jefferson on July 26, 1794, with this force in such good condition that Wayne at once (July 28) moved forward to Fort Defiance. There is historical record that it was one-half of Scott's force—variously estimated by historians of that date at 1100 to 1600 men—that Wayne chose to circle the Indian right wing at Fallen Timbers, and attack them on the rear. Whether or not this historical designation is correct, it was that movement which the Indians subsequently

---

[22]Amer. State Papers, v., 243.
[23]Ibid., 234.
[24]Ibid., 238.
[25]Dillon, *History of Indiana*, 1:312.

declared threw their forces into quick rout, and gave Wayne his decisive victory in less than an hour after William Sloan, a Clermont County boy, Wayne's own bugler, sounded the call to advance to the attack.

Considerable time was spent by the "van" at Slab's Camp on the Bullskin Trace where tradition says slabs or puncheons were used in making camping quarters. Two soldiers died during this encampment and were buried two hundred yards north of it. The location of their graves has been held in memory by each generation of the patriotic people of that community. Recently, when this camp site was dedicated, a duplicate of the Blanchard original thirteen-star flag was raised on the site by the Daughters of the American Revolution of Blanchester, and the Willing Workers of Edenton, and the graves of these unknown soldiers were honored by patriotic services, preliminary to the placing of a marker to their memory. At West Woodville, a short distance from the trace, preliminary services were held on January 28, 1928, dedicating the site of the fight which took place between Smalley's "van" and the Shawnees of that vicinity in 1793, and a thirteen-star flag marks the site.

Enactments of the first Ohio legislature established "the Xenia State Road" over the entire length of the Bullskin Trace, and appropriated funds for its immediate improvement. The unsettled conditions on our north border line and on the Great Lakes, made an open and usable roadway from the Ohio River, north to Detroit, a military necessity. Events of the War of 1812 fully justified this prophetic vision. It is fortunate that the road was ready when the conflict came, for as soon as the War of 1812 was declared, Perry's fleet on Lake Erie had to be supplied with provisions and ammunition. Isaac Blanchard, who afterwards became a resident of New Richmond, took the contract to haul supplies, which were boated down the Ohio River to the mouth of the Bullskin Creek. From there, his caravan of fifteen wagons bumped over the new corduroy road on its way to Sandusky.

For nearly two years, Blanchard kept hauling these

supplies. Eight horses were hitched to each wagon, and each wagon had two men, then called witnesses, who were well armed with old flint-lock rifles to defend themselves from the wild animals and the British in the northern part of the state. The first wagon carried a flag of thirteen stars, which is now in possession of Isaac Blanchard's grandson, William Blanchard, of Edenton.

Excepting the marks of the old trail here and there, about all that is left to tell the story of these heroic days of conflict, are a few old flint-lock rifles and horse-pistols, some gunpowder horns which the soldiers of those days have handed down to the present generation, and a few cannon-balls and rusted bayonets picked up from these camp sites of years ago.

REVEREND ROBERT ARMSTRONG

The first pastor—1803-1821—of the Massie's Creek and Sugar Creek congregations, Greene County, Ohio.

The first public library in the present bounds of Ohio was in circulation at Belpre in 1795. The first book printed in Ohio, then the Northwest Territory, was the *Maxwell Code*. The printing of this small octavo volume of territorial laws was done by William Maxwell; the binding by his wife—in Cincinnati, 1796.

In Drake's *Picture of Cincinnati and the Miami Country*, printed there in 1815, the author notes the progress of the writing and printing of books and pamphlets:

Ten years ago, there had not been printed in this place, a single volume; but since the year 1811, twelve different books, besides many pamphlets, have been executed.[26]

The Ohio Archaeological and Historical Quarterly gives the interesting story of the genesis in 1803, of the Coonskin Library at Ames, Ohio, and its successor, the Western

---

[26]Drake, Daniel. *A Picture of Cincinnati and the Miami Country*, 153.

Library Association.[27] In *Pioneer Biography* is found a detailed account of the first library meeting at Cincinnati in 1802. $340.00 was raised by subscription for the Cincinnati Library. With Lewis Kerr as librarian, its organization was completed March 6, 1802.[28] These were the first three public circulating libraries in the Northwestern Territory.

Rev. Robert Armstrong, however, brought with him to Greene County,[29] a library that was large and representative to a degree hardly to be expected in a minister of that period—1803 to 1821. The doctrinal theology of the old Scotch Associate communion, his denomination, was well represented, but not more so than was other best literature of the past. He was a graduate of the University of Edinburgh, and naturally received there the liberal viewpoints reflected throughout all his pastoral ministrations to his two Greene County congregations. After his theological training under the Presbytery of Edinburgh, he was assigned to the new mission field—the United States. Some of his books came with him over seas, across the Alleghanies, into the heart of Kentucky, and then to Old Chillicothe, where they found a final resting-place among friends, to whose spiritual life he was a true pastor, and into whose intellectual uplift he and his library entered. Libraries were small in size and few in number in the final years of the Northwestern Territory. This one was probably, for a few years at least, the Territory's largest individual book collection. It certainly was, if taken together with that of his near neighbor, James Galloway. It is pleasing to know that these books were made available to all who then desired to read, and tradition relates that these were many. The influence of this library was noted in the statement of Howe, "that more books have been sold and read in this county than in any other of the same population in the state."

Mr. Armstrong's intellectual ability is evidenced in the outlines of a sermon preached by him to his congregation

---

[27]*Ohio Arch. and Hist. Quarterly*, 26:58-77.
[28]McBride, James. *Op. Cit.*, 1:43, 104-105.
[29]Howe, Henry. *Op. Cit.*, 1847, 196.

at Massie's Creek, Saturday, April 18, 1818, evidently a preparatory service preceding communion. The sermon was a strong presentation of the truths suggested by the unusual text he chose, and is notable from the fact that, in its discussion, no sectarian or doctrinal elaboration is found. The notes, made by Major James Galloway, Jr., were usual for the period. Many pioneer listeners were industrious notetakers at their pastor's Sabbath discourses, and freely discussed them afterwards, both in their homes and at neighborhood gatherings.

The following sketch of the life and labors of Rev. Robert Armstrong in the mission-fields of Kentucky and Tennessee, previous to his ministerial work as stated pastor, which began in 1803 in Greene County, Ohio, is furnished by Rev. Dr. Jesse Johnson, professor of church history, Xenia Theological Seminary. Dr. Johnson's historical data are drawn largely from McKerrow's *History of the Secession Church;* Scouller's *Manual of the United Presbyterian Church;* the *Christian Magazine* for 1799, pp. 187-188 and 569-572; and Reverend Armstrong's letters written home, subsequent to 1803.

The narrative of Andrew Galloway, in the Xenia *News,* 1859, reprinted in the Xenia *Torchlight,*[30] furnishes a pen-picture of this remarkable cleric and his pioneer ministrations in Greene County, Ohio:

Rev. Robert Armstrong was born in Midholm, Roxboroughshire, Scotland, and was graduated at the University of Edinburgh. He studied theology with Archibald Bruce at Whitburn; was licensed in the autumn of 1796 by the Associate Presbytery of Kelso, and ordained June 15, 1797, by the same. He was both licensed and ordained with the intention of going to America. In 1796 some Scotch Seceders, living near Lexington, Kentucky, applied to the Synod for a preacher, and in answer Mr. Armstrong and Mr. Andrew Fulton were sent in the summer of 1797. They tarried during the subsequent winter in western Pennsylvania, and arrived in Kentucky in the summer of 1798. On the 28th of November they organized, according to instruc-

---
[30]Xenia *Torchlight*, September 17, 1873.

tion, the Presbytery of Kentucky, subordinate to the General Associate Synod of Scotland. Armstrong was installed April 23, 1799, as pastor of Davis' Fork, Miller's Run and Cane Run, and so labored until the autumn of 1804,[31] when he and his three congregations became so heartily sick of slavery that they rose *en masse* and migrated to Greene County, Ohio. Here they were organized into two congregations, Massie's Creek and Sugar Creek, and on the 2nd of September the Presbytery ordered him to take charge of them without the formality of re-installation. In 1811 he gave up the Sugar Creek branch and continued at Massie's Creek until January 9, 1821, when he resigned with the intention of going to Flat Rock, Indiana; but before he could accomplish this he died October 14, 1821. He was remarkable for the smallness of his body, being short in stature and slight in form, but possessed of a vigorous mind and good attainments. He received a very respectable vote in the Synod of 1821 as the only competitor of Dr. Ramsay for the Professorship of Theology.

The account of the appointment of Mr. Armstrong and another minister, Andrew Fulton, by the Anti-Burgher Associate Synod of Scotland as missionaries to Kentucky, and of the organization of the Kentucky Associate Presbytery is of interest:

This year (1796), an application was made to the Synod, by some of the inhabitants of the State of Kentucky, to send out missionaries to that part of America. The application was favorably entertained by the Synod, and two of their preachers, Messrs. Andrew Fulton and Robert Armstrong, having expressed a willingness to undertake the mission were appointed to be ordained and to proceed with all convenient speed to the place of their destination. Instructions were given to them, that so soon as they should arrive in Kentucky, they should constitute themselves into a presbytery, in immediate subordination to the Synod, under the designation of "The Associate Presbytery of Kentucky." The Presbytery of Kelso was instructed to write a letter to the brethren of the Presbytery of Pennsylvania, accounting for these two brethren being missioned not in a state of subordination to that Presbytery; and the Presbytery of Perth, through whom the application had

---

[31] In 1804, Rev. Mr. Armstrong married Nancy Andrew, in Tennessee.

been made to the Synod, was appointed to write a suitable address to the inhabitants of Kentucky. To defray the expense of the mission, a collection was appointed to be made in the several congregations under the inspection of the Synod in Britain, so as that these young men may be conveyed to the scene of their labor in such a manner as may be for the credit of religion and of the Synod. These brethren set sail for America in the end of summer, 1797. During the course of the following year, intelligence was received from Pennsylvania expressive of the high gratification which the brethren belonging to that Presbytery felt in the mission to Kentucky, and declaring their readiness to cooperate with their brethren in Kentucky, so far as circumstances might permit. The Pennsylvania brethren also intimated that they had it in contemplation to disjoin themselves into several presbyteries, and to erect a transAtlantic synod, maintaining the same connection with the General Synod, in Scotland, as they now did in their presbyterial capacity.

During the summer (1799), intelligence of a gratifying kind was received from the two missionaries, Messrs. Armstrong and Fulton, who had been sent to Kentucky in 1797. They arrived in that province in the month of March, 1798; and though they had considerable difficulties to encounter at first, and appear to have been discouraged by the general state of the country, yet a great and an effectual door was speedily opened unto them. More applications were made to them for sermons than they were able to answer. As soon as circumstances permitted after their arrival, they constituted themselves into a presbytery. This took place at Cane Run, on the 28th of November, 1798.[32] The following account of the early difficulties and prospects of this mission extracted from the letters of these individuals, cannot fail to be interesting:

We set sail (says Mr. Armstrong, in a letter dated 5th December, 1798) from Pittsburgh for Kentucky, on the 21st February, 1798; and, after a passage of nine days, arrived at Limestone,[33] on the first of March. Limestone is 500 miles from Pittsburgh. The weather was for the most part cold and stormy, and our accommodation in the boat very indifferent. It was so much crowded with horses, baggage,

---

[32]The original minute-book of this Presbytery, in Mr. Armstrong's handwriting, is in the possession of Xenia Seminary.
[33]Now Maysville, Kentucky.

and merchant goods, that there was scarcely any place in it where we could stretch ourselves to sleep; and, except a part of two nights, when we stopped the boat and went ashore to a house, I slept little, and never pulled off my clothes. On one occasion, the darkness of the night rendering it dangerous to continue sailing, we fastened our boat to the bank of the river, and Mr. Fulton and I went in search of a house to lodge in. After traversing the woods of what is called the Indian shore, on the right hand side of the Ohio River, going down for a considerable time, we found that our search was in vain; for no inhabitants could be seen. There was a good deal of snow on the ground: we could not sleep on board, and we wanted rest somewhere. The only shift which now remained was to cut up logs for a fire. Three of us, Mr. Fulton, another young man, and myself, went to work and kindled a fire as well as we could. I then chose a place to lie upon; and after scraping away the snow, and cutting up a piece of log for a pillow, I wrapped myself in a blanket, and lay down to sleep. When we had rested thus for about two hours, a great fall of wet snow obliged us to decamp, and again remove to the boat.

When we set sail at first, the river was low, and our vessel grounded, sometimes on shallows, sometimes on rocks; then all hands (myself only excepted), were obliged to assist, and jumping into the river, while water reached to their loins, to force her off with long poles. Such a situation was not, in a cold frosty night, you may judge, very tolerable. There were only six men on board, which made it necessary for Mr. Fulton and me to take our full share of watching and rowing; this, as we generally sailed night and day, was labour sufficient.

A severe cold, contracted very suddenly at Pittsburgh, threw me into a slight fever, from which I had not fully recovered when we set sail down the river; and this circumstance, through the kindness of the owner of the boat, procured for me the indulgence mentioned above; yet I got perfectly well during the passage and landed at Limestone free from any bodily complaint whatever, except that I felt wearied and sleepy.

We staid ten days near Limestone, in the house of Alexander Hamilton, an old Scotch Seceder from Haddington. We were yet seventy miles from the place of our destination, and wanted horses to carry us along. There is scarcely any such thing as horses to hire in this country; and, owing to the deepness of the roads, in some seasons, it is almost impossible to travel on foot. But here, as in everything else, we experienced the kindness of Providence, and were agreeably extricated from this difficulty; for Mr. Hamilton gave us one horse, and a Roman Catholic, to whom we were introduced, gave us another for upwards of fifty miles; and, at the same time, a letter of introduction to a gentleman of the Baptist persuasion, with whom he was connected. From this gentleman's house we sent back our horses; and he showed his kindness by detaining us with him as long as he could, and then gave us horses to Cane Run, where Mr. Goodlet resides.

We had now finished our journey; but our difficulties seemed only to begin: for besides other discouraging circumstances, we scarcely knew of any in all this western part of the world, to take us by the hand or submit to our ministry. At first I regretted that one of us had not remained in Pennsylvania, where there was great need for him. But God, who often, for the accomplishment of his own gracious designs, works by such means, and in such manner, as short-sighted mortals cannot understand, disappointed our fears; and we were soon convinced that the General Associate Synod has been directed to the most proper measure in sending out two ministers. The hand of God in this matter was seen and acknowledged in different parts of the country; for, though our beginnings were small, a great door has been opened here for the preaching of the gospel; and there are petitions for sermons which it is impossible for us to answer to the satisfaction of the people; and though the people that submitted to our ministry at first, if they had all resided in our settlement, would have made but a small congregation, there is now every reason to think that those under our inspection would afford sufficient work for four ministers; two in Kentucky and two in the State of Tennessee, which lies on the south-west of Kentucky.

Reverend Armstrong continued his relations as missionary pastor of the three Kentucky churches until 1803, when he accepted the call of Massie's Creek and Sugar Creek pioneers in Greene County, Ohio, to become their stated pastor. The prosecution of the call, and his installation as their minister took place in 1804. The building of the first two log churches following his coming, and notes throwing light on his unusual personality are found in a communication to the Xenia, Ohio, *News*, written by

Andrew Galloway, Esq., one of the members of his Massie's Creek charge at that date.[34] A quotation from it follows:

    The first church edifice of the Associate Congregation of Massie's Creek was built on about three acres of land donated by James Stevenson for church and cemetery. It was built of round hickory logs, the bark peeled off. It was thirty feet square and covered with clap-boards, knees and weight-poles; the interstices between the logs were filled up with cat and clay; it was without gallery or loft of any kind, and the floor was composed of Mother Earth. In it there were neither stoves nor chimney; there was but one door, and it was in the center of one end of the house. From the door there was an aisle that ran to the foundation of the pulpit in the center of the other end. The pulpit was composed of clapboards, on a wooden structure; on each side was a window of twelve eight-by-ten lights. It was seated with two rows of puncheons, from twelve to fifteen inches broad and twelve feet long, split out from poplar near by; they were from four to six inches thick, and hewed on the upper side with a broad axe, and smoothed off with a drawing-knife or a jack-plane; in each end and center there were uprights some three feet long, mortised in, and on these uprights, from two to three slats were pinned and formed quite a comfortable back. These seats had four substantial legs like a stool; one end of them stood against the wall, the other end extended to the aisle.

    This edifice was on the north bank of Massie's Creek, about four miles from where it empties into the Little Miami River. Men and women rode on horses, or walked, for there was no other means of locomotion, from two to twelve and some fifteen miles to this house; sat through two sermons, and returned home without seeing or smelling fire in the coldest weather.

    About the year 1812-13, a second house of worship was built of hewed logs, distant from the first one some 150 feet. (At this date, the country had improved, and several mills had been built). This church was about fifty feet wide; was floored, and ceiled with half-inch poplar boards. In it there were four pews, and the balance of the seats were those from the first edifice. This house became too small for the congregation and its increase; one side of it was taken out, and the width increased about twelve feet. This building was occupied until the stone edifice now used by

---

[34]Xenia *News*, January 29, 1859.

PIONEER STORIES

Rev. J. P. Smart, was built, about two miles distant from the first site. This first site is now occupied as a cemetery. In it are the remains of Mr. Armstrong and of a large majority of the congregation who were members at its commencement. Out of Massie's Creek, Sugar Creek, and Xenia congregations of the Associate Church, and Xenia Associate Reformed congregation, has sprung the nucleus of almost all the congregations in the United Presbyterian Church in the West.

One hundred and twenty-five years after the call of Reverend Robert Armstrong to pastoral work in Ohio; on the afternoon of August 26th, 1928, the first day of the Greene County, Ohio, Home-coming, the pioneer worship of Rev. Armstrong's congregation was repeated in remembrance of the Faith of our Fathers and their simple and heartfelt worship of God. The Sugar Creek United Presbyterian Church, which has been in continuous and active organization since Rev. Armstrong's pastorate, formed the organized body of this afternoon's congregation. With them came many of the descendants of the original communicants of both Rev. Armstrong's congregations; home-comers from every section of the United States, and some from foreign lands—it was a large congregation of the sons and daughters of Greene County.

The historic address, visualizing the pioneer period of the hour's worship, was given by the writer. The sermon, with a description of preparations for the communion period services of 1804, was given by the Rev. H. B. McElree of the Second United Presbyterian Church, Xenia, Ohio. The precentor, Mr. Edwin Galloway, who led the congregational singing, used Rouse's version of the Psalms, and "lined out" two lines at a time, as was the custom of the Massie's Creek Seceder Church, in which his ancestors worshipped.

The collection was taken by the elders and deacons of the Sugar Creek United Presbyterian Church, who have been in unbroken and active succession as such since being organized by Rev. Armstrong in 1804. They used the "handle and poke" receptacles of the pioneer period for the taking of the collection.

OLD CHILLICOTHE

Thomas Wildcat Alford, great-grandson of the Shawnee chief Tecumseh, and the guest of the Home-coming Week, and of this congregation, was present on the rostrum. Among other valued services to his nation, the Absentee Shawnees, now permanently resident in Oklahoma, he had recently completed, after 25 years of study, the translation of the four gospels into the Shawnee language. In honor of this great work for his people, who have no biblical translation, the offering of the day, amounting to nearly $125.00, was devoted toward the paymen of its publication. When the offering was presented at the altar, Chief Alford arose and received it for the purpose designated, and offered a heartfelt prayer in Shawnee, beseeching God's blessing on the great congregation who had succeeded his people in this beautiful land, and who were sending this message of love and salvation to them now.

This was the historic moment of the Home-coming of 1928, and of the dedicatory services of the pavilion in the park at Xenia, Ohio, which bears the name of Chief Alford's nation, once the proud owners of this land.

KENTON, THE PATRIOT

An interesting story, illustrating General Kenton's patriotism, which was outstanding and always in evidence, has been preserved as one of the incidents of his visit, in 1824, at the home of his friend, James Galloway, Sr., near Old Chillicothe. This visit, which was incident to a journey the general was making to Kentucky, gave opportunity for these two comrades to renew their friendship of former years, and once more recall their adventures in Kentucky before and after the days of 1782. In this short visit, they renewed in memory their part in the stirring events of Clark's and Logan's campaigns and the strenuous days in the Kentucky settlements when, sometimes together and sometimes quite far apart, they defended the blockhouse forts against the attacks of the Shawnee Indians and their allies. At the time James Galloway, Sr., left Kentucky with

HOME OF OREN AND MARTHA NORTH, OLD CHILLICOTHE—NOW OLDTOWN, OHIO

From this porch, in 1834, Simon Kenton described his captivity and run of the gantlet, after taking seven Shawnee horses, in 1778. The author is standing by the porch.

his family, and established a home at Old Chillicothe in 1797, General Kenton was a rich man. His home place of 1000 acres at Washington, Kentucky, was only a small part of his Kentucky possessions. It was known to his host that he had met with financial reverses since that time, but it was impossible for him to realize, as he subsequently learned, the extreme pinch of poverty then endured by General Kenton, or that this distinguished patriot had actual lack of food and clothing, except as provided by the generosity of a relative, who was almost as poor as the general himself. At the time of this visit, his final assets, which consisted of some hill land in Kentucky, had been forfeited through lack of funds to meet the taxes as they came due. In this extremity, he secured a poverty-stricken horse and a disreputable saddle and bridle, and started to Frankfort, Kentucky. If he could get there, he would venture a personal appeal to the legislature to remit his forfeitures, and release his lands from tax liens then due the state he had served with such signal courage and devotion, when it needed his services most.

The American Pioneer gives this interesting account from which we quote:[35]

After supper, Mr. Galloway, who had seen his horse, wretched saddle and bridle, and his tattered garments, said, "Kenton, you have served your country faithfully, even down to old age; what expedition against the British and savages was ever raised in the West, but you were among the most prominent in it? Even down to the last war, you were with Harrison at the taking of General Proctor's army in Canada; an old gray-headed warrior, you could not stay at home while your country needed your services; and, look, how they have neglected you! How can you stand such treatment?" Kenton rose from his seat, casting a fierce and fiery look at his old friend Galloway; clinching his right fist, and with a stamp of his right foot, he exclaimed with warmth, "Don't say that again; if you do, I will leave your house, and never again call you my friend."

Kenton passed on to Kentucky, and to Frankfort, where the legislature was in session, with all his troubles

---

[35]*The American Pioneer*, 2:155.

hanging over his head, in order to petition the legislature to remit the forfeiture of his land for taxes; which, he said, if he could sell for six and a fourth cents an acre, it would be doing "mighty well"!

On Kenton's arrival in Frankfort, at first no one recognized him, for Kenton's old friends had nearly all gone to the world of spirits. The roughly clad old man, with tattered garments, passed to and fro. At length General Thomas Fletcher, a senator from Bath County, recognized the old warrior; he took him by the hand, led him to a tailor's shop, had his measure taken for a full suit of clothes and bought him a new hat. On the adjournment of the legislature, Kenton was taken to the capitol and into the representative chamber, placed in the speaker's chair, and there was introduced to a crowded assembly of legislators, judges, officers of government and citizens generally, as the second great adventurer of the West. His lands were released from forfeiture, through memorials then forwarded; Congress soon after granted him a pension, and the last time I saw the old man, in 1832, he was wearing the same suit of clothes, and I *believe* that the *same hat* was still on his *head!*[36]

Kenton's Run of the Gantlet

Kenton's first "run of the gantlet" occurred at Old Chillicothe on the Little Miami River, after his capture at the Ohio River. Its course across the level prairie is one half-mile in length. Six hundred Indians formed the lane of the gantlet which ended at the council-house. The double line, between which Kenton ran for his life, was armed with sticks and staves, and some had knives and tomahawks with which to strike him. As he sped toward the council-house, which was his "city of refuge," many called him "horse-thief"—an appellation which stuck, in a joking way, with many of his pioneer friends and acquaintances long after Indian times in Ohio. General Kenton's own statement, unquoted for many years, reveals his motive and purpose. "I never in my life," he said to William Patric, an early Urbana, Ohio, historian, "captured horses for my own use,

---

[36] Compare Kenton, Edna. *Simon Kenton*, 307-310.

but would hand them over to those who had lost horses by Indians' thefts; nor did I ever make reprisals on any but hostile tribes who were at war against white settlers."[37]

The Kenton Elm

General Simon Kenton and General Simon Rains both were related to the Greene County pioneer family of John Lucas, Sr. In the Xenia *Gazette*, July 8, 1896, one of the descendants of this family gives interesting personal history, excerpts of which are here given:

One peculiarity not usually alluded to was the manner in which General Kenton wore his hair—in a queue. Many times, it has been the pleasure of this writer to hear the venerable pioneers, W. A. Smith of Jamestown, Ohio, and Grandma Sarah Bales relate, that when Kenton visited their home, which he often did, she took great pride in dressing his hair. During the period from 1800 to 1821, when these visits were most frequent, when he was standing it reached to the calves of his legs. As a reward for her services, General Kenton agreed to attend her wedding should she ever be married. This he did in 1813. Sarah Lucas Bales, alluded to above, was the daughter of John Lucas, Sr. Her mother was a sister of General Simon Rains. The Kenton and the Rains families were neighbors in Virginia before Kenton had to run away from that state.

Grandmother Bales often told the story, of a visit in 1809 to Xenia, 12 miles away from her father's farm in Caesar's Creek Township, Greene County, Ohio. She, with her father and mother and Uncle Simon, as he was called in the family, made this trip along the trail which is now known as the Hoop Road. When they approached the present location of the Lauman schoolhouse, three miles southeast of Xenia, General Kenton had them all dismount, and took them to a large elm tree of very heavy foliage, which stood north of the schoolhouse. It was about 500 feet east of the location of Mr. Walter Nash's present residence. He there recounted one of the stirring incidents of his life as a scout and Indian fighter. During one of these forays into the Shawnee Indian territory about Old Chil-

---

[37] Kenton, Edna. *Op. Cit.*, 99.

licothe, he became separated from his party, and endeavored to make his retreat alone. The Indians, however, struck his trail, and pursued him on horseback. When Kenton first heard them, he was near this great elm, into the top of which a large wild grapevine had securely trellised itself, reaching across from the top of a smaller hickory tree growing near by. He pulled himself up the hickory tree by this vine, and thence overhand into the elm after he had confused his trail by backtracking. The Indians approached in great glee, his trail indicating that they were near their victim. Covering a trail by backtracking was skillfully done in those days by both pioneers and Indians. In this case, General Kenton was successful and was so securely hidden by the dense elm and grapevine foliage that he was not discovered. The pursuing party of Indians remained some hours under the very tree which sheltered him while he observed them examining every possible means of escape except the one he adopted. The Indians finally gave up the search and returned to Old Chillicothe.

The writer remembers this tree. It was a noble elm which should be standing today, one of Ohio's historic monuments. He was taken to see it when a boy by his father, the late Major James C. Galloway, who related to him, as they sat under the widespread branches and dense foliage, substantially the same story of its part in General Kenton's escape as that given above.

THE CAPTIVITY AND ESCAPE OF DANIEL BOONE

The Shawnee narrative of the escape of their star prisoner, Daniel Boone, whom they always admired, and whose name and deeds still live in their traditions, is one of the Northwestern Territory's finest human interest tales. It is a part of the stirring story of his capture, and the four months he spent with them—their adopted son.

Boone's captivity at Old Chillicothe, his adoption as a son by Black Fish, the leading civil chief of the Cha-lah-kaw-tha tribe of the Shawnees, and his escape to warn Boonsborough of what he believed to be an impending attack by 400 warriors who gathered at Old Chillicothe, were among the notable incidents of his career. American writers give substantially in its entirety the account of his capture by the Shawnees, his escape after four months of rather agreeable captivity, and his strenuous overland journey to Boonsborough in time to warn the settlement and repair its dilapidated fortifications. The expected attack did not occur, but a 12-day siege of Boonsborough, August 7th to 20th, 1778, did occur later under the leadership of Captain Duquesne and eleven other Frenchmen.

The American narratives are incomplete to students familiar with the safeguards which are known to have been thrown around Boone to prevent his escape, so specially urgent at that time. Old Chillicothe was swarming with a war-party preparing, he believed, to move against his home settlement in Kentucky, but in fact on their return journey from an unsuccessful invasion in Virginia. Any unexplained absence of Boone—who had accepted adoption with its obligations—from the village, for a half-day or a night, would have started pursuit by bands of Indian trailers, impossible for him to have outrun in his four-day journey to his home, the direct overland distance of which is fairly estimated at 160 miles from Old Chillicothe. Instinctively his objective would have been determined, and from out of the hundreds of Indian warriors available, the surest and fleetest marathon trailers in America would have been chosen to track Boone and recapture him.

The Shawnee explanation of Boone's escape accounts for the time necessary for him to get so far on his way as to be beyond successful pursuit; it also proves that strategy, Boone's well-known characteristic, did not fail him at this time. There is no Shawnee tradition that they undertook to trail him after they felt certain that he had escaped. They relate that Boone was sent out by Black Fish to locate and drive back the tribe's horses to their usual stockade near the village. These horses, when not needed, were turned loose to pasture at will in the forest. They followed an old leader horse with a bell strapped to his neck. The sound of a bell always carried far in the quiet of the forest, especially at evening time, and was of great assistance in locating the horses when they were to be brought in.

Boone found the drove, and removed the bell from the lead horse's neck. Then after some delay, he returned to the village and reported to Black Fish that he had not been able to find the horses. The chief ordered him to go back and find them, and not to return till he could bring them in. This gave Boone the necessary freedom to make his getaway, together with a lapse of time that left his trail old and uncertain, even if the Indians could have found the point from which it started. Successful pursuit was consequently impossible with a man as skillful as Boone in "covering and backtracking."[38]

Boone's Own Story

January 1, 1778, I went with thirty men to the Blue Licks on Licking River to make salt for the different garrisons.

February 7th. Hunting by myself, to procure meat for the company, I met a party of 102 Indians and two Frenchmen marching against Boonsborough. They pursued and took me; and next day I capitulated for my men, knowing they could not escape. They were 27 in number, three having gone home with salt. The Indians, according to the capitulation, used us generously. They carried us to Old Chelicothe, the principal Indian town on the Little Miami.

On the 18th of February we arrived there, after an uncomfortable journey in very severe weather.

On the 10th of March, I and ten of my men were conducted to Detroit.

On the 30th, we arrived there, and were treated by governor Hamilton, the British commander at that post, with great humanity.

The Indians had such an affection for me that they re-

---

[38]Boone is believed to have followed the Bullskin Trail which bore directly south from Old Chillicothe to the mouth of Bullskin Creek at the Ohio River. A monument, with appropriate legends, marks this trail at Edenton, Clermont County, Ohio. The fact that Boone did not make his escape on one of the Shawnee horses easily available to him is explained by the easily followed trail left by a horse, and that when mounted, he could not "cover and backtrack" in case of close pursuit.

fused £100 sterling offered them by the governor, if they would leave me with the others on purpose that he might send me home on my parole. Several English gentlemen there, sensible of my adverse fortune, and touched with sympathy, generously offered to supply my wants, which I declined with many thanks, adding that I never expected it would be in my power to recompense such unmerited generosity. The Indians left my men in captivity with the British at Detroit.

On the 10th of April, they brought me toward Old Chelicothe, where we arrived on the twenty-fifth day of the same month. This was a long and fatiguing march, through an exceeding fertile country, remarkable for fine springs and streams of water. At Chelicothe, I spent my time as comfortably as I could expect; was adopted, according to their custom, into a family where I became a son, and had a great share in the affections of my new parents, brothers, sisters and friends. I was exceedingly familiar and friendly with them, always appearing as cheerful and satisfied as possible, and they put great confidence in me.[39] I often went a-hunting with them, and frequently gained their applause for my activity at our shooting matches. I was careful not to exceed many of them in shooting; for no people are more envious than they in this sport. I could observe in their countenances and gestures the greatest expressions of joy when they exceeded me; and, when the reverse happened, of envy. The Shawanese chief took great notice of me, and treated me with profound respect, and entire friendship, often entrusting me to hunt at my liberty.[40] I frequently returned with the spoils of the woods, and as often presented some of what I had taken to him, expressive of duty to my sovereign. My food and lodging was in common with them, not so good indeed as I could desire; but necessity made everything acceptable.

I now began to meditate an escape, but carefully avoided giving suspicion.

Until the first day of June, I continued at Old Chelicothe, and then was taken to the salt springs on Scioto, and kept there ten days making salt. During this time, I had

---

[39] Boone's adopted name was Sheltowee, meaning Big-turtle.

[40] During Boone's time the hunters' prices for pelts were: Deer skins (best in summer) $1.00. Beaver (winter best) $2.50. Otter $3.00 to $5.00. A horse load of deer hides was 100 pelts. Buffalo, bear and elk hides were too bulky for horse transport, and were of little value and had no market.

hunted with them, and found the land, for a great extent above this river, to exceed the soil of Kentucky, if possible, and remarkably well watered.

On my return to Chelicothe, four hundred and fifty of the choicest Indian warriors were ready to march against Boonsborough, painted and armed in a fearful manner. This alarmed me, and I determined to escape.

On the 16th of June (1778) before sunrise, I went off secretly and reached Boonsborough on the 20th, a journey of one hundred and sixty miles, during which I had only one meal. I found our fortress in a bad state, but we immediately repaired our flanks, gates, posterns, and formed double bastions, which we completed in ten days. One of my fellow prisoners escaping after me, brought advice that on account of my flight, the Indians had put off their expedition for three weeks.

About August 1st, I set out with nineteen men to surprise Paint Creek Town on Scioto. Without four miles we fell in with thirty Indians going against Boonsborough. We fought, and the enemy gave way. We suffered no loss. The enemy had one killed and two wounded. We took three horses and all their baggage. The Indians having evacuated their town and gone all together against Boonsborough, we returned, passed them on the sixth day, and on the seventh arrived safe at Boonsborough.

On the 8th (August, 1778) the Indian army, four hundred and forty-four in number, commanded by Capt. Duquesne, and eleven other Frenchmen, and their chiefs, came and summoned the fort. I requested two days consideration, which they granted. During this, we brought in through the posterns all the horses and other cattle we could collect.

On the 9th, in the evening, I informed their commander that we were determined to defend the fort, while a man was living. Then they proposed a treaty, and said if we sent out nine men to conclude it, they would withdraw. The treaty was held within sixty yards of the fort, as we suspected the savages. The articles were agreed to and signed; when the Indians told us, it was their custom for two Indians to shake hands with every white man in the treaty, as an evidence of friendship. We agreed to this also. They immediately grappled us to take us prisoners, but we cleared ourselves of them, though surrounded by hundreds, and gained the fort safely, except one that was wounded by a

MEMORIAL TO DANIEL BOONE AND 27 SALT MAKERS

*Erected by Dr. William A. Galloway at Oldtown.
Greene County, Ohio, 1931*

heavy fire from their army. On this they began to undermine the fort, beginning at the water-mark of Kentucke river, which is sixty yards from the fort. We discovered this by the water being made muddy with the clay, and countermined them by cutting a trench across their subterranean passage. The enemy discovering this, by the clay we threw out of the fort, desisted.

On the 20th day of August (1778), they raised the siege.

During this dreadful siege, we had two men killed, and four wounded. We lost a number of cattle. We killed thirty-seven of the enemy, and wounded a great number. We picked up one hundred and twenty-five pounds of their bullets, besides what struck in the logs of the fort.[41]

CONCERNING STEPHEN RUDDELL

Mrs. W. T. Lafferty of the University of Kentucky, adds an important chapter to Kentucky church history, which shows the assistance given in Stephen Ruddell's notable and devoted services as a Baptist missionary worker among his adopted brothers, the Shawnees. His sterling character is manifest at once upon reading his letter to Benj. Drake on Tecumtha.[42] His handwriting is that of a man of moral and mental poise, and his composition, which he did not attempt to correct, is that of a clear and ready thinker. Mrs. Lafferty was fortunate in obtaining the loan of the old Cooper's Run Baptist Meeting-house Sessions' Record, beginning in 1784, and, with her characteristic generosity, has selected such portions of it as are of interest to this story:

I was about to give up the quest. I was afraid the book had been lost, but on Sunday I went to see the owner of it, who found it and allowed me to bring it home with me. It is an old hand-tanned leather book seven and one-half inches by twelve, whose yellowed pages are of hand-made paper, scarcely lighter than the faded home-made ink used by the five clerks who kept the minutes from June, 1787 to July,

---
[41]*Ohio Arch. and Hist. Quarterly*, 13:271-273.
[42]See page 127.

1829. They were good penmen, all of them, and must have been expert in trimming their quill pens to a fine point.

The book begins with the declaration of faith in which capitals are abundantly misused. Then follow the names of "the members," "when received," "when dismissed," "when died," and "when excommunicated." This list includes the negroes, as well as the white members, and such are invariably written, "Negro Winny," "Negro George," "Negro Juno," "Negro Phyllis," etc.

Each minute begins formally with the statement, "At a church meeting held at Cooper's Run Meeting-house, the 4th Saturday in —— month, after prayer proceeded to business as follows:". As there were few accessible courts of justice in those days, all the offenses and misdemeanors of members were tried before the discipline committee of the church. In reading through, I find the names of people whose descendants are influential citizens today, "Up before the church" for "slander," "whispering," "gambling," "fiddling for dancing," "dancing," "drinking to intoxication," "immorality," "quarreling with neighbors," etc. The clerks who have kept these records were James Garrard, son of the governor of the state, James Brown, Edmund Montjoy, William Corbin and Simeon Kirtley.

At the meeting held on September 12, 1801, Stephen Ruddell "gave his membership to the church." At a meeting February 13, 1802, "paid by the church 18 shillings for the Indian Mission, likewise gave three Dollars to Brother Stephen Ruddell for his attendance with the above missionary."

Which indicates that Stephen Ruddell had had a predecessor.

At the church meeting held May 9, 1807, Ruddell made the following report in writing concerning his mission to the Shawnee Indians:

"The report of Stephen Ruddel on his Mission to the Shawnese Indians appointed by the church of Christ at Cooper's Run September 13, 1806 Sheweth that your Missionary agreeable to the request of the Church proceeded on his Mission on September 19 last, and reached the place of destination on 2nd of October following where he found a number of the Indians collected with an expectation of my arrival. Although a number of them had left the Assembly in order to hunt and provide for their winter's Sustenence. Such as remained I preched to on the 3rd day following.

They appeared to be very attentive and desirous to be informed and instructed into the knowledge of the Christian religion which they expressed to me the day following and further to confirm the truth of what they said in aprobation of the Doctrines delivered to them in my Sermon they gave me a String of beads as a token and evidence of their friendship for the Society who had sent me on a Mission so desirable to them, which they desire the Society will accept of through me, your Missionary; and further your Missionary attempted to remove some fears respecting the Justice of the Government towards them which he did so satisfactorily to them that they as an evidence of their entire satisfaction gave him another String of Wampum which is requested to be present to you. Your Missionary believes that if prudent and proper measures were adopted to enlighten their minds the present temper of mind which they appear to possess (with the blessing of God) would be attended with great Success to the Gospel and greatly beneficial to those poor unenlightened Savages. Signed, Stephen Ruddel."

Continuing, the minute records: "The two Strings of Wampam mentioned in the above report was received by the Church through Brother Stephen Ruddle and was ordered to be deposited among the Church papers, also agreed, that we will encourage Brother Ruddle on a farther Mission to the Indians; that Brother Eastin inform the churches at Indian Crick, flat Lick, and green Creek of the Same, in order that Contributions be made for Brother Ruddle on Said Mission, that Brother Thomas Smith inform the Church at Summerset for that purpose—Also that Brother Montjoy write to the Church at Jack's Creek on that Subject."

The Brother Eastin referred to was the moderator and his name was Augustin Eastin, a man who took a prominent part in the religious discussion of that day.

The preacher at Cooper's Run Meeting-House was paid 35 pounds a year.

At a Church meeting held at Cooper's Run on the 10th of February, 1810, it was "Agreed that the Subject of Brother Stephen Ruddle's Ordination be postponed to next meeting."

At a certain meeting held at Cooper's Run on Saturday 10th of March, 1810 "the Subject of Br. Stephen Ruddell's Ordination was taken up. And it was agreed that he should be ordained to the ministry of the Gospel. And that the

Saturday before the 2nd Sunday in April be set apart by fasting and prayer to Almighty God for said purpose."

If there was a meeting held in April, it was not recorded in the church book, for the next minute is May 12, 1810. After that there are frequent references to Isaac Ruddell, who was the father of Stephen, but I have not been able to find another item concerning Stephen.

This old church is still in the possession of a descendant of the Garrards. I have been able to persuade the owners of similar church books to place them in the Baptist Theological Seminary of Louisville or in the Kentucky State Historical Society of Frankfort for safe-keeping. I wish this one could be placed in the State Historical Society also.

CAPTAIN THOMAS BULLITT

The first white man known to have visited Old Chillicothe on the Little Miami River was Captain Thomas Bullitt, a Virginian of Fincastle County—now Kentucky. In 1773, he came down the Ohio River with a party of surveyors and settlers to a point not far from Bullskin Creek in the present Clermont County, Ohio. There he debarked and camped his party, while he journeyed alone for sixty-five miles inland to find the Shawnee Indian settlement and interview its chief. There is a tradition that he located his camp near the old Indian Bullskin Trace. This trace led north from the mouth of Bullskin Creek, directly to Old Chillicothe. By any other course he would have encountered forest and undergrowth conditions, all but impassable for such an inland journey.[43]

Prior to 1778, when Colonel John Bowman sent Simon Kenton with Montgomery and Clark to scout the Miami country, the location of this Indian village was not certainly known to Kentucky pioneers. Early in 1778 the location of Old Chillicothe and an Indian trail leading to it from the Ohio River became known to Daniel Boone and his party, who were captured while making salt at the Blue Licks. The distance from this point on the Licking River in Ken-

---

[43] Collins, Lewis. *Historical Sketches of Kentucky*, 453-454.

tucky to Old Chillicothe is about one hundred miles. The salt-makers were taken prisoners by the Shawnees on February 7th, 1778. They arrived at Old Chillicothe on February 18th, 1778. Less than ten miles a day appears to have been the rate of travel on this return march, where the prisoners were all strong men. Boone states that, "The Indians, according to the capitulation, treated us generously." The same daily mileage was maintained when Boone and ten other salt-makers were taken from Old Chillicothe to Detroit for ransom. Twenty days were occupied in this journey of two hundred miles. They left Old Chillicothe on March 10th and reached Detroit, March 30th, 1778.[44]

Captain Byrd, on his return march to Detroit, after destroying Ruddell's Fort and Martin's Fort, on the Licking River, Kentucky, June 1780, averaged less than four miles per day. This slow rate was, no doubt, due to the large number—470— of captured men, women and children, and the large amount of plunder obtained at the forts by the Indians and carried on to Detroit. When hunting in large parties, distance between camps was short. Mixed party hunting expeditions often occupied an entire season and extended to distant points. All such journeys were unhurried, unless seasonal or other changes hurried them back to their own territory.

The Scioto or Salt Trail, which connected Old Chillicothe with the Scioto River Shawnees, must have been known, however, to early pioneers who, like Isaac Donalson, were among the first white captives of the Shawnees in the Miami country.

Captain Bullitt's interesting experience with the Shawnee chief, Black Fish, after he had reached Old Chillicothe, and the record of this chief's favorable attitude toward the survey and settlements Bullitt desired to make at the falls on the south side of the Ohio River—now Louisville, Kentucky—may be found in *Notes on Kentucky* or Howe's *Historical Sketches of Ohio*.[45] On this visit, Black Fish,

---

[44] See "Boone's Own Story," on page 260.
[45] Howe, Henry. *Op. Cit.*, 1847; 190-191.

for his nation, granted to Captain Bullitt the right to settle permanently on the south side of the Ohio River, reserving only the privilege of hunting there. The Shawnee attitude at that date—1773—was evidently still in harmony, as to permanent settlement, with the first Fort Stanwix Treaty.

A PIONEER FUNERAL

The funeral services on the death of John Townsley were held on December 27th, 1827, with interment at the Stevenson graveyard.

The following story of his funeral, in the vicinity of Old Chillicothe one hundred years ago, was found among the valuable historical notes of the late Dr. Clark M. Galloway. It was given to him by his Uncle Robert Kendall who, as a boy, accompanied his father, William Kendall, to the funeral:

A large assembly of people, from a wide range of the surrounding country, came at the appointed time to the home of the deceased; some afoot, others on horseback, or in four-horse Conestoga wagons where roadways had been opened. All came to pay sincere respect to this valued pioneer's memory and to comfort the members of the afflicted family, as far as lay in their power.

The pioneer's last service for those he loved was surrounded with limitations and hardships difficult for us to realize in the light of the luxuries of the modern burial service. There were no coffin factories in those days. The carpenter or the cabinet-maker came for the measurements of the deceased and built his coffin from strong and selected oak lumber. The deceased was dressed in "his fine suit of clothes," and reverently placed in this unlined box. The coffin handles, when possible to obtain them, were individual ones. The plain board lid was fastened in place with long screws. One has difficulty now in visualizing the family's task of preparing enough food for the large concourse of people—and their horses—that came to the funeral of any prominent citizen.

The deceased was John Townsley, builder of the first log schoolhouse in Greene County, Ohio, in 1804. He was a prominent man, a large landholder, and was the first teacher in the schoolhouse that he built.

There had been a cold rain and sleet for several days. The earth was soaked with water and the streams were bank full. William Kendall and his son—then only a lad—mounted their horses in early morning and rode through the woods until they reached their destination, two miles east of Cedarville, nine miles from their home. The mud was fetlock deep on their horses. Both riders were wet through and chilled to the bone when they arrived.

There was a long service at the house, and lunch was served for all in attendance. Afterwards, the four-horse Conestoga wagon with cover was brought out to carry the deceased and the members of the family to the graveyard, nine miles distant. The wagon also carried axes to cut out fallen trees and limbs that might obstruct the way; a mattock, spades and shovels for digging the grave. Following this wagon were other covered Conestoga four-horse wagons filled with friends; the horsemen came after the wagons. Thus in the cold rain, the sad procession wended its tedious way to "God's Acre," there to perform its last duty to a citizen, a neighbor, a friend, and a relative.

It was late in the afternoon, after pulling through mud half a wheel deep in places, and fording Massie's Creek that ran into the wagon beds, that they, at length, reached the Stevenson graveyard.

The horsemen dismounted and, forming relays, soon finished digging the grave. The coffin was quickly lowered by straps. A few appropriate remarks were addressed to the mourners and their friends by the minister. After the singing of the Twenty-third Psalm and a short prayer, closing with the benediction, the wagons quietly faced homeward, and the horsemen disappeared in the forest trails.

In this pioneer graveyard of four acres rest the remains of John Townsley and eleven other soldiers of the American Revolution; twenty-six soldiers of the War of 1812, fourteen of the Civil War, and two of 1898—fifty-four soldiers in all—the noted Scotch Associate minister, Rev. Robert Armstrong, and many members of the pioneer families who first settled central Greene County, following the Treaty of Greenville, in 1795.

INDIAN STORIES

INDIAN JOE

THE SHAWNEE Indian of the pre-Revolutionary period was a village dweller. No evidence appears in the histories of the Northwest Territory campaigns, or was found by explorers or missionary priests, who preceded this period by almost a century, that Indian life had ever been characterized by individual or family location apart from their village settlements or from each other. Civic evolution here, largely due to environment, did not succeed in developing a status beyond the commune. Subsequent Shawnee Indian history becomes an interesting sociological study when viewed from this angle. His transposition from a community life as ancient as his nation's oldest tradition, has been to involuntary isolation—imprisonment for him—on eighth- or quarter-section farms individually owned and operated. Quite naturally, the mental attitude of the aged Indian, who has known both the freedom of the great reservation and the limitations of the prairie farm, is that of rebellion against acreage limitations. "The call of the wild" in the heart of the aged child of nature who has not forgotten its lure, becomes a living emotion that cannot be stilled within the limits of the line fences of his farm, especially since, in the ancient days of his fathers, limits lay far beyond the sky-line in every direction about him.

The Ohio habitats chosen by the Shawnees were locations of natural beauty and easily-induced fertility. The valley of the Muskingum and Scioto Rivers and the Little and Great Miamis were choice spots to those who came out of Virginia and Kentucky to conquer and possess them. In that stirring period which ended at Greenville in 1795, the command, "Thou shalt not covet," was more honored in its breach than in its observance.

INDIAN STORIES

When the time came for the red man's eviction, the first lap of his long trek destined to end in Indian Territory, the land of his reestablished home, was to the Auglaize country. The interesting map photostat,[1] reproduced from Drake's *Picture of Cincinnati and the Miami Country* (1815), shows the southern boundary of this Indian country which lay in the northern section of Ohio.

The removal of the Shawnees from Old Chillicothe was attended by manifestations of great grief when they bade farewell to the beautiful valley at Oldtown, where many of them had been born and had grown to mature age; had established their own home wigwams and, very near by, had laid their loved ones in final rest. Few of the white settlers ventured into the circles of Indian grief and mourning at Old Chillicothe during the final days before the tribe's removal to the Auglaize country in northern Ohio. A number of these Virginia and Kentucky pioneers had personally participated in one or more of the military campaigns, from 1779 to 1794, against the Shawnees. Many of these men and their families established neighborly relations with the Indians who remained at the village after the Treaty of Greenville in 1795, and were not fully satisfied that the Indians had been fairly treated in their compulsory change of location.

One Indian only, of the Shawnees at Old Chillicothe, refused to go with his nation on its removal to the Auglaize country. He was a cripple, but was also an expert tanner, an art much needed by the pioneers settled about his old home. He was given a home and welcome by Aaron and Hannah Paxson, who were comfortably situated in a pioneer home less than two miles from Old Chillicothe. Here, Indian Joe remained till his death some years later. He contributed much to the comforts and necessities of his white neighbors with his arts in tanning. When he finally passed away, he was buried in the manner he had desired, by the white neighbors whose names appear among the best of Greene County's early pioneer settlers. Attorney W. A.

---

[1] Reproduced opposite page 102.

271

Paxson of Jamestown, Ohio, a grandson of Indian Joe's hosts, has contributed this interesting narrative:

Indian Joe, the very last native Indian of the tribe, lived at Oldtown or Old Chillicothe. His death took place at my grandfather's home about the year 1855. He was crippled and refused to go with the tribe when they left for the Auglaize Reservation. He knew my grandfather, who could talk the Indian language, and came to him late in the fall and asked to stay during the winter. My grandfather would not turn him away, and I do not know how many years he remained there; but I do remember when he died. He would always go away in the spring after the weather was settled. He never said where he was going, but he took his blanket, buffalo robe, some bacon and bread and fishing-tackle, and set out and did not come back till along in the fall. He would never sleep in a bed, but wrapped up in his robe and blanket, he would lie down in front of the fire-place in the kitchen. One year we had a very early spring, and after "Old Baldy" had put out his leaves "as big as a squirrel's ear," Indian Joe left. In about two or three weeks, we had a severe cold spell, with snow and a return of winter. Old Joe came back with a very bad cold, which developed into pneumonia. My grandmother doctored him, but he grew worse and died. This occurred about the first of May, and there was snow on the ground. He said he did not want to be placed in a coffin, but wished to be wrapped in his robe and blanket and buried in the ground. He also wanted his fishing-line and hooks and some bacon and bread buried with him. I remember that my grandfather and some of the neighbors, Uncle Aaron Beal, Andrew Walls, Uncle Billy McIntosh, Adam Routzong and David Keifer wrapped him all nicely in his robe and blanket, put the things he asked for with him, hauled his body on a sled across the prairie to an old burying-ground on my grandfather's farm, and buried him there.

He used to tan skins, especially ground-hog skins, some with the hair or fur on, and some without it. He called this fine, tough product, "whang leather."

He told me that the sun came up out of a ground-hog hole up at Hickory Point, a small grove on the eastern side of my grandfather's farm, and that it set behind the big stone on Steel's Hill, where he said the sun went behind the rock to the westward. He showed me a ground-hog hole up at those woods, where it had been worn smooth, and he said that it was the sun coming out that made it smooth.

This tree that he called, "Old Baldy," was the largest chinkapin tree that I ever saw, and it was just across the road from my grandfather's gate. To prevent the tree being cut, he set his fence over a considerable distance. He used to call it "the summer wagon-shed." I do not know if it is still standing. Old Indian Joe would not leave in the spring till that tree leafed out, and he said that for many, many moons, it had never lost its leaves by the frost; but the year he died, the leaves on most all of the trees were killed, and that was the only time I ever knew it to happen. As I write, I can, in fancy, see the poor old man as he used to sit out in the yard with his skins. Sometimes he would become talkative and tell me about the Indians, how they lived; and that, when they died, they went to the happy hunting-grounds, where they were not disturbed by white men. He said that some white men were good, and that my grandfather was one of the good ones.

Old Joe's primitive method produced a perfect tan of all native wild animal hides. For the purpose of facilitating his tanning operations, he hewed a couple of troughs out of the straight-grained trunk of a large oak-tree. Into these troughs, he would put the ingredients for his tanning processes and the hides he would be working on. He hewed out one of these troughs, which would contain more than a barrel, for my grandmother to use as a receptacle for the soft soap which she made every spring. Soft soap was made each year at every pioneer home. All of those homes used wood for cooking and heating purposes, and the lye from the ashes was the only alkali used for domestic soap-making. Another well-finished trough, considerably longer and holding perhaps two or three barrels, was used as a watering-trough by my grandfather, and was placed below the spring-house, where the water ran in at one end and out at the other. This was the watering-trough for all the horses and cattle of my grandfather's farm. No stock ever had finer running spring water every day in the year. Down below this old spring-house, which was also used as a wash-house, there was quite a bog. Indian Joe would gather a lot of willows from along Ludlow Creek, place them in this bog, and, after leaving them there for a while, would take them out and strip the bark from them. He would use these strips to weave baskets of various sizes and kinds. Out of the larger willow-bark strips, coarse and strong feed-baskets were woven; and from the smaller strips, ladies' dainty work-baskets were woven. These baskets could be found in some of the homes around my grandfather's old home for years afterward.

Making soap in pioneer days was an interesting process. On a foundation of two cross logs, a dug-out trough was placed for the lye drain. One end of four-foot boards rested in the trough, the other end against a surrounding frame railing five feet square, and about the same height above the trough. This made a V-shaped ash-hopper. When both ends of the V were made tight with short boards, the hopper was ready to receive and store the ashes of the household's winter fires.

By April, the hopper would be filled, and then would come the "tug of war"—carrying the water from the spring to keep these ashes wet to make the lye for the soap. My grandfather and the hired man, if they were not too busy, would carry the water up the hill from the big watering-trough at the old spring. Of course, I wanted to help, at first, but I could not carry a large bucket full, so I hunted up a smaller bucket that would hold perhaps a gallon. I was nimble, and could make two or three trips to my grandfather's one, until I would get tired. One day, I began "loafing on the job," saying, "Oh, I can't carry very much at a time," and my grandfather said to me, "Oh, mony a mickle makes a muckle." I was then urged to keep up the good work.

Joe used different materials and methods for tanning various skins, according to the purpose for which the skin was to be used. For making the "whang leather," he generally used the skin of the ground-hog, as it was so much tougher than any other. He always used the brains of the slain animal in his process. When the neighbors brought him a ground-hog skin to tan, he always had them bring, at least, the head of the animal, if not the whole carcass. Then I have seen him sit for hours at a time and manipulate this skin and brains over and over until the entire brain substance was completely absorbed into the skin, after which the leather remained pliable, and was not, apparently, affected by time or weather. He would also use an ooze made from oak bark and leaves, which he would pound up in an old iron kettle till well macerated. After soaking the hides in this ooze for a long time, he would then take them out and "man-handle" them, that is, just rub and stretch them. He would use what was known as the mesentery fat, which my grandfather would let him have when they

INDIAN STORIES

butchered the hogs—sometimes as many as a dozen at a time—and any old tallow from the beeves that were killed from time to time.

The tanning which was done by Indian Joe was notable for the fineness and durability of the leather after he had finished it. The pioneer community in which he made his home considered itself fortunate in having him to do all of this sort of work for it. The ordinary pioneer tanning amounted to a process of softening the leather so it would be usable. Howe gives the pioneer method.[2]

So it was that I, as a little boy, would sit and watch Indian Joe, and fetch and carry for him anything that he might need or want, while he told me stories of the old days of his people.

Once he told me the Indian folklore story of the sun, moon and stars; how the Great Spirit, whom I came to know as God, was the first man who ever lived; that He lived in a big mansion away up in the sky; that the sun, moon and stars were His family; the moon was His wife who watched over the star children while He slept at night; that He never died, for there was no one big enough to kill Him, and that He would live forever.

In his naive, Indian way, he told me that the jack-o'-lanterns that glowed over the Ludlow Run bottoms, below my grandfather's house, were little stars which had come down too low and gotten their wings damp with the fog, and could not fly back again to the other stars where they belonged. He said the lightning bugs that came by the thousands every summer, were the jack-o'-lanterns' little boys and girls, who came to visit them and tell them all the news up in the star-land where the poor jack-o'-lanterns could never go again.

These stories well illustrate the vivid imagination pos-

---

[2]Howe, Henry. *Historical Collections of the Great West*, 216: "Every family tanned their own leather. The tan-vat was a large trough, sunk to the upper edge in the ground. A quantity of bark was easily obtained every spring in clearing and fencing land. This, after drying, was brought in, and in wet days was shaved and pounded on a block of wood with an ax or mallet. Ashes were used in place of lime for taking off the hair. Bear's oil, hog's lard and tallow answered the place of fish oil. The leather, to be sure, was coarse, but it was substantially good. The operation of currying was performed by a drawing-knife. The blacking for the leather was made of soot and hog's lard."

sessed by the Sons of the Forest, when they desired to exercise it.

THE SECOND BEND IN THE RIVER

A Great Leader's Secret

The period of Tecumtha's visits to James Galloway's home began in 1797, and did not cease until about 1809, when he began his notable campaign to build an Indian confederacy for the preservation of his nation's hereditary home in the Northwestern Territory. Rebecca Galloway consequently "grew up" from a girl of six years to a young woman of about seventeen during the time of his visits to her father's home. There are no sentimental traditions. The girl was intellectual, and the man's attitude was that of deep-seated admiration for the mentality which he had observed as it developed in her.

Many pioneer girls were married at sixteen or before. The duties and environments of these girls led to early maturity and to matrimony—the only career open to them. In this romance, the point of special contact was the mental outlook of both. There was a disparity of more than twenty years in their ages—years to him of experience with men and affairs of both races, and with his own nation's problems. They were also years of experiences of the kind which lead men to be more readily influenced by the subtle power of mind, than by the evanescent beauty of face and form. Without doubt, it was this mental viewpoint that held him, although, as elsewhere described, she was physically attractive. The man's appearance and manners, which have already been described, must have made him attractive to a girl of her type and age, in an environment of books which both liked. The book-shelf has had its romance in history, and this one was a repetition rather than a precedent.

After Tecumtha had given the girl a canoe to use on the beautiful little river which flowed past the door-yard of her father's home, very naturally personal instruction was necessary to teach her skill in its use and management. The girl proved to be an apt pupil and Tecumtha a willing teacher.

She was a lover of flowers, and no canoe trips were ever made for instruction without flowers being gathered; some for her home adornment, and some with roots and soil carefully lifted to be transplanted about the home doorway.

No season is given for the time of this story, and none is needed, for the flowers of this fertile valley were everywhere abundant and beautiful in color, both in the prairie and forest. They bloomed in profusion from early spring until late autumn. It was the time of one of Tecumtha's visits, when the discussions had not centered about her English instructions, but had been carried on with the girl's father and several other Revolutionary soldiers, who were near neighbors and frequent visitors in his home. The talk had been about the second Fort Stanwix Treaty and its aggressions, which threatened the home interests of Tecumtha's own people. As the discussion proceeded, the portent of what was soon to happen in Northwestern Territory history, seemed to cast its shadow across the little gathering of friends. The girl listened for a while, then grasping the paddle of the canoe from its rack on the wall, she called to Tecumtha to come with her to see a new kind of tree about a mile up the river, near which were also some new and strange flowers to get for the door-yard flower-bed. He arose at once to go with her; but as he did so, one might have observed unusual concern in his glances at her as he asked if the tree was near the bank of the river, at its second bend above.

To this she answered, "Why, yes, you seem to know something about it. Come on, and stop talking about things that ought never to happen. Come on, and let's go to the tree. What was it that made you ask about its location, Mr. Tikomfa Chief?"—a name she sometimes playfully called him, and which always pleased him.

"You have to tell me about it when we get there, all

about it, *now mind; not half around,* please, like you Indians do when you do not want your paleface friends to know your secrets."

Although spoken playfully, the girl touched a notable and universal Indian characteristic in her last sentence. For a moment, he gazed at her as though he would read her thoughts, but made no answer as he followed her in silence down the pathway which led to the canoe "pier"—a magnificent sycamore, with branches far overspreading the river bank, and a strong, smooth root, that reached out into the river, so the canoe could nestle itself alongside, while it waited for its mistress to step easily into it.

"You get in first," Rebecca commanded, "for I'm going to show you I can do real well at paddling. Then you will be proud of your pupil even if her face is pale."

All lovers are biddable in this their time of concession, and most sweethearts are commanding in their time of brief supremacy. Happy are those for whom this mirage never wholly fades away. No words were spoken as the girl swung the canoe into midstream and, with graceful movement of body and arms, paddled it against the current. She seemed determined to win his approbation. He, happy in her presence, forgot for a time a somber determination to effect an Indian confederacy, which had been whipped into fresh activity by the discussion at the girl's home with his host and the other guests.

There is some one hour in every girl's life when she radiates all the power of her endowments. As Rebecca rounded "the second bend in the river," and turned the canoe into a good bank landing, she could not realize that such an hour had come to her, and that she was face to face with her manifest destiny; that portentous events in her country's history were soon to hang on the slender threads of the decisions of her heart.

"Come!" she said, as the canoe made landing, and she quickly stepped out of it. "The tree is just around the hill, and the flowers are there, too. Maybe you'll know what they are. I don't. Anyway, there is nothing like them that I can find in the woods."

"Here they both are," she cried, as she ran ahead of him. "See the blossoms on the tree, how beautiful they are, and the flowers, there, what are they? I never saw anything like them."

She stooped over and picked up something under the tree. "It looks good enough to mash and eat," she exclaimed as she handed it to her companion, "and I believe I will," she declared as she grasped a small stone lying at her feet to use for a hammer.

With a quick movement, he was at her side. "Come over to this stone and sit down, and I will tell," he said, "for I did not expect you would ever find them. You should not know the tree and flowers are here; they are nowhere else near. Why did I not kill what might do my pale friends harm? Will you listen, then forget?"

The girl looked earnestly at a face of power and determination she had never seen in him before. As though impelled by an unseen, but irresistible power, she slowly nodded her head in assent.

"The tree and the flowers shall be destroyed that no harm may come to you or your family," he declared. "It is the pact of peace. Now you are our care, no harm can come to you."

Alarmed at this strange and unexpected warning, she exclaimed, "Tell me what it is and what you mean! What kind of a tree is it? Are it and the flowers poison? Tell me quickly!"

He quieted her alarm with the first few words of the remarkable story he then related to her. In a voice of authority she had never heard before, he asked, "Will this I tell you be for you, and you only?"

"Yes," she replied, "it is your wish, and it will be for my ears—and should you consent, for one other only."

Then he paused, and as though addressing himself, he presently began. "It is the Indian's secret! He suffers pain as you palefaces do. He fears the wound, the torn arm and leg; but this you have found, if prepared right, quiets pain. The red man takes the powder of the flowers and leaves, or of that other fruit that you held in your hand, into battle with him. If the bullet bites or the arrow pierces, the potion quiets the pain. If the warrior falls in battle, it eases him. What you had in your hand is the best. With it, the pain of the fire at the stake is little. If wounded, the warrior can be removed to a place of safety without pain. This powder is as powerful to quiet pain as your opium is, but does not do the harm it has done. No paleface knows its power. It is our secret. If the Indian loves, he speaks the truth; but if he does not, he is silent."

There is a time in every life when the events of the hour press hard, and silence is the spirit's own retreat. No further words were spoken as they walked slowly back to the canoe. As she stepped into it, she passed the oar, and left it for his own skilled hands to use. With a few strong strokes, he drove the canoe into midstream, where the current almost floated it down to the girl's pioneer home. It was evident from the sober lines of her face that she had been profoundly impressed with the secret she had promised to keep, and with his confidence which had inspired its utterance. After a while she spoke with all the directness she could command.

"Do you recollect," she said, "the things next my heart that we talked about during your last visit here? I want to talk about them again. I shall keep the secrets you gave me today, and reveal them at last to some one of my own blood who may be worthy, and through him in the same way of succession, and so await the time your Great Spirit speaks for their release for humanity's sake; but you must promise me whatever conditions of war or conquest may arise in the future, that, as your sister Tecumapese and I have so earnestly beseeched you, you will throw all your power against the massacre of women and children, and of men who have surrendered, or who are hopelessly overpowered."

No word of immediate assent was given by this man who was soon to become his race's greatest war-leader, and to mark the ending of his brilliant career by the notable exercise of the humanities in battle, for which the girl was pleading. As the canoe drifted near to her home, his face

THE SECOND GALLOWAY PIONEER HOME

The barn at the left is on the exact location of the first cabin built in the fall of 1797 by James Galloway, Sr.

became lighted with the finer emotions of his soul, but he still remained silent till they neared the home "pier."

Then she heard the words from him that she had so longed to hear. "I promise, little paleface girl, I promise!" Fort Meigs has given history the story of the faithful fulfillment of this promise to the girl he loved.

One hundred and twenty-five years later, a great chemist—a master of the materia medica of the American botanical field—in company with a descendant of the girl, was driving in a beautiful section of Southern Ohio, long noted for numerous tumuli of the mound-builders and as the former home of their successors, the American Indians. A small tree and some flowers attracted their attention and they stopped to examine them. These proved to be isolated specimens of the flowers and the tree which had grown at "the second bend of the river." Closely scanning the doctor's face, the chemist asked him if he knew about them.

"Yes," the doctor replied, "they played a part in one of America's historic romances 127 years ago. They produce the Indian's anodyne for pain and suffering—his opium. I feel sure from your question," he said to the chemist, who was examining the blossoms he now held in his hands, "that you must have isolated an active principle from both."

"Our laboratory," he replied, "has isolated a narcotic element from each of them."

Both men now became engrossed in study of the plant. Quite naturally, one was interested in its botanical structure and pharmacology, as determined in his laboratory, while the thoughts of the other reverted quickly to events at "the second bend in the river," long years before. The chemist, observing that the doctor's face betrayed his anxiety to verify the ancient tradition of the narcotic use of either or both plants, pointed out an interesting and peculiar botanical structure present in the plant.

"An active principle," he went on to explain, "is obtained from the secretion of the peculiar capsule of the flower of the plant. Its structure and secretion, in that respect, are not unlike the capsule of the white poppy, which after its first incision, furnishes the juice from which the best opium of commerce is made. The plant was once indigenous to large areas of our country, and the narcotic products of its capsule unquestionably became known and was used by American Indians for alleviating pain. At the date when your tradition of its use began, it was probably so long established in their materia medica, that the date of its discovery by them will never be known to us. I am anxious, however," the chemist continued, " to learn what you know of the narcotic effect of the berries of the tree, which also has been indigenous in as large sections of North America as the erythroxylon coca in the mountain districts of Peru."

"Ah!" spoke the doctor, "how well we both know the story of that plant and its alkaloid cocaine to be one of the outstanding romances in American medicine. The story of the product of the tree is almost as interesting. Its secret was evidently not so well kept by the Indians, for one of America's pioneer country doctors, whose name became immortalized by his daring work in surgery, became aware of the narcotic value of the berry, ten grains of which, when properly prepared, gave his patients the same narcotic reaction as three gains of opium, and without the unhappy *sequelae*. Whether he used it as the anodyne of choice in his great operations is not known to history. Presumably, he used it in appropriate cases, as their needs required. Like the savants of another race and period, he guarded his secret as too dangerous to release to those who might easily procure it from the forests of his period, and use it to their own harm. The incidents of our outing, today, hark back to the archives of history, do they not?" the doctor exclaimed, as he looked at the plant and then the tree-shrub.

The chemist replied, "I think I know the story, but if so, it is well worth repeating. Then, again, it may be entirely new to me, so please go on."

With a feeling that it would be "a twice-told tale" to his friend, the doctor proceeded:

"More than 1000 years ago, savants of China are said to have discovered the explosive force of gunpowder and, in formal council, considered what dangers would be loosened if its control could not be maintained. With solemn consideration of the interests of humanity it was their duty to protect, they buried the dangerous discovery, together with other worthy, but dangerous things, which men would misuse to their destruction, were they intrusted to their keeping."

The doctor looked far across one of Ohio's beautiful landscapes, and presently spoke again to his companion: "Many blessings," he said, "are double-edged."

"Yes," the chemist replied, "humanity is yet too frail to stand alone."

The knowledge of the power for human harm contained in the alkaloids of the flowers and the tree these two friends found growing by the roadside is forbidden release from the laboratory records of a great chemist, and from the heart of his friend, a country doctor.

NON-HEL-E-MA, SHAWNEE PRINCESS

By Dr. LOUISE PHELPS KELLOGG,

Historian of the State Historical Society of Wisconsin

In the spring of the year 1780, there appeared at Fort Pitt a French officer of distinction, who had come to America to offer his services to the cause of the United States. Colonel Augustin Mottin de la Balme for two years had been acting, under appointment from Congress, as inspector-general of cavalry in the Continental Army. Now he had come to the West on a mission for France and her representative in America, Chevalier de la Luzerne. La Balme planned to travel throughout the Ohio and Illinois country in order to learn the disposition of the French inhabitants therein, and to encourage them to stand firm for the Franco-American alliance; he also intended to visit the Indian villages in order to assure the chiefs that their former father, the French king, wished them to adhere to the cause of the "Big Knife," and not to take orders from the British at Detroit. At Fort Pitt, La Balme concerted with Linctot, one of Clark's agents for Indian affairs. He left for the West with three Frenchmen and "a Shawnee princess, somewhat old."[4]

It is with this escort of the French traveler that we are here concerned. Who was this Shawnee princess and what may be known of her career? Without doubt, she had had a life full of adventure and danger, and so far as we know, she was the outstanding woman of her tribe. Her tribal name was Non-hel-e-ma, and she was a sister of the celebrated chief Cornstalk, who in 1774 led the Shawnees against the whites in the well-known Battle of Point Pleasant.

The Frenchman's description of her age, *"un peu suranne,"* leads us to believe that she was at the time he met her near her sixtieth year. Thus it was probable that she was born in the early twenties of the eighteenth century. At that time her tribe did not live in the Ohio Valley, but was scattered throughout the South, some villages being on the Cumberland River (called on early maps, the Shawnee); some on the upper waters of the Savannah River, Georgia; some in Florida;[5] while Shawnee villages were also located in western Maryland and central Pennsylvania. Cornstalk and his sister were members of the Mequochake clan of the tribe, the group to which belonged the priests or medicine men of the nation. This seems to have been the division that dwelt at Oldtown, Maryland, whither they had been led about 1698 by a French deserter. If Oldtown was the birthplace of Cornstalk and Nonhelema, they soon removed to the upper Ohio, where in 1728 was a village of the Shawnees to which Pennsylvania traders found a way.[6] Here the Shawnees were on debatable land, claimed by both the French and British crowns. The year

---

[4] *Ill. Hist. Collections*, v. 166.

[5] Black Hoof, the noted Shawnee warrior told an Indian agent that he was born in Florida about 1720, and remembered bathing in the ocean.

[6] Draper MSS. 1B119.

after the Shawnees settled on the Ohio, three of their chiefs went with the other Indian delegations to visit the governor-general of New France at Montreal; he urged them to remove their villages nearer to the French-allied Indians, and finally chose for them a site on the Wabash River close to the Kickapoo and Mascouten.[7] At one time some of their number went to live near Detroit, but the majority of the tribe would not abandon their homes on the Ohio, and there when the Pennsylvanian group removed from the Wyoming Valley, they were constantly visited by English traders.

We do not catch a single glimpse of Nonhelema during all these growing years, when her two brothers, Cornstalk and Silverheels, were negotiating alternately with French and British officers. From her later career it would seem that she leaned to the side of the alliance with the French, and was much impressed with their officers, who visited the Shawnee villages. Meanwhile, she grew very tall and vigorous. So large she was that the English dubbed her the "Grenadier Squaw," since she carried herself like a grenadier soldier at the head of his troop. At the usual age she married and had at least one daughter.[8]

About 1747 the Mequochake-Shawnees left their villages on the Allegheny and the upper Ohio for the Scioto; at the mouth of that river they built a substantial village of log houses, part of which lay on the south side of the Ohio, but the council house and larger number of huts lay on the north.[9] This was Nonhelema's home for about ten years; then a terrible flood in the Ohio River caused the tribe to abandon the Scioto village site and to remove farther up the river to the Pickaway Plains, at first called "Great Plain of Maguck," as the habitat of the Mequochake or Maguck-Shawnees.[10] On these plains, one of the most fertile and beautiful sites in Ohio, the Shawnees built several towns,

---

[7] *Wis. Hist. Collections*, xvii, 64, 383.

[8] Thwaites & Kellogg. *Frontier Defense on the Upper Ohio* (Madison, 1912), 195.

[9] Darlington. *Gist's Journals* (Pittsburgh, 1893), 44.

[10] Charles Hanna. *The Wilderness Trail* (N. Y., 1911), i, 148.

and Cornstalk and Nonhelema each had a village, located on either side of Scippo Creek.[11] There the tribe prospered, obtained many cattle and horses, planted large fields of corn, and lived at ease. A visitor to their towns about this time speaks of them as cheerful and merry, laughing and joking with one another.[12] Among the French, too, they were spoken of as "gentle in character and consequently easier to govern than all other Indians."[13] Great must have been the change wrought in these people by the French and Indian War and its successors, when they became the most feared and most terrible tribe of the Ohio Valley.

Cornstalk apparently adhered to the French interest, for in 1759 he went on a raid against the Virginia frontier, at the very time others of his tribe were making peace with the English at Fort Pitt. He was also in a marauding party during Pontiac's Conspiracy and his sister Nonhelema kept a number of the captives at her village.[14] When Colonel Bouquet moved into the Indian country after the defeat in 1764 at Bushy Run, Cornstalk was one of the hostages exacted to ensure the deliverance of white captives held in the Shawnee towns. Bouquet remarked on the "sullen haughtiness" of the Shawnee chiefs, and also spoke of their affection for their white captives, and their grief when surrendering them next year at Fort Pitt. In all these events Nonhelema had her share.

The decade that followed the pacification of the Ohio country in 1764 was a momentous one for the Shawnees. Despite their submission to the English authorities, they chafed under the restrictions placed upon them by the British officers and by the Iroquois. Cornstalk began arranging a confederacy of the western tribesmen, and is credited with drawing together, about 1767, a large congress of Indians on the Scioto plains, when they aired their grievances and uttered defiance against the Iroquois and

---

[11] Map in Draper MSS. 15J92; see also Thwaites and Kellogg, *Dunmore's War* (Madison, 1904), 301.

[12] Journal of the Rev. David Jones, 1772-1773 (N. Y., 1865), 71.

[13] *Wis. Hist. Collections*, xviii. 12.

[14] Dunmore's War, 432; Hanna, *Op. Cit.*, 11, 388.

the English. Sir William Johnson sent his deputy, George Croghan, to bring the Ohio tribesmen back to their allegiance. Croghan had been known to the Shawnees for a score of years, and at his summons a large number of chiefs joined the Delawares and the western Iroquois in a great council at Fort Pitt in the spring of 1768. Apparently Cornstalk did not go, as his name does not appear in the list of Shawnee chiefs present at that time. Hardman and Nimwha were the Shawnee spokesmen; at first they were defiant, but finally joined in a submissive treaty, which Croghan succeeded in negotiating.[15]

Peace once more reigned for a brief time on the Pickaway Plains.

It was during this interval of quiet that the Shawnees on the Scioto were visited by missionaries of the Moravian sect. In 1772, David Zeisberger made his first visit to this region, and relates that the Indian teacher or priest was greatly impressed with his message.[16] Draper in his manuscript notes identifies this Shawnee priest as Cornstalk. The next year, when Zeisberger took a second journey to the Scioto villages, the chief was exasperated against all white people, and no mission could be begun.[17]

It seems probable that it was during one of these visits of the Moravians that Nonhelema became interested in the Christian doctrine, and gave her assent thereto sufficiently to become baptised. The name, Catherine, was conferred upon her (hence she was frequently called Katy by the whites), and in her later conduct and forgiving spirit she showed that she had embraced far more of the spirit of Christ than many so-called Christians among her white contemporaries. We have no record that Cornstalk was ever baptized, but he exemplified in his last days the Christian virtues of forgiveness of enemies, and calmness in the face of a shameful death. He visited the Moravian mission on the Muskingum twice after the Battle of Point

---

[15] *Colonial Records of Pennsylvania*, ix. 514-517.
[16] *Ill. Hist. Collections*, xvi. 323-324.
[17] G. H. Loskiel. *History of the Mission of the United Brethren* (London, 1794), iii. 82, 92.

Pleasant, once with a retinue of thirty persons, including his wife, the next year with one hundred.[18] No doubt his sister accompanied him on these visits.

We come now to the events of the war in which Cornstalk chiefly distinguished himself, Dunmore's War of 1774. The Shawnees had never been satisfied with the settlement of 1768; they were still more annoyed, when later in that year, the Six Nations met Sir William Johnson and consented to a new boundary-line, which deprived them of a considerable portion of their hunting-grounds south of the Ohio. This grievance with the unlicensed encroachments of whites, especially Virginia settlers far down the Ohio, aroused the fears of the Shawnees that they would soon be driven from their homes. In 1772, the British government in an effort at economy, evacuated Fort Pitt and withdrew its garrison. The Indians interpreted this action as caused by fear on the part of the authorities, and believed that the West was to be left to the uncontrolled animosities of the frontiersmen. Cornstalk again called a council at the Scioto, and an Indian war loomed upon the horizon.

At this juncture, Sir William Johnson called on the Six Nations to exert pressure on the Ohio Indians to keep the peace.[19] In 1773 the unrest had so far subsided that Johnson wrote to England, that the Shawnees seemed on the whole to be the best-behaved of all the western tribesmen. They were, however, alarmed at the numbers of settlers from Virginia going down the Ohio, and at their disorderly conduct.[20]

The hostilities of the spring and summer of 1774 were accentuated by the rivalry between Pennsylvanians and Virginians over the western boundary, and by the rash energy of Captain Connolly, the agent of Virginia's governor. He declared a state of war, April 21st, and barbarities occurred between both races. The Shawnee chiefs

---

[18] G. H. Loskiel. *History of the Mission of the United Brethren* (London, 1794), iii. 107, 113.
[19] *N. Y. Colonial Documents*, viii. 262, 281, 314, 467, 476.
[20] *Ibid.*, 396.

endeavored to restrain their warriors; Cornstalk and his brother, Silverheels, in May, escorted a party of traders to safety at Fort Pitt, and in answer to his summons, visited Colonel George Croghan at his home. Before they could hold a council, a mob of frontiersmen rushed upon the Indian camp and seriously wounded Silverheels. After this disaster, all hope of arranging a pacification fled. Governor Dunmore called out the Virginia militia, and himself took command of the eastern division. The southwesterners, under General Andrew Lewis, marched down the Great Kanawha to a rendezvous with Dunmore's forces at its mouth.

Cornstalk, head chief of the Shawnees, and his sister, Nonhelema, were not in favor of war; they knew that their forces were not sufficient to cope with the armies the white men could raise, but they could not restrain their warriors, who eagerly clamored for revenge. When he found that their own country was to be invaded, Cornstalk showed military skill by deciding to strike one wing of the invading army before it could be united with the other. Lewis's forces were the nearest, so early on the morning of October tenth, Cornstalk and his braves made a surprise attack on the frontiersmen at Point Pleasant. For a whole day the conflict raged, and Cornstalk's stentorian tones could be heard urging his warriors to be brave and to stand fast. Finally at nightfall the Shawnees withdrew their forces, retreating to their villages, and carrying their wounded with them. There they waited in sullen dread for the outcome of the matter.

As Lord Dunmore with his division approached the Pickaway Plains, both Cornstalk and Nonhelema went to meet him and begged for peace. This for the "richest, proudest, and bravest of all the Indian nations,"[21] was a deep humiliation. The Shawnees had prepared to burn their towns, and many had crossed the Scioto in readiness for flight. Dunmore, however, when he reached the Pickaway Plains, and built Camp Charlotte on their eastern border, received Cornstalk's peace overtures graciously,

---

[21] *American Archives*, 4th Series, i. 1015.

much to the dissatisfaction of Lewis's division, which had come up from the mouth of the Great Kanawha. This western army marched within three miles of the Grenadier Squaw's town, where the main group of the Shawnee warriors had prepared to make a stand. There Lewis was halted by messengers from Dunmore, who reported that negotiations for peace were well advanced, and ordered that no attack should be made. With deep reluctance, Lewis's men drew off and returned to their former battle-field, where they left a small fort and garrison to protect that frontier.

Dunmore, in the meanwhile, considered that the Shawnees had been punished enough. He exacted from them promises that they would deliver all prisoners and captured horses, that they would not cross the Ohio to hunt, nor molest any boats going down that stream, that they would keep the trade regulations, and refrain from attacks on the whites at any place. The Shawnee chiefs eagerly accepted these mild terms and delivered hostages to the governor to secure the peace treaty. As the governor and his forces after the conference at Camp Charlotte withdrew, Cornstalk and his sister courteously accompanied Dunmore as far as the Hockhocking River.[22]

For the brief remainder of his life, Cornstalk loyally kept the terms of his treaty with Lord Dunmore, and also came to Pittsburgh in 1775 to make peace with the colonists' delegates. William Wood, who was the messenger inviting the Shawnees to the treaty, asked them to "bring some of your wise women along with you."[23] Thus it seems probable that the Grenadier Squaw took part in this first important treaty made by the Americans with the Western Indians.

It was in accordance with the terms of this treaty that Cornstalk and his son, Elinipsico, went, October, 1777, to Fort Randolph, at the mouth of the Great Kanawha, to bring word that he was no longer able to restrain his war-

---

[22] *Dunmore's War*, 308.

[23] Thwaites and Kellogg. *Revolution on the Upper Ohio* (Madison, 1908), 59.

riors, and that they intended to join the raiding parties instigated by the British. For some months before this, Nonhelema had been bringing information to the Americans and carrying messages to her people, thus being loyally true to the obligations she had assumed.[24] For these actions on her part she was disowned by her people, who even before Cornstalk's mission to Fort Randolph had removed their council fire westward to Old Chillicothe, near Xenia, Ohio.[25]

It does not seem that Nonhelema was present at Fort Randolph, when her distinguished brother and his son were so cruelly done to death in a moment of mad passion on the part of the frontier militiamen. But with this murder all hope of reconciliation with the Shawnees fled. What could the poor woman do, but turn to the whites when her own people had driven her off?

In her petition to Congress in 1785 she says: "Your petitioner at the commencement of the hostilities perpetrated by his despotic Majesty, the King of Great Britain, on the United States, avowed a different disposition from the rest of her friends and brethren, the Indians generally, and abstracted myself from them and took refuge in the garrison of Fort Randolph, belonging to the State of Virginia; into which garrison your petitioner took forty-eight head of horned cattle, which were taken for the use of the garrison without making me any compensation for them, also a number of horses, and was obliged to leave a very considerable Property behind me, which my brethren would not suffer me to remove."[26]

Thus repudiated by her own people, and driven from her well-loved home, she saw herself obliged to accept the grudging hospitality of the very people who had murdered her nearest relatives. "Through the hospitality of the different commanding officers in this western country, I was allowed," she writes, "at some times a part of a ration of provision at the public expense." For such service she gave

---

[24]*Frontier Defense*, 26.
[25]*Ibid.*, 25, note 56.
[26]Draper MSS., 14S158-160.

what return she could, acting as interpreter, and painting and disguising the white messengers, who in the spring of 1776 went to warn the border of the approach of a hostile Shawnee party. When the more responsible militia officers wished to send a message of excuse to the tribe for the dastardly murder of the defenseless Cornstalk, they asked Catherine Nonhelema to carry their document to the Shawnee chiefs, well knowing that no white man would be permitted to approach the towns.[27]

Thenceforward the Shawnee princess, homeless and propertyless, dragged out a somewhat forlorn existence around the fortified posts of the West. In 1779, Fort Randolph was evacuated by the garrison and burned by the Indians as soon as the troops were removed. Nonhelema drifted to Fort Pitt, whence, as we have seen, she went in 1780 with LaBalme to the western country. Perhaps she hoped that under the aegis of the French ambassador her own people would receive here once more. Where she spent the next years we do not know. General George Rogers Clark in 1783 recommended sending "the Indian woman to the Shawnee."[28] Probably this was Nonhelema, who in an interval of peace might venture to visit her tribal friends.

At the close of the Revolutionary War, Clark and Richard Butler were chosen commissioners to make peace with the northwestern Indians. In November, 1784, they summoned the tribal chiefs to Fort McIntosh on the upper Ohio. The Shawnees refused to be present or to treat with their recent foes; but one poor Shawnee woman appeared asking help from the white people, with whom she had so loyally kept faith. Richard Butler had been a trader at the Shawnee towns before Lord Dunmore's War, Clark had favorably known Nonhelema, and both officers agreed to present her petition to Congress and to endorse her request, "for two thousand acres of land on the west side of the Scioto river, above the old Pickawee town, where she once resided and had goods, houses and fields, where her mother

---

[27]Kellogg. *Frontier Advance on the Upper Ohio, Wis. Hist. Collections*, xxiii, 69.

[28]*Ill. Hist. Collection*, xix. 223.

is buried, which she says is a great motive to her particularly fixing on that spot. She also thinks of collecting her relations, and withdrawing them from the Shawanoe nation to that place if granted."[29] Clark and Butler both signed this petition, and when in New York in the summer of 1785, presented it to the President of Congress. The original document addressed to the commissioners of the Indian Affairs was endorsed by several prominent citizens of Pittsburgh, who state that the petitioner had lived among them for several years and had been properly behaved. They knew she had lost considerable property, because of her adherence to the American cause.

Before any answer came to her petition, Nonhelema had determined to throw in her lot once more with her own people. Peace between the United States and Great Britain had been declared, the Indians were nominally pacified, she would once more live among the Shawnees. The Mequochake-Shawnees had long left the Scioto, and had established their towns on the head waters of the Miami, near the present Ohio city of West Liberty, in Logan County. The head chief was Moluntha of her own clan, probably a close relative. The Grenadier Squaw, with her daughter and son, were domiciled at this village late in 1785. Thence the Shawnees went to negotiate with the United States at Fort Finney, at the mouth of the Great Miami. Clark and Butler were again the commissioners. Fanny and Morgan, Nonhelema's children, were used as messengers to their people, who showed the greatest reluctance to come to the council.[30] At last the chiefs came in, accompanied by a great concourse of women and children, and the treaty was signed in January, 1786, promising firm peace between the United States and the Shawnee people. Nonhelema was no doubt with her relatives at this Treaty of Fort Finney.

Neither party to the treaty was really sincere; the Kentucky people were so exasperated against the Shaw-

---

[29] Draper MSS., 14S158.
[30] Butler's Journal in Craig, *Olden Time*, ii. 490, 500, 509.

nees, that every murder on the frontier was attributed to their agency. The Shawnees had no real desire to be at peace; they were constantly instigated by British agents to maintain their rights, and to repel all activity of American surveyors. or land seekers north of the Ohio. Alexander McKee had a village near that of Moluntha and Nonhelema, and constantly instigated the warlike spirit of the Shawnees.

Once more Nonhelema attempted to prevail upon her Shawnee friends and relatives to keep the terms of the treaty at Fort Finney. In the autumn of 1786, most of the Shawnee warriors were on the war-path prepared to meet the expedition of General George Rogers Clark along the Wabash River. But Clark had ordered Colonel Benjamin Logan to make a supporting expedition against the Shawnee towns on the Miami; Logan enlisted eight hundred Kentuckians, who made a swift march and surprised the Shawnees, now destitute of their defenders. The Mequochake town of Moluntha was the first to be attacked; the chief was captured with the women of his family, among whom was Nonhelema.[31] Once again this Shawnee princess experienced bad faith and treachery on the part of the white frontiersman; Moluntha, a prisoner and unarmed, was struck down, killed, and scalped by the bloodthirsty McGary. Logan, and his men were horrified at this act, but although McGary was later court-martialed, the penalty imposed upon him was light.[32]

The Indian prisoners were carried to Kentucky by Logan's men, and kept at Danville in an outhouse during the winter. Although we have many accounts of travelers and residents who saw these poor Shawnee captives, none of them mentions the Grenadier Squaw by name. Colonels Daniel Boone and Robert Patterson made arrangements for exchange.[33] In May, 1787, Captain Wolf, a Shawnee chief,

---

[31] Lytle's narrative in Howe, *Historical Sketches of Ohio* (N. Y., 1876), iii. 351. Lytle says the chief and his three wives, one of whom was the famous Grenadier Squaw. The militia man was no doubt mistaken as to their relationship.

[32] Draper MSS., 12S133-139.

[33] Ibid., 1MM162, 2MM6; 14073.

brought to Kentucky nine white prisoners to exchange for Indians; by August, all the captives had been released.

After her return from captivity, we hear nothing more of Nonhelema. Whether the strain of the winter had been too much for her strength and she died not long after her return home, or whether she removed with that portion of her tribe that went in 1787 and 1788 to live in Spanish territory on the west side of the Mississippi, we do not know. Her brother's son, Peter Cornstalk, was one of the emigrants, and was living on Apple Creek, Missouri, as late as the War of 1812.[34]

Wherever Nonhelema passed the evening of her life, it was doubtless among her own people once more, honored for her wisdom and courage, and consoled for her misfortunes. It is difficult for us of a different tradition to estimate the character of an Indian woman. That in her early days Nonhelema had been a bloodthirsty savage seems proved by the fact that the burning-ground of the Shawnee captives was a part of her village on the Scioto. That on becoming a Christian and being baptized she was sincere, appears by her keeping faith with the whites after the treaty, even to losing her home and her standing with her people. She proved herself a woman of affairs by the prosperity of her village on the Scioto and by the part she took at Lord Dunmore's treaty of Fort Charlotte. Later, as an exile and as captive, she retained her personal integrity and endured affliction without complaint. Among those to whom the historians of Ohio should give a meed of praise stands Nonhelema, the Shawnee princess.

THE TWO WYANDOTTE CAMPS IN GREENE COUNTY, OHIO

An interesting contemporary estimate of the fighting spirit of the Wyandotte warrior is quoted from General William Henry Harrison's discourse in 1837, before the Ohio Historical Society:

---

[34] Louis Houck. *History of Missouri*, i. 212.

When General Wayne assumed the position of Greenville, in 1793, he sent for Captain Wells, who commanded a company of scouts, and told him that he wished him to go to Sandusky and take a prisoner, for the purpose of obtaining information. Wells (who, having been taken from Kentucky when a boy and brought up amongst the Indians, was perfectly acquainted with their character) answered that he could take a prisoner, but not from Sandusky! "And why not from Sandusky?" said the General. "Because," answered the captain, "there are only Wyandottes there!" "Well, why will not Wyandottes do?" "For the best of reasons," said Wells, "because Wyandottes will not be taken alive!"[35]

Captain Wells' estimate of the fearlessness of the Wyandottes is corroborated by Jonathan Alder's manuscript description of the Battle of Fallen Timbers:

After Wayne's light horse had circled around the end of their line and attacked them from the rear, the Indians found themselves completely surrounded. All who could, made their escape. The balance were all killed, which was no small number. Among these last were all the Wyandottes, with one or two exceptions, that lived at Sandusky when I went to inform them of the expected battle.

Jonathan Alder lived among the Indians, but did not wish to fight. He was sent as a messenger to Sandusky to notify the Wyandottes of the approaching battle, and remained there until the battle was over.

The woodland lying immediately north of Old Chillicothe was one of the two camp grounds of the Wyandottes in Greene County, Ohio, when they were removed to their western reservations. They were the last of the tribes to camp here, and rested for several days before continuing their westward trek. The reader is referred to contemporary history for the story of grief and heartache that these and other Indians suffered at the time of their forced removal from the land which had been their home for generations, and the burial-place of their loved ones. The

---

[35] *Transactions of the Hist. and Phil. Society of Ohio*, Pt. 2, v. 1, 266-267.

WOODLAND IN WHICH WYANDOTTE INDIANS CAMPED DURING REMOVAL BY THE GOVERNMENT TO A RESERVATION IN KANSAS

These woods are on the east side of the Springfield-Xenia Highway, at its junction with the Clifton Pike, Greene County, Ohio. Clark's expeditions camped here in 1780 and 1782, and Harmar's forces, in 1790

INDIAN STORIES

same woodland was the camping-place of General Harmar on his advance, and his retreat after his disastrous campaign of 1790, and of General George Rogers Clark in his expeditions of 1780 and 1782.[36]

Local tradition recites that a number of the pioneer white boys of the neighborhood went to this Wyandotte camp to have some fun wrestling and jumping with the young Indians. The white boys proved rather too much for the Indian boys, and considerable commotion was raised as they hurried away to their wigwams. A pioneer citizen and Indian fighter, who happened to be present, warned the white boys to make a quick getaway, for the Indians were preparing to take their scalps. They were none too soon in doing this, for as the boys were leaving, the Indians came out with tomahawks and scalping-knives in hand, and were restrained from pursuit with great difficulty by the officers and military escort in charge of the tribe.

These Wyandottes, numbering about 700, were transferred to Kansas and Indian Territory under government supervision in 1843. At that time, they were but a remnant of a once powerful tribe. Before the day of their departure, they quietly performed the last sad rites for their dead. The ceremonial farewell to this land of their fathers and their own home, was enacted with the composure characteristic of this tribe in all its known history. These final duties performed, their chiefs announced they were ready to begin their long trek to their new home.

Their supplies were furnished by the government. On the route, in July, 1843, after an easy march from their last camping place near Old Chillicothe, they halted, pitched their wigwams and prepared their teams and wagons for a night's rest. This second camp in Greene County occupied all the southern part of Bellbrook, and the adjacent land to Sugar Creek. The government Conestoga wagons in which their household effects were moved overland to the Ohio River, were provided with large, round, white covers fastened at each end with draw-ropes. These wagons

---

[36] Winter's *History of Northwest Ohio*, 1:174-185.

would carry about two tons with safety. Leather water buckets were used in large numbers for watering their teams and carrying water for cooking purposes. When a halt was ordered, it was a sight to see how quickly the wagons were unloaded and the wigwams erected. A large number of extra horses and some cattle helped to make up the long procession. All the team horses had hame bells, and when in action they made a beautiful chime, as there were about a dozen of various sized bells on each horse. Some of the saddles and harness were very beautiful, being trimmed in gay colors. Several of the chiefs were richly decked out, as they were very fond of gay colors and fine trappings. The chiefs were quite dignified and some of them could speak English.

WEH-YAH-PIH-EHR-SEHN-WAH

Blue Jacket—Marmaduke Van Sweringen

This famous Shawnee Chief was in command of the allied forces which signally defeated General St. Clair in 1791. He was second in command to the great Miami chief, Little Turtle, at the Battle of Fallen Timbers, 1794, the last stand of his nation in the Northwestern Territory. The story of his capture by the Shawnees, his adoption by them, and his subsequent rapid rise to the position of war-chief is quoted from the narrative of his kinsman, Thomas J. Larsh. Larsh was a grandson of Marmaduke Van Sweringen's sister, Sarah. The ultimate details of this history of Chief Blue Jacket and his descendants were obtained from Rev. Charles Blue Jacket's daughter, Mrs. Sally Gore. Quite naturally, the story bears evidence of the pride of Larsh in the culture of his Indian kinspeople, a feature brought out in his paragraph description of Rev. Charles Blue Jacket. This story is followed by another story of the chief, touching quite a different angle of his life. It occurred, in part, at the home of James Galloway, Sr., after this doughty warrior had attended his nation's final treaty of peace at Greenville, and had buried his tomahawk for all time.

INDIAN STORIES

His name was Marmaduke Van Sweringen. I cannot now recall the given name of his father or the place of his nativity, except that it was in western Virginia. He had brothers, John, Vance, Thomas, Joseph, Steel and Charles, and one sister, Sarah, and perhaps more. Marmaduke was captured by the Shawnee Indians when out with a younger brother on a hunting expedition, some time during the Revolutionary War. He was about seventeen years of age when taken, and was a stout, healthy, well delevoped, active youth, and became a model of manly activity, strength and symmetry when of full age. He and a younger brother were together when captured, and he agreed to go with his captors and become naturalized among them, provided they would allow his brother to return home in safety. This proposal was agreed to by his captors, and carried out in good faith by both parties. When captured, Marmaduke, or Duke, as he was familiarly called, was dressed in a blue linsey blouse, or hunting-shirt, from which garment he took his Indian name of Blue Jacket.

During his boyhood, he had formed a strong desire for the free savage life as exemplified in the habits and customs of the wild American Indian, and frequently had expressed his determination that when he attained manhood, he would take up his abode with some Indian tribe.

I am not able to fix the exact date of this transaction, except by approximating it by reference to other events. It is traditionally understood that Marmaduke was taken by the Indians about three years before the marriage of his sister, Sarah, who was the grandmother of the writer of this article, and who was married in the year 1781. Although we have no positive information of the fact, traditional or otherwise, yet it is believed that the band or tribe with which Blue Jacket took up his residence lived at that time on the Scioto River, somewhere between Chillicothe and Circleville.

After arriving at his new adopted home, Marmaduke, or Blue Jacket, entered with such alacrity and cheerfulness into all the habits, sports, and labors of his associates, that he soon became very popular among them. So much was this the case that before he was twenty-five years of age, he was chosen chief of his tribe, and as such, took part in all the councils and campaigns of his time. He took a wife of the Shawnees, and reared several children, but only one son. This son was called Jim Blue Jacket, and he was a rather dissipated, wild and reckless fellow, who was quite well known on the upper Miami River during and after the War of 1812. He left a family of several children, sons and daughters, who are now living in Kansas, with one of whom, Charles Blue Jacket, the writer of this, has long kept up a correspondence.

I first saw Charles at the time the Shawnee nation was removed from Ohio to Kansas under the conduct of the national government in 1832. He is a well-educated and intelligent gentleman, and in all respects,—feature, voice, contour and movement—except as to his darker color, is an exact facsimile of the Van Sweringens.

Charles Blue Jacket has been a visitor at my home in Ohio, not above eleven years ago, and exhibits all the attributes of a well-bred, polished, self possessed gentleman.[37]

Chief Blue Jacket was the guest, for several weeks in 1800, of James Galloway, Sr., at his home near Old Chillicothe. He was accompanied by several other Indians. Interest was attached to the visit, because of its unusual character, and also from the fact that later, descendants of Chief Blue Jacket's Virginia family, the Van Sweringens, and those of James Galloway, Sr., became related by marriage. Blue Jacket's lineage was known by his host, and for the time being, during his stay, much of his acquired Indian traits were dropped and in their place, some of his family's notable characteristics became apparent. He was an agreeable guest, and considerate at all times of the pioneer hospitality he enjoyed.

The mythical silver mines of the Shawnee Indians, as then described, were located in Greene County not far from Old Chillicothe. Stories of their existence have been handed down, as told by both reliable and unreliable white men held captive. These prisoners were marched, always blindfolded, for what seemed a few hours, along the course of Massie's Creek, east from the village, where they waited under guard until laden with heavy sacks of what they believed to be silver-bearing ore, which they were compelled to bear back to Old Chillicothe. Various attempts to slip their blindfolds enough to see something of the location

---

[37] *Kansas State Hist. Soc. Transactions*, 1877.

were, in a few instances, successful to a degree. The story, with a map of two of the "mine" locations, is well described by Professor Roy S. King, of the University of Arizona, in an interesting narrative, *"Silver Mines of Ohio Indians."*[38] For many years after their removal to the Auglaize Reservation, small parties of Indians returned every summer to Greene County, and stopped for a few days' camp in the glen at Yellow Springs, now part of the campus of Antioch College; then passed on to the location given in Professor King's narrative, and thence to well-marked locations noted by pioneers, where excavations had been made before their time at Caesar's Creek, southeast of Xenia. Early explorations of two excavations in the glen at Yellow Springs showed vertical shafts with evidences of timbering in one of them. Evidence of excavation at one site is still apparent. The writer does not believe that the outcropping Clinton limestone, forming this glen, is ore-bearing. Nevertheless, while a student at Antioch College, he uncovered, by blasting near the falls on the east fork of Yellow Springs Creek, which runs through these grounds, a half-inch vein, from specimens of which a small "bead" of silver was found in the residue by a competent assayer at Cincinnati. There were traditions of mythical silver mines, also, in Kentucky. It was the locating of one of these mines on Red River in Kentucky that brought Blue Jacket and his party to the home of James Galloway, Sr., in 1800. The story of his visit was given to Benjamin Drake by Major James Galloway, Jr., deputy surveyor of Virginia military lands, a banker and large land owner and a well-known writer of that period, under the pseudonym of "Pioneer, Jr." Drake quotes the story here given, in his *Life of Tecumseh*:

In the spring of 1800, Blue Jacket and another chief whose name I have forgotten, boarded for several weeks at my father's, in Greene County, at the expense of a company of Kentuckians, who engaged Blue Jacket, for a valuable consideration, to show them a great silver mine, which tradition said was known to the Indians as existing on Red River, one of the head branches of the Kentucky. A Mr.

---

[38] *Ohio Arch. and Hist. Quarterly*, 26:114-116.

Jonathan Flack, agent of this company, had previously spent several months among the Shawanoes, at their towns and hunting-camps, in order to induce this chief, to show this great treasure. At the time agreed on, ten or twelve of the company came from Kentucky to meet Blue Jacket at my father's, where a day or two was spent in settling the terms upon which he would accompany them; the crafty chief taking his own time to deliberate on the offers made him, and rising in his demands in proportion to their growing eagerness to possess the knowledge which was to bring untold wealth to all the company. At length the bargain was made; horses, goods and money were given as presents, and the two chiefs with their squaws were escorted in triumph to Kentucky, where they were feasted and caressed in the most flattering manner, and all their wants anticipated and liberally supplied. In due time and with all possible secrecy, they visited the region where this great mine was said to be emboweled in the earth. Here the wily Shawanoe spent some time in seclusion, in order to humble himself by fastings, purifications and *pow-wowings* with a few to propitiate the Great Spirit; and to get his permission to disclose the grand secret of the mine. An equivocal answer was all the response that was given to him in his dreams; and, after many days of fruitless toil and careful search, the mine, the great object so devoutly sought and wished for, could not be found. The cunning Blue Jacket, however, extricated himself with much address from the anticipated vengeance of the disappointed worshippers of Plutus, by charging his want of success to his eyes, which were dimmed by reason of his old age; and by promising, on his return home, to send his son whose eyes were young and good, and who knew the desired spot and would show it. The son, however, never visited the scene of his father's failure; and thus ended the adventures of the celebrated mining company of Kentucky.[39]

Historians of his period and officers in command of the forces that eventually conquered the Shawnees and determined their final status at the Treaty of Greenville in 1795, speak in respectful words of Blue Jacket's ability and reliability whenever he committed himself or his nation. Such qualities were characteristic of his progenitors, and also of his descendants. Blue Jacket's failure to locate the

---

[39]Drake, Benj. *Op. Cit.*, 40-41.

mythical Kentucky silver mines is the only story of record where he failed to fulfill his agreement. There are phases of Indian psychology the white man has never been able to interpret. The reader is referred to the story of William Smalley, and the paragraph which describes the Indian's reaction to the remodeling of "White Warrior's" former home.[40] A possible explanation of Blue Jacket's mental complex in the final days when he failed to complete his agreement, may be found there. The white man has never been able to understand the concepts of the red man. His prescience remains his own, as do other features of his endowment which have escaped us. The Indian at Old Chillicothe located and obtained ore by some process, said by white prisoners to be from nearby mines. He never revealed their location or his process of securing whatever was contained in them. All that is known of either has been related by Professor King and the writer. When boys, we played about the mystic location of the two round, stone-filled holes he describes. They are near the foot of "the devil's back-bone," a quite high ridge, with a declivity down to the bank of Massie's Creek not far from the old King Mill site. The legend of the lost silver mine was one with the legend of Sleepy Hollow to our boyhood imagination. It has faded under the shadows of modern material tumult until now it has all but taken its flight from the realms of gripping traditional stories.

LEGEND OF THE FIRST MEETING OF THE CHA-LAH-KAW-THA AND THA-WE-GILA CLANS OF THE SHAWNEES[41]

The Definitions of Pa-waw-kona (plural) or Pa-waw-ka (singular) (which is spelled as Pvwrkvn, or Pvwrkv in the Shawnee)

(a) The latter form is singular, and inanimate; and

---

[40]See page 237.
[41]Told to the writer by Thomas Wildcat Alford at his home, Shawnee, Okla.

the former is also singular, when animated; but it is the plural of the inanimate form. This is an individual form of the *Meesawmi* for any person, rather than for a group, and is limited to the death of the person; it is to be acquired or earned by worthy accomplishments or personal preparation of an individual, rather than as a free gift of the Great Spirit, whose favor is indicated through an animal, fowl, or anything, by noise, groan, or action as auspice of such creature, to the one who earned it for the right use, as his *o-pawawka* (possessive case). Through its possession, individual inspiration and aid from the Great Spirit are obtained, for the service of the hour, as that of the physician in his ministrations for mankind, and the warrior for defense of his country or his honor, which he reiterates under all circumstances in whisper or in his heart before taking action.

(b) God, if you deserve Him, will appear to you through any form of good you may have in mind, and whatever that appearance is, it will, if you need and have earned it, become your *Pa-waw-ka*, and through it you can appeal for power in whatever right way you need to use such power, so contributing to your success in any undertaking. It is an individual *Mee-saw-mi* to be earned, rather than a gift.

The Definition of Meesawmi
(*which is spelled as Mesrmi in the Shawnee*)

(c) The *Meesawmi* is a *free gift* of the Great Spirit with which He originally endowed each clan composing the Shawnee nation, the potency or inspiration of which always remains with the clan as its very life and inspiration. It is represented by some material thing; what it is, no one knows save those who have the right and authority to open the same after having gone through with the ceremony connected with it, which very seldom is done, unless it is absolutely necessary. A strange thing about the *Meesawmi* of the two chief clans, out of which comes the national chief, is that it never is kept in the wigwam (*wegiwy*) of the chief who has charge of it. It is always on his premises somewhere—sometimes on top of a pole set in the ground. It is wrapped with layers of buckskin, and covered over with some common material to protect it from the elements. The ground about the pole is always carefully swept, and no weed is there allowed to grow. The *Meesawmi* is held sacred and secret by all, and it is considered wrong for anyone to talk about it outside or in public. Therefore, no one, save the chiefs who have charge of it, knows about it. Just recently, and then only in an indefinite manner, could one get information from any Shawnee Indian who thinks well of his nation. This is especially true among the oldtimers.

The Definition of Umsoma
(*which is spelled as Umsomv, singular, in the Shawnee*)

(d) This *Umsoma* is a good genius, or representative, of an attendant spirit, which is an animal or other creature, whose actions or characteristics are represented in the name of a person.

Ten days after a male child is born, he is given a name, identifying the good genius to which he belongs. When grown, it becomes his duty to defend, in social affairs only, against all disparagement of his good genius, all those persons belonging to the same division of the *Umsoma* as his own. If the child is a female, she has to wait two more days before she receives her name, and her duty in social affairs is the same as man's in reference to her *Umsoma*. It seems that every one has the right to engage in defamation and disparagement of members and their good geniuses of every other division of the *Umsoma* but his own. It is considered disgraceful and unmanly for any one to be offended by members of other divisions, and to underrate his own good genius and members thereof; and is considered manly to be able to return like for like, and to retain all composure. This is a source of great jollity among the Shawnees in their visits and gatherings.

The Divisions of the Umsoma

(e) *Umsoma* is divided into six divisions, and each is represented by a group of animals, fowls, creatures or reptiles, as follows:

1. *Msaywaywi-lani*, horse-man; composed of animals with hoofs.
2. *Patakuthidaywi-lani*, round-footed man; composed of animals of round feet or paws.
3. *Palawi-lani*, man of fowls; composed of fowls of all kinds.
4. *Theypodewi-lani*, raccoon-man; composed of animals with oblong feet, like raccoon and bear.
5. *Kahgilaywi-lani*, turtle-man; composed of turtles of all kinds.
6. *Patahginaythi-lani*, rabbit-man, composed of rabbits and others of its kind. This latter is about extinct. At least, it is not popular.

THE SHAWNEE LEGEND

The following Shawnee tradition of their exodus was the basis of Tecumtha's interest—noted elsewhere in this story—in the exodus of the children of Israel across the waters of the Red Sea as he heard it read from the Bible in the home of James Galloway, Sr. It is noteworthy that this tradition is purely native. It is free from coloration of historical and other writings, which became known to them later, and became blended, to an extent, with other migratory history, into the texts of the exodus traditions of several other Indian tribes.

It is the tradition of the Shawnees that one of their clans, the Cha-lah-kaw-tha, did not originate in America as the other clans did, but in the beginning it was created and dwelt in a foreign country, and that later it migrated across the waters, and entered America. At that time, on this continent, Tha-we-gila was the Shawnee clan out of which the chief ruler of the nation was chosen. At a later period, the Tha-we-gila was traveling west (or east). The traditions do not agree in this one respect as to direction. About the same time, the Cha-lah-kaw-tha clan, migrating west (or east) toward America, came to an end of the land in which they lived, and found there thick, unbroken ice. They traveled as far as they could on this ice. Finally, coming to the end of it, they encountered an open shallow sea, the width of which was not great.

The chief, or head of the Cha-lah-kaw-tha clan then called on each one of his people to name their *Opa-waw-kon-wa* (plural and possessive). These were given as he requested, and out of these he chose the Grizzly Bear and the Turtle, as they were most used to the water.

Those Shawnees, for whom these two animals were *Opa-waw-kon-wa*, at once entrusted themselves in this exodus to their backs, and were thus carried through the water to the dry land across the strait, thereby becoming the leaders of the people in this part of their exodus. In that way, the Cha-lah-kaw-thas were landed on American shores and continued their journey on land eastward (or westward). In the meantime, the Tha-we-gila clan journeyed westward (or eastward) until one evening it came to a small brook, and camped for the night.

While lying down on the ground to sleep during the dark hours of the night, they heard the voices of a people approaching them from the opposite side of the brook. They listened in silence, on the caution of their chief and leader. To their great surprise, they found that the language of those approaching them was their own Shawnee. Finally, the people coming near stopped on the opposite side of the brook, prepared their meal, and camped for the night, in the same manner as the Tha-we-gila had done, and not knowing of their presence so near them.

Early the next morning, the Cha-lah-kaw-tha was surprised to find a camp of people on the opposite bank, and at the same time, the Tha-we-gila chief demanded to know who these strange travelers were, and how they knew the Shawnee language, which he had heard them use in such perfection during the night.

Thereupon, the Cha-lah-kaw-tha chief related where he had come from; how they came across the waters from their distant home and entered America, and that he and his people were Shawnees, whose blood was unadulterated.

The Tha-we-gila chief then inquired if he had a

Meesawmi, to which the Cha-lah-kaw-tha chief replied that he had. He was then questioned as to the powers it possessed, and upon learning them, the Tha-we-gila chief determined that each clan of the Shawnees, there gathered at this strange meeting, possessed *Meesawmis* of equal power; but to determine if there was any difference in the power of these two *Meesawmis,* it was agreed by the chiefs of each clan that they would submit their *Meesawmis* to tests of power the next morning—the tests to be of equal character. On the morning of the tests, Cha-lah-kaw-tha was requested to test first, so its chief prepared a small bow and arrow with a sharp point, and said that his test would be to shoot at the sun, and if it turned bloody, this would show the power of his *Meesawmi.* At noon, in the presence of the people, he shot this little arrow at the face of the sun. The face of the sun turned bloody red and the atmosphere became dark for a while. Then it cleared. The Tha-we-gila then tested his *Meesawmi.* Preparing a still smaller bow and arrow, he took a wooden basin filled with water, and set it in the midst of the two clans. He shot at the reflection of the sun in the basin. At this shot, the water became bloody red and the air darkened as before. After a while, it cleared. Upon the completion of these two tests, both chiefs and the people of both clans declared the power of each *Meesawmi* to be the equal of the other. Then they grasped hands and acknowledged both clans to be equal, and there decreed that the chiefs of the Shawnee nation were thereafter to be chosen only from one or the other of these two clans, whose *Meesawmis* had shown that they were of equal power.

The other three clans were never included in this pact.

The May-ku-jay clan, out of which all true Shawnee medicine men came, has lost its *Meesawmi,* and has ceased to exist, leaving at this time—1926—four clans in the Shawnee nation:

1. Tha-we-gila.
2. Cha-lah-kaw-tha.
3. Pec-ku-we, or Peckuwetha.
4. Kis-pu-go, or Kis-pu-go-tha.
   (Tecumtha's clan).

The principal or national chiefs in the civil government of the nation always come out of the first two clans, as their *Meesawmis* were equal.

It is interesting to note that from the time of this tradition, the other three clans became subordinate. Tecumtha sprang from a subordinate clan, the Kis-pu-go-tha. This lack of hereditary chieftainship explains Tecumtha's experiences in his rise to power. A close study of his career leads his historical estimate into the field of leadership rather than chieftainship—a distinction and difference heretofore recognized, but not explained in our histories. Little was heard of his early influence and authority among the Shawnees in times of peace, because the tribe's *Meesawmi* was not a chieftainship endowment by the Great Spirit. There seemed to be a Kis-pu-go-tha status among the Shawnees like that among the Jews 1926 years ago: "Can any good thing come out of Nazareth?" It was only in times of war that the Kis-pu-go-tha were expected to produce chieftains. At that time, an accredited war-leader was expected from it, even though, as in Tecumtha's case, the chiefs of the nation were tardy in acknowledgment. It was the young men of the Shawnees and allied tribes who early recognized his leadership, and flocked to his support.

THE INDIAN BOY'S PREPARATION FOR HIS *OPA-WAW-KA*

A Shawnee boy was usually given long and often rigid preparation by his father before he was deemed worthy to receive his *Opa-waw-ka*. Alford gives this account of his preparation to earn his own *Opa-waw-ka*:

His father's abode was near a creek in which there was a deep "hole." One October morning the father called him into his presence and, with solemn admonitions and instructions, informed him that the time had arrived in his and his younger brother's lives, when they must prepare to become possessed of the material object with which they could approach and receive power and help from the Great Spirit in times of need—their *Opa-waw-konwa* (plural). They were instructed to repair to the family wigwam and strip themselves completely; run naked from the wigwam to this deep place in the creek and plunge into it; then return and dress. This they did each morning from the pleasant autumn day when they received their father's instructions, until the depth of winter. As the winter came on, the task grew harder. Ofttimes the boys had to break the ice before they could take the plunge, and very often the winter's cold and the icy water was a severe test of courage and endurance for their little naked bodies, but their father's directions remained unchanged, and their own obedience unswerved. They were being disciplined in obedience and reverence for the command of their earthly father, to make them worthy to receive the protection and loving care of the Great Spirit.

On the morning of their final plunge, their father informed them that the time of their preparation was at an end. He instructed them, this time, to dive to the bed of the creek, close both hands over whatever they touched, and bring whatever they grasped to him without opening their hands. This they did, and from what was contained in their grasp, he selected a *Pa-waw-ka* (singular) for each one—a material emblem to be an intermediary as between them and their Great Spirit, and to be so used when they were in need of His help and direction.

Methods of selecting *Pa-waw-kona* were varied. Two types of them are noted in the narrative of the exodus of the Chalah-kaw-tha clan. To these "sons of the forest," as to their palefaced enemies, the intermediary was "the way of safe conduct" to the assistance of the Great Spirit, from whom needed protection was to be received in times of trouble if, as with us, they had conducted their lives in the light of His revelations. Their belief in divine assistance through an intermediary seems to have no point of contact in their traditional history with our own. Nevertheless, it leads quite directly to the same conclusion: special manifestations of the Great Spirit's love and care for all His children are available whenever they may be in need of help, a concept broadly held by many races of mankind.

One may well inquire, where and when did these Shawnees realize the power of the mediator in the subtle interdependence of spirit and mind, as directing them to "the way of safe conduct?" The answer is not difficult to those who can interpret the language of the great out-of-doors, or to those who pause a moment and visualize the historical "retreat" there of the Master of Nazareth. God's great out-of-doors is potent with the power of final determination, and is still the open sesame to the inspiration of the spiritual equivalent when human emergencies press hard. From the theo-philosophy of this narrative, one gathers a significance, unperceived by those with whom he contended, in Tecumtha's declaration to General Harrison at Greenville:

"The earth is my mother, and I will rest on her bosom."

She is not changed, nor does she ever withhold her concepts of *wisdom* from those who woo her with *understanding*.

APPENDIX

SHAWNEE VOCABULARIES OF 1818, 1854 AND 1926

THE vocabulary of 1818 is taken from the *Archaeologia Americana*, Vol. I, Transactions and Collections of the American Antiquarian Society, 1818, William Manning, Publisher. That of 1854 is taken from the United States Government Report, *Explorations for a Railroad Route from the Mississippi River to the Pacific Ocean*, Chapter 2. In the *Report upon the Indian Tribes* by Lieut. A. W. Whipple, Thomas Eubank and Prof. William W. Turner, 1855, Chapter 2, they state that: "These vocabularies are of interest to ethnologists if studied in connection with *'Schoolcraft,'* Second Volume, and Gallatin's *'Synopsis'*."

As noted elsewhere, lack of Shawnee records compelled the white pioneers to use phonetics and phonetic spelling, and resulted in many errors. These are corrected, where of like definitions, by the Shawnee vocabulary of 1926 which, to an extent, parallels that of 1818. This vocabulary, 1926, was prepared by Thomas Wildcat Alford, and is authentic in so far as given.

To preserve the fast-fading language of his nation, and for the religious instruction of his race, Mr. Alford has recently completed a translation of the four Gospels. This has been a specially hard task because of the great difficulty in translating the spiritual meanings of many important passages in the Gospels from our language to his—a difficulty well known to all translators. Mr. Alford's translations are his special contribution to the permanent preservation of his people's language, which has been passing slowly, but perceptibly, and would otherwise soon be gone.

The vocabularies named above are cited here in the hope they will be of value to students of Indian lore and language.

APPENDIX

VOCABULARY OF THE LANGUAGE OF THE SHAWANESE, 1818[1]

One, Negote
Two, Neshwa
Three, Nithese
Four, Newe
Five, Nialinwe
Six, Negotewathwe
Seven, Neshwathwe
Eight, Sashekswa
Nine, Chakatswe
Ten, Metathwe
Eleven, Metathwe, kitenegote
Twelve, Metathwe, kiteneshwa
Thirteen, Metathwa, kitenithwa
Fourteen, Metathwe, kitenewa
Fifteen, Metathwe, kitenealenwe
Sixteen, Metathwe, kitenegotewathwe
Seventeen, Metathwe, kiteneshwathwe
Eighteen, Metathwe, kitensashekswa
Nineteen, Metathwe, kitenchakatswe
Twenty, Neeshwateetueke
Thirty, Nithwabetueke
Forty, Newabetueke
Fifty, Nialinwabetueke
Cat, Posetha
Turkey, Pelewa
Deer, Peshikthe
Raccoon, Ethepate
Sixty, Negotewashe
Seventy, Neshwashe
Eighty, Swashe
Ninety, Chaka
One Hundred, Tepawa
Two Hundred, Neshwa-tepawa
Three Hundred, Nithwa-tepawa
Four Hundred, Newe-tepawa
Five Hundred, Nialinwe-tepawa
Six Hundred, Negotewathwe-tepawa
Seven Hundred, Neshwathwe-tepawa
Eight Hundred, Sashekswa-tepawa
Nine Hundred, Chakatwse-tepawa
One Thousand, Metathwe-tepawa
Two Thousand, Neshina Metathwe-tepawa
Three Thousand, Nethina Metathwe-tepawa
Four Thousand, Newena Metathwe-tepawa
Five Thousand, Nialinwa Metathwe-tepawa
Dog, Weshe
Horse, Meshewa
Cow, Methotho
Sheep, Meketha
Hog, Kosko
Girl, Squithetha
Child, Apetotha
My Wife, Ncewa
Your Wife, Keewa
Bear, Muga
Otter, Kitate
Mink, Chaquiweshe
Wild Cat, Peshewa
Panther, Meshepeshe
Buffalo, Methotho
Elk, Wabete
Fox, Wawakotchethe
Muskrat, Oshasqua
Beaver, Amaghqua
Swan, Wabethe
Goose, Neeake
Duck, Sheshepuk
Fish, Amatha
Canoe, Olagashe
Big Vessel, Misheolagashe
Paddle, Shumaghtee
Saddle, Apapewee
Bridle, Saketonebetcheka

---

[1] *Archaeologia Americana*, 287-292.

APPENDIX

Man, Elene
Woman, Equiwa
Boy, Skillewaythetha
My Husband, Wysheana
Your Husband, Washetche
My Father, Notha
Your Father, Kotha
My Mother, Neegah
Grandmother, Cocumtha
My Sister, Neeshematha
My Brother, Neethetha
My Daughter, Neetanetha
Old Man, Pashetotha
Young Man, Meaneleneh
Chief, Okema
Great Chief, Kitchokema
Soldier, Shemagana
Hired Man, Alolagatha
Englishman Englishmanake
  (by the Shawanese)
Englishman, Sagonas
  (by the Ottawas)
Frenchman, Tota
American, Shemanese,
  or Big Knives
The Lake, Kitchecame
The Sun, Kesathwa
The Moon, Tepethkakesathwa
The Stars, Alagwa
The Sky, Menquotwe
Clouds, Pasquawke
The Rainbow, Quaghcunnega
Thunder, Unemake
Lightning, Papapanawe
Rain, Gimewane
Snow, Cone
Wind, Wishekuanwe
Water, Nipe
Fire, Scoote
Cold, Wepe
Warm, Aquetteta
Ice, M'Quama
The Earth, Ake
The Trees, or the Woods,
  Metequeghke
The Hills, Moqueghke
Bottom Ground, Alwameke

Prairie, Tawaskote
River, Sepe
Small Stream, Thebowithe
Pond, Miskeque
Wet Ground, or Swamp,
  Miskekopke
Good Land, Wesheasiske
Poor Land, Melcheasiske
House, Wigwa
Council House,
  Takatchemoke Wigwa
The Great Spirit, or Good Spirit,
  Wishemenetoo
The Bad Spirit or the Devil,
  Matchemenetoo
Dead, Nepwa
Alive, Lenawawe
Sick, Aghqueloge
Well, Weshelashamamo
Corn, Dame
Wheat, Cawasque
Beans, Miscoochethake
Potatoes, Meashethake
Turnips, Openeake
Pumpkins, Wabego
Melons, Usketomake
Onions, Shekagosheke
Apples, Meshemenake
Nuts, Pacanu
Nut, Pacan
Gun, Metequa
Axe, Tecaca
Tomahawk, Cheketecaca
Knife, Manese
Powder, Macate
Lead, Alwe
Flints, Shakeka
Trap, Naquaga
Hat, Petacowa
Shirt, Peleneca
Blanket, Aquewa
Handkerchief, Pethewa
Pair of Leggins, Metetawawa
Eggs, Wawale
Meat, Weothe
Salt, Nepepimma
Bread, Taquana

APPENDIX

Kettle, Acohqua
Sugar, Melassa
Tea, Shiskewapo
Medicine, Chobeka
I am very sick, Olame ne tagh, que, loge
I am very well, Ne wes, he, la, sha, ma, mo
A Fine Day, Was he kee, she, ke
A Cloudy Day, Mes, quet, wee
My Friend, Ne, cana
My Enemy, Mat, che, le, ne, tha, tha
The Great Spirit is the Friend of the Indians, Newecanetepa, Weshemanitoo
Let us always do good, Weshe-catweloo, Keweshelawaypa

SHAWNEE VOCABULARY, 1854

From "*Explorations for a Railroad Route from the Mississippi River to the Pacific.*"

God, ou-wis'-i-man-i-toh' = Uwasi Mvnatu. (Mvnatu is the name the Shawnees use for God. The word Uwasi Mvnatu, as given here, means Good God as distinguished from Mvci Mvnatu, Bad God or Devil).
Devil, match'-i-man-i-toh' = Mvci Mvnatu
Man, il-le-ni' = Ilani
Woman, s'squaw-o-wah' = Iqawv
Boy, s'sque-lai-thi-thah' = Squilvwahfefv
Girl, s'sqaw-the-e-thah = Sqahfafv
Infant, child, ah-be-lo-tha-ki = Vpaluhfafv
Father, No-thah' = Ufimv. (The word N'uhfv, or Ni uhfv, as given here as No-thah, means my father).
Mother, nik-yah' = Ni giv (Means my mother).
Brother, Jai-nai-nah'
Sister, Nit-que'-quai-o-mah
Son, ni-qui-thah' = Ni qihfv (Means my son; Uqihfimv is son).
Daughter, dah-nai-thah = (Ni) Drna'hfv = (my) daughter, with Ni left out, Udrnfimv.
Husband, oui-se-ah = Wahsiv (Also means my husband; Nhrkvnv is husband).
Wife, ni-wah (Also means my wife. Nhrkvnah-qa is wife).

Indian, del-noi-eh'
Head, oui-i-si'
Hair, oui-thai-ah'
Face, e-shi-que-chi'
Forehead, lah-oui-ki-leh'
Ear, h'tow-wa-ca'
Eye, s'ski-si-coh', ski-she-quih'
Nose, ki-tschar-si
Mouth, ki-tor-ni'
Tongue, ki-lar-ni'
Tooth, ki-be-tar-leh'
Beard, qui-ni'-lu-nar-o-lih'
Neck, k'quai-e-ka-ker
Arm, ki-neh-ki
Hand, ki-leh-chi'
Fingers, ki-leh-chi'

APPENDIX

Nails, x-kas-sah'
Body, ni-i-yah'
Belly, beh-quoi-tah'
Breasts, ul-le-ne'
Man's privates, pas-sah-tih
Woman's do, mas-sih
Leg, t'kar-chi'
Foot, ni-thi-chi'
Toes, ni-thi-tah-lish'
Bone, h'kah-nih'
Heart, ki-te-hi
Blood, ps'qui
Town, village, ou-te-ou-wel'
Chief, ou-ki-mah'
Warrior, ne-noth-tu'
Friend, ne-kah-noh'
House, hut, oui-qu-ah'
Cup, tip-hi-cah'
Kettle, s'couth-quoi'
Bottle, oui-tha-quuc-quoi'
Arrow, il-le-na-lui'
Bow, il-le-nah-qui'
Axe, hatchet, te-kah-ah-kur'
Knife, mah-ne-thi'
Canoe, boat, ou-la-kai-i-sih'
Moccasins, shoes, m'ki-thai-nah'
Bread, te-whoir'
Pipe, calumet, h'quoi-a-ker'
Tobacco, t'thai-a-mer'
Sky, s'spem-e-ke
Sun, ki-sah-thoi'
Moon, te-beth-to-kish-thoe'
Star, ah-la-ah-quoi'
Day, qui-si-qui'
Light, te-o-pah'-cou-li'
Night, te-beth-ki
Darkness, pai-bai-ke-char'
Morning, pi-ai-tah-cou-tha-mou'
Evening, pak-e-se-mou
Spring, me-loh-cak-me'
Summer, ni-pai-n'oui'
Autumn, pah-co-tai'
Winter, pai-pou-n'oui'
Wind, p'si-cah-n'oui
Lightning, pah-pah-n'oui
Thunder, nen-nem-ki
Rain, que-mou-ah-n'oui

Snow, co-o-nah'
Hail, p'ou-quoi-mah'
Fire, s'cou-te
Water, ne-bi'
Ice, ki-pat-te-nui'
Earth, land, a-shis-ki'
Sea, k'chi-cak-mi'
River, t'hi-bi'
Creek, small river, meth-to-qui
Lake, p's-ske-o-qui'
Valley, ki-kah-ka-mi-ka-tui'
Hill, ma-quoi-ki
Mountain, p'sske-mu-quoi-hi-ki
Island, me-ne-thi'
Stone, rock, she-quo-nur'
Copper, ou-thow-o-qu-quah'
Iron, pou-cou-pe-lo-qui'
Maize, tar-mi'
Tree, te-qui'
Wood, ut-e-qui
Leaf, sis-qui
Bark, ou-la-ge-qui'
Grass, p's qui-te-qua-loh'
Oak, wah-bah',-co-me-shi'
Pine, s'she-quoi'
Flesh, meat, oui-or-thi'
Beaver, er-meh-quoi'
Otter, quit-ta-teh'
Bison, buffalo, p'thu-thoi
Deer, p'sceke-thi'
Bear, pu-quoir
Wolf, ptwe-o-wa'
Dog, with-si
Fox, wa-cu-cha-thi'
Squirrel, an-e-quoi
Rabbit, hare, pet-a-ke'-ne-thi
Snake, man-e-toh'
Bird, ouis-ke-lo-tha'
Egg, oua-oui'
Goose, ska-ki'
Duck, shi-shi-a-puh'
Pigeon, poi-i-tha-ki'
Partridge, que-qua-la-soi-tha-ki'
Turkey, pe-le'-o
Fish, no-me-tha'
White, wuh-ker-ne-kah'
Black, p'cat-e-wah'

APPENDIX

Red, p'squaw-oui'
Blue, pski-pah-cah'
Yellow, ou-thow-wa'
Green, pski-pah-cah'
Great, big, psai-wi'
Small, little, match-squa-thi'
Strong, oui-shi-cat-tu-oui'
Old, pas-shi-tu-e-tha'
Young, mai-ah
Good, oui-sah'
Bad, mat-ou-oui-sah'
Handsome, u-le-thi'
Ugly, mat-e-thi-i-thi
Alive, life, li-nou-e-oui'
Dead, death, ne-poi', chi-pah'
Cold, oue-bi
Warm, hot, ah-quoi-te-ti'
I, ni-la'
Thou, ki-luh'
He, yah-ma
We, ni-la-weh'
Ye, ki-luh-weh'
They, la-neh-ke
This, la-yah-mah
That, la-nah
All, tscha-yah-ki
Many, much, met-chi'
Who, ne-thow-we
Near, ma-ketch-e-ne-lu
Over, kit-te
To-day, e-no-ke-kah-she-ki-ki'
Yesterday, u-la-o-co
To-morow, wah-pah-keh'
Yes, hah-hah'
No, mat-tah'
One, ne-co-ti
Two, ni-e-sui
Three, t'thoui'
Four, ni-e-oui'
Five, ni-ah-la-nui
Six, ni-co-toi-thi
Seven, ni-shaw-thi
Eight, t'tha-shik-thi
Nine, tcha-cat-thi
Ten, net-a-thi
Eleven, kit-te-ne-co-ti'
Twelve, kit-te-ni-e-sui
Thirteen, kit-te-t'thoui
Twenty, ne-suoi-pit-a-ki
Twenty-one,
   ne-suoi-pit-a-ki-te-ne-co-ti
Thirty, t'thoi-pit-a-ki
Forty, ni-e-oi-pit-a-ki
Fifty, yah-ba-noi-pit-a-ki
Sixty, ne-co-toi-a-shi
Seventy, ne-shoi-a-shi
Eighty, thaw-a-shi'
Ninety, tscha-a-ka'
Hundred, te-pe-e-weh'
Thousand,
   meta-the-ne-the-pe-a-weh'
Eat, oui-then-e-luh'
Drink, men-e-luh
Run, me-me-qui-luh
Dance, men-i-e-de-luh'
Go, weh-pe-theh
Come, pe-e-wah'
Sing, na-ca-mo-loh'
Sleep, ne-pah-loh
Speak, atch-mo-loh
See, ni-ne-e-meh'
Love, dah-que-le-mah
Kill, tschi, tsi
Walk, pam-the-loh'
Bury, ne-pe-ka'
Canadian river, Ki-ne-e-ti'

The vowels and letter combinations of this vocabulary have the following sounds, as given by Mr. Whipple:

Long *a* is sounded as in father; short *a* as in fat.
Long *e* is sounded like *a* in face; short *e* as in met.
Long *i* is sounded as in marine; short *i* as in pin.
Long *o* is sounded as in go; short *o* as in got.

APPENDIX

Long *u* is sounded like *oo* in food; short *u* as in but.
ai has the sound of the *i* in line.
ow or *au* is sounded as in the word now.
g is always hard, as in go.
ch or *tch* is sounded like *ch* in church, or *tch* in witch.
qu is pronounced as in queen.
h' prefixed to a word denotes a very strong aspiration.
s' prefixed shows that the word begins with a sharp, hissing sound.
t' prefixed indicates that the tongue is to be pressed forcibly against the teeth.

Sound of Letters of the English Alphabet in the Shawnee Indian Language, 1926

By Thomas W. Alford

All letters have each but one sound, and all the consonants have the same sound as in English, except *f*, *r*, and *v*, the sound of which in English is not found in the Shawnee language. The last two (*r* and *v*) are used as vowels, and *f* in place of the *th* sound common to both English and Shawnee. Also the sound of the last letter in the alphabet is not found in the Shawnee, and is therefore entirely left out.

Vowels

The vowels in the Shawnee language are seven in number and are *a, e, i, o, r, u* and *v*; and the sound of each follows:

A is sounded as *a* in bay, hay, hate.
E is sounded as *ee* in see, seen, seed.
I is sounded as *i* in pin, sin, chin.
O is sounded as *o* in mole, note.
R is sounded as *aw* in paw, law, haw.
U is sounded as *oo* in took, cook, book.
V is sounded as *u* in luck, tuck, duck.

APPENDIX

Consonants

B, same as in English.
C, (*tsi*) as *ch* in English, chin, chip, church.
D, same as in English.
F, as *th* in English, the, thin, they.
G, same as in English, but is always hard, as in give, got.
H, same as in English, but is often silent when followed by a consonant and represents a short silence or more aspirate pause.
J, same as in English, jail, Joe, just.
K, L, M, N, P, Q, S, T, W, X all have the same sound as in English.
Y, is pronounced as in yes, yet.

VOCABULARY OF 1818 (*Archaeologia Americana*)
CORRECTED TO MODERN SHAWNEE

One, Nakuti
Two, Neswi
Three, Nfwi
Four, Nyawi
Five, Nyrlvnwi
Six, Nakutwvhfwi
Seven, Neswvhfwi
Eight, Nfwrsigfwi
Nine, Jrkvtfwi
Ten, Matvhfwi
Eleven, Matvhfwi-gita-nakuti
Twelve, Matvhfwi-gita-neswi
Thirteen, Matvhfwi-gita-nfwi
Fourteen, Matvhfwi-gita-nyawi
Fifteen, Matvhfwi-gita-nyrlvnwi
Sixteen, Matvhfwi-gita-nakutwvhfwi
Seventeen, Matvhfwi-gita-neswvhfwi
Eighteen, Matvhfwi-gita-nfwrsigfwi
Nineteen, Matvhfwi-gita-jrkvtfwi
Twenty, Neswr-pitvgi
Thirty, Nfwr-pitvgi
Forty, Nyawr-pitvgi
Fifty, Nyrlvwr-pitvgi
Sixty, Nakudwrsi
Seventy, Neswrsi
Eighty, Nfwrsi
Ninety, Jrkv
One hundred, Tabawa
Two hundred, Nesana tabawa
Three hundred, Nfana tabawa
Four hundred, Nyawana tabawa
Five hundred, Nyrlvna tabawa
Six hundred, Nakutwvhfana tabawa
Seven hundred, Neswvhfana tabawa
Eight hundred, Nfwrsigfana tabawa
Nine hundred, Jrkvtfana tabawa
One thousand, Matvhfana tabawa
Two thousand, Nesana-matvhfana tabawa
Three thousand, Nfana-matvhfana tabawa
Four thousand, Nyawana-matvhfana tabawa

APPENDIX

Five thousand, Nyrlvna-matvhfana tabawa
Dog, Wihsi
Horse, Msawa
Cow, Mfofwv (as applied to all kinds of cattle)
Sheep, Magefv
Hog, Kusku
Cat, Bosefv
Turkey, Palawv (as applied to all kinds of turkeys and chickens)
Deer, Psagfi or Pisagfi
Your wife, Gewv
My husband, Wahsiv or Wahsivnv
Your husband, Wahsivni, or Wahsivnv
My father, Ni uhfv, or N'uhfv
Your father, Ki uhfv, or K'uhfv
My mother, Ni giv
Grandmother, Huhkumfimv, or Kuhkuci
My sister, Nit iqamv (if spoken by man); Ni janinv (if by woman)
My brother, Ni janinv, (if spoken by man); Ni usgemv (by woman)
My daughter, Ni drnahfv
Old man, Pvsidofv, or Gigi 'lani
Young man, Mvyrni 'lani
Chief, Ugimv
Great chief, Msi ugimv
Soldier, Svmrkvnv
Hired man, Vlolrkvni 'lani
Englishman, English-mrnv
Frenchman, Dodewi 'lani
American, Msi Mrnfi (great creature with big knife). Takuhsiv is now used to apply to all white people.
The Lake, Ini msgaqi
The Sun, Inv gesagi, gesvhfwv; or Inv gesagi gesfwv; which means the day satellite, as distinguished from the moon, which is Tapahgi Gesvhfwv, or Gesfwv, the night satellite. The Shawnee word Gesvhfwv, or Gesfwv, is a common name for the sun and moon.
The Moon, Inv tapahgi gesfwv, or Gesvhfwv (the night satellite)
The Stars, Nihki vlrqvki
The Sky, Ini manqvtwi
Clouds, Brfqvhki
Racoon, Ifapvti, or vfapvti
Bear, Muqv, or M'qv
Otter, Gitvta
Mink, Srqawahfi
Wild Cat, Pasiwv
Panther Msi-pasi
Buffalo, Pvqvci mfofwv, or Belasgi mfofwv, or Pvfulu
Elk, Wrpiti (White butt)
Fox, Wrkucahfi
Muskrat, Usvsqv
Beaver, Vmahqv
Swan, Wrpafi
Goose, Wrpacigiahfv (other than Canada goose)
Duck, Sihsepv
Fish, Nvmahfv
Canoe, Ulvgasi (boat of any kind)
Big Vessel, Msi Vlvgasi (if big boat is meant)
Paddle, Jomrti
Saddle, Vpvbewa, or Msawawi vpvbewa (Vpvbewa means any kind of a seat, chair, bench, etc.)
Bridle, Fvgituna-picikv
Man, Ilani
Woman, Iqawv
Boy, Sgilvwahfefv
Girl, Sqahfafv
Child, Vpaluhfv
My wife, Newv
The Rainbow, Inv Ukunvqv
Thunder, Nanamgi (personified)
Lightning, Bapvgi
Rain, Gamuwrgi
Snow, Gonv

APPENDIX

Wind, Mahsigikvgi
Water, Napi
Fire, Skuta
Cold, Wapi (applies to weather); Tigilwv (to person); Tikvnwi (to things not personified)
Warm, Vhqvtata (to weather); Gesowafi (to person), and Gesowv (to things not personified)
Ice, M'qvmv
The Earth, Ini Vsisgi; or Ini Vsisgi-drmqa; or Yalakuqvh-kvmigigi
The Trees, Nili mtaku
The Woods, Nili lr mtaqihgi
The Hills, Nili maqvhgefiki
Bottom Ground, Lwrmagi (low ground); Yapvgrmahgigi (flat ground); Dapgr-mahgigi (level ground)
Prairie, Tvuskuta (it is prairie); Dauskudagi, Prairie (n).
River, Fepi
Small Stream, Fepuwahfi
Pond, Msgakunahi
Wet Ground, or swamp, Mskakupgi
Poor Land, Mvci Vsisgi, or Mvci Vsisgihi
Good Land, Uwasi Vsisgi
House, Wegiwv
Council House, Tapuwa-wikv or Msi Kvmiqi (Temple)
The Great Spirit, Inv Msi Ilafewanv; or Inv Msi Ucvjrlvhqv; or Good Spirit, Uwasi Ilafewanv; or Uwasi Ucvjrlvhqv; or Good God, Uwasi Mvnatu
The Bad Spirit, Inv Mvci Ilafewanv; or Mvci Ucvjrlvhqv, or The Devil, Inv Mvci Mvnatu
Alive, Ianvwawi (applies to person); Ianvwaweiv (to things not personified)
Dead, Napwv (to person); Naboiv (to things not personified)
Sick, Vhqiluga (to person); Vhqilugaiv (to things not personified)
Well, Uwasi lrsvmvmu (to person); Uwasi lrsvmvmoiv (to thing)
Corn, Drmi
Wheat, Kvwvsqi
Beans, Mskucihfvki
Potatoes, (Irish), Myrsihfvki
Turnips, Wrwiah-paniv. The word Upamyaki, or Openeake as given, is the common name for all kinds of tubers.
Pumpkins, Wrpiku
Melons (Water), Sgitvmaki
Onions, Sagrkuwesv
Apples, Msi-minvki
Nuts, Pvgrnv
Nut, Pvgrni
Gun, Mtaqv
Axe, Taghrkv
Tomahawk, Cvgi-taghrgrfv
Knife, Mrnahfi
Powder, Mkvta (if gunpowder is meant)
Lead, Vlwi, or Hvlwi
Flints, Srkugrnv
Trap, Nvqrkv
Hat, Patvghowa (head gear)
Shirt, Betanikv; or Lrmagi Betanikv. (Betanikv means a garment of any kind)
Blanket, Vqewa; or Hvqewa
Handkerchief, Pfewa
Pair of Leggins, Nakudwa-lanv Mvtadrwvli; or Mvtadrwvli
Eggs, Uwrwvli
Meat (flesh), Wivufi
Salt, Napi-pami (water grease)
Bread, Tvkuwhv
Kettle, Vhkuhqv
Sugar, Malrsi
Tea, Msisgi-Wrpu (leaf juice)
Medicine, Ujapihgi
I am very sick, Nit vhqiluga ulrmi

APPENDIX

I am very well, Ni uwasi lrsvmvmu ulrmi
A Fine Day, Uwasi gesagi cahi
A Cloudy Day, Bofqvtwi grsagigi
My Friend, Nihgrnv
My Enemy, Ni mvdaladewanv
The Great Spirit is the Friend of the Indians, Nili Msi Ucvjrlvh- qvli, nileni wihgrnwrli nihki masqi-lokv-yacki lanvwaki.
(These last two words mean, red-skinned people, and take the place of the Anglo-Saxonized name, Indian)
Let us always do good, Wahi mosvtvwi uwasi lvwe-drku.

THE TRANSLATION OF THE FOUR GOSPELS

by THOMAS W. ALFORD

"*THE FOUR Gospels of Our Lord Jesus Christ, in Shawnee Language*", by Thomas Wildcat Alford, was published by Dr. William A. Galloway, Xenia, Ohio, 1929. One edition—500 copies—was published and was a gift to the Shawnees by the publisher through the translator.

There were never any prospects for material reward for this work, which has called for many long, tedious hours of hard, mental labor; nothing save the joy and satisfaction of accomplishing my object. I fully realize that, under our present system of commercialism, this would be called foolishness, and the idea of obtaining joy and satisfaction in saving a language that would otherwise be forgotten, lost, is liable to be called under the same system, egotism or selfishness. Be it so.

My people are among those who once owned this vast country; they were strong and brave and virtuous according to their knowledge. If they have failed to live up to the standards of the white race, they at least have fought for their convictions. Who can say that in future generations they will not contribute something of untold value to the life of our nation?

Surely strength of character is a commendable trait, and our white friends would very well profit by some of our tribal teachings, such as loyalty, perseverance and self-reliance; perhaps future generations will crave some know-

APPENDIX

ledge of these people—will search to find their natural tongue.

Anyway, the Shawnee language is full of majesty and sweetness, and I have done all that I could to preserve it in its purity and beauty.

DESCENDANTS OF TECUMTHA (or TECUMSEH)

(Prepared in 1930)

TECUMTHA and his wife, Monetohse, left two sons: Nay-thah-way-nah who died in 1840, and McLaughlin or Mah-yaw-we-kaw-pa-we, who died in 1868.

Nay-thah-way-nah married So-com-se, who died in 1867 in Oklahoma. To them were born six children, two boys and four girls, one of the latter (a twin-sister of number 3 below) was killed in infancy by the kick of a horse during the year of 1827. The remaining five grew up to manhood and womanhood. Their names follow:

1. Naw-swaw-pa-ma, who died in 1856, and her husband, Nocks-kaw-way, who died in 1860.

2. Pa-se-quaw-mea-se, who died in 1857, and her husband, Kyan-thaw-tah, who died in 1850.

3. Way-lah-skse (a twin), who died in the summer of 1869 near what is now the city of Shawnee, Oklahoma. She was the wife of George Wildcat Alford, Sr., or Gay-tah-ke-pea-se-ka, who died Sept. 25, 1877, near the same city at the age of 52 years.

4. Jim Fry, or Wal-kos-ka-ka, who died in 1872 in the same state, at the age of 41 years, and his wife, Jay-ney-quay, who died in 1876 in the same state, at the age of 39 years.

5. Big Jim, or Waw-paw-meap-to, who died in Mexico, Sept. 30, 1900, at the age of 66 years, and his wife, Metho-tay-se, who died in 1876 in the state of Oklahoma.

McLaughlin, or Mah-yaw-we-kaw-pa-we (the other son

APPENDIX

of Tecumtha), married Mrs. McLaughlin, or Taw-pa-ma, who died in 1873. To them was born the following named daughter:

6. Mrs. Washington, or Pea-taw-pea-se, who died March 5, 1912, near Skiatook, Oklahoma, at the age of 99 years; and her husband, Thomas Washington, Sr., or Way-nay-peas-ka-ka, who died in 1884 near the same place.

Now the descendants of these six GRANDCHILDREN of Tecumtha, mentioned above, in the order of their names, follow:

1. To Naw-swaw-pa-ma and her husband was born Nay-cah-twah, who died March 4, 1892, in Oklahoma, at the age of 47 years. She married four times and left three children now living, whose names are Webster Tyner, age 57 years; Lucy Williams, nee Ellis, or May-lo-now-o-se, age 51 years, and William Ellis, or We-se-kih-se-mo, age 48 years. Also several of her grandchildren are now living.

2. To Pa-se-quaw-mea-se and her husband was born Thomas Washington, Jr., better known as "Long Tom", or Wayl-way-way-se-ka, who died June 22, 1906, eight miles north-east of Shawnee, Okla., at the age of 59 years, and left six children, two boys and four girls, who are still living: Mrs. Fannie Tarhorty, or So-we-pea-se, age 58 years; Mrs. Hattie Dirt, or Hol-o-tah-we-pea-se, age 50 years; Ella Washington, or Mkahtay-wah-com-se, age 47 years; Mrs. Rose McClellan, or Ne-thaw-pea-se, age 44 years; Walter Washington, age 37 years, and Willie Washington, age 35 years. Also several of his grandchildren are now living.

3. To Way-lah-skse and her husband were born four children, two boys and two girls: Mrs. Nancy Hood, or Ah-lay-maw-pa-ma, now living, age 72 years, who has four children and several of her grandchildren now living; Thomas Wildcat Alford, or Gan-waw-pea-se-ka, now living, age 70 years, who has eleven children and several grandchildren now living; David W. Alford, or Bay-me-taw-pea-se-ka, who died near Tecumseh, Okla., Sept. 28, 1900, at the age of 37 years and left his son, Webster Alford, now living, age 37 years, who has three children living; Mrs. Nellie

APPENDIX

Hood, or Nah-wah-taw-pea-se, now living, age 59 years, who has no children.

4. To Jim Fry, or Wal-kos-ka-ka, and his wife was born Joe Longhorn, or Taw-peas-ka-ka, who died Nov. 2, 1896, at the age of 38 years and left three children now living: Allen Longhorn, or Nah-haw-peas-ka-ka, age 43 years, who has two children living: Mrs. Ferdie Forman, or Mo-sah-tah-waw-pes-se, age 39 years, who has also two children living; Mrs. Lydia Warrior, or Ke-way-pea-se, age 36 years, who has four children living.

5. To Big Jim, or Waw-paw-meap-to, and his wife were born two children: Little Jim, or To-tom-mo, now living, age 58 years, who has three children and several grandchildren also living; and Lah-lah-waw-pea-se, or Lo-pah, who died Feb. 20, 1909, at the age of 33 years, and left her daughter, Mrs. Sallie Gibson, or Pay-maw-com-se, now living, age 29 years, who has two children living.

6. To Mrs. Washington, or Pea-taw-pea-se, and her husband were born two children: William Washington, or Way-the-path-ka-ka, who died near Skiatook, Okla., in Jan. 1923, at the age of 63 years and left one daughter, Mrs. Rosa Gibson, or Ke-kaw-com-se, now living, age 47 years, who has three children living; and Mrs. Fannie White, or We-se-kaw-com-se, who died in 1886 and left one son, Thomas White, or Quay-tah-waw-com-se-ka, now living, age 46 years, who has two children also living.

AFFIDAVIT

State of Oklahoma
Pottawatomie County } SS:

We, the undersigned, members of the Absentee Shawnee Tribe of Indians and members of the Business Committee for said Tribe, do hereby certify, on honor, that most of the facts stated above .... were given us from mouth to ear by our parents, grandparents and elders before their death; some were from our own people living to-day; some were

APPENDIX

obtained by our own personal efforts for many years from other sources within our reach; and from our own knowledge and belief; all these have been recorded and kept in the *Shawnee Family Register* of our Tribe by our custodian, Thomas Wildcat Alford, where all these facts can be found to-day; and

We further certify, on honor, that a copy of said *Register*, only, however, that portion of which mentions the names of the allottees of land and their parents, was obtained by the U. S. Government through the Indian Office in 1903 for the use of the Shawnee Indian Agency at Shawnee, Oklahoma, where it now remains, and that these facts stated above regarding our great Warrior Chief Tecumtha and his descendants are true and correct to the best of our knowledge and belief.

Witnessed our hands this the 13th day of August, A. D. 1931

GAN-WAW-PEA-SE-KA or THOMAS W. ALFORD
NANA-QUAW-COMS-KA-KA or THOS. B. HOOD
NAH-KE-PEAS-KA-KA or JACOB BUCKHEART
QUA-LAY-PATH-KA-KA or JOHN E. SNAKE

Committeemen

AUTHORITIES QUOTED

Alder, Jonathan, 296
Alford, Thomas Wildcat, 14, 16, 18-42 54-66, 152-153, 163-165, 170-201, 206, 215, 303-310
American Pioneer, 87-88, 89-90, 255-256

Benton, Thomas H., 104-105
Bodley, Temple, 93
Boone, Daniel, 260-263
Bourassa, Joseph N., 153-154
Bradford, John, 76
Burnet, Jacob, 2, 5, 219
Bushnell, David I., Jr., 159-160

Clark, George Rogers, 77-78, 84-85
Croghan, George, 39

Dane, Ralph, 20
Dills, R. S., 85-86, 225
Drake, Benjamin, 109-110, 146, 149-150, 301-302
Drake, Daniel, 245
Drake. Samuel G., 112
Draper Manuscripts, 13, 49, 85, 91, 110-111, 114-116

Eastman, Charles, 13
Eggleston, Edward, 159

Flint, Timothy, 8

Galbreath, C. B., 224-225
Galloway, Andrew, 247-248, 252-253
Galloway, Clark M., 268-269
Galloway, James, Jr., 68
Gist, Christopher, 201, 202-204
Graham, A. A., 4
Green, Thomas M., 93, 94

Hamin, P. S., 227-228
Harrison, William Henry, 98, 295-296
Harvey, Henry, 204-206
Hatch, William Stanley, 118-119, 126, 154, 159

Hildreth, Samuel P., 207
Howe, Henry, 93, 101, 166, 275 footnote

James, James A., 68-69, 70, 82
Johnson, Cave, 82-83
Johnson, Jesse, 247

Kellogg, Louise Phelps, 50 footnote, 283-295
Kenton. Edna, 81, 256-257
King, Roy S., 301
Kratz, George Davenport, 4-5

Lafferty, Mrs. W. T., 49-53, 263-266
Larsh, Thomas J., 298-300

MacLean, J. P., 142-143, 145
McBride, James, 99-100
McFarland, R. W., 17
McGrew, Thomas F., 71-74, 216
McWhorter, L. V., 111-112
Mills. William, 119
Moorehead, Warren K., 112-113

O'Neall, George T., 239-240

Paxson, W. A., 272-275
People's Press, The, 98

Randall, E. O., 113, 116
Renick. Felix, 16
Ruddell, Stephen, 110-111, 115, 127-134

Sheldon, Addison E., 208-209
Shetrone, H. C., 113
Slagle, Henry, 117-118

Vancleaf, John W., 83

Western Annals, 242-243
Williams, John, 16
Withers, A. S., 93
Wright, Thomas Coke, 217-219

Xenia, Ohio, Gazette, 257-258

INDEX

Absentee Shawnee Business Committee on Tecumtha's birthplace, 108, 116-118; memorial to Tecumtha, 120-121; function of, 125
Adena, home of Thomas Worthington, 210, 213
Advertising, first in Northwest Territory, 220-221
Agriculture, Shawnee, 183-184; early in Ohio. 211, 213
Ahkuwila, Shawnee chief, 28, 32
Ahquiloma, Shawnee chief, 32, 34
Alford, Thomas Wildcat, Shawnee historian and committeeman, 125, 127 footnote. 143, 254; renewal of Tecumtha's pact with Galloways, 167, 169
Allegheny country, center of Indian influence, 28, 31, 33
Armstrong, Rev. Robert, 245-253
Auglaize River country, Shawnees in, 41, 271; Indian supply base, 44, 67 footnote; described by Wayne, 102

Bales, Sarah Lucas, 257
Baptists in Kentucky, 263-266
Basket-making, Shawnee, 187
Big Jim, 116
Black Fish, Shawnee chief, 14, 114, 258, 259; in Battle of Oldtown, 56, 62; and Thomas Bullitt, 267-268
Black Hoof (Catahecassa), Shawnee chief, 12, 14, 35, 62, 71, 142, 284 footnote; burial, 204-206
Blanchard, Isaac, 244-245
Blue Jacket, Shawnee chief, 12, 213, 215 footnote, 298-303
Blue Jacket, Charles, 300
Blue Jacket, George, 143
Books of pioneers, 124, 246; first in Ohio, 245-246
Boone, Daniel, 81, 85, 88, 294; last years of, 7-9; captivity at Old Chillicothe, 10, 12, 258-262, 266-267; at siege of Boonsborough, 262-263
Boonsborough, Ky., siege of, 14, 58, 259, 262-263

Bouquet, Colonel, 286
Bowman, Col. John, expedition against Old Chillicothe, 14, 43, 48-49, 101, 266; in Battle of Oldtown, 55-66
Braddock's defeat, 35
British. *See* English
Bryant's Fort, Ky., 53; siege of, 80
Buffalo Trace, 102, 241
Bullitt, Capt. Thomas, 201, 266, 267-268
Bullskin Trace, 15, 103-104, 122, 236, 239, 242, 244, 260 footnote, 266
Burial customs Shawnee, 198-199, 204-206; pioneer, 230, 268-269
Burnet, Jacob, 1-5
Butler, Richard, 292, 293
Byrd, Capt. Henry British officer, invasion of Kentucky, 49-52, 67, 68-69, 78, 267

Canada, Kentucky captives in, 52, 267
Canals beginning of in Ohio, 212
Catahecassa. *See* Black Hoof
Centinel, The, 219-222
Charlotte, Fort, Treaty of, 290
Chartier, Peter, 29, 32
Chiksika, brother of Tecumtha, 12 106, 129, 131
Chillicothe (*see also* Old Chillicothe), origin of name, 15-17; towns so named, 15-17, 23, 38-39, 43-44; in Ross County, Ohio, 112, 209, 210. 213
Churches, pioneer, 252
Cincinnati, 71, 81, 85, 87, 89, 221-222, 234, 245-246
Clark, George Rogers, conquest of Northwest Territory, 1-2; last years of, 2-3; expeditions against Shawnees, 43, 66-70, 79-86, 100, 294; in Battle of Old Piqua, 71-78; semi-centennial of 1782 expedition, 86-90; invasion of Wabash country, 90, 94, 294; Indian commissioner, 292-293
Clay, Green, 89

331

INDEX

Clothing. *See* Dress
Conestoga Indians, 26, 29
Cooper's Run Meeting-house, records of, 263-266
Cornstalk, Shawnee chief, 12, 58, 284-291, 292
Crawford, Col. William, expedition against Indians, 79-80
Creek Indians, 23
Croghan, George, 287
Culture, Indian, 144

Dances, Shawnee ceremonial, 190-194
Daughters of the American Revolution, 11, 14 163, 165, 244
Delaware Indians, 25-39 *passim*, 78, 79
De Vaudreuil, Marquis, 28
Dress, pioneer militia, 47; Shawnee, 197
Dunmore's War, 288-290
Dwellings. *See* Homes, Tepee, Wegiwa

Education, Shawnee, 171-172, 176, 179-180, 309-310; pioneer, 268
English, and Indians, 19, 24-40 *passim*, 49-52, 54 68-69, 80, 114, 261, 285-291, 294
Eskipakithiki, ancient Shawnee town, 18-19

Fallen Timbers, Battle of, 44, 132, 241, 243-244, 296
Fighting, Indian methods, 45, 57, 67 72-78, 96-97; pioneer methods, 60-61, 62-63, 72-73, 91
Finney, Fort, Treaty of, 293-294
Food of pioneer militia, 60, 72, 81, 82; Shawnee, 183-189
Fremont, John C., 104
French, and Indians, 19, 24-40 *passim* 54, 259, 262, 285-286; La Balme's mission, 283-284
Fulton, Rev. Andrew, 247-251
Funerals. *See* Burial customs
Fur, trade, 26-27, 35; prices of, 261 footnote

Galloway, James, Sr. 10, 11, 16; deposition on Old Chillicothe, 83 footnote; Clark semi-centennial, 86-87 footnote, 88-90; settled near Old Chillicothe, 121; home of, 121-123; visits of Tecumtha, 122-124; pact with Tecumtha, 166-169; visited by Kenton, 254-255; Blue Jacket's visit, 300-302
Galloway, James, Jr., 11, 86 footnote, 247; visit of Blue Jacket, 301-302
Galloway, Major James C., 258
Galloway, Rebecca, 10, 121; wooed by Tecumtha, 123-125, 135-139, 166, 276-280
Games, *See* Recreation
Girty, Simon, 65, 70 233; in Battle of Old Piqua, 73, 76
Gnadenhutten, massacre of, effect on Indians, 58, 79-80
Gordon, Governor, of Pennsylvania, 26, 29, 30, 35
Government, Shawnee tribal, 180-183
Gravier, Jacques, 27
Greene County, Ohio, court records quoted on Old Chillicothe, 11, 83 footnote; Shawnee and pioneer trails, 15, 101-105, 122, 223-224, 236, 239; histories of, 86 footnote; pioneer settlements 119, 121-122; militia, 225-226; Scotch Associates, 246-248, 251-253; Home-coming of 1928, 253-254; first school, 268; Wyandotte camps, 296-298; Shawnee silver mines, 300-301, 303
Greenville, Treaty of, 121, 134, 140
Grenadier Squaw. *See* Nonhelema

Hamilton, Henry, British governor of Detroit, 2, 260-261
Handicrafts, Shawnee, 187, 273-275; pioneer 274, 275 footnote
Hardin, Col. John, with Harmar's expedition, 96-99
Harmar, Gen. Josiah, expedition against Indians, 43, 44, 83, 94-100
Harrison, William Henry, denounces the Prophet, 149-150; Battle of the Thames, 155, 156, 158; on Tecumtha's death, 159-161; at Fort Meigs, 212
Harrodsburg, Ky., 48, 53, 69
Highways, development of, 104-105, 212, 214
History, pioneer, difficulties of, 93, 242; Shawnee, 164, 170-171
Homes pioneer, 121-123, 227; Shawnee, *see* Tepee, Wegiwa
Hunt, Josiah, 217-219

INDEX

Hunting, pioneer, 218; Indian, 267

Illinois, Shawnees in, 24

Iroquois Indians, 21, 24-28, 32-36 *passim*

Jackson, Joseph, 64

Jefferson, Thomas, opinion of the Prophet, 141-142

Johnson, Col. Richard M., as Tecumtha's slayer, 154, 161; speech on Tecumtha's death in Battle of the Thames, 155-158

Johnson, Sir William, 287, 288

Johnston, John, 113

Jones, John Gabriel, 76 footnote

Kansas, Shawnees in, 41, 42

Kaskaskia Clark's capture of, 2

Kawkawatchikay, Shawnee chief, 25, 26, 29-31, 36-38

Kelly, Benjamin, 114, 122-123

Kenton, John, 89

Kenton, Simon, last years of, 4-7, 254-256, 257; run of the gantlet, 10, 11, 256; affidavit in circuit court, 11-12; scouting activities, 11, 48, 59, 70, 81 footnote, 84, 266; Clark semicentennial, 86-90; with Logan's expedition, 101-102; on Tecumtha's birth, 113, 118-119; attack on Tecumtha, 132-133; visits James Galloway, Sr., 254-255; Kenton elm, 257-258

Kenton Trail, 101, 104

Kentucky, Shawnees in, 18-19, 24, 27, 202; pioneer conditions, 45-47; Indian raids, 48, 58; forts in, 48, 49, 52-53, 58; British-Indian invasions, 49-52, 68-69, 80, 267; militia, 67 (*see also* Militia); Associate Presbytery, 248-249; Baptists, 263-266

Kirker, Gov. Thomas, commission to Indians, 109, 147, 213-214

La Balme, Col. Augustin Mottin de, 283-284

Land, defective records, 9 footnote; owned by Washington, in Ohio, 15; claims of Absentee Shawnees, 42 footnote; demand for, 202; public sale, 211

La Salle, and Indians, 24

Leather, tanning, 273-275

Libraries, early in Ohio, 245-246

Licking River, mouth of, rendezvous of pioneer forces 59, 69, 81, 82

Liquor, Shawnee attitude on, 35-36, 127, 182

Little Turtle, Miami chief, 12, 97, 142, 298

Logan, Benjamin, expedition against Shawnees, 43, 90-94, 100-101, 294; public estimate of, 58; in Battle of Old Piqua, 72-74; with Clark's 1782 expedition, 81

Logstown, Pa., Shawnee town, 31, 37, 39

Lower Shawnee Town, 23, 38, 285

M'Cracken, Captain, 89

McGary, Capt. Hugh, kills Moluntha, 91-92, 294

McKee, Alexander, 294

Manawkyhickon, Delaware chief, 30

Manete, wife of Tecumtha, 125

Marriage customs, Shawnee, 196-197, 199-200, 202-204

Martin's Fort, 51, 53

Maryland, Shawnee settlements in, 25, 26, 284

Massie's Creek Church, 252-253

Maxwell Code, 220, 245

Maxwell, Nancy Robbins, *See* Robbins, Nancy

Maxwell, William, 219-226, 227, 229-232

May-thah-way-nah, son of Tecumtha, 125

Medicine Shawnee knowledge of, 175-176, 279-280, 281; pioneer practice, 229-230

Meesauwmi, Shawnee token of life, 21, 40, 41, 54, 304-305, 308

Meigs, Fort, siege of, 212

Methotase, mother of Tecumtha, 108, 115, 129, 165

Miami Indians, 30, 102, 234-235, 240-241

Miawawluway, Shawnee chief, 25

Militia, pioneer, equipment of, 46-47, 60, 72, 81, 82, 90, 98; in Greene County, Ohio, 225-226

Missouri, Shawnees in, 40-42, 56, 61-62

Moluntha, Shawnee chief, 293; capture and death, 91-92, 94, 294

Moravians, massacre of Gnaden-

333

INDEX

hutten, 58, 79-80; mission to Shawnee Scioto villages, 287

Names, personal, Indian, 171, 216 footnote
Newspapers, pioneer, 219-222
Nonhelema, Shawnee princess, 91, 284-295
Northwest Territory, conquest of, 1-2, 149; legislature, 3, 219-220; Washington's interest in, 15; slavery forbidden, 210; first newspapers, 219-222; first books, 220, 245-246

Occupations, Shawnee, 173-174, 183-184
Ohio, Indian villages in, 23, 38-39, 43-44, 68, 79 footnote, 84, 90-91 footnote, 92, 239, 270, 285-286, 293; agriculture, 211, 213; first canal, 212; War of 1812, 212, 244; seal, 213; printing, 219-222, 245; libraries, 245-246
Ohio River, boundary of Indian lands, 14, 15, 202; Shawnees on, 31, 202, 285; travel on, 249-250
Oklahoma, Shawnees in, 42, 164, 181
Old Chillicothe (see also Oldtown), persons connected with, 1, 10-14, 44-45; location and size, 10-14, 44-45, 61, 83 footnote, 121, 266; Tecumtha's birthplace near, 10, 14, 40, 54, 108, 110-111, 114, 115, 117-118, 120, 128, 163-165; settled by Shawnees, 39-40, 164; Shawnee migrations to and from, 40-42, 121; invasions of, 43-49, 55-67, 69-70, 77, 78-79 footnote, 81-86, 99-101; pioneers settled near, 119, 121-122; Shawnee removal from, 271
Old Piqua, See Piqua, Old
Oldtown, Battle of in 1779, 54-66; Clark's order before battle in 1782, 84-85
Opessa, Shawnee chief, 25, 26, 31

Pact of Peace, between James Galloway, Sr., and Tecumtha, 166-167; renewal of in 1926, 167-169
Panther, The, Indian chief, 213, 215-216 footnote

Patterson, Col. Robert, 83, 118, 294
Paxtan, Pa., Shawnee town, 37-38
Peace with Indians, unsuccessful attempts, 94-95, 292
Penn, Thomas, and Shawnees, 33, 36, 38
Penn, William, treaty with Shawnees, 25-26
Pennsylvania, Shawnee settlements in, 25-39
Philadelphia, Indian treaty of 1715, 26
Pickaway Plains, Shawnees on, 23, 39, 285-286; in Dunmore's War, 289-290
Piqua (also see Piqua, Old), origin of name, 17, 22-23; towns so named, 17, 44, 68, 79 footnote, 81-82, 84
Piqua, Old, on Mad River, 44, 68, 102, 216; Battle of, 71-78, 84; as Tecumtha's birthplace, 109-110, 111, 113-116
Pitt, Fort (Pittsburgh), 286, 287, 290
Point Pleasant, Battle of, 40, 45, 289
Powhatan, 20
Presbyterians, Scotch Associate, 121-122, 247-253; United, 253
Printing, early in Ohio, 219-222, 245
Prophet, The. 12, 106, 112 footnote, 127, 129; mission of, 139-151, 213-214; sacred slab, 151-152
Psychology, Indian, 141, 148-149, 151, 159, 170, 303
Pucksinwah, father of Tecumtha, 12, 37-40, 54, 106, 111, 114-115, 128-129, 164

Rains, General Simon, 257
Recreation, of Shawnees, 172-173, 193-196
Religion, among pioneers, 122-123, 136-137, 247, 248-253, 263-266; of Shawnees. 139-149, 152, 177-179, 190-194, 237, 275, 303-305, 309-311
Revolutionary War, in Kentucky, 50-52, 267
Robbins, Nancy (Mrs. William Maxwell), 226-229, 231
Rock, Thomas, Shawnee committeeman, 116-117

INDEX

Rogers, Joseph, 76
Roundhead, Wyandotte chief, 213, 215 footnote
Ruddell, Capt. Isaac, 50-51
Ruddell, Stephen, 53, 110-111, 122-123, 139, 213, 215, 263; missionary to Indians, 264-266
Ruddell's Fort, 52-53

St. Asaph's, Ky., 50 footnote, 53
St. Louis, Mo., 40
Scioto River, Shawnees on. *See* Pickaway Plains.
Scioto Trace, 102-103, 267
Scotch Associates, *See* Presbyterians
Scott, Gen. Charles, with Wayne's campaign, 240-242, 243-244
Seal of Ohio, 213
Seneca Indians, 33
Shakers, report on the Prophet's mission, 140, 142-145
Shawnee Indians, council-house of, 10, 13, 16, 62, 164; characteristics, 12, 13, 18, 56, 59, 286, 202; at Old Chillicothe, 13, 39-40, 121; migrations and settlements, 14, 24-42, 61, 121, 284-285, 293; "Absentee", 14, 41, 42, 181; expeditions against, 14, 43-49, 55-78, 81-86, 90-101, 294; language, 16, 168-169; clans, 17, 21-23, 181, 306-309; early history, 18-21; relations with French and English, 19, 24-40 *passim*, 54, 285-290, 294; divisions, 21-22, 40-42, 54, 56, 164; and the Iroquois, 24-35, 286; relations with Delawares, 25-39 *passim;* and the Conestogas, 26, 29; attitude on liquor, 35-36, 127, 182; type of villages, 44, 45, 270; trails of, 101-105; religion, 139-149, 152, 177-179, 237, 275, 303-305, 309-311; rearing of children, 171-172, 176, 179-180, 309-310; recreation, 172-173, 193-196; occupations, 173-174, 183-184; dwellings, 44, 174-175; medical knowledge, 175-176, 279-280, 281; government, 180-183; food, 183-189; handicrafts, 187, 273-275; records of time, 164, 189; ceremonial dances, 190-194; marriage, 196-197, 199-200, 202-204; dress, 197; burials, 198-199, 204-206; songs, 200-201; removal from Old Chillicothe, 271
Silverheels, Shawnee chief, 285, 289
Silver mines, Shawnee, in Greene County, Ohio, 300-301, 303; in Kentucky, 301-302
Slab, sacred, 151-152
Slab's Camp, 244
Smalley, William, 232-239, 242, 244
Soap-making, pioneer, 274
Sports. *See* Recreation
Stanwix, Fort, Treaty of, 14-15, 202
Stevenson graveyard, 252, 253, 269
Susquehanna River, Shawnee settlements on, 25-38 *passim*

Tecumapese, sister of Tecumtha, 12, 106, 158
Tecumtha (Tecumseh), 12, 17, 37, 311; birthplace, 10, 14, 40, 54, 107-120, 128, 163-166; family, 106, 108 115, 129; place in history, 107, 309; burial place, 108, 152, 153; memorial to, 120-121; in Galloway home, 122-124, 166; courtship of Rebecca Galloway, 123-125, 135-139, 166, 276-280; appearance, 125-127; described by Stephen Ruddell, 128-134; break with the whites, 136, 138, 147-151; death, 152-161; legend of return, 162-163; pact with Galloways, 166-169; in Worthington home, 213-215
Tennessee, 18
Tenskwatawa. *See* Prophet, The
Tepee, 44-45, 174
Thames, Battle of the, Tecumtha's death in, 152-161
Thomas, Governor, of Pennsylvania, 34-35
Thurston, Col. R. C. Ballard, owner of manuscripts on Clark, 82
Time, Shawnee records of, 164, 189
Tippecanoe, Battle of, 148
Toh-tah-mo, Shawnee chief, 125
Tools, used by Indians, 13, 45
Townsley, John, funeral of, 268-269
Trails, Indian and pioneer, 15, 101-105, 122, 216-217, 223-224, 236, 239, 241-242, 244, 245

335

INDEX

Umsoma, Shawnee personal genius, 165, 171, 195, 214-215, 305-306
Urbana Road, 101, 104

Villages, Indian, how built, 44-45, 74; in Ohio, *see* Ohio
Vincennes, Clark's capture of, 2
Virginia, claim to Tecumtha's birthplace, 112
Virginia Military Reservation, 104, 202, 209

War of 1812, 212, 244
Washington, George, land owned in Ohio, 15; orders to Harmar, 95-96; commission to Miami Indians, 234-235, 242-243; orders to Wayne, 235-236
Washington, Thomas, Shawnee committeeman, 116-117
Wayne, Anthony, in Auglaize country, 102; training army, 235-236; movements of forces, 238-242, 243-244

Waynesville, Ohio, encampment of Wayne forces near, 238-242
Wegiwa, 170, 174-175
West Woodville, Ohio, battle with Shawnees near, 239, 244
Wigwam. *See* Wegiwa
Winchester Trace, 102, 104, 122, 239
Witchcraft, the Prophet's campaign against, 145-146
Women, pioneer 208
Worthington, Thomas, 109, 147 footnote, 209-215
Wyandotte Indians, 78, 79, 80; characteristics, 296; camps in Greene County, Ohio, 296-298
Wyoming Valley, Shawnees in, 30-31

Xenia State Road, 103-104, 236; supplies to Perry over, 244-245

Zane, Betty, 226
Zeisberger, David, 287

www.ingramcontent.com/pod-product-compliance
Lightning Source LLC
Chambersburg PA
CBHW030315100526
44592CB00010B/442